WRITE TO LEARN

WRITE TO LEARN

SIXTH EDITION

DONALD M. MURRAY

HARCOURT BRACE COLLEGE PUBLISHERS
FORT WORTH PHILADELPHIA SAN DIEGO NEW YORK AUSTIN ORLANDO SAN ANTONIO
TORONTO MONTREAL LONDON SYDNEY TOKYO

Publisher	Earl McPeek
Acquisitions Editor	Julie McBurney
Product Manager	Laura Brennan
Project Editor	Mary Mayo, Louise Slominsky
Production Manager	Serena Barnett
Art Director	Linda Wooton

Cover Image © 1998 Pierre-Yves Goavec

ISBN: 0-15-505448-1
Library of Congress Catalog Card Number: 98-70007

Address for Orders
Harcourt Brace College Publishers, 6277 Sea Harbor Drive, Orlando, FL 32887-6777
1-800-782-4479

Address for Editorial Correspondence
Harcourt Brace College Publishers, 301 Commerce Street, Suite 3700, Fort Worth, TX 76102

Web site Address
http://www.hbcollege.com

Harcourt Brace College Publishers will provide complimentary supplements or supplement packages to those adopters qualified under our adoption policy. Please contact your sales representative to learn how you qualify. If as an adopter or potential user you receive supplements you do not need, please return them to your sales representative or send them to: Attn: Returns Department, Troy Warehouse, 465 South Lincoln Drive, Troy, MO 63379.

Printed in the United States of America

8 9 0 1 2 3 4 5 6 7   066   9 8 7 6 5 4 3 2

Harcourt Brace College Publishers

....

To Minnie Mae

who shares my words and my life

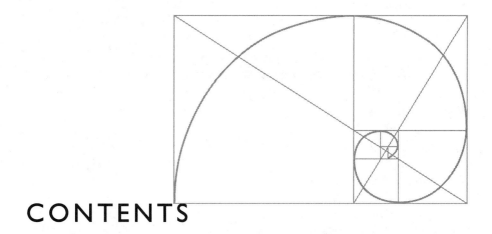

CONTENTS

....

CHAPTER 2
READ AS A WRITER 44

....

CHAPTER 3
SEE AND WRITE 67

CHAPTER 4
FOCUS 94

....

CHAPTER 5
EXPLORE   118

....

CHAPTER 6
PLAN   138

....

CHAPTER 7
DRAFT   172

....

CHAPTER 8
REVISE TO EXPLORE MEANING   202

·······························

CHAPTER 9
EDIT TO CLARIFY MEANING   224

·······························

CHAPTER 10
FIT YOUR PROCESS TO YOUR TASK   240

CHAPTER 11
READ WRITERS' WRITING 263

....

CHAPTER 12
IN THE WRITER'S WORKSHOP   290

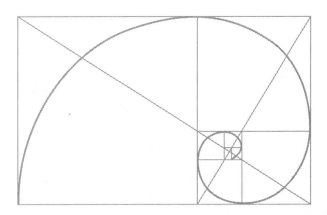

PREFACE

Novelist Graham Greene asked, "Isn't disloyalty as much the writer's virtue as loyalty is the soldier's?" Well, I've been a loyal soldier and a writer aggressively disloyal to what I have published. I have especially enjoyed turning traitor on each edition of *Write to Learn,* and in this sixth edition, I have again practiced what the title preaches and continued my lifetime apprenticeship to the writing craft. Revision—re-seeing—is my delight. I have revised and relearned throughout the book. I cannot read what I have written unless I can do it with cursor in hand, cutting, adding, reordering, clarifying what I read. I have revised the sixth edition page by page.

A NEW EMPHASIS ON READING

Reviewers of the fifth edition challenged me to place more emphasis on reading and the new Chapter 2, "Read as a Writer," responds with an extensive examination of how the writer reads before, during, and after writing. Writers must read as they write, but it is a very special kind of reading that interacts with the writing process. This chapter describes and demonstrates these special and rarely described skills that are essential if a student is to write and rewrite effectively.

A NEW EMPHASIS ON SEEING

I have long been interested in the fact that most effective writers visualize as they write: They see and write what they see. Visualization is fundamental to most writers, yet I do not know of a textbook on composition that introduces and develops this important technique. I draw as well as write and have studied how artists as well as writers see—and how they see through drawing and writing. The new Chapter 3, "See and Write," will help students visualize as they write.

A NEW LOOK AT REVISION

In Chapter 8, "Revise to Explore Meaning," I have developed a new look at revision that will help students and their teachers see revision in a new and practical way. This new approach presents strategies that make the revision process logical and rational.

NEW QUESTIONS AND ACTIVITIES

Because I am no longer in the classroom on a daily basis, I invited a superb teacher of freshman English, Mary Hallet of the University of New Hampshire, to write new questions and activities for most of the chapters. They have added immensely to the quality and the practicality of the text.

NEW CASE HISTORIES

I have added a new student case history—an argument for teenage access to the Internet—by Emma Tobin. This case history chronicles my teaching of Emma during the drafting of her essay; and it includes her reactions to my instruction.

I have also added a powerful personal essay on anger by a distinguished writer and teacher of writing, Christopher Scanlan, director of writing for the Poynter Institute for Media Studies in St. Petersburg, Florida. He expands his revealing and candid case history with professional counsel for student essay writers.

INSIDE COVERS

We have continued the index, "Help for Your Writing Problems," on the inside front cover as well as a reference list of "Writing Techniques" placed on the inside back cover.

USING *WRITE TO LEARN* WITH *READ TO WRITE*

Read to Write is a reader organized around the major components of the writing process and emphasizes the relationship between reading and writing. Although *Write to Learn* is designed to be used alone or with other readers, *Read to Write* was written after *Write to Learn,* and each book supports the other. They have the same process and a similar attitude toward the act of writing.

THE INSTRUCTOR'S MANUAL

I write my own instructor's manual to help teachers with the practical problems of the classroom. It is based on my own experience as a teacher and on the experiences of instructors who have used *Write to Learn* in many different types of institutions and courses, with students at varying levels of accomplishment. It is specific, practical, and designed to help both beginning and experienced instructors in realistic teaching situations. This manual can be obtained by contacting your local Harcourt Brace sales representative.

ACKNOWLEDGMENTS

I write each morning by myself but I am never alone. I am part of a writing community that inspires and supports me. Minnie Mae, who started mailing out the manuscripts I was burning when we were married, is my first reader and constant supporter.

Laurie Runion has again been involved in the conceptual development of this edition, as well as its chapter by chapter, page by page, paragraph by paragraph, sentence by sentence, word by word execution. She has suggested, commanded, demonstrated, supported, and corrected with perception, wisdom, and good humor. It is her book as much as it is mine and it is a joy for me to be allowed to collaborate with her.

Christopher Scanlan of the Poynter Institute in St. Petersburg, Florida; Donald Graves in Jackson, New Hampshire; Brock Dethier of Utah State University in Logan, Utah; Thomas Romano of the University of Miami in Oxford, Ohio; Elizabeth Cooke of the University of Maine at Farmington; Michael Steinberg of Michigan State University in East Lansing, Michigan; and Ralph Fletcher of Birmingham, Alabama are as close as the telephone, e-mail and fax. They always share, respond, listen, laugh, and understand.

At the University of New Hampshire I have learned from and with many colleagues. Those who have especially stimulated and helped shape my thinking during the writing of this edition were professors Thomas R. Newkirk and Lisa Miller.

The other members of my private writing community who appear behind my computer screen each writing morning, shaking their heads no and yes, smiling or frowning, include Driek Zirinsky of Boise State University, Evelynne Kramer of the *Boston Globe,* Bonnie Sunstein of the University of Iowa, Elizabeth Chiseri-Strater of the University of North Carolina at Greensboro, and Lad Tobin of Boston College.

In the sixth edition I am especially indebted to Mary Hallet for her questions and activities, Emma Tobin and Christopher Scanlan for their instructive case histories, and Geoffrey Chang for his writing on computer art.

I have been given wise counsel by those who reviewed the fifth edition and made valuable suggestions for the sixth: Larry Burton, University of South Alabama; Sherie Coelho, Antelope Valley College; Bobbie R. Coleman, Moorpark College; Eileen Donovan-Kranz, Boston College; Marion Hogan Larson, Bethel College; Joan Spangler, California State University—Fullerton; Gil Tierney, William Rainey Harper College; and Karen Uehling, Boise State University.

I owe special thanks to the staff at Harcourt Brace: Michael Rosenberg, former Executive Editor for English; Julie McBurney, Acquisitions Editor for English; Mary Mayo and Louise Slominsky, Project Editors; Serena Barnett, Production Manager; and Linda Wooton, Art Director.

WRITE TO LEARN

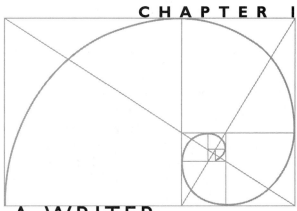

CHAPTER I

WRITE AS A WRITER

Write now. Don't wait for an idea. Of course you don't know what you are going to say or how you are going to say it. That's the terror and the joy of the writing experience.

Turn on the screen or pick up a pen or pencil, and start putting words on paper. Write what comes to your fingers; write what you hear yourself saying silently to yourself. Don't worry about spelling or grammar or mechanics or form yet. Worry about those things later, not now. Don't worry about being silly or stupid or clumsy or accurate or sensible, not now. Worry about those concerns later.

Write fast. Outrun all the censors in your head—teachers, parents, friends, editors, critics—who tell you what you have done wrong. To balance on a two-wheeler and get somewhere, you have to pedal fast. Velocity makes balance possible. It is the same thing with writing. You have to write fast to say what you did not know you needed to say.

What will you write? You don't know. Most of all, writers write to surprise themselves, racing into the unknown in search of the known.

You will find words to express the hidden feelings that you did not know you had felt. Today's writing reveals the conflict between what your parents said and what they meant to say; a quick first draft recovers the specific information that contradicts what you thought you believed. Your feelings about last night's party, described now in detail, expose a significance you do not expect; the page produces information that you did not know your mind had collected; memories connect what has seemed, until now, random and unconnected. Writing, you have answers that need questions, solutions that hunger for problems, simplicities that become complex and complexities that become simple.

The writer writes to live life a second time, a third, a fourth, each life richer, more fully experienced on the page than in reality. The writer writes to feel, to think, to learn.

I emphasize personal writing for several important reasons:

1. We have to write from an abundance of information. Effective writing grows from what we know, what we don't know we know, what we want and need to know. Later we may write as doctors, police officers, historians, business executives, social workers, engineers, physicists, military officers, politicians, legislators, but as students we must begin to learn to write from what we know now: the personal, individual lives we have lived and are living.

2. When we write about personal experience, readers can share and understand what we are saying. They can identify with what we are trying to say, the problems we are facing and their solutions. If we wrote about convertible debentures, the Chaucerian pause, Morison's theory of gaseous diffusion, only specialists could understand what we are trying to say and how we might say it.

3. It is important for all of us to learn how to use language to explore, understand, and share the individual human experience for ourselves—and for each other. We need to discover how we view the world in which we live and what we think and feel about it. We need to examine the world, thinking through writing, and we need to speak out, testifying, celebrating, persuading—participating in the continual remaking of our world.

Personal writing does not preclude scholarly, corporate, scientific, legal, governmental writing. What we learn in personal writing we can adapt to impersonal writing. Of course, we should realize that most detached, objective professional and academic writing is personal. The language may be impersonal but the point of view toward the world and the writer's opinion of the world are still intensely individual.

On a personal note—pun intended—I have been hired by corporations and government agencies to draft or revise technical documents because I am an expert at personal writing. I can take those lessons and apply them to other writing tasks, and so can you.

Of course there are days when the computer screen remains empty, the page blank, and so I have developed some techniques that will lead me to the writer's essential discovery draft. I start with a **LIST.**

I think back to an event, a person, a place that I keep remembering. I list whatever comes to mind. Nothing is too trivial, too stupid: specific details, phrases, sounds, fragments of conversation, colors, smells, tastes—anything. I want to see what is revealed when the compost heap is turned over.

I'm going to demonstrate how making lists works for me. Join me but don't copy me. My list will differ from yours, it should, and if I write another list tomorrow, it will differ from the list I wrote today. Create your own list from your own world.

I found myself going back into my childhood as I began putting fragments of language down on paper. Here is today's list:

Vassall Street

Six years old

Grape arbor

Uncle Will's car

Up on blocks

Back stoop

New house

Painting the back steps with water

Apple tree

Can't play with neighbors

Vacant lot

Car radiator drained

Secret place behind the garage

House of childhood

Under the porch

Bible

Sickly

Fight with Walter Almeda

This list—written in private language—was meant to be read only by me. Each of those simple words or phrases gives off a personal meaning for me. "Sickly," for example, reminds me of my childhood illnesses and the long, dreamy weeks in bed convalescing in the days before miracle drugs; "under the porch" was where I first discovered that girls are constructed differently from boys; the "apple tree" was the first tree I learned to climb; I recall the Depression New England custom of draining a car's cooling system and putting it up on blocks from January through March, and it reminds me of my uncle's open Buick and the slow, windy, chilly Sunday afternoon drives in the days before a car had a heating system; the haunting image of myself "painting the back steps with water" reminds me of the imaginary games I played with Grandma Smith when I was very young.

I am going to use that list to find a **FOCUS**. The writer needs to focus as much as a photographer does. The photographer doesn't shoot without looking;

the photographer looks, then takes a picture. The writer uses language to look at the world and find something worth exploring in writing.

To find my focus, I look at the list and interview myself, asking questions that may help me see the possibilities hidden within my list:

- What surprises me?

    "Painting the back steps with water" brings back a whole afternoon filled with details: I can see the backyard, the people beyond the backyard, the water drying on the thick, worn back steps, Grandmother towering over me.

- Where's the tension?

    "Can't play with neighbors" brings back memories of tension with our neighbors. We were Scots and Protestant; they were Irish and Catholic; that difference worried my family, and their worry became a mystery for me.

- Where's the conflict?

    Between the way I was supposed to behave and what I did "under the porch" and in the "secret place behind the garage."

- What makes me feel happy, sad, angry, amused?

    I remember my thrill at climbing the apple tree and seeing my familiar world all new.

- What makes my memory itch? What do I keep thinking about when my mind wanders?

    The scene of my painting the back steps with water.

- What do I need to understand?

    I need to understand the power of the image of my painting the back steps. I wonder what's so important about that afternoon.

Ask yourself the questions I did, or any others that come to mind, to find your focus. I'm going to focus on the scene on the back steps. Now that I have my focus, I'm moving to the next stage of my writing process and **EXPLORE** it.

A focus can be explored in many ways. You may have to go and observe your subject, interview someone who was involved, visit the library, and make entries in a notebook that you can read when it comes time to write. In my case, I began watching the movie of my childhood that is stored in my head. I traveled back in memory until I found myself near my childhood home and drove around the block several times, remembering what a long and wobbly trip that was on my first two-wheeler (that trip might make an essay), remembering a bright blue, Depression bike made out of leftover parts by the local blacksmith, remembering the only African American in my Yankee hometown (that might be a story, too).

This movie runs when I go for my walk, while I wait for my wife in the car, during the commercials of a Celtics game, in all sorts of nooks and crannies of time during the day. Usually I make notes, but I didn't need to in this case. In memory I visit the kitchen with the great, black cast-iron stove. It was my job to bring up the filled coal hopper from the cellar and keep a supply nearby for Grandmother. I went down to the dark, spider-webby coal bin and heard again the terrifying roar as a ton of coal slid down the chute from the truck. I went back up to the pantry where I grabbed the edge of a jelly bowl and pulled hot jelly over me, wasting, in a moment, an entire grape harvest. I could see the pattern in the kitchen's linoleum floor, the black soapstone sink, the ice box with the drip pan I hated to empty.

For days I live in that house in memory, storing each memory against the time when I will write. I know I have a rich abundance of material to draw on as I write. That's all I need to know. It is time to **PLAN.**

There are many ways that I plan, but the most common is to write as many first sentences as possible—three, five, eleven, seventeen—until I find one that interests me enough that I can see the sentence that will follow, sometimes even the sentence or paragraph beyond that. That's all and that's enough. I write to discover, to be surprised, to experience, to find out; I write to learn.

I find myself writing:

I return to the house of childhood and find myself alone on the bottom step of the back stoop, scratching words in the dust with a stick. I am the writer I will become.

    Conditions of writer alienation—can't play with Catholic kids

    Grandma, paintbrush, and water

That's all I need to ignite a draft. The image is strong and compelling: a child writing words in the dust with a stick. But I am "inspired" to write even more by the sentence that follows: "I am the writer I will become." That sentence sparks my note "conditions of writer alienation—can't play with Catholic kids." It sets up the tension that will ignite a draft. I know I want to find out what I have to say, and I know it will involve the scene in the next note about painting the steps. It is time to begin a **DRAFT.**

Writers call the attempts they make to write *drafts.* These attempts are experiments, sketches, trial runs. Sometimes a writer has to finish many drafts—my personal record is eighty-six versions of a poem. Three drafts is common, but sometimes one draft is all the experienced—or fortunate—writer has to write. The writer also uses the word *draft* as a verb to describe the action of writing a version of a piece that may have to be rewritten—drafted—again: "I'm drafting an essay." "First, I draft my articles." "I draft to find out what I have to say."

Drafting is best done at top speed. Remember when you rode your first two-wheel bike? You had to pedal fast, even if the speed scared you, because velocity made it possible for you to balance the bike. Velocity is as important in writing a draft as it is in riding a bicycle.

Writing with velocity keeps you ahead of the censor, the doubter within, the grammar police, and the state trooper of spelling who all apply premature criticism to a draft. Writers must first produce drafts; then they can be critical.

Speed also causes the accidents of insight and language essential for effective writing. You don't know what you are going to say? Good. You don't know what you are saying? Even better: Write to discover what you have to say. This counsel contradicts common sense. Each craft is that way.

Common sense told me to stand up and run from the German machine gun during World War II; the soldier's craft taught me that because machine guns rise as they fire, it is best to stay low and run toward the firing machine gun. Common sense—and some teachers—tell us to know what we have to say before writing and to write it down slowly and carefully, not making mistakes. The experienced writer knows that learning is hidden in the mistakes, that we discover what we have to say and how we can say it from fast-written prose. Try it. You'll see it on your page and in my draft that follows.

I began with the scene of myself sitting on the bottom step painting with water. My commentary throughout this draft is thought out and was inserted after I finished the essay as a way of articulating what I did instinctively—and at top speed, writing this draft in less than forty-five minutes the way you might write an in-class paper.

I sit alone on the bottom of the back stoop of the house at the corner of Vassall Street and Billings Road in Wollaston.

When I do not know where to start, I usually begin with description.

I can almost make out the words I try to scratch in the dust with a stick. Am I the writer I will become?

Changing the second sentence into a question makes an enormous difference. It creates suspense: The reader is invited to explore the subject with the writer.

I have the ideal condition for a writer: alone in a world made strange. We have rented a whole house in a new neighborhood and the family has undergone a change in fortune I do not understand. I have left behind the Airedale that terrified me on Grand View Avenue, but I know there will be new terrors here.

Now I know I have a piece worth writing. The first sentence of the paragraph puts my personal experience in a larger context: What are the conditions of creativity? That single sentence makes me be specific about those conditions in the specific terms of my life then. I also experience the surprise caused by velocity when I write about an "ideal" condition. I had expected sadness, unhappiness—but "ideal"? I find that word interesting and have to write on to discover what it means.

Recently I drove past the house, circling the block to see if the significance of that haunting memory would come clear. The back steps were still there, and so was I.

The reader travels at my side.

I am alone, fenced into an unfamiliar backyard. As so often happens to us who are at the autumn of life, I am both in the car in this Sunday afternoon and back in 1930, within the mysterious world of half-remembered childhood.

At my age I see what is and what was at the same time, as if one photograph was printed on top of another. I share my double vision with the reader, placing both the experience and my reflections on it in specific time frames.

There is a boy next door, a girl across the back fence, a great variety of boys across the street, but I am told they are Catholic and I am Baptist and I am not to play with them.

I define the peculiar nature of my alienation, knowing that readers will translate the prejudices of my childhood into those of their own childhoods.

I don't understand what those words mean but I know my family is serious about this, and something terrible will happen to me if I break their commandment.

Later, of course, I did break it, and I found that the other children were not supposed to invite a Protestant—another word I did not understand—into their homes. Our parents' prejudices do not automatically become ours, but I am left with a sense of alienation, of my own difference; that is another condition of most writers.

I show the reverse prejudice but decide not to go on—in this draft—to explain how I found the alien mothers often more affectionate than my own. I emphasize my feeling of difference, pointing out this common condition among writers.

But this day, on the bottom step, I have not broken my parents' law and Grandmother, seeing me sitting alone, suggests I paint the back stoop. She gives me an old paintbrush and a can of water and I paint the steps.

Looking back at those two simple sentences, I realize how long it took me to learn my craft and simply reveal a scene. No flourishes here, just ordinary words revealing an ordinary scene that will, through the writing that follows, become extraordinary.

I easily enter the world of make-believe and paint; Grandmother returns to admire the painting I have done. But even at the time there was something special about the task, and perhaps that is why I remember each stroke of the brush, how the wood darkens and how soon it fades.

I remember my innocence—my ignorance—when I wrote these words. Now it seems inevitable to me, but at the time I was only describing a feeling—a hope, a guess—that there was something significant in painting the back steps with water.

I suspect there was an end to innocence that afternoon. I had made a choice between the world of reality and the world of imagination. I chose imagination.

This is the crucial paragraph in the draft. If a draft works for me, I push what I am writing to a deeper level of meaning about halfway through. I go further than I—or the reader—expect, finding an insight that intrigues and lingers in the mind after the reading is done. This insight—generated by velocity—is the reason I write: to discover meaning in experience.

I would soon be six and I knew there was only water in the can and Grandmother knew I knew and yet we could share, that afternoon, the satisfying illusion of a job well done.

I keep the essay rooted in the specifics of my experience, allowing its importance to rise from them.

I would soon start first grade at the Massachusetts Fields School and it would not go well, perhaps because my imagination made it possible for me to enter the book and become a character, often a character new to the story who traveled his own path through the book, a path the teacher could not see.

Effective writing creates a conversation with the reader. The reader asks what happens because of the decision to choose imagination. I say, "Oh boy, I'm glad you asked that question" because I, the writer, want to hear my own answer.

When the teacher pointed to a map, my imagination ran up the pointer and into the map, exploring under the canopy of the rain forest, unable to hear the teacher's questions. When we studied the Revolutionary War I became a boy of Boston, in 1775, three cornered hat and all, a busy printer's apprentice, unavailable for class discussion.

I make my school experience active. I do not tell about it—I show it—revealing it to the reader who may then remember his or her own classroom hours.

Looking back I wonder how I got through school at all; I attended school but rarely remained in the class. Imagination provided my text.

In writing this essay, I am discovering a new answer to a question I keep asking myself: Why did I do so badly in school, dropping out of high school twice and finally flunking out?

I lived—and still live—in the geography of memory and fantasy, what may have been, what may yet be. I am still the small, lonely boy painting the back steps with water, and I wonder if in giving me water and a paintbrush, my grandmother hadn't given me the gift of imagination that has been my trade ever since and causes me to remember that afternoon so many years ago with such clarity.

I weave back to the opening scene, to what followed school and suggest a reason why I remember that image so clearly.

Now it is time to **CLARIFY**. I read the draft out loud, hearing it as a reader would, making small changes to make my meaning clear. I then ran it through the spell checker on my computer, had my wife read it, and sent it off to Evelynne Kramer who was then my editor at the *Boston Globe*. When she called the next day, she said she liked it, but she was not sure what it meant. I paid attention to her reaction; I have learned to respect, trust, and depend on her. If she was not sure what it meant, readers certainly wouldn't be sure.

You may not have a computer with spell check, a wife who is a good reader, or a professional editor, but you can be your own editor, reading what you have written over as a stranger to be sure what you have written will be understood. If you are lucky, you may be able to find a good test reader, a person who can read your early drafts as readers will read your final ones. That person—a classmate, a fellow writer, a friend—will help you see the strengths as well as the weaknesses of your draft and will help you recognize what needs to be added to make the paper clear to a reader. This test reader may be critical but the comments should be supportive. My own condition for test readers: They make me want to write when I leave them.

I read the draft over and agreed with my editor. I had been too close to the subject and started too abruptly. I decided I had to step back and put the story in a context the reader could understand. First I made a statement, and then I gave a number of personal examples in the second paragraph that I hoped would spark memories in readers' minds.

Here is the new beginning as the essay was published:

• ALL MY ROADS LEAD BACKWARD •

Each of us is haunted by images from our childhood that have a mysterious attraction we cannot completely understand.

One image I often remember—and dream—is the green crusted pilings at Salem Willows that slide upwards as I sink, almost drowning. And the brown wallpaper of the small downstairs room into which I was locked, the day I could not go to the Brockton Fair. The huge tire and drive chain of the Mack dump truck rolls toward me on Billings Road. The hammer after it left my hand and my uncle falling, that is all.

Over sixty, reflecting back on the life we have lived, we examine these haunting images, perhaps even returning to the place where they occurred in the hope of discovering meaning—or at least the reason they are so immediate after all these years.

In one recurring scene I see myself sitting alone on the bottom step of the back stoop of the house at the corner of Vassall Street and Billings Road in Wollaston.

....

DISCOVER THE WRITING PROCESS

Now you and I have experienced a writing process. There is, however, not one writing process but many. This book is organized on one writing process—the one I most often find effective for me. But I adapt it according to the writing task, my experience with that task, and the way my head works that morning. Sometimes I write away with a river flood of fluency, other days I build a draft slowly like a bricklayer. No matter. I am a writer. I write. And you should as well. Change your process as your thinking style evolves, as you face a new writing task, or as you become more experienced with a particular writing task.

The process used in this book is:

Focus

The writer chooses a way to look at the subject, focusing on one aspect of the topic.

Explore

The writer researches the subject either formally or in the informal way I did in memory, seeking out the specific details from which to construct a meaning from the confusion of information.

Plan

The writer sketches a trail map for the draft, usually finding a lead or starting point, then some landmarks that may appear along the way.

Draft

The writer drafts quickly to outrun the censor and cause those instructive failures that reveal the meaning of the subject, surprising the writer—and the reader—with an unexpected insight.

Clarify

The writer clarifies meaning by revising (reconsidering form and structure) and editing the language (reading each line aloud) so the reader will understand what the writer has learned about the subject through writing about it.

The next chapters discuss reading as writing and seeing as a writer, because those skills are the foundations on which this process is built. The book then goes through the process chapter by chapter.

Writing is both an art and a craft. This process is not something to be followed rigidly, step by step. There are times when the writer may begin by drafting or exploring to find a focus. As Eudora Welty says:

> The writer himself studies intensely how to do it while he is in the thick of doing it; then when the particular novel or story is done, he is likely to forget how; he does well to. Each work is new. Mercifully, the question of how abides less in the abstract, and less in the past, than in the specific, in the work at hand.

We all know why writing often goes off track—"I began at 2:00 A.M. Sunday night after a busy weekend," "The dog ate my notes," "I found out how I shoulda written it after I finished." To improve your writing, concentrate on when the writing goes well: Write down the conditions and the processes you followed during your best writing experiences, the attitudes you had as well as the techniques you used, a record of the environment in which the writing took place.

WRITE IN A DAYBOOK

The environment in which much of my most creative writing takes place is the *daybook*. The daybook competes with the computer as my most valuable writing tool. Even the name *daybook* is important to me. For years, I tried to keep a journal. I imagined I was Gide or Camus. But I wasn't either of those writers, and what I wrote was not perceptive but pompous, full of hot air, hilarious to read, and utterly useless to me as a writer. At other times I tried to keep a diary, but then I found myself recording only trivia—the temperature, or whom I met, or what I ate.

I don't know where I heard the term *daybook,* but a number of years ago I found myself using the term and writing every day—well, almost every day—in a ten-by-eight spiral notebook filled with greenish, narrow ruled paper, with a margin line down the left. This worked for me. I write on my lap, in the living room or on the porch, in the car or an airplane, during meetings at the university, in bed, or sitting on a rock wall when resting during a walk. A bound book doesn't work for me. I find a spiral book convenient and easy to handle; and since I write in all sorts of light, indoors and out, I find the greenish paper comfortable. I chose the size because it fits in the outside pocket of the bag I carry everywhere.

The organization is simply a day-by-day chronology. When I change the subject I write a code word—novel, poem, talk at St. Anselm's, children's book?—in the left-hand margin. That way I can look back through the book and collect all the notes I've made on a single project or concern.

I often write in the daybook during the first fifteen minutes of the day before I eat breakfast; then I keep it near me all day long. If something occurs to me, I make a note during a television commercial or in a meeting, or while walking, or in the car. I almost always make a note about the next day's writing before I go to bed.

How I use my daybook varies from time to time. Since I now do most of my writing using a computer, my daybooks have pages or paragraphs I have printed out and pasted in so I can read, reconsider, and play with the writing during spare moments. All the writing in the daybook is a form of talking to myself, a way of thinking on paper. Much of my "spontaneous" writing can be tracked through years of daybooks in which I have thought and rethought, planned and researched, drafted and redrafted its movement from interesting fragment to possible draft.

Here are some of the items you might see in my daybook:

- Questions that need to be answered
- Fragments of writing seeking a voice
- Leads, hundreds of leads, the beginning lines of what I may write
- Titles, hundred of titles
- Notes from which I have made lectures, talks, or speeches
- Notes I have made at lectures, talks, or speeches of others; also notes I have made at poetry readings, hockey games, and concerts
- Outlines
- Ideas for stories, articles, poems, books, papers
- Diagrams showing how a piece might be organized or, more likely, showing the relationships between parts of an idea
- Drafts
- Observations
- Quotations from writers or artists
- Newspaper clippings
- Titles of books to be read
- Notes on what I have read
- Pictures I want to save
- Writing schedules
- Pasted-in copies of interesting letters I've received or written
- Lists, lots of lists
- Pasted-in handouts I've developed for classes or workshops

I don't use the daybook in any single way. Anything that will stimulate or record my thinking, anything that will move toward writing goes into the daybook. When a notebook is filled—usually in about six weeks—I go through it and harvest a page or two or three of the most interesting material for the beginning of the next daybook. When I'm ready to work seriously on a project, I go back through past daybooks and photocopy pages that relate to the subject I'm working on.

The daybook stimulates my thinking, helps me make use of small fragments of time, which on many days is all the time I have to write. There is no sign of struggle. I'm not fighting writing, I'm playing with writing. If it isn't fun, if nothing is happening, I stop and wait until the magic begins. The daybook also keeps my writing muscles in condition; it lets me know what I'm concerned with making into writing; it increases my productivity.

If you decide to keep a daybook, make it your own. Don't try to follow anyone else's formula. And don't write it for another audience. It's a private place where you can think and where you can be dumb, stupid, sloppy, silly; where you can do all the bad writing and bad thinking essential for those moments of insight that produce good writing.

Your daybook might not—should not—be like mine. It may be a file stored in a computer. From time to time, I have kept a computer file called JOURNAL. The poet Mekeel McBride's daybook is a bound sketch pad in which she draws and paints as well as writes. I envy her and have tried to imitate her, but it doesn't work for me. I know other writers who use file cards, tiny pocket notebooks, huge accounting ledgers, scraps of paper stuck in file folders in a drawer, a paper compost heap that flows from desk to floor. And some writers keep only mental daybooks in which they make notes of the world and rehearse the writing they intend to do, trying out one approach and then another in their minds. There is no one way and no correct way to write well; there are many ways and it is your job to find what works for you and be ready to switch when it stops helping you write well.

The playwright Marsha Norman says:

> But I'm really writing all the time, I'm afraid, even when I'm not at my desk. You'll notice there are little pads of paper everywhere? It works for me to write down the things I want to know. Regarding a character, the progress of a scene. . . . Even before I begin to write, I will say, "These are the things I must know before I start to write." I'll simply make a list of questions. Over the course of the next couple of weeks or months I'll get the answers to those questions. Even when I do rewrites, I just make a little question that says, "How is another way to say this?" Then I will put the paper away. It may be on the back of a grocery list, but once I write the question down, I never forget it. I do have a prodigious memory, and that helps. So I don't need to keep track of all these pieces of paper, I just need to have them around. The answer will end up on some other piece of paper. Gradually, in the course of getting ready to write, those pieces of paper collect, and pretty soon I have a whole box of them.

Fear.

I don't like that word. It is a strong word but the person who says it is weak.

Or perhaps strong enough to admit it.

Fear.

The shadow companion who rises with you when you get up in the night. The person you meet unexpectedly when you turn the corner. The twinge of pain in the left arm, the morning when you can't remember a proper noun. The reality that rises from the obituary page.

Fear.

What we try to avoid, deny, ignore.

Fear is physical - a queasiness, a shakiness, a dizzyness, a kind of feaver

Fear increases the symptoms of what is wrong, magnifying them.

As men, we have been taught to deny ourselves. Someone recently mentioned the "wounding" men do to each other in joining the squad, the

This is an example of daybook free writing, in which I explore a topic that is on my mind—in this case *fear*—to discover what I feel about a passing thought or emotion.

team, the management group. The "kidding" may be harsh but we learn to take it, ignore how we feel, and we learn to dish it out.

Ignoring our true feelings—hurt, anger, aching, fear—may serve us well in getting ahead in a corporate world out on football field competition but it doesn't help when we have to confront our weaknesses—how we feel—and analyze it.

The very act of reading ourselves, in males of my generation, feels feminine, although we all know what is the toughest sex.

Although this beginning eventually became a *Boston Globe* column, I try not to have a restrictive intention or expectation while free writing. I simply write quickly to see what I have to say and to discover what form it may take. The result may become fiction, poetry, or a column. While this bit did become a column, it also fertilized some ground in which poems have grown.

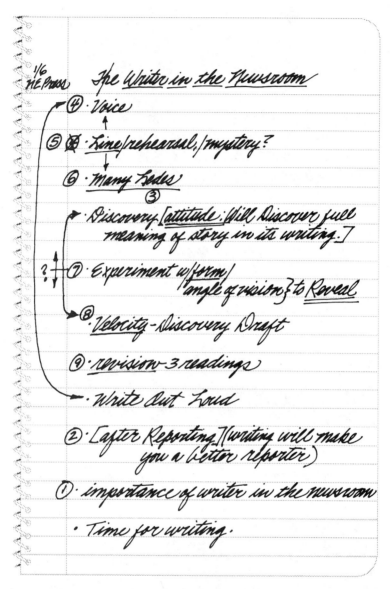

On this page of my daybook, written in a restaurant while waiting to meet someone for lunch, I worked on a talk I was going to give twelve days later at a New England Press Association convention. This example shows the way I usually prepare a talk, a magazine article, a business memo, the chapter of a textbook. I list the elements that may be appropriate as they come to mind, then manipulate them into a meaningful shape, cutting some, adding others, and reordering—and reordering, and then reordering.

The list, ordered and reordered, is as important to the creative act as it is to the supermarket shopping trip. As these entries demonstrate, I make use of fragments of time and put the ideas into a savings account so I can withdraw them when I have an hour or two in which to write.

ice bends to branch

① skid laughing
② how I walk
③ ?

I no longer ski, skate, slide —
except unexpectedly—but I welcome
snow, cold, gray skies, the
Natural round of seasons

Bagelry—cultural center

Charlie—nuts, etc

squeak of snow

snow high

snow house, snow forts
skiing
sledding   quiet
snow wars

laughing

slide?

miller's market
truck

jeep in ridge

1-27

over sixty, I wobble, sliding
small stepped, teetery-
tottery, ice & snow

I usually begin my day by being one of the first customers at The Bagelry, where I consume a bagel and a large, black coffee and solve the problems of the world with an early rising friend. He didn't show up on this snowy morning, so I took one of the paper bags on the counter and started brainstorming my memories of snowstorms when I was young. I am never bored—not if I can get my hands on pen and paper.

When I finished breakfast, I folded the bag, stuck it in my pocket, and took my walk. During my daily exercise, the ideas I had scratched down continued to bubble away in my conscious and subconscious. When I got home, I sat down at the computer and drafted a column that was published under the title "All Hail the Snow." The next day I wrote a poem that was ignited by my brown-bag notes, and it soon divided into two poems as I continued to explore my worlds of snow.

Throughout this text, in each chapter, I indicate how you can use the daybook to stimulate and support your writing. Translate what I say to whatever form of written, drawn, or mental note taking and rehearsal helps you.

The method of capturing, connecting, and developing ideas is not important, but the act of capturing, connecting, and developing is.

....

FIND YOUR OWN WRITING TERRITORIES

When we write we explore personal territories. Willa Cather said, "Most of the basic material a writer works with is acquired before the age of fifteen." Some of your best writing may come from these territories, as did my essay on painting the back steps.

These territories—or themes—are the ones I keep returning to when I am alone. In mining these territories I have found a lifetime of writing:

School and writing. I was always fascinated by pen and paper, obsessed with the mystery of how words and lines could create and clarify a world. I read books, studied pictures, and did badly in school. I did not learn in the way that the "bright" kids learned and thought I was dumb. My motivation to become a teacher and to write books about writing and the teaching of writing came from my personal struggles in the classroom; I wanted to understand how writing was made so that I could help students like myself explore our world through writing.

Family. Like most families, mine had difficulties—problems, tensions, conflicts—I could not understand when I was young. Much of my writing today deals with family: my grandparents and parents who are dead, my daughters, their husbands, and our grandchildren; the daughter we lost when she was twenty. I keep writing about family to celebrate and to understand.

Sickness, aging, and death. I had a sickly childhood. The grandmother with whom I lived became paralyzed when I was very young, and I helped take care of her until I went to college. I wrote many magazine pieces about health issues, and now I write a weekly column for the *Boston Globe*—"Over Sixty"—that documents my own aging.

War. I was in combat as a paratrooper during World War II and am still trying to deal with the internal conflict of pride and shame experienced during my own months in combat. The Pulitzer Prize I received was for writing on military affairs, and my columns and poems constantly find their way onto the battlefield. The novel I am writing explores the effect of war on those who appear to survive it.

List the subjects that make you itch. What do you think about when you are driving alone in the car, taking a walk, tuning out the people you're with at dinner or a party, doing errands or the laundry, while listening to a boring lecture? What keeps you awake nights? What do you try to avoid thinking about? Donald Barthelme said: "Write about what you're most afraid of."

Of course much of the writing you do in school or at work concerns territories dominated by teachers or employers. It is important to try to make the territory your own, to turn any assignment so you can write with confidence—and to find an abundance of specific information on which you can draw.

FIND YOUR OWN MYSTERY

Our best subjects come from the mysteries in our lives or in the topics we are exploring with language. Grace Paley said, "We write about what we don't know about what we know." Many of us know a parent, uncle or aunt, teacher or neighbor whose life was changed by the Vietnam War, but often we do not know the details or the nature of the change. That individual's personal history is a mystery that might help us to understand them—and the nature of war—if we could explore it.

Seek and confront the mysteries in your life to find writing subjects. The mysteries may be personal: Why did I return to a spouse who abused me? What was the effect of my parents' drinking on my life? Or they may be impersonal: What makes it possible for a heavy metal plane to fly? Why does one product sell while a similar one sits on the supermarket shelf?

Some of the mysteries that have led me to write:

- How can I feel both pride and shame at my combat experience? This unresolved mystery has produced columns and poems as well as the novel on which I am currently working.
- Why didn't I do well in school? How might school have been made meaningful to me? This mystery led to articles and books I have written on teaching.
- How is writing created? This mystery has fascinated me from grade school to today and has led to nine published books about writing.

The mysteries may be small or large, personal or impersonal, but they engage our minds. They present problems we need to solve and provide us with unexpected answers as we watch our words appear on the page or screen.

TECHNIQUES FOR DISCOVERING SUBJECTS

There are many other ways to discover the mysteries that will produce effective subjects. Play with them to see what works for you.

Brainstorming

One of the best ways to discover what you already know is to brainstorm. When you brainstorm you write down everything that comes into your mind as fast as you can. You don't need to be critical; you do want to be illogical, irrational, even silly. You want to discover what is in your mind. You want to be surprised.

Here I have brainstormed about my childhood to see what other topics I may have overlooked that need to be explored in writing. I'll start with the geography of childhood and see where it leads me as I list as fast as I can, not worrying if I am silly or stupid. Brainstorm beside me in the margin of the text. There's plenty of white space. You may discover a subject you want to explore through writing. My list is personal; I'm writing about my childhood. Your list doesn't have to be. Brainstorm any topic, personal or impersonal, with which you have some experience to see if there's something you wish to explore.

Now to brainstorm:

- Geography of childhood
- The block
- The vacant lot
- Empty stores
- Cellar hole
- Under the porch
- Playing doctor
- Sex mis-education
- Behind the garage
- Dogs, Airedale, Chow, scared
- Uncle
- Grandmother collapses
- Alien WASP—white Protestant in Irish Catholic neighborhood
- School
- Nearsighted
- Sat in back row
- Glasses
- "Four-eyes"
- Turn the other cheek—beaten up on playground
- Muddy Ducks

- Fights
- Seriousness of games
- Red Sox, Bruins
- Snow
- Sleighs
- Uncle Will's car up on blocks in winter
- His Buick
- The Sunday drive
- Almost drowning
- Fear of water
- Sickly childhood
- Days in bed—good
- Reading
- Friends who lived in walls
- Fantasy
- Temper—threw hammer at uncle, he fell
- Grandmother's paralysis
- Day I pulled hot jelly over me
- Wood stove
- Mystery of basement
- Mystery of attic
- Den
- Brown, color of *my childhood*

That took eight minutes. It's possible to brainstorm for a much longer time, but I find short spurts—fifteen minutes, ten minutes, five minutes—are more productive. You can also brainstorm together with another person or a group of people. The important thing is not to censor what you say, not to judge it, not to really understand it—but to let it come.

This brainstorming list is printed simply as it came. I didn't prepare for it, except by living with my grandmother until I went off to college. I had to let it come.

After you have brainstormed, look at what you've written to see what surprises you or which items connect. These surprises and connections remind you of what you know and make you aware of meanings you hadn't seen before.

It is important not to worry about how the brainstorming list is written. Don't worry about spelling or penmanship or sentences; it is a time to write in a sort of private language of code words that stand for particular meanings in your own mind. When the phrase "turn the other cheek" appeared on my brainstorming list, it reminded me of all the years—from grade one until grade six—when my mother would instruct me not to fight but to "turn the other cheek." If I really believed in Jesus, she said, the fists of the other boys would be held and they would not smite me. Apparently, I was never able to believe enough, because their fists kept hitting me and I lived in fear, humiliation, and guilt at my lack of faith. All that and much, much more would pour out if I wrote about that phrase in a column, novel, or poem; but the simple phrase "turn the other cheek" would be enough to hold it in reserve for another writing session.

I brainstorm before I write important letters or memos. I brainstorm class lectures and novels. I brainstorm articles and poems and textbooks such as this. I also brainstorm before I decide to buy a car or take a job or choose a vacation. Brainstorming shows me what I know, what I need to know, and what the connections are between what I know and don't know.

Looking for Surprise. I look at the list to see what surprised me. Whatever you are brainstorming—an academic paper or a job application letter—first go over the list to see what surprises you, to find out what discoveries you have made.

The surprise doesn't need to be enormous. I am surprised by:

- Under the porch
- Playing doctor
- Sex mis-education
- Behind the garage

I don't remember what happened behind the garage, and that's enough of a mystery for me to start to explore my childhood world when I first became aware of sex—I thought the facts of life ridiculous when I first learned them, and, in fact, they are.

I also note:

- Seriousness of games
- Red Sox, Bruins

That is all it takes to remind me of the importance of being a sports fan in a town like Boston. It was one of the few subjects that connected me with my father and my uncles—the world of men—and the emphasis on sports and competition probably marked me more than I know. If I write about that subject, I may discover its importance.

An old theme for me but a new twist:

- Sickly childhood
- Days in bed—good

What have we lost because of miracle drugs? Convalescence. I am nostalgic for the long, lonely hours of fantasy and the reading that helped make me a writer.

Looking for Connections. Next I look for connections between the items on my list. I draw lines connecting related entries, creating little bunches that may lead to a subject:

- The vacant lot
- Empty stores
- Cellar hole

Child's delight in playgrounds created by construction and business failures in the Great Depression.

- Alien WASP—white Protestant in Irish Catholic neighborhood
- Turn the other cheek— beaten up on playground
- Fights
- Seriousness of games
- Almost drowning
- Fear of water
- Sickly childhood

Might explore the terrors of childhood.

- School
- Nearsighted
- Sat in back row
- Glasses
- "Four-eyes"

Might reconstruct the school world of a nearsighted kid when you got beaten up for wearing glasses.

Mapping

Another form of brainstorming that often works is mapping. You put the subject or topic you want to think about in the center of the page and then draw lines radiating out from it when another idea occurs to you. These lines branch off, capturing the fragments of information that you have unknowingly stored in memory.

A map of thoughts I have about my childhood is on page 24.

How Mapping Leads to Writing. That map took less than ten minutes to create, about the same time as the brainstorm list, but it produced different information. I rediscovered the red quarantine cards that were placed on the door when anyone had scarlet fever or measles; this memory might lead me into the territory of childhood disease before miracle drugs. The map also made me aware of how much I learned about the world came in the form of stories—from the Bible, from Grandma and the uncles, from the street, from the classroom. Then there was the role of music—my family's hymns and Sousa marches, my jazz and the beginning of my interest in classical music—I could write a musical geography of my childhood.

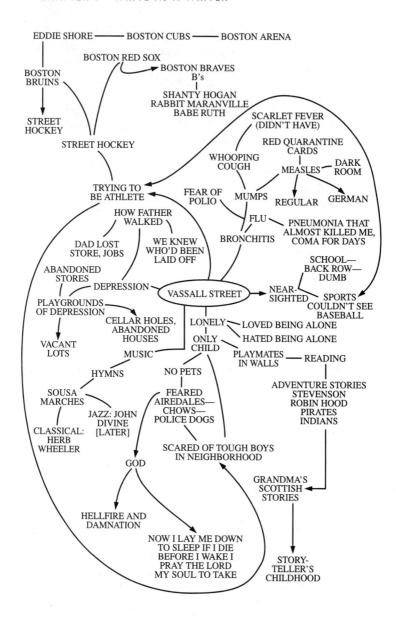

Making a Tree

Another helpful technique to discover what you already know and don't know you know is to draw a tree. The chart on page 25 reveals the branches that can grow from a single idea.

This technique gives you a way of breaking down a subject or letting a subject expand. Some writers who use trees successfully place the central idea at the

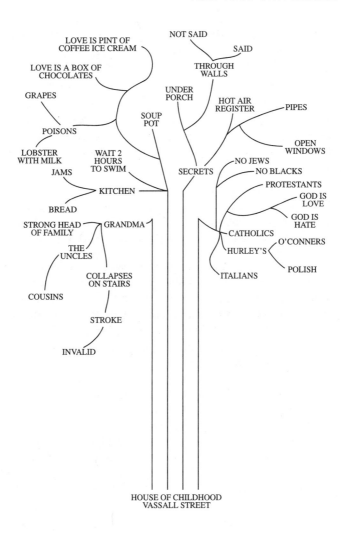

top of the page and let the tree grow down, whereas others place the central idea at the bottom of the page and let the tree grow up. Both produce excellent results.

This tree took five minutes to create, and it produced some new insights. I discovered the larger complexity of religions with which I grew up and their contradictions, the food myths that were important in my childhood, and the role of secrets in our family.

Free Writing

Another technique I have found productive is the free writing with which this chapter opened. To free write, sit down and let the writing flow; see if language will start to reveal something that unexpectedly interests you—an event, person, place, idea, feeling. Suspend critical judgment, as you do when brainstorming or mapping, and look for something to happen.

I'm never sure that anything will happen when I free write. But it really doesn't matter. Some days the writing comes, and some days it doesn't. If free writing doesn't work right away, I try brainstorming or mapping, or staring out the window, or turning to another project, or getting a cup of tea, or taking a walk, or otherwise creating an interruption. It is important in doing creative work to step back from the draft, the canvas, the score, the lab experiment—just far enough to gain perspective, to allow the subconscious to percolate. But in a few minutes I'll return to my desk, and something will work.

Now I'll free write, aware that my free writing looks more polished than the beginning writer's. It is. I refuse to fake it for the purpose of an example, but don't worry if your free writing is a lot sloppier than mine. It should be.

> I don't think I was ever alone in that house of childhood. Mother was a woman of the streets, shopping, always shopping, chatting with friends, having lunch with them. She hated housework and cooking; she loved going out. And yet, although Grandma was there singing hymns in the kitchen; and Uncle Will was at his desk, keeping the books for one customer or another; or Father was at the dining room table organizing sales slips from the store and Mother was in the living room reading a woman's magazine; I remember being alone in that house. I had hiding places. My own room, under the dining room table, between the bushes and the house, behind the sofa, at the top of the stairs in the dark, in the empty coal bin.
>
> I must have been a strange little boy, always listening, always making up stories, always trying to understand the tensions between the four adults with whom I lived. They were all so self-centered they gave me a lot of room—space, we'd call it today. I drove by the house and it is smaller, much smaller, than I remembered. I suppose I was never more than a few feet from anyone, and yet that loneliness is real. And the silence. We did all our hurting with turning away, what was not said, was our favorite weapon.

That few minutes of writing certainly took me where I did not expect to go, giving me a whole new vision of my childhood on Vassall Street.

Velocity in free writing is important; write fast so that you say what you do not expect to say. Also, note that free writing isn't really free. It starts to take you somewhere, to tell you what to say and how to say it. After free writing, look back to see whether you want to follow any of your paths, to explore them so the writing stops being private and can go public to readers. Decide whether you want to share with others what you are discovering. If you do, you'll find that the more personal the writing, the more specific and private, the more it will spark memories and ideas in your readers' minds.

Free writing is just as valuable a technique to use as a starting point for a term paper, an historical essay, or a review of scientific literature. It's a way of thinking in which you can preserve the flow of thought.

Interviewing Yourself

Develop your own "itch list" to help you find a subject. Here are some of the questions I ask myself to discover what I want to "scratch" next:

- What has surprised me recently? What do I need to know?
- What would I like to know?
- How are things different than they used to be? How will things be different in the future?
- What have we lost?
- What have we gained?
- What do I know that others need to know?
- Who would I like to get to know?
- What's not happening that should?
- What's happening that shouldn't?
- Who would I like to see at work?
- What process do I need to know?
- What process would it be fun to observe?
- How can I switch my position so I will see my world differently?
- What have I read, heard, thought that confuses me?
- What connections are being made that surprise me?
- How is peoples' behavior changing?
- How are beliefs changing?
- What makes me mad?
- Sad?
- Happy?
- Worried?
- Frightened?
- Content?
- What do I expect to see, hear?
- Why?

....

START THE WRITING HABIT

The myth: Published writers—screenwriters, playwrights, novelists, poets, nonfiction writers, short-story writers, as well as composers and artists—lead lives of Bohemian excess, smoking stuff, drinking stuff, and chasing stuff all night long.

The reality: Writers write; the artistic life is a life of discipline. Gustave Flaubert said, "Be regular and ordinary in your life like a bourgeois so that you may be violent and original in your work." Flannery O'Connor testified, "Every morning between 9 and 12 I go to my room and sit before a piece of paper. Many times I just sit for three hours with no ideas coming to me. But I know one thing: If an idea does come between 9 and 12, I am there ready for it."

Sounds simple, doesn't it? It isn't. Getting the writing done day in and day out, despite interruptions, phone calls, obligations, duties, responsibilities, inertia, exhaustion, poor health, bad weather, invited and uninvited guests, too much drinking, too much eating, or too little eating, wars, storms, births, deaths, marriages, divorces, travel, letters that come and letters that don't come, and a million other problems, is what separates the writer from the hope-to-be writer.

TIME

We have two kinds of writing times: fragmentary and insulated. Fragmentary time is the few minutes you have before a class begins, sitting in a doctor's office, waiting for a friend to show up for lunch, waiting for a bus, or during the commercials while watching TV. Insulated time is the half-hours, hours, hour-and-a-halfs, two hours you are able to shut out the world—in your room, the library, an empty classroom. Obviously, we have much more fragmentary time than we have insulated time, and it is important that we make use of both kinds of time. The focusing and planning I do is performed mostly in small fragments of time that can be measured only in minutes, sometimes in seconds. This writing is done in my head and in my daybook. It isn't a question of hours but of minutes.

Try it yourself before class begins, waiting for a friend at the student union, during a commercial break on television, waiting for the campus bus, during a coffee break at work, or as a short break from studying; see how long it takes to brainstorm five essay titles, write a lead paragraph, draft a description, focus on a definition, sketch an anecdote, or even outline an article. I suspect you will find that when you thought you worked ten, or fifteen, or twenty minutes, you've worked two minutes, or four, or ninety seconds.

If you make good use of those fragments of time, then you'll be able to write when you have a stretch of uninterrupted time. For most writers an hour is good, but not good enough. Two hours is plenty; three hours is heroic. During those times unplug the phone, lock the door; do not read, plan, edit, nap or eat—just write.

The time of day is important. Most young writers start writing late at night but end up writing in the morning—the early morning—when their minds are fresh and the world is least likely to intrude. Goethe said, "Use the day before the day. Early morning hours have gold in their mouth."

The time of day, however, is not as important as habit. Most productive writers—there are exceptions—establish a routine and write at the same time every day. They know the time and the people around them know the time. Alberto Moravia says:

> When I sit down to write—that's between 9 and 12 every morning, and I have never, incidentally, written a line in the afternoon or at night—when I sit down at my table to write, I never know what it's going to be until I'm under way. I trust in inspiration, which sometimes comes and sometimes doesn't. But I don't sit back waiting for it. I work every day.

Do not attempt long, exhausting writing sessions. Few writers are productive in that way. Most writers write regularly for one to three hours every day, and those are considered full-time writers. You may have to try for an hour a day or half an hour. Philip Larkin says:

> I don't think you can write a poem for more than two hours. After that you're going round in circles, and it's much better to leave it for twenty-four hours. . . . Some days it goes, and some days it doesn't go. But over weeks and months I am productive.

Once you have produced a draft, fragmentary time can serve you again. I find it better to edit in short bursts. If I edit more than fifteen minutes at a run I tend to be kind, far too kind. In these slivers of time, early and late in the day, I can cut, insert, reorder, and perhaps decide that I need another draft when I have a few hours of insulated time.

PLACE

It helps to have a place where you go to write. It should be a place where you can leave your work lying out and come back to it later, where you have your tools at hand and you have the climate that you prefer.

Ross MacDonald said, "I took my lifelong tenancy in the bare muffled room of the professional writer where I am sitting now, with my back to the window, writing longhand in a spiral notebook." I like to look up from my writing and see a view. Other writers, such as Ross MacDonald, turn their backs to the view. I need music when I write; other writers need silence. Create a place of your own where you can shut the door and be alone.

That's an ideal many students can't achieve because they have families or roommates. Joyce Carol Oates says, however, "If you are a writer, you locate yourself behind a wall of silence and no matter what you are doing, driving a car or walking or doing housework, which I love, you can still be writing, because you have that space."

It isn't easy to create that internal space, but it can be done, as Lois Duncan points out:

Now I keep a typewriter with a sheet of paper in it on the end of the kitchen table. When I have a five-minute lull and the children are playing quietly, I sit down and knock out a paragraph. I have learned that I can write, if necessary with a TV set blaring on one side of me and a child banging on a piano on the other. I've even typed out a story with a colicky baby draped across my lap. It is not ideal—but it is possible.

Donald Graves has been able to write in a dormitory room with pneumatic drill construction going on next door or in a small summer cottage filled with family, friends, and dogs by using earphones and listening to Beethoven at top volume to insulate himself from the surrounding world.

Find ways to detach yourself from the world and go to that place where you can "hear" the writing. Depending on your personality, that place may not be the ideal artist's cabin high in the Rockies. I wrote most of one novel in a park, either sitting in the car or at a picnic table far out of the range of my mother-in-law's voice. I like to write in coffee shops and diners where no one knows me, and where there is a stimulating but unobtrusive background life that I can observe or ignore. When I was an undergraduate, my favorite writing places included the top row of the empty football stadium, a pleasing assortment of rocks on the Atlantic coast, a special table in the library, and an empty classroom late at night. Find the places where you can hear your voice as it speaks from the page.

CONDITIONS THAT INVITE WRITING

I have to cultivate conditions that encourage writing. I do this by looking at what conditions I experienced when the writing came easily, when I was ready to write and the writing flowed almost effortlessly. Yes, there are such days.

Expectation

I expect to write. My attitude predicts my performance. The swimmer who goes to the starting block prepared to lose will lose; the writer who does not expect a draft will not write one. I have to recall when I have written easily before to expect that the draft will come.

Demand

External. A deadline helps—a line beyond which you are dead if you don't deliver. No excuses. I am lucky because I start the week with a Monday morning deadline on my column. All week I know that I will sit down Monday morning and produce a column, and I do. My editor expects it; I expect it. An external demand that requires a finished product can make all the difference between a published writer and a wish-I-were-published writer.

Internal. I also have an internal demand. I need to write to understand the life I have led and am leading. Catherine Drinker Bowen explains, "Writing is a kind of double living. The writer experiences everything twice. Once in reality and once in that mirror which waits always before or behind him." Compare it to what happens to you when you go over last weekend's party in your mind or in conversation with a friend, recreating what you did and didn't do, should have and should not have done or said to find out what it means. I write to discover who I am and what the life I am leading means. I must write.

This statement doesn't mean just personal writing. Lawyers write briefs to find out how past judicial decisions impact their cases; business people write reports to discover where profits are being made or lost; insurance investigators write to find out if their companies must pay claims; scientists and engineers write to find out what experiments taught them and what future experiments need to be performed.

Rehearsal

Sometimes I come to my desk stupid, empty, drained of anything to say and then, if I just plunge in and write blindly, I may receive a good piece of writing that surprises me; but most times I come to my desk having rehearsed what I may say, the way I would rehearse an employment interview. I go over fragments of language, strategies of development and communication in my conscious and subconscious mind. I talk to myself, I dream, I imagine what I may say, sometimes making notes, often just letting the random fragments of writing circulate through my mind. It is all brought together as I start to draft.

Forgiveness

To write, I have to write as well as I can write today, accepting the fact that I cannot write as well as I'd like to or as well as I imagine other writers are writing. I keep rereading the wise counsel of poet William Stafford:

> I believe that the so-called "writing block" is a product of some kind of disproportion between your standards and your performance. . . . One should lower his standards until there is no felt threshold to go over in writing. It's easy to write. You just shouldn't have standards that inhibit you from writing.

> • • •

> I can imagine a person beginning to feel he's not able to write up to that standard he imagines the world has set for him. But to me that's surrealistic. The only standard I can rationally have is the standard I'm meeting right now. . . . You should be more willing to forgive yourself. It doesn't make any difference if you are good or bad today. The assessment of the product is something that happens after you've done it.

Velocity

To balance a two-wheeler I have to pedal fast; to outrun the censor and to cause the accidents of insight and language that mark good writing, I have to write fast.

Ease

I try to write with ease, relaxed, allowing the words to flow through me naturally. If I do this, the draft will instruct, telling me what I should say and how I should say it. The evolving draft will take its own course, exploring experience as it is relived. If I am patient, receptive, open to surprise, the draft will tell me what I have to say. E. M. Forster said: "Think before you speak, is criticism's motto; speak before you think is creation's."

Write easily. Relax. Allow the writing to pass through you. Do not force, strain, or intend, but receive. The cliché says, "Easy writing makes hard reading" but the experienced writer knows the opposite is true—graceful, fluid writing makes easy reading.

All of these conditions and attitudes help get me to start writing. They aren't all in place every day but enough are so that I begin each day writing, and that writing gives me the wonderful surprise of hearing what I didn't know I knew. That's what keeps me writing.

....

HEAR THE VOICE OF THE DRAFT

Voice is style and tone and more. It is the human sound that arises from a written page. Voice is rhythm and beat, inflection and emphasis, volume and pause; it is the manner in which the author speaks; it is the flow of what is spoken; it is the emotional content of writing, it is energy and force; it is the presence of an individual writer speaking to an individual reader. Voice is the most important, the most magical and powerful element of writing. During writing and revising, the writer hears the voice of the draft and tunes it to the meaning being developed and made clear.

One way to hear the voice of the draft is to speak aloud while writing. Then you will hear the tone of what you are saying, the background music that communicates mood and emotion. You can do this by "silently" speaking what you write, as I am doing now. Then you will be able to hear what you are writing—and tune the voice of the draft to what is being said.

Voice is magic but not mysterious. From another room, you can recognize the voices of those with whom you live; you know if they're mad, sad, having a good time, asking, rejecting, commanding, pleading. You can accomplish the same effect through your writing. You establish a voice that arises from the page.

Read aloud—and I mean right out loud—the first sentences of the following passages to hear their voices:

· THE JOY LUCK CLUB ·
Amy Tan

My father has asked me to be the fourth corner at the Joy Luck Club. I am to replace my mother, whose seat at the mah jong table has been empty since she died two months ago. My father thinks she was killed by her own thoughts.

Amy Tan's voice takes you right into her world. Her father's command establishes a new relationship with his daughter, who is "to replace my mother" (his wife). The next sentence explains why this new relationship and the last sentence creates a mystery; he does not have a conventional, 1990s, American cause of death such as cancer or heart disease. The narrator's voice is direct, simple, spare of emotion, neither resentful of her father nor sad for the loss of her mother; it is the voice of a young observer of life who is recounting an event that has significance to discover its full implications.

· PROSPECT ·
Bill Littlefield

Scouting was a funny thing for me to get into, the way both Alice and I felt about travel. But I'm damned if the business wasn't full of guys who didn't like to fly, even though there was an awful lot of flying involved, and guys who said they hated to drive, too, though sometimes they'd drive all day and all night. There were guys who said they got stomachaches when they had to sell a boy's parents on the idea of him signing, and others who claimed they'd rather go to the dentist than fill out all the paperwork their clubs required. But we will put up with almost anything for the chance to do something that offers us joy. And when you get older you will fly, or drive, or stand on your head to be in the presence of that thing, which is a fleeting thing.

This is the garrulous voice of an old baseball scout retired in Florida. We hear in this voice an old man who has spent his life sitting in the stands chatting with other old baseball players.

· THE REMAINS OF THE DAY ·
Kazuo Ishiguro

It seems increasingly likely that I really will undertake the expedition that has been preoccupying my imagination now for some days. An expedition, I should say, which I will undertake alone, in the comfort of Mr. Farraday's Ford; an expedition which, as I foresee it, will take me through much of the finest countryside of England to the West Country, and may keep me away from Darlington Hall for as much as five or six days. The idea of such a journey came about, I should point out, from a most kind suggestion put to me by Mr. Farraday himself one afternoon almost a fortnight ago, when I had been dusting the portraits in the library.

Now we hear a radically different voice, the formal voice of a British butler, created by a young writer recognized as a master stylist.

• THE MERRY ADVENTURES OF ROBIN HOOD •
Howard Pyle

In merry England in the time of old, when good King Henry the Second ruled the land, there lived within the green glades of Sherwood Forest, near Nottingham Town, a famous outlaw whose name was Robin Hood. No archer ever lived that could speed a grey goose shaft with such skill and cunning as his, nor were there ever such yeomen as the sevenscore merry men that roamed with him through the greenwood shades.

This is the old-timey voice of one of my childhood's favorite books. It is a traditional storyteller voice that attempts to imitate a minstrel, preserving oral history.

• THE THINGS THEY CARRIED •
Tim O'Brien

First Lieutenant Jimmy Cross carried letters from a girl named Martha, a junior at Mount Sebastian College in New Jersey. They were not love letters, but Lieutenant Cross was hoping, so he kept them folded in plastic at the bottom of his rucksack. In the late afternoon, after a day's march, he would dig his foxhole, wash his hands under a canteen, unwrap the letters, hold them with the tips of his fingers, and spend the last hour of light pretending.

O'Brien, perhaps the best of the Vietnam novelists, uses a reportorial voice, somewhat detached, that allows him to reveal the horrors of war—in this case a soldier's loneliness and distance from the woman he loves.

• BELOVED •
Toni Morrison

124 was spiteful. Full of a baby's venom. The women in the house knew it and so did the children. For years each put up with the spite in his own way, but by 1873 Sethe and her daughter Denver were its only victims. The grandmother,

Baby Suggs, was dead, and the sons, Howard and Buglar, had run away by the time they were thirteen years old—as soon as merely looking in a mirror shattered it (that was the signal for Buglar); as soon as two tiny handprints appeared in the cake (that was it for Howard). Neither boy waited to see more; another kettleful of chickpeas smoking in a heap on the floor; soda crackers crumbled and strewn in a line next to the doorsill.

> *Another storyteller's voice that recreates an oral tradition on the page. No reader can escape the power, energy, force of this voice by one of our most respected writers.*

• WILDFIRE •
Richard Ford

In the fall of 1960, when I was sixteen and my father was for a time not working, my mother met a man named Warren Miller and fell in love with him.

> *Richard Ford, another of our most respected writers, has created a sentence of utter simplicity that reveals, in a few words, a very complicated story that would be told—and explored—by a sixteen-year-old narrator.*

Each of these voices is different but each is true to the author and to the story the author is telling. Each one makes me want to listen, to read on. Each writer has an individual voice that comes from such influences as genes; ethnic, religious, and regional heritage; social and economic class; and educational background. The important thing is to take that personal voice and tune it to the meaning of the text. All of these examples of voice serve the meaning of the text. Think of a musical score that tells you when to be scared, when to laugh, when to be sad. The music of written language does the same thing: It tells you what to think and feel.

WRITING ON A COMPUTER

The great advantage of the computer is that it makes it easy to write badly. Good writing is the direct product of bad writing. Unless we write badly, we say only what we have said before in the way we have said it before. On the computer it is easy to rush ahead of meaning, of clarity, of grace, of tradition, of correctness to where we find what has not yet been said, at least by us, in forms and voices we have never explored.

At *Time* magazine we were given great, thick, soft lead pencils and forced to write by hand. The editors wanted us to slow down and craft our stories with constipated care. That may have been good advice for a magazine that had a strong style, that wanted to speak in a familiar and recognized voice, but not for me. I did a bad job at *Time* because I wrote out of fear and caution, trying to please, trying to be someone I was not.

Before *Time* and afterward, when I wrote by hand or typewriter, I wrote carefully. I did not want to suffer the tedious job of typing a new, clean draft—or asking my wife to type it for me. But with the computer I could race ahead of my censors, surprising myself and finding—in the bad writing—the writing, as Chip Scanlan says, that only I could do.

I write with velocity, surprising myself with what appears on the screen. Then, once I have discovered what I have to say and how I may be able to say it, I can write and rewrite, shaping and crafting my lines until they are clear to me—and to a reader.

The computer also makes it possible for me to write right over what I have written, developing the text with layers the way oil painters often work. This method of revising—described and demonstrated on pages 182 through 186—is made easy by the computer.

IN THE WRITER'S WORKSHOP

The hardest thing I had to do even to become a writer was believing that I had anything to say that people would want to read.   ALICE MCDERMOTT

There is in you what is beyond you.   PAUL VALERY

When my writing is going well, I know that I'm writing out of my personal obsessions.
BHARTI MUKHERJEE

I never know what my stories are about until they are finished, until they choose to reveal themselves. I merely feel their power, how they breathe on me. I try not to write them. I prefer the rush of having them write me.   KATE BRAVERMAN

That is the pure pleasure of creation—the not knowing that leads you to the knowing.
BOBBIE ANN MASON

If you want to be a tuba player you get a tuba, and some tuba music. And you ask the neighbors to move away or put cotton in their ears. And you probably get a tuba teacher, because there are a lot of objective rules and techniques to both written music and to tuba performance. And then you sit down and you play the tuba, every day, every week, every month, year after year, until you are good at playing the tuba; until you can—if you desire—play the truth on the tuba.

It is exactly the same with writing. You sit down, and you do it, and you do it, and you do it, until you have learned how to do it.   URSULA K. LE GUIN

You always play the same way. You can't play different from who you are. Maybe you growl now, but your personality, intelligence, feeling, they don't change. I think it was Matisse who said, people have one idea and they're going to deal with it forever.
WYNTON MARSALIS

I write every day, in the early morning. I become melancholy if I don't. Writing is really more of an obsession than a habit. WILLIAM TREVOR

What I've found and what I believe is that everybody is talented. It's just that some people get it developed and some don't. STEPHEN SONDHEIM

For a couple of years I was waking up at five every morning to write for a few hours before going to work. That was when I knew what I wanted to say but didn't know how to say it. When I finally found the right voice, it took me only a month to write the novel. I'd take my eight-month-old son out in the stroller for a walk, and while he was looking around at the trees and grass in the park, I'd be thinking about what I was going to write next. Then I'd come home and write when he napped. I did exactly what a friend once told me to do—I never used my child's nap time for anything but writing. EVE HOROWITZ

I think I'm trying to keep myself from being bored. When I think about why I would be a writer, why I should continue to be a writer, it seems to me one of the few things you can do where you're never bored. GISH JEN

I don't plan my writing. What comes out is usually quite surprising. I write to find out what I'm thinking. JOHN ASHBERY

I have the feeling that if I don't write, the previous day disappears. . . . one writes to recover what has been lost. ISABEL ALLENDE

QUESTIONS ABOUT WRITING AS A WRITER

What is all this about a process for writing? I don't have a process and I still get As on my essays.

Everyone has a writing process, but the process is invisible since writers usually write alone. Because writing is a closed-door activity, we have no way of knowing the difficulty an author has with finding a topic or how many times she revises before publication.

We forget too that using a computer has made the process of writing less apparent, since we now can perform multiple tasks at one sitting: drafting, focusing, and drafting again; editing, deleting, and planning; revising, focusing, and drafting once more. When a writer finishes, we usually see only the result: a proofread product, typed, tidy, and ready for the reader's eye.

It's certainly true that some writers (and you may be one of these) can sit down at the computer and hammer out something worthwhile without much effort. But if asked to explain in detail how they compose, even these writers would define some sort of process. They sift through information and focus on an angle for their topic. They revise, insert, delete, and move text around, pausing to read what they have written before moving on. It is the rare accomplished writer who does not finally read a printed copy of a draft with pencil in hand, looking for ways to make a story or essay even better.

If you are getting straight *A*s on all your writing, that's great! Your process is working for you. But you might want to ask yourself another question: Is your writing publishable? If the answer is no, it may be time to take your writing to the next plane, to push yourself beyond what is expected of you at school and to think of becoming the best writer you can on your own terms. Concentrate more on planning and revision. Write for yourself instead of for your teachers.

I've already explored my writing process in high school. Don't you think it's a waste of time to do it again in college?

No. Process means fluidity and growth, something that is always evolving, always in flux. While you are probably a more insightful writer from having paid attention early on to your writing process, you will never be finished exploring, changing, and improving the way you write until you draft your final sentence. Since you will be writing in one form or another throughout your life, that final sentence (we hope!) is a long way off.

You may want to think about it this way: You don't finish learning when you finish college. Each new experience becomes part of a longer, continuous process of analyzing and making meaning, of revising the way you view the world and the way you think about older experiences. Likewise, your experiences at college will be different from your high school experiences. You are probably already reprocessing what you know and what you think, even though you may have been at college for only a very short time. Since writing is a way of thinking, learning, and revising, your particular process will change as you change.

Besides, your writing assignments at college will most likely be much different from those in high school, and you will want to adapt your process accordingly. As you explore different disciplines and juggle an increasing number of deadlines, you will have to experiment with different processes. What worked for you in high school may not necessarily work for you now.

So if process means flexibility, why do I have to follow all the steps of the process in the order that you have them in this book?

You don't. Following a procedure is a good way to get started and move through a draft, and it's a good idea to work through the steps in the order you find them here as a way of beginning and thinking about your process. But it's not the only way. While you will probably complete each step of the process before you are through (and your teacher may insist on this), don't think of these steps as guideposts along a straight and narrow road. Think of them as points along a circle or spiral, sites that you will most likely revisit or pass again on your journey as a writer.

Writing should be an exciting, adventuresome activity. It should be full of surprises, unexpected opportunities, twists in the trail, surprising views, new challenges. You can always vary a method of working and go back to it when you need to. A writing method should never make a writer follow a discipline of writing that ignores the evolving life of a draft.

How about academic writing, essays I have to do for other classes? How will following a process help me if my teacher assigns a topic?

From a practical perspective, following a process of focusing, planning, drafting, revising, and editing will get you from Point A to Point B. It will force you to set a schedule and meet deadlines. Instead of writing your paper the night before class (or not turning it in at all!), you will have a polished product to hand in on the day it is due. This kind of agenda will also be helpful if you get a job that requires reports and other written products.

But aren't English teachers the only ones who use a writing process?

No. If you ask professors in different fields to talk about essays or books they have written, or if you see all their drafts, you will find that published writing evolves through an extensive process of focusing and revision. You will also discover that your professors rely on editors who proofread their work before it is published. None of these professors sits down at the computer and fires off a perfectly polished product the first time around.

What if my teacher won't let me write from my point of view or use the pronoun I when I write? What if she thinks it's too personal?

Even if you do not say *I,* you imply it in all your writing. It is the *I* who is behind every bit of information that goes into your paper and who makes the decisions regarding genre, focus, and angle. While the *I* may receive feedback and suggestions from other readers, that is the person who ultimately sits down to write the piece.

It would be great if you could come right out and say "I think . . ." in all of your papers. But if you can't, try not to distinguish too greatly between personal and academic writing when working through your writing process. All writing is revealing; all writing is personal. While a writer may be distant and detached, his or her choice of words, details, and focus can show what he or she thinks. Even the most "objective" academic writer reveals some sort of relationship with the people and ideas he or she writes about. The long and the short of it is, you don't need to say *I* to write from your own perspective or to make your writing your own.

ACTIVITIES FOR WRITING AS A WRITER

1. Start a writing process log or daybook, picking out a notebook that feels comfortable to you and is the right size so that you can have it with you most all the time. Doodle in it, write in it, paste things in it, record observations and thoughts, ideas and drafts for titles, leads, ends, middles. Create outlines and diagrams. Don't worry about neatness or correctness—this is a place to have fun. Talk to yourself, think to yourself, find out what you are seeing, hearing, feeling, thinking and what it means.

2. Select a writing partner in class and set aside a specific time, fifteen minutes to a half-hour each day, to write one another via campus mail or e-mail. Make the main topic of correspondence the craft of writing, but don't be afraid to just talk about life in general; this is where good writing starts. Discuss subjects that you want to write about and ask questions about these subjects. Comment about the actual act of writing too: where you sit, your ideal writing environment, when you are most productive, when you are not. Support each other through each stage of writing and help each other "power" through writer's block. Keep copies of your correspondence, and collect them in a binder at the end of the semester. Write a preface about your writing process and your semester as a "pen-pal."

3. Find a brainstorming "room:" a cafe, dorm room, lounge area, or even a spot outside by a river or under a tree. Make it your own. Settle into your space with notebook or personal computer and reserve an hour or so each day just for free writing or brainstorming. Make a daily appointment with your spot, and commit yourself to keeping it for at least a month.

4. Come up with a list of five nouns and ask your writing partner to do the same. Exchange lists and write for five minutes apiece about each word, paying particular attention to sensory details and any memories the words evoke. Choose one of these and brainstorm with your partner about ways to expand it.

5. Join an Internet bulletin board or newsgroup. Explore the hundreds of topics these boards cover and choose two or three that interest you. Make a point to read and respond to the posted entries at least once or twice a week. Be attentive to various "posts," jotting down what you agree or disagree with, what you learn from them, and what you can add. Then post your own thoughts.

6. Collaborate with a group of classmates on a TV script for a drama or sitcom. Look at the credits of your favorite shows and note how many writers collaborate together on a show. As an alternative, check network Web sites on the Internet, where you can find all kinds of information about popular programs. Decide how you will collaborate on the script, and elect a recorder who will keep a detailed record of the process you used in writing the script.

7. Invite a local writer—a newspaper columnist, poet, novelist, or essayist—into your classroom. Read selections from the writer's work, and ask the writer to bring in drafts and to talk about his or her writing process. Be prepared with questions about drafting, planning, focusing, and revising. Have on-hand copies of publications by the writer, and refer to specific chapters and passages as you talk.

8. Visit the home or museum of a literary figure where drafts of the author's writing are on display, or check out a biography of an author from the library. Often such displays and biographies track the various stages of a famous work from beginning to end, from idea to publishing. Make a report to your group or class about the writer's composing process.

9. Check out the many writers' chat areas and bulletin boards on the Internet. "Listen" to the conversations among writers about drafting and revising, how they write, when they write, and where they write. Talk with them about your own processes, and choose a mentor from among them. You will find that most writers in these groups will be more than eager to discuss your work.

10. Write in your daybook about a project you have completed that made you proud. How about a speech you wrote and delivered as valedictorian? A car's engine you rebuilt during the summer? A dinner you cooked for your parents' wedding anniversary? The skis you refurbished last winter? When you have finished writing, list the steps you took in planning and carrying out your project. When did you first think of it? Did you have to gather information or do some research in order to complete it? Did you have to revise your plans as you went along? How much time did it take? Was the final product worth it? Was it well-received by others? When you have finished, compare the process of completing your project to the process of writing. How was it similar or different?

11. Choose a passage from a piece of autobiographical writing by a professional author, one that you think conveys a sense of his or her voice. Make copies and pass them around in a small group; ask your groupmates to do the same. Omit any information about the author or the

title of the piece. Try to guess from the passage what the narrator is like. What kind of voice does the writer have? How old do you think the writer is? Is the writer male or female? Write up a profile of the narrator in your daybook.

12. Take a piece of your favorite writer's work and imagine the different stages it must have gone through before it was published. Try to step into your author's shoes and imagine how he or she got started. Pretend you're that author and plan the piece from beginning to end.

13. If your school has a writing center or lab, ask to sit in on a couple of tutoring sessions and listen to conversations about writing. If you can't actually listen in, then make an appointment with the director of the center or a writing tutor to talk about the various ways people go about writing and how tutors at the center help them through the process. Jot down your observations and then write an entry in your daybook comparing your own writing process with those of others.

14. Write a letter to a class partner about a writing project you have in mind and how you want to approach it. As you take the project through its various stages, write memos to your partner reporting on your progress. Pay special attention to the various phases of your writing process and how you move through, repeat, skip, or merge them. At the end of the semester, join with your partner in "publishing" a small book of your work.

15. Write a paper quickly the last minute before class. Don't bother to go back and reread, revise, or edit it. Make copies of your paper and pass them out in a small group. Read the paper aloud and then discuss what needs to be done with it. What process will your paper have to go through to make it better?

16. Hold a "bad" writing contest. With a group of classmates, write a short essay that you consider dull, unfocused and . . . well . . . just generally bad. Exchange your bad essays with another group. Using the stages of the writing process outlined in this chapter, write up a list of suggestions for the authors of each essay and how you think they could improve it. Don't get stuck on grammatical and spelling errors at this point. Think about the gist of the piece, and read it with an eye toward planning, focusing, and drafting.

17. Imagine your writing as a house and draw a blueprint. Don't worry about being highly technical and accurate. Just divide the stages of writing into "rooms" (brainstorming, free writing, and mapping, for example, might be the doors and entrance ways to your house), and furnish the rooms with details about each step. As you write your essay, keep

track of where you have to change your blueprint. Which rooms get the most use? Which do you visit the least?

18. Create the perfect writing area. Splurge on inspirational posters, artwork, a comfortable chair, the right pens and pencils and paper. Go to yard sales or flea markets to buy all the extras that will spiff up your special corner. Make it a place you will want to return to again and again. If you need music while you write, have your stereo and headphones nearby; if you like privacy, enclose the space with a screen. Post pictures of family and friends or of writers whom you admire around your computer or writing desk.

19. Talk to professors in your major or area of interest about writing in that discipline. Ask them to tell you about any articles they have written, how they went about planning and drafting them, and how they revised them. Find out what kind of feedback they got from friends, colleagues, and publishers that helped them put together their final drafts.

20. Retype a couple of pages from a published author's work on a typewriter or computer. LISTEN to the rhythm of the sentences as you rewrite them. Think of the words you are putting down and how the author chooses them. Pay attention to punctuation and the stylistic choices the author makes. Then rewrite the passage. Change or add punctuation or leave it out; drop or add details, or go off on a tangent of your own. Move the middle paragraph to the beginning or change the ending. Choose one scene or detail to write about extensively and omit others. Note when and how the focus of the essay shifts as you fiddle with it.

21. Make a list of teachers you remember. Next to their names, jot down writing assignments you associate with them. Select two or three names from this list and in your daybook write as quickly as you can about the teachers, what you learned about writing from each one, and how you began, sustained, and completed each writing assignment for that teacher. Be humorous or serious or reflective, but try to trace your writing process through each teacher and each writing assignment.

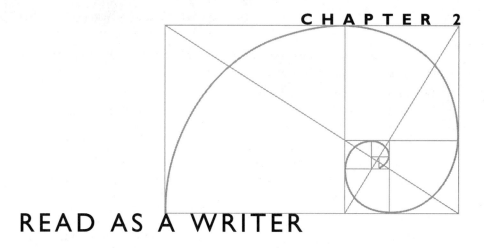

CHAPTER 2

READ AS A WRITER

Readers don't have to be writers, but writers have to be readers—skillful readers of their own evolving drafts and insightful readers of the masters who can teach them how to develop their craft.

Writers must be able to read what they haven't yet written—so they can write it. They also must read what they are writing while it is being written. Finally, they must read what they have written to see if a reader will understand.

Writing and reading continuously interact during the writing process. Writers move in close and then stand back, developing a double vision as they read the words they have just written and, at the same time, remember the entire draft to see how each word changes the whole piece of writing and how the evolving whole affects the meaning of the word. This lightning-fast, instinctive reading can be developed by beginning writers who already do the same thing in conversation, hearing what they have just said and reading its effect, word by word, phrase by phrase on their listeners.

Writers also read other writers for information, delight, escape, instruction, inspiration and, most of all for craft. We imagine the problems the writer faced, the possible ways of solving them that were considered, rejected, or, as the successful draft demonstrates, used. We should not read with envy or as competitors. Of course there is competition in the arts, but it is always inappropriate, always a lack, a weakness, a failure of faith in the craft we share. We do not—or should not—paint or compose or write against each other. We have joined the guild because we celebrate our world, and we should take nurture, instruction, and delight in the celebrations of others. We cannot copy others but we can discover how their craft, processed through our own experience as people and as writers, can improve our craft.

READ YOURSELF

Writers read their lives to discover what they have to say and what they need to explore through writing. They live their lives with constant awareness, using all their senses to record moments consciously and subconsciously, storing in memory what they may not, at the time, have been aware they saw or heard, thought or felt. Writers not only live their lives with heightened awareness but respond to their lives, putting events in the context of what has gone before and what may follow.

I am never bored even when sitting on a bench at the supermarket waiting for my wife to finish the shopping. I read the *world,* noticing how many customers leave items with the checkout clerk because they cannot pay for them. I see the young mother with children use food stamps and imagine their life. I see the elderly widow with the old fashioned purse; she unfolds her dollars and hunts for the correct change while people in line roll their eyes. I am amused. They will become their mothers as my wife has—and as I have become the parents I thought I had escaped. That observation led to an essay.

Sitting in front of the checkout counter, I read memory, zooming back in time to Miller's Market, the small neighborhood grocery store in which I worked. During the Great Depression of the 1930s, that store sold most of its groceries on credit, and when I went to work—Friday afternoon and night, Saturday from six in the morning to midnight—I found my parents' names on the bad risk list— another essay. I remember the few fresh vegetables available when I was a boy— peas for a few weeks, no broccoli, winter squash, no zucchini, only iceberg lettuce, packed in ice. Remembering, I see my blood on the lettuce as my fingers became numb and awkward with cold, and the sharp trimming knife slipped in my hand—still another essay.

I not only collect specific, revealing-to-me details from life and from memory, but I respect my feelings and my thoughts. I react to life welcoming the unexpected, the contradictory, even the uncomfortable. As the novelist E. L. Doctorow says, "Every time you compose a book your composition of yourself is at risk. You put yourself further away from whatever is comfortable to you or you feel at home with. Writing is a lifetime act of self-displacement." Writing is not recording thoughts. It is thinking. Writing is not recording feelings. It is feeling. Writing is not recording living. It is a double living, a reading of experience that tells the writer—and perhaps readers—what it is like to have lived this life—and what it means. Reading our lives reveals their significance.

....

READ WHAT ISN'T YET WRITTEN

Writing begins long before a single word is written. When I receive a writing assignment or when I am looking for something I need to write, I wander about in what one writer has called a *state of skinlessness*. I observe a mother cruelly lecturing her small son in a parking lot and remember when I wished I was adopted. I laugh as I overhear a person say, "Now you take my God-damned religion" or find out the Guilford College football team is called "the Fighting Quakers."

Writers write before writing, playing with language, thoughts, and feelings in their mind, a kind of talking to themselves. Writing usually begins with a fragment of language or an image. The picture of the mother and son in the parking lot keeps reappearing in my mind until I have to deal with it. It is an itch that needs to be scratched. The same thing happens with what I call "the focusing line," a word or a phrase, rarely a sentence, that privately contains something that itches. The elements that signal there may be a topic in a line include:

- A surprise, something I do not expect to see, remember, think or feel:

    When I left home for college, I knew I would never live at home again. I was glad.

- A contradiction, something that runs counter to what I have believed:

    It was good that I was an only child. It prepared me for infantry combat.

- News, something I didn't know before:

    I learned that seventy percent of the people in the world are unable to read.

- A trigger, something that sparks a memory or an obsession:

    I hear a daughter say to her child what I said to her thirty-something years before, and I also hear my grandmother, long dead, in her voice.

- A conflict or tension between the elements in the line:

    The Fighting Quakers—What is it like to be taught peace and to play a violent sport?

- A question I must answer:

    I wrote in my daybook the question a tow-truck driver asked me, "How close did you get to the Germans in the Battle of the Bulge?"

- A problem to be solved:

    How do writers read?

- A new point of view that changes my vision of the world:

    I wrote in my daybook space between the bullets *and saw my war differently than I ever had before as I wrote a poem that begins:*

I run down long, thin corridors of air
between bullets that passed unseen,
but twice kissed my cheek . . .

Here is a column I have just written. Read it, and then I will reveal some of
the ways I—and my editor, Irene Sege of the *Boston Globe*—read the draft to produce this publishable version.

Each August there comes a day, perhaps with a whiff of fall in the air, when I
become seventeen, getting ready to go to college. I know I will never live at
home again.

I am glad.

When I was twelve, the family doctor pierced the myth of a good Christian home and said, "Donald, you do not have to be like your parents."

I accelerated the natural teenage process of separation, eventually leaving
my father's church for a more liberal one, seeking jobs that gave me financial
independence instead of my parents' constant debts, exploring the Irish
Catholic and Orthodox Jewish neighborhoods in which we lived and about
which I had been warned.

Now, I told myself, I am going to have a chance to earn my way through
Tilton Junior College, in Tilton, New Hampshire, by serving as a dormitory
monitor and by playing football. I am going to complete the design of a new
Murray, far from my childhood homes in Quincy and Winthrop, making myself
into someone, anyone, different from my parents.

I remember walking up the hill to West Hall laden with luggage that
seemed as light as the rifle I would carry in combat little more than a year
later. It was 1942 and I knew I'd better complete my redesign in a hurry.

In my room that first night I got out the chart I had clipped from *Esquire*
and learned, finally, how to tie a Windsor knot. When I went down to the
lobby to wait for supper, I discovered how much more I had to learn.

Even the first year boys seemed at home in their sports jackets, slacks and
Windsor knots. My hands felt huge, too large for pockets, but the others casually stuck one hand in a pocket, gracefully gesturing with the other. My
hands flopped like fresh caught fish.

My accent was south of Boston, theirs more polished. They sauntered
while I hesitated and almost stumbled. Their humor was dry and savage. They
laughed immediately at the quick thrust and parry. I laughed at the wrong time
or too late.

So I began, like most teenagers, to reject the style of my parents by copy-
ing the style of my peers, trading one conformity for another. I don't think I
ever learned to dress, saunter, smile like a preppie, and I don't think I became a jock although I was first string right tackle. In basketball I spun
around and made a basket—two points for the other team—and sat out the
season.

But I had many good teachers and one great one whose name I will always
remember, Mortimer B. Howell. I still have the battered green copy of

Thomas Hardy's *Return of the Native* above my writing desk. I open it and read my seventeen-year-old penciled handwriting "Irony: 1. A sort of humor or light sarcasm in which the intended meaning is opposite to the literal meaning, 2. A state of affairs or events the reverse of what was, or was to be expected; as, the irony of fate."

In May, when I had to leave school early for the Army, Mort Howell handed me a copy of the *Christian Science Monitor.* He had sent them one of my editorials from the Tiltonian. They published it, and he said, "When you come home from the war you will be a writer."

It was the gift of a life I came home and lived.

And in living the life of a writer that was far different from my father's retail-store, Baptist-deacon life, I thought I had escaped my family.

And, in some way, I have. I pay my bills on time. I own a house, a single-family house, and I own a car. I hug my wife, my daughters and my sons-in-law, my grandchildren, and, sometimes, surprised friends.

Recently, an academic organization honored me, and in the recognition I saw more evidence of how far I have come from my father, who never even went to high school.

But then, as people onstage paid embarrassing tribute to me, I realized that in a religious setting instead of an academic one, they could all have been talking about Dad.

He had a mustache and I have a beard. He passed out Bible verses, and I pass out writers' quotations. Somehow during my long trip to escape, I have become my father after all. The people who spoke made me, at last, proud of him.

Now this is how I began that essay in an early draft:

When I left home for college, I knew I would never live at home again. I was glad.

> *That was a gift. My first lead. I knew I had a column because it contained a tension, a surprise, a complication that I needed to explore: ". . . I would never live at home again. [Then one beat and the surprise] I was glad." But then in writing the final draft, I realized that I had to set up the piece to justify publishing it in August, as I wanted to do, and to establish my age. The lead was also a bit abrupt. The edited lead established a more reflective tone that would be appropriate to the essay. I also lengthened the beat by making it a paragraph break to emphasize the surprise.*
>
> *I liked my lead but tried a number of other leads to test that one: "The students return to Durham, New Hampshire, the college town in which I live, and I am again seventeen, going off to college. I know I will never live at home again. And I am glad . . ." But that didn't have the reflective quality I wanted.*
>
> *I tried another and crossed it out:* ~~As the students and faculty, younger each year, pour into Durham, New Hampshire, from the south, west,~~

~~north, and east I am again 17 again, going off to college. I know I will never live at home again. And I am glad.~~ *Finally, I decided on:*

Each August there comes a day, perhaps with a whiff of fall in the air, when I become seventeen, getting ready to go to college. I know I will never live at home again.

I am glad.

Then I read the next paragraph aloud.

When I was twelve the family doctor told me, "Donald. You do NOT have to be like your parents." I walked the two miles home, two feet off the ground. Free at last.

I read this over—out loud—and left it alone. It is just as important NOT to change as it is to change. Earlier I had written: "Or eventually. I moved from my deacon father's fundamentalist Baptist church to a 'liberal' Baptist church. I dropped out of school [twice] and returned to flunk out. Now I was going to junior college to play football and to design myself, to make myself what I did not know." Although all of that was true, it cluttered up the page, did not advance my meaning. It had to go.

I kept reading the piece, word by word, phrase by phrase, sentence by sentence making sure that what I said was as true as I could make it and as clear. I didn't worry about grammar and mechanics, knowing that if I made myself clear I would be following the traditions of the English language, and if I strayed—and was clear—that would probably be all right. My editor would be the referee and blow the whistle if necessary.

As I write these words, I am seventy-three years old and still learning to write. I count that a blessing. I learn to write by writing and reading what I have written, and I learn by reading what others have written.

READ TO HELP

When I ask colleagues or editors to read drafts in process, I find it helpful to establish the agenda. I tell them the type of reading I want. Many of the problems—and tensions—between writer and test reader occur because the writer has one unspoken expectation and the reader another. The writer may need to know if the subject is clear, and the reader may leap over that issue and start correcting spelling.

I tell my readers-in-process what I expect from them. I may say, "I know the writing isn't polished yet, but do I have a subject and do you care what I have to say about it?" Or I may say, "The topic is set, but do the parts of the piece move forward logically, do I answer your questions when you ask them?" Or "I think the subject and the order are set, but I don't know the voice and clarity. Do you have time to give it a careful line-by-line reading?"

When others come to me with drafts, I ask them to tell me what kind of reading they want. Most people will say, "I want you to be hard on me. Tell me what's wrong." They may even mean it, but then you have to tell them there's no right or wrong but many rights and many wrongs. It all depends. You can't tell them what to do. You can suggest some of things you might do—depending. Depending on what? The subject, the writer, the reader, the purpose, the genre, and all the other elements that affect a piece of writing.

And remember the hierarchy of problems: The writer must find a limited, well-researched topic before problems of structure and language can be addressed. Then problems of form and order have to be solved before problems of voice can be solved. Finally, the writer and any test readers can address questions of voice, grammar, usage, mechanics, spelling, typography, and neatness.

READ OTHERS

When I read other writers, it is always with a kind of double vision. I read for information, for escape, for delight, for instruction, and I also read for craft. I am able, as a fellow writer, to imagine how the page might have been written, to see the problems faced by the writer and to imagine other solutions.

I do not—at least I try not to—read competitively. I am not writing against anyone. I am not writing to win. I take pleasure in all those who write better than I do, and I also take instruction.

It can be useful to keep a reading journal in which you interact with the text, questioning what the writer says—doubting, developing, running ahead of the writer, dropping behind, going back, connecting what is said and how it is said with your writing and the writing of others. I taught my freshman English students how to write in the margins of books they own and mar-up the text, underlining, drawing connecting arrows, entering into an intellectual or artistic dialogue that makes the books their own. I still have the books I read in freshman English with the notes from my reading and from class discussions recorded in pencil. I often visit that young me and may respond again to the text, keeping the book mine.

Again, as when I read my own drafts, a hierarchy of reading overlaps elements without losing their distinct identities. The arrangement is however, often reversed. First I hear the voice, then I become aware of the form, and then I read for content.

READ FOR VOICE

When I read for voice I am looking for the individual behind the page, the author I can trust and believe, the author who will be my companion and guide through the subject.

READ FOR ORDER

Now that I have met the writer, my guide, I want to be shown a way through the piece, a clear trail through the material that I can follow at an appropriate pace. I don't want to be rushed, and I do not want to dawdle; I want time to listen, absorb, and learn—and I want to keep moving.

READ FOR CONTENT

Finally I want to be served an adequate portion of specific, accurate information in a context that I can understand and that reveals the significance of the material. I want to be changed by my reading: entertained, informed, persuaded, inspired.

....

STUDENT CASE HISTORY: JULIE SCHUM

Read the following student paper by yourself, ignoring my commentary, then read it with me as I demonstrate what a writer reads in the writing. It was written in an undergraduate course in critical analysis of literature for Dr. Brock Dethier when he was on the faculty at the University of New Hampshire. The student, Julie Schum, is a science major who wants to be a writer concentrating on science and environmental issues.

· KATE'S RESISTANCE TO DOMINANCE BY PETRUCHIO IN *THE TAMING OF THE SHREW* ·
Julie Schum

I had one strong response upon reading Kate's submissive speech at the end of Shakespeare's *The Taming of the Shrew:* I don't buy it.

> *This is an academic paper, an excellent literary research paper, but the writer's voice is established in the first sentence. The writer has a strong point of view and her own unique way of expressing it. I hear her voice as a promise of a strong and lively point of view.*

Something seemed funny about the strong female character, who had been the star of Shakespeare's play, her scalding wit an equal match for any of the male characters', suddenly forsaking her independent nature and calling upon all women to become submissive to men. I didn't believe her. I wasn't convinced. Her words were telling me one thing, while her actions and the fact that hers is the voice delivering the critical and longest speech in the play seemed to contradict that message.

> *The author makes a statement, then immediately documents it. I sense an order that will take me through a reading of a play I haven't read in*

decades. I feel I will have a guide that will make each point clear and give me time to consider it.

My reading of *The Taming of the Shrew* left me with the feeling that Shakespeare's purpose in the play was not to encourage men to dominate women and women to be submissive to their husbands. Shakespeare was dealing with an issue facing his audience at the time. The play seems to be a reflection of the cultural change from a time when women kissed their husbands' feet as part of the wedding ceremony to a time when many women chose not to marry and to speak up for themselves in the patriarchal society. To the audience of the 1590s, Kate's final speech would have sounded old fashioned, possibly reminiscent of the good old days, but would not be interpreted as a message to women to be submissive or for men to abuse their women into submission.

The author puts her topic into literary, historical, and social contexts. I feel sure that she has something important to tell me and that she will satisfy my hunger for accurate, specific information that will stimulate my thinking.

Lynda Boose points out in her article "Scolding Brides and Bridling Scolds," . . .

I'm relieved. This isn't just going to be the author's opinion off the top of her head. She is going to cite objective, scholarly authorities to support her position.

. . . that Kate's statement,

". . . place your hands below your husband's foot.
In token of which duty, if he please,
My hand is ready, may it do him ease" (V.2 176–178),

Good. I do not have the play in front of me, but I am going to be given evidence from within the text so I can hear the lines and see if they support the writer's thesis.

. . . is an allusion to an actual pre-Reformation marriage ceremony in which the bride must kiss her husband's feet in an act of submission and obedience, a ritual which was removed from the Book of Common Prayer in 1549.

The lines from the play are put in context. My guide through the piece—the author—is answering my questions as I ask them.

Boose believes Shakespeare used the patriarchal, outdated reference in Kate's speech because, "on the one hand, it inscribes the concluding Kate and Petruchio marital relation as an anachronism; and yet, on the other, by idealizing and romanticizing that model, it imbues it with the nostalgic value of a vision of social order imagined as passing away"

(195-6). By this interpretation, the audience would have taken the taming of Kate as exaggerated, an old fashioned ideal of submissive women, not as a model Shakespeare was encouraging them to follow. Men in the audience may have cheered Kate's final speech, but most would have done so with a sense of fantasy and nostalgia, knowing that they would never see their wives making such a speech. Seeing Kate's speech in historical context gives me a different perspective on the injustice of the speech and its impact on women's role in society. Knowing that the audience was probably not convinced by the explicit theme of taming women allows me to see beyond the blatant sexism of the plot to the more implicit themes of the play.

> *Here the author skillfully leads me to her conclusion and then, in the next paragraph, establishes and defines—definition is very important—an important theme.*

One of these themes is the importance of language and the ability of women to have power through speaking. Kate is considered a shrew because of the language she uses and her disregard of what is socially acceptable for her to say. Bianca, on the other hand, plays the role of the socially acceptable woman—she is silent. Karen Newman makes the observation in her article "Renaissance Family Politics and Shakespeare's *The Taming of the Shrew*" that, ". . . Kate refuses her erotic destiny by exercising her linguistic willfulness. Her shrewishness, always associated with women's revolt in words, testifies to her exclusion from social and political power. Bianca, by contrast, is throughout the play associated with silence" (90).

> *Each point is made clearly and then documented. I am instructed in writing and rewriting this chapter by the author's skill in this process.*

The contrast in the speech of the two sisters is shown clearly by comparing Petruchio's courtship of Kate to Lucentio's courtship of Bianca. In the first exchange between Kate and Petruchio (II.1 182-271), Kate is the instigator of the quarrel and gets the better of Petruchio through puns which mock his attempt to treat her as an object of exchange. She uses words to resist his efforts to dominate her. Newman agrees that, "[Kate] takes the lead through puns which allow her to criticize Petruchio and the patriarchal system of wooing and marriage" (94). In the exchange between Bianca and Lucentio (III.1 31-43), Bianca simply repeats the words Lucentio says to her. Newman feels that Bianca is conforming to the accepted role of women by not speaking. She says, "[Bianca's] revelation of her feelings through a repetition of the Latin lines [Lucentio] quotes from Ovid are as close as possible to the silence we have come to expect from her"

(94). Kate is considered a shrew because she uses wild language and linguistic wit to resist being treated like a commodity. Bianca is favored by suitors because she is quiet, complacent, and submissive. In this instance, language is the tool Kate uses to break away from being traded among men by her father.

> *Go through the rest of the research paper by yourself, with a partner, or with several of your classmates, noting just what the author is doing, paragraph by paragraph. Read it aloud and hear the writer's voice. Outline it to see the logical trail she carves through the material. Write out her thesis and the points she makes to see the significance of what she is saying.*

As Petruchio tries to tame Kate, a major tactic he uses is intentionally misunderstanding what she says. By changing the meaning of her words, he takes away her power to be independent. After the quarrel when Petruchio and Kate first meet, Petruchio negates Kate's power by telling Baptista that Kate has agreed to marry him and that she loves him when they are alone (II.1 278–310). Baptista believes Petruchio, and Kate is powerless to fight against being treated like an object by her father and Petruchio. She must marry Petruchio, who forced himself upon her and defeated her independence by ignoring her ability to speak.

Petruchio intentionally misinterprets the meaning of Kate's words again when she wants to stay at the wedding feast (III.2 198–238). Kate clearly tries to resist his power to control her by saying,

"The door is open, sir, there lies your way,
You may be jogging whiles your boots are green.
For me, I'll not be gone till I please myself" (III.2 209–211).

Petruchio ignores her will, and the fact that she's angry about being humiliated at the wedding, and claims that he is rescuing her from thieves, saying,

"Fear not, sweet wench, they shall not touch thee, Kate" (III.2 237).

He says this in the same breath that he calls her

"my goods, my chattels, she is my house,
My household stuff, my field, my barn,
My horse, my ox, my ass, my any thing" (III.2 229–231).

His tactic of dominating Kate in this scene is to rob her of her independence as a human being by ignoring her words.

Petruchio's strategy continues when they reach his house. Newman says, "Kate is figuratively killed with kindness, by her husband's rule over her not so much in material terms—the withholding of food, clothing, and sleep—but the withholding of linguistic understanding. As the receiver of her messages, he simply refuses their meaning; since he also has material power to enforce his interpretations, it is his power over language that wins" (95). Kate still struggles to maintain her independence through words. In the scene with the tailor, Kate tells Petruchio that she will not be silenced:

"Why sir, I trust I may have leave to speak,
And speak I will. I am no child, no babe.
Your betters have endured me say my mind,
And if you cannot, best you stop your ears.
My tongue will tell the anger of my heart,
Or else my heart concealing it will break,
And rather than it shall, I will be free
Even to the uttermost, as I please, in words."

As Petruchio withholds food and sleep from Kate, she becomes more willing to be civil to him, realizing it's the only way she'll stay alive. Still, she doesn't lose her wit and her confidence to be outspoken and contradict Petruchio.

The conversation between Kate and Petruchio on the way to Padua is a relief to me. It shows that Kate has not been conquered in the sense that she still has her wit and her ability to speak. Newman says this exchange shows Kate is having fun playing along with Petruchio's games (95–96). She refers to the pun Kate makes when saying to Vincentio,

"Pardon, old father, my mistaking eyes,
That have been bedazzled with the sun" (IV.5 145–6).

"Sun" in this case, is a pun referring to Petruchio, who referred to himself as his mother's "son" earlier in their conversation.

Kate retains her sharp verbal abilities through the end of the play. Even when Kate gives her monologue on how to be a good wife, it is Kate who is speaking and telling the audience what she feels. She has retained her individuality at least to the extent that she contradicts the other two wives and addresses the audience with the longest and most climactic monologue in the play. Newman says, "Kate's having the last word contradicts the very sentiments she speaks" (99). Newman also notes that even though one shrew is tamed, two more reveal themselves: "Bianca and the widow refuse to do their husbands' bidding, thereby undoing the sense of closure Kate's 'acquiescence' produces" (100).

Because Kate does not lose her power to speak, it seems that Shakespeare is showing us that Kate is not ultimately defeated by Petruchio. The play leaves the audience with an uneasy feeling that the conflict of men not being able to dominate their wives is not resolved. This is further supported by the historical context of Kate's final monologue and how the contemporary audience would have responded to that as a fantasized, unrealistic basis for the situation to wrap up. Historically, this play reflects the feeling of English society in the 1590s. According to Newman, "The period was fraught with anxiety about rebellious women" (91). Other historians have identified the era as a "crisis of order" which was based on a fear of women rebelling against their submissive role in the patriarchal culture (Newman 90). Boose adds that there was a sudden increase in witchcraft trials and other court accusations against women documented in this time period. There was also an increase in the instances of crimes that are typically female, "scolding," "witchcraft," "whoring," "brawling," and "dominating one's husband" (184). These historical records of punishment show the strength women were showing in beginning to overcome their submissive role in society and the magnitude of the threat these women posed to men.

Boose observes, ". . . what is striking is that the punishments meted out to women are much more frequently targeted at suppressing women's speech than they are at controlling their sexual transgressions" (184). This social phenomenon is reflected in *The Taming of the Shrew,* when Kate is considered a shrew because she speaks freely, and in the way Petruchio tries to dominate her by suppressing her ability to speak.

Also in the play, there are several references to Kate that could imply accusations of witchcraft. After Kate yells at Baptista for making deals with Bianca's suitors, Hortensio says,

"From all such devils, good Lord deliver us!" (I.1 65).

When Baptista scolds Kate for attacking Bianca, he says,

"For shame, thou hilding of a devilish spirit" (II.1 26).

Kate is associated with the devil, probably like many women in England at that time, because she is a threat to male authority.

The punishments that Kate receives from Petruchio—public humiliation at her wedding, humiliation at the wedding feast— also resemble the historical customary punishment of "scolds" and "shrews." Boose refers to these as Kate's "shaming rites" (192).

Looking at the play from this historical perspective shows that Shakespeare's purpose in *The Taming of the Shrew* was to reflect what was going on around him in society. The audiences who saw Shakespeare's play probably recognized Kate's outspoken, shrewish behavior in women of their time and identified with Petruchio's quest to dominate them and restore the order that society once knew. Many men probably cheered Kate's final speech wishing their women would adopt such attitudes. But, by showing the audience Petruchio's inability to truly dominate a shrew, the play showed the present and future of the gender struggle—that for one tamed shrew there were two more untamed, that the days of a woman professing her submission and inferiority to her husband were gone. Despite the content of Kate's final monologue, it seems the primary theme of *The Taming of the Shrew* is that men should beware because the shrews will not be tamed.

> *Note the strong ending written not with rhetorical flourishes but with solid, specific information that weaves all the strands of the research paper together and leaves at least this male thinking about women to today and the women in his life—his wife, his daughters and granddaughter, his women friends. Shakespeare speaks to us today because he dealt with the fundamental issues of men and women, then and now.*

• WORKS CITED •

Boose, Lynda E. "Scolding Brides and Bridling Scolds: Taming the Woman's Unruly Member." *Shakespeare Quarterly* 42 (1991): 179–185, 194.

Newman, Karen. "Renaissance Family Politics and Shakespeare's *The Taming of the Shrew*." *English Literary Renaissance* 16 (1986): 86–100.

Shakespeare, William. *The Taming of the Shrew*. Ed. G. R. Hibbard. London: Penguin Books, 1968.

The author's teacher, Brock Dethier, wrote at the end of the paper: "A. Excellent. Best research paper I've seen this semester." It is a superb example of academic writing that is more than that—simply good writing—and we can all take instruction and inspiration from good writing.

We read ourselves, and by understanding the challenges on our own pages, we are able to read other writers with a special insight; in reading others, we bring a new perspective to the reading of our drafts.

....

YOUR DAYBOOK

Your daybook is not only a place to begin writing, but a place to record your reading for craft and your response to that reading. Paste in examples of good writing from others. In my current daybook, I find part of an essay by Joseph Brodsky and an excerpt from an interview with Jan Burke; a few paragraphs from an article about Jorie Graham; poems by Eamon Grennan, Thomas Lux, and John Updike; articles by Ellen Gilchrist, Elissa Ely, Gabriel Garcia Marquez, Carolyn Heilbrun, and Judy Troy; quotations from Mary Gordon, David Storey, and Amos Oz; an article about Dr. Seuss, and the first two paragraphs of the novel *School for the Blind* by Dennis McFarland, which establish the voice of the entire book.

Your daybook can also be a reading journal, a place where you record your reactions to reading your own drafts as well as the published writing of others.

YOUR COMPUTER

The Internet allows you to read writing by many others, published and unpublished. There are sites where writers publish and other sites that include interviews with writers about their craft. The computer allows you to interact with these texts before or after downloading.

You can easily revise the texts, seeing what the writer has done by trying— and often failing—to improve the draft. Play with the prose of others, seeing what the writer did by undoing it or adding to it, changing the order, the point of view, the genre, or the voice. You can also read interviews with writers and in some cases chat with authors or editors.

Emma Tobin, whose case history of an article about the Internet appears on pages 310 to 325, says she uses America Online. "I go into 'Instant Novelist,'" she tells me, "While I am there, I can write stories, and have them responded to by some good writers, and some terrible writers. (That's just the way it goes. . . .) I meet writers that way if I respond to one of THEIR stories in a way that interests them. If they're intrigued, they might respond, and we might start a friendship. Really the only other place I go to meet writers is a 'Reading/Writing' chat room."

Some of the places I go include Book Report on AOL and bookstores such as Amazon.com and BarnesandNoble.com that offer news about books, chats with writers, reviews, interviews, readers' responses, and, often, sample chapters.

The *New York Times* Internet site [www.nytimes.com/books] presents its book reviews, stories about authors and the book business, and interviews with writers. It has a tremendous archive of materials. So does the site for the C-Span program Booknotes [booknotes.org]. You can also contact most magazines, newspapers, and television networks easily. I find book publishers very helpful—www.harbrace.com, www.putnam.com, www.randomhouse.com, www.harpercollins.com, www.greywoldpress.org, www.godine.com.

There are also writer's organizations such as Poets and Writers [pw.org] that have a great deal of helpful information for writers. Sites such as www.lit-arts.com or writer.net provide all sorts of links with other organizations, writers, communities, schools, and publishers. The Internet has almost unlimited possibilities. I typed *writers resources* into the Alta Vista search field and came up with 2,127,997 documents!

And don't forget Oprah Winfrey and her book club, which has had an enormous impact on the book business.

IN THE WRITER'S WORKSHOP

When you're reading, you're writing. MARY GORDON

For most of us I believe the voice gradually emerges, coming out of all that we have read (I don't mean mimicry, of course, rather the combined influence of thousands of voices), from the exquisite discipline of writing itself, and from who we are at the most fundamental level, from our souls, if you will. FRANK CONROY

I read everything that I write aloud. First, the paragraph. Then, the page. Then, the chapter. And finally, I read the whole book aloud. Because I want to hear my voice reading it, and I need it to sound natural. ISABEL ALLENDE

I think that one of the things that gives pleasure in reading—at least gives me *pleasure in reading—is the sense of the presence of a storyteller, whether it's fiction or nonfiction. I think we can use terms like "voice" or "style," but a large part of it is the sense that there's someone behind the scenes adroitly pulling the strings, the reader's realizing with pleasure that there's someone there. Not that the narrator, or the storyteller who may stand behind the narrator, has to be an obtrusive presence, but the reader's sense of that presence, the reader's pleasurable sense of that presence, is something that I feel is fundamental.* TRACY KIDDER

I'll write about three pages, then go to the typewriter and type that out. Then the next day I'll read those three pages again and maybe not like them, and go back to the notebook—write it out, make changes and then retype it. NEIL SIMON

When I'm working on a book, I start each day by re-reading everything I've written up to that point. This is easy at the beginning, very time-consuming at the end. It's the way I find easiest to slip back into the emotional locale of the book. I need to know where I was before I figure out where I'm going. DIANE ACKERMAN

It's a very queer thing how craft *comes into writing. I mean down to details. Par Example. In* Miss Brill *I chose not only the length of every sentence, but even the sound of every sentence. I chose the rise and fall of every paragraph to fit her, and to fit her on the day at that very moment. After I'd written it I read it aloud—a number of times—just as one would* play over *a musical—trying to get it nearer and nearer to the expression of Miss Brill—until it fitted her.* KATHERINE MANSFIELD

I will read something seemingly utterly unconnected with what I am writing about, and suddenly I will see a connection—a nugget of information, an insight, a comparison, a metaphor. . . . I still read everything aloud. I have a fundamental conviction that if a sentence cannot be read aloud with sincerity, conviction, and communicable emphasis, it is not a good sentence. Good writing requires good rhythms and good words. You cannot know whether the rhythms and the words are good unless you read them aloud. Reading aloud is also the easiest way to see that prose tracks, that it runs on smoothly from sentence to sentence, idea to idea, section to section within the larger whole. Reading aloud also makes the mind consider connotations of words and perhaps above all their relations to each other. RICHARD MARIUS

Ever since I was first read to, then started reading to myself, there has never been a line read that I didn't hear. As my eyes followed the sentence, a voice was saying it

silently to me. It isn't my mother's voice, or the voice of any person I can identify, certainly not my own. It is human, but inward, and it is inwardly that I listen to it. It is to me the voice of the story or the poem itself. The cadence, whatever it is that asks you to believe, the feeling that resides in the printed word, reaches me through the reader-voice. I have supposed, but never found out, that this is the case with all readers—to read as listeners—and with all writers, to write as listeners. It may be part of the desire to write. The sound of what falls on the page begins the process of testing it for truth, for me.

Whether I am right to trust so far I don't know. By now I don't know whether I could do either one, reading or writing, without the other.

My own words, when I am at work on a story, I hear too as they go, in the same voice that I hear when I read in books. When I write and the sound of it comes back to my ears, then I act to make my changes. I have always trusted this voice. EUDORA WELTY

For me, writing—and reading—are ways of seeing: *I have a sharply visual imagination and love to see by way of words.* JOYCE CAROL OATES

What murders writing is reading. The death of writing is reading. Reading back over what you have just written and realizing you could make it better and halting your forward motion down the page in order to go back and try to improve on the first part rather than marching resolutely raggedly bravely onward down to the bottom of that page and up to the top of the next one without letup until, however imperfectly, you have stuttered out whatever you may have thought you had to say.
SHANA ALEXANDER

I read for the pleasure of learning how to write. V. S. PRITCHETT

QUESTIONS ABOUT READING

I'm afraid I don't read enough books to become a good writer. Is this necessary?

Writers who read books usually have a knack for language, a sense for what looks and sounds right on the page just from having seen writing that works over and over again. And certainly the more you read in your field, the more skilled you will become in recognizing the features of particular genres and the vocabulary you will need to succeed in your major. But don't too readily separate your personal activities from your scholarly life, your "everyday" writing from your academic writing.

You don't have to be a voracious reader of books in order to write. Think of magazine and newspaper writers. They may be avid readers, but their material is usually the stuff of everyday experience. And the same is true of the writers whose work you read in English classes. They too are readers of life.

How do I learn to "read" life?

Learning to observe life closely is like learning to see those crazy "Magic Eye" illustrations. While these optical illusions seem dull on the surface, they have a lot of stuff going on underneath. When you first glance at them, you notice only flat, one-dimensional pictures. But as you hold the images closer and adjust your eyes, three-dimensional figures and patterns emerge. The initial images become richer, more colorful, and more textured.

Reading life is the same. It's all a matter of adjusting your eyes and your senses. Imagine the world as a kind of optical illusion that obscures its own richness. Tease out its fullness by paying close attention to what goes on around you, by writing about what you notice, by reading between the lines for what's obvious and also for what's not.

But how will all this help me when I have to write a formal essay for another class, something other than a personal story or an essay about everyday experiences?

Analyzing what you are most familiar with not only helps you hone your observational skills; it also helps you appreciate the validity of your own viewpoint. The more you analyze and interpret, the more you will realize that you have something to say and that what you have to say is worth listening to. As you rely more on your own judgment and less on the proclamations of "experts," your new strength and confidence as a reader will spill over into your writing.

Will reading well help me with grammar and good sentence structure? Aren't these the most important things in writing?

Writing well is much more than writing grammatically; it's bringing depth and thoughtfulness to images, concepts, and ideas—to what you read in a book or to what you experience in the world. This is not to say that writing "correctly" is not important. But your main goal in reading should be to immerse yourself in the writer's imagery and ideas, to participate in a kind of conversation with the writer that helps you make sense of what you are reading.

Use your daybook or reading journal as a way of seeing and responding to all your readings, academic and otherwise. When you observe closely anything and anybody—hazing on campus or the economy of Africa, grandma Harriet or Harriet Beecher Stowe, the surfer on the beach or the writer at her desk—you learn to look for the unusual, the commonplace, the ironic, the tragic, the humorous. You search for what is and what isn't, for what should be and what will never be. You recognize patterns and images. You learn different ways of communicating, seeing, and being—a skill that serves you well no matter how and what you write about.

I love to write, but I hate to write book reports or essays about literature for English classes. Even when I think I know what my teachers want, I'm sure that my reading is always wrong.

There is no one way to read literature. We've had it drummed it into our heads that we have to be experts in order to understand "works of art." That's why we feel intimidated when we bring our own experience as writers, readers, and human beings to literature. But writers who read, and readers who write, view reading as an active process. By responding honestly to what you read, you can become a kind of partner with the authors whose books and poems you're assigned.

That partnership is strengthened when you keep a reading journal that tracks your reactions and responses to readings. Talk with or back to the author, essay, or book. Clarify confusing or difficult passages by writing about them, by working through them bit by bit. You will find that you have plenty of worthwhile commentary when you have finished reading.

`Isn't it possible to read too much into something? Do we have to examine everything? Can't we just write?`

By all means just write! Don't wait until you have "profound" thoughts to put pen to paper, fingers to keyboard. Writing is thinking and reading deeply and critically comes with writing. It is writing. That's why we write first.

Writing well and living well take energy and inquisitiveness, a zest for exploration and finding out. Can we read too much into anything? No, I don't think so. Sometimes we may be afraid that exploring and analyzing will mean we can no longer appreciate or have fun doing everyday things and casually observing life. But if we want to live deeply, we have to read deeply. Writing as we read, or reading to write, allows us to interpret and make sense of our lives. Think of this kind of reading and writing as a way of living, a way of being in the world with all senses engaged. We never worry about living too much or breathing too much. We shouldn't worry about "reading too much into things," about making meaning of our worlds and lives.

Observing, free writing, brainstorming, drafting, planning, focusing, revising, and editing—all of these activities allow us to write about what we read from every perspective, to poke and probe life from all angles. You won't like what you read less. You'll probably find that you appreciate it more.

....

READING ACTIVITIES

1. Choose a piece of reading you have in your backpack or bag—registration instructions, a textbook, the school newspaper, a syllabus, whatever—the more "everyday" the better. Work with a partner on a close reading of this piece: Analyze it from every perspective and try to read "too much" into it. Is the writer of the text you chose detached, friendly, condescending, involved? How can you tell? What words does the writer use to evoke a particular tone of voice? Who is the writer's audience?

What is the focus of the piece? Play around with the piece, making it flowery, dramatic, funny, or sad. Reflect on, poke fun at, or argue with what the writer says. Record your responses to the reading in the margins, between the lines, or on a separate piece of paper.

2. Start a reading journal in your daybook or in a separate notebook. Reserve a special section in it for memorable, provocative, or disturbing passages. Share these with the class and talk about why you wrote them down. Did they make you think? Have you had experiences that gave them special meaning? Did you find them beautiful, ugly, upsetting? What struck you as particularly significant about these passages?

3. Use your reading journal to make sense of essays and stories you read not only for your writing class, but also for your other classes. Read each piece twice. Draw a line down the center of a page and jot down responses to your first reading on the left-hand side. Note what works in the essay, what strikes you as interesting, challenging, tragic, or ironic, what moves you, persuades you, enlightens you or makes you laugh or cry. Make sure to note the confusing parts of the essay as well. Then record your response to your second reading on the right-hand side. What do you see this time around? Do the confusing areas become clearer to you? Are there other areas that seem less clear? What other responses do you have?

4. Use your reading journal or daybook to "converse" with an author you admire. Imagine how he or she might respond to your questions and jot down the answers you think the writer would give. Then stage a mock interview with your writing partner. Play the role of the writer and have your partner interview you. Answer your interviewer's questions from the perspective of the writer. Switch roles.

5. Brainstorm a list of favorite childhood books, stories, poems, or nursery rhymes, what you remember about them, through reading them or having them read to you. How old were you? Where were you? Were you alone or did you have sisters and brothers with you? Then free write about your childhood reading experiences and see where it takes you.

6. Exchange freewrites in small groups, and select passages from each that you like. Compose responses telling why you like the passages. Then go around the room and read one passage aloud each, explaining why you chose it. Publish a class newsletter of memorable passages.

7. Choose a passage out of a magazine or newspaper that catches your eye and read it to the class or a small group. What is it about this passage that grabs your attention? Is it the way it begins? The topic itself? The kind of information the author uses? Its tone of voice? Did it make you laugh or cry, "see," "touch," or "hear"? How?

8. With a partner, read a short article in a popular magazine, such as *Rolling Stone, Sports Illustrated,* or *Cosmopolitan.* Articles in these magazines do not include bibliographies or "Works Cited" pages, but their writers collect information. Figure out the kind of reading the author of your article had to do in order to get his or her information. What kinds of books, magazines, or other documents and sources did he or she use? Are these sources available to you? If so, how would you go about getting access to them?

9. Bring in a recording of a favorite comedian and listen to the timing and the rhythm of the comedian's delivery. Then choose a humor writer such as Dave Barry, James Thurber, or Molly Ivins and do the same thing. Read for the rhythm and timing of the writer's sentences. Where in the writer's essay does this sense of sound work? How does it work? What kinds of choices about language does the writer make?

10. Bumper stickers, billboards, slogans, even the wording on baseball caps "tell" on the people who write them, post them, wear them. Sometimes they are full of humor and contradictions. A bulletin board in front of a church, for instance, announces the morning sermon: "Jesus Walks on Water." "In Search of Jesus," the board laments that evening. In your daily treks around campus and town, get into the habit of reading signs and jotting them down in your daybook. Read them for surprises, insights, and humor. Read them for how they sound and how they work together, for what they say as well as what they don't (but should) say about the people who display them.

11. Celebrate "literal" day. Exchange papers in groups, then pick out familiar figures of speech and imagine how they would "read" to someone from another planet or culture. In an episode of *Third Rock from the Sun,* for example (a sitcom about aliens posing as humans), an exasperated earthling told an extraterrestrial, "You take the cake!" "I don't want the cake," the alien replied. "I want you!" Brainstorm a list of other common sayings that would be senseless or just plain crazy if we read them "literally" as the alien character on television did.

12. Go walking at dusk just before nightfall. Glance into the lighted windows of houses and think of what you see as snapshots. Read as many details as you can. Notice the father in the kitchen chopping vegetables for dinner, the woman reading a book in an armchair next door, the bluish light of a television in the window across the street. Listen for conversations and attune your nose to smells. When you get back home, make a detailed list of what you saw, smelled, and heard.

13. Pick a place where students gather: the dining hall, the post office, the entranceway to a lecture hall. Observe a group closely, how they stand,

what they wear, how they speak. Read body language: How close to each other do they stand? Do they touch? What kinds of expressions do they have on their faces? Are they friends? Casual acquaintances? How can you tell? What kinds of moods are they in? Do they laugh, wrinkle their brows, turn abruptly and walk away? Do they seem shy, outgoing, nervous? Jot down details and figure out which ones are the most "telling."

14. Select two objects you are carrying or wearing that you can share with the class—something in your backpack, perhaps, or a piece of jewelry. Place the objects, along with those of your classmates, on a desk or in a box at the front of the room. From this collection choose two items other than your own. Draw a line down the middle of a page in your daybook or reading journal. On the left-hand side of the page, write down every detail of the objects you can think of: size and shape, how they feel in your hand, what they're made of, their color, weight. Are they worn or rusted? Old or new? On the right-hand side of the page, interpret these details. Make up a story about the objects and owners from what you have observed and then have the objects' owners tell their own histories.

15. "Eavesdrop" on an Internet chat room. Follow one conversation through from beginning to end. How do the participants build on contributions to the conversation? What words or phrases do they repeat? How much of your reading of the conversation makes you feel like an insider or an outsider? What other kinds of information would you need to be a fully informed reader and writer in the chat room?

16. In your reading journal or daybook, collect interesting, humorous, or disturbing one-liners or passages from Internet chat room conversations. Arrange them into a poem or free write about them. Save them for topic ideas.

17. Examine the faces of different people on a subway or bus, or in another public area. List the details of these faces as fully and quickly as possible without seeming too intrusive. Later, see if you can transform the wrinkles, lines, blemishes, expressions, glasses, and jewelry you observed into a descriptive essay or story about each person.

18. Brainstorm or map a list of printed or written texts you remember reading within the last few weeks: newspapers, magazines, graffiti on walls, music lyrics, advertisements on buses, campus directions. Then make a second list of words, sentences, or information you remember from these sources. Circle a few that you might select as topics for research or future writing, and have your classmates ask questions about them.

19. Think of something you've read that changed your life or simply came back to haunt you. Or think of something you read during an important,

unhappy, or celebratory period of your life. Write about the details of where you were when you read the piece and how it affected you. What words and phrases do you remember? Did your reading of the piece prompt you to take an important step or action? What might have happened if you had not read the piece? How would your reading differ now as opposed to when you first read it?

20. Read a poem aloud in small chunks, covering up the unread portion as you go and pausing after each bit to write a response in your daybook or reading journal. Respond honestly, thoughtfully, and specifically to every chunk you hear. Does an image move you or make you laugh? Can you interpret the poet's voice and mood by the words he or she uses? Does the poem make sense to you as you read and consider more of it? How do you respond to the sound and rhythm of the poem? In what direction do you think the poem is taking you? Savor each line and when you finish, read the entire poem aloud and write a final response.

21. Look ahead to the activities in the following chapters to jump-start your writing.

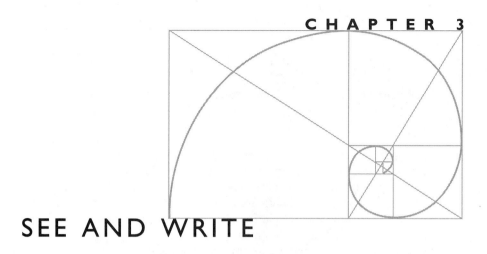

CHAPTER 3

SEE AND WRITE

If you ask young children to write a story, they are as likely to hand you drawings as bits of prose. They know instinctively what their teachers in the upper grades and college seem unable to understand: Writing is a visual art—writers see, then write. The few children who will become published writers continue, despite school, to see with the mind's eye, then write. They know from daily experience at the writing desk that writing is a special way of seeing.

Although published writers see what they write, I do not know of any composition textbook that connects writing and seeing. We are the victims of the academy, which separates the visual arts—drawing, painting, sculpture, photography—from the language arts—writing, reading, speaking.

THE CRAFT OF VISION

The writer's purpose, as novelist Joseph Conrad said, ". . . is, by the power of the written word, to make you hear, to make you feel—it is, before all, to make you see." To make others see, writers must first see themselves. Each day I exercise my observation muscles. I watch the predawn light make black lace of the winter branches in the woods behind my house; on my morning walk I pay attention to how the far away yellow day lily grows large as I approach it, until I can see the other colors that rise from its throat; I notice the young police officer's practiced, police academy stroll up to the car he has just pulled over; I record the way my wife, as we watch the evening news, makes a sharp comment, then waits to smile until I get her double meaning; before falling off to sleep I walk down the path I took sixty summers ago to the lake, remembering how the water looked when I could not swim and feared the lake, and how the black water grew to a light blue-green when I could dive, even swim all the way to the raft under water. I fall asleep swimming underwater with a bright ceiling of reflected sunlight above my head.

Specific sensory details that rise off the page and resonate in the reader's mind are vital to lively, effective writing. Listen to one of the best writers about the natural world, Diane Ackerman, who is also a novelist and poet:

> . . . [W]hen I go out on an expedition, I take with me small, spiralbound yellow notebooks. They don't have very many pages in them, but that doesn't matter. If I fill one of those notebooks, I'll be able later to write something of 20 or 30 pages. All I put in the notebooks are sensory details. I don't put in what happened because I can remember what happened when, and I don't put in what people said, because I can always interview them later. The things I will not be able to remember are the sensory details—the color of the light on the water, the way the eyelashes flicked, how somebody walked across the sand, the sound of a mother seal calling to her young.

For years I would look at something ordinary, the parking lot uptown, my familiar rock wall, the people waiting for a concert to begin, and write down a hundred or a hundred and fifty specific details:

Lady with hat

Looks like salad bowl upside down

Remember when women wore hats

Silk stocking

Gloves

How his face changes when he sees a customer

Salesman's mask

Greedy smile

Slimey voice

Firm handshake

All con men have firm handshakes

Look you in the eye

Dad trained me to look him in the eye

Have firm handshake

She rises from car as if she were rising from swimming pool

Liquid movement

She flows

Shy smile

But her eyes are not shy

Eyes like switchblade

As quick as a switchblade

Today I do not often formally write down the specifics. I don't need to because I have years of list making behind me. But you need to. Go to an ordinary place—where you are right now, where you would normally go next, where you waited for a friend yesterday. Start writing down specific, revealing details. You will discover that when you look at an ordinary place, event, or person and observe carefully, it becomes extraordinary.

I live my life collecting revealing details. I study my woods and pay attention to the dancing maple branch from which the squirrel has just leapt, then follow his acrobat course, racing along highways in the air only he can see. I pay attention to this morning's distance between the neighbor couple who first walked arm in arm laughing, then hand in hand listening to each other, now a yard apart, silent. Aging myself, I notice the signs of others' aging—the gray hair sneaking up under the dye job, the way a hand trembles, the step that is unsure, shuffling out ahead to find the curb.

I may still write down what I observe in my daybook, but most of the time I allow it to sift into memory unconsciously. It will remain there forgotten until it is recalled by my writing. Then it will appear on the page surprising me. The more I see, the more that is stored in memory like money in the bank, reading to be withdrawn when it is needed. I cannot promise you that if you develop the craft of vision that you will become a writer—or an artist—but I can promise you that you will rarely be bored.

THE SEEING I

The craft of vision begins with respect for your own point of view. This requirement sounds easy but it isn't. When I came into teaching, I was warned that my students would be selfish, self-centered, inflated with their own importance, and there were a few through the years that fitted that stereotype—but very few.

The biggest problem was a modesty so extensive, I thought it had to be false. It wasn't. Most of my students didn't believe they had anything to say worth saying. They didn't respect themselves and the individual points of view from which they saw their world, therefore they didn't see or didn't pay attention to what they saw. If they saw—felt, thought—it, then it must not be special.

This was true of almost all my students, including the soldier wounded in Vietnam; the woman caring for her dying mother, her father, and her brothers and sisters—while going to school; the welfare mother of nine children who was returning to college; the man who left the ministry to become a writer; the professional fisherman; the victim of marital violence; the woman who was first mate on a three-masted schooner that had weathered a hurricane in the Caribbean; as well as all the other students who had lived their more quiet lives that were still filled with material for effective—and significant—writing.

The writer Sandra Cisneros tells us to, "Write about what makes you different." Wise advice that took me a lifetime to understand. All that made me strange—and sometimes frightening—to my family and weird to my teachers and classmates, made me a writer. I didn't know that as I stumbled through school, dropping out then flunking out of high school. I thought I was strange, different and yet dull, uninteresting, boring, blah. I did not know the importance of everyone's seeing I. You have already lived extraordinary lives. Take inventory:

What's your ethic background?

Racial?

Religious?

Are you adopted?

If so, what do you know about your background?

What don't you know?

What do you want to know?

What do you not want to know?

If you know your grandparents, write a line describing each one.

Do the same for your parents or stepparents.

Where did you grow up?

What do you know how to do?

What would you like to know how to do?
    List your jobs.
    List your skills.

Describe your world.
    What do you feel about your world?
    What do you think about your world?

As you travel into yourself and your world, you will discover your personal angle of vision and be surprised at how much you know and how it influences your vision of the world. As you write, you will learn to respect your own individual way of looking at the world.

SEE WITH THE SEVEN SENSES

The writer needs to exercise the seven senses—sight, hearing, touch, taste, smell, memory, imagination. I'll pick a nearby subject, and while I'm recording it with my senses, you should pick your own subject and do the same. I look out my office window at the woods behind the house, the rock wall, the abandoned wood pile, the great tree stump that has become a banquet table for a huge pileated woodpecker, and then I spot my wife's compost piles just beyond the rock wall where she turns garbage into fertilizer to my disgust. It is such an unlikely subject, and I feel so strongly about it, I must pay attention.

SIGHT

My wife used to make a square of yard-long pieces of wood, stacked alternately so the garbage would be contained and yet receive the air essential to good rotting. Now the wood has rotted as well, and she just builds up circles of garbage—peels and shells and pizza crusts and leftover, cooked zucchini and green, moldy bread, banana skins and apple cores and spaghetti and a green-spotted custard pie.

HEARING

I heard the "caw-caw" of the crows after a Wednesday dumping as they advertise what we had for Sunday dinner and before. We have no secrets from our gossipy crows.

TOUCH

One of my chores as a boy was to carry out what Uncle Will called "the swill"— the slimy, slithery, ick in Mother's leaky sink garbage container. Now we have a garbage disposal unit in our sink, but my gardener wife keeps a plastic box in which she stores compost. When I have to carry it out, I do it at arm's length so I can't see the disgusting waste, what had to be cut away, what was rotting, what we weren't allowed to eat, what we refused to eat. I don't allow my fingers to touch the damp, gooey mess.

TASTE

Taking out the compost, I taste last Saturday's supper—how great it had tasted at 7 p.m. and how it rose in my throat at 3 a.m., burning, sour, rancid. Its memory rises from the compost.

SMELL

My wife lifts the cover off the kitchen compost box, and a stink, thick as pea soup, heavy as a wet tarpaulin, pushes down my throat then rises up inside my nose.

MEMORY

During one trip to the compost bins, a sweetish stench this time, I remember the afternoon in Berlin, at the end of the war, when they opened a subway where hundreds had been buried in an air raid months before—the sweet perfume of death spread across the city, street by street.

IMAGINATION

I hate to garden, but I imagine I am a gardener and see in the death of plants, birth. At the top of the compost pile, a small green shoot, a single leaf, new life rising from what was discarded, tossed away to return to earth.

....

WRITE TO SEE

Wallace Stevens, the poet wrote, "The tongue is an eye." When we write, we see. As the words spin forth, we discover scenes in memory that we had forgotten or only half remembered. Language recovers vision.

I start thinking about my grandmother, with whom we lived and who was the most powerful person in my world until she had a stroke—we called it a "shock" then—and was leaving her paralyzed and bedridden for the rest of her life. I remember the shiny gloss of the skin on the left hand she could not use and write that down, remembering in the writing the delicate colors of the skin, like the iridescent inside of an oyster shell.

I see her wispy crown of white hair and remember back until it was auburn and twisted into a knot on top of her head. She always said her hair was "not red but auburn" even when it was turning gray. How proud she had been of her hair, of her strength, widowed with five children and raising them in a foreign land. She told me stories of how, as a girl, a bull had attacked, and she drove sewing scissors up its nose, saving her companions and herself, and how, when her husband was alive but away on business and a robber with a six-gun wanted the mill's payroll, she broke his wrist with one stroke of her cane and got Alec, her oldest to run for the constable. But the woman I see is imprisoned in her bed, and I start to write what I do not know; my fingers on the keyboard become an eye. I do not think about writing but concentrate on seeing and recording what language sees.

> After school, I wash Grandma's legs that will never walk and, looking away, my hand moves upward, under the covers, following her geography, missing nothing.
>
> *I feel the experience of washing her in my right hand and feel her embarrassment and mine at our necessary intimacy. I go back to see more by writing, focusing on the action, not its meaning.*
>
> I dip the face cloth in the dishpan, rinse, return as she talks of washing the dead when she was a girl in the Hebrides.

I remember more of the stories she told me when she was a girl on an island off the western coast of Scotland, a girl who was old for her years and trained by her mother, my great-grandmother, to care for the ill, the dying, and the dead. I continue the interaction between memory and language by retelling her stories.

A banging on the cottage door in the night and a shouted name, waking the animals.

I follow the story, traveling through geography to Scotland and through time to the mid-1800s. I am surprised by what I write.

Death always comes just before dawnlight, and she gathers her twice-washed bindings, wraps herself in her Black Watch shawl.

The dark, black-and-green shawl always lay on her bed. I was fascinated by it. Her uncle, for whom I was named, had fought, according to family legend, with the famous Scots Black Watch regiment against Napoleon at Waterloo.

To walk alone across the island's dark shadowed fields, watching out for bulls.

I remember that story of the scissors.

The closing of the eyes, the tying up of the jaw, the scrubbing away of all that was soiled in the dying.

My memory of what she said is woven together with what I have heard, seen, read. This will be my duty to Grandma upon her leaving. Actually, she died when I was overseas in combat, but as a boy I imagined I would wash her after she died. It was not, as I remember it, a terrifying thought, but an appropriate act of love and respect. I return to the simple description of my actions. That is where the power of writing often stays.

I empty the pan, fill it with warm water from the whistling kettle and attend her other side.

I am pacing out the story. I move from her paralyzed side to the side that is still alive, and I am really surprised by what I write.

My hand touches the foot that can still be tickled, then circles up.

All that is unsaid, is said. All the times we laughed, all the times she played with me when I was young, all the human caring that passed between us as I continue washing.

What might be a paragraph in a social worker's report about a troubled teenager—which I was—who had to wash his grandmother becomes a celebration of living and dying in the writing. She had passed on her inheritance from her mother to me: I could do what had to be done. That act predicted some of what I had to do as I lived my life in the war and afterward, when I was alone with my other grandmother when she died, and when I had to give both my parents and a daughter the release of death after I made a lonely, necessary decision.

I find I have written a poem:

The Passing on of Care

After school I wash Grandma's legs
that will never walk and, looking away,
my hand moves upward, under the covers,
following her geography, missing nothing.

I dip the face cloth in the dishpan,
rinse, return as she talks of washing
the dead when she was a girl in the Hebrides:

A banging on the cottage door in the night
and a shouted name, waking the animals.

Death always comes just before dawnlight,
and she gathers her twice-washed bindings,
wraps herself in her Black Watch shawl
to walk alone across the island's
dark shadowed fields,
watching out for bulls.

The closing of the eyes,
the tying up of the jaw,
the scrubbing away
of all that was soiled
in the dying.

This will be my duty
to Grandma upon
her leaving.

I empty the pan, fill it with warm water
from the whistling kettle and attend
her other side. My hand touches
the foot that can still be tickled,
then circles up.

THE FOCUSING LINE

I write an essay for my newspaper column every week, work continuously on a chapter of one book or another, and write at least two poems a month, several articles a year, and half a dozen or so talks that turn into writing. They all start with a focusing line, an image, a mental picture that intrigues and haunts me, or a written line, a fragment of language that I know contains a piece of writing. Once I have the line, I can start writing immediately or wait until I have time. The spark will be there.

Most of the time, the focusing line is a response to life, but if I have a specific assignment, I still seek a line of my own. I continue to live my life in a state of passive awareness, a receptive alertness in which I absorb the life I am living and pay close attention to my reactions to that life. Certain signals within a line compel me to pay attention and to write.

CONFLICT

The most common beginning point is a conflict or tension within the line. Guilford College in North Carolina is a Quaker school, dedicated to nonviolence, but its football team is called the Fighting Quakers. I wrote in my daybook, "I had an ordinary war" and started writing a book about the extraordinary that becomes ordinary in war.

SURPRISE

I read what I do not expect. I write "they should stay in the graves" and report on a true and disturbing human feeling: my anger at those who I have loved and lost that will not be forgotten.

WORRY

I noted "My daughters were proud" when I became violent in an automobile confrontation. The police thought I was right to attack the other driver but I felt within myself the paratrooper-trained ability to kill. I wrote about my fear of what is within us.

JOY

I wake in the morning and take delight in "the coming of light." My writing celebrates the moment of waking—*carpe diem,* seize the day.

CONNECTION

I observe my grandson's "war games" and connect his play at war to my playing in war, when those who fell down dead did not jump up laughing. One of the most important things the writer does is to connect what is not usually connected so it reveals meaning.

PERSONAL TERRITORIES

Each of us have territories that we are compelled to explore, places where we find meaning. My personal territories are a childhood that was strange and full of questions I have not yet answered, a fascination with the creative process and language, the war, school where I did so badly and later returned as a teacher, my experience in combat and what I discovered about the enemy: myself. I read a story, for example, advocating the tracking of students—separating them by potential ability in high school; in response, I write down the single word line—*tracked*—and later write a column about how it felt to be categorized by a thirteen-track-school system and how it marked my life in a bad way.

POINT OF VIEW

I write "skinny, bespectacled kid" and see myself as others saw me. As a grandfather, I also see myself when I was a boy or a young father. I see my daughters when they were the ages of their children, hear them saying now what we said to them—and I have a piece to write.

VOICE

The experienced writer hears the music that reveals the emotional content, or even the meaning of a piece, in just a fragment of language. You will too after you become used to listening to your language as you write. "I meet my cousin's son. He steps out of the photograph of my father taken before I was born." I hear a reflective music in that line, a thinking back and musing music that makes me think of the childhood my father never had and how that experience shaped him—and perhaps me.

NEWS

On my friend Chip Scanlan's bulletin board I see a clipping from the May 1997 issue of *Mature Lifestyles* and copy it. Each item makes me see my world differently in a way that might lead to writing:

> If we could shrink the earth's population to a tiny village of exactly 100 people, and if we kept existing population ratios the same, our village would look like this:
>
> - There would be 57 from Asia, 21 from Europe, 14 from North and South America, and 8 from Africa.
> - 51 would be female; 49 would be male.
> - 70 would be nonwhite; 30 would be white.
> - 70 would be non-Christian; 30 would be Christian.
> - Half of the entire wealth would be in the hands of only six people from the United States.
> - 80 would live in substandard housing.
> - 70 would be unable to read.
> - 50 would suffer from malnutrition.
> - One would be near death, and one would be near birth.
> - One would have a college education.

Other focusing lines might reveal a potential genre—a research paper, a memo, a short story—I should write. I might discover a need I have that others might need to know, as well. I might see a pattern of behavior that should be exposed, an answer without a question or a question without an answer—until I write it.

Writing is not apart from living. We had just completed a visit with close friends, Kathy and Tom Romano from Ohio, when he e-mailed bad news. A routine checkup isn't routine; Kathy has to have a mastectomy. I talked to them on the phone and by e-mail after they received the terrifying diagnosis, and was impressed by the way they were handling it. I formed the image of the sharp edge of a shadow across a field and imagined stepping over it as I had in combat, passing from fear to calm. I heard a line in my head: "crossing the edge of fear." With combat, the deaths of our daughter and our parents, with our own terrifying surgeries, I have realized that people handle such situations as my friends have with courage and strength, and they need to have that strength recognized and reinforced.

Without planning, I sat down and wrote them the following e-mail online:

This I know: That people have come through what you have come through in the way you have, have grown stronger. You should take comfort and strength in the fact that we all have choices to make—roads to go down and roads not to go down. The way you have handled this prepares you to handle the other tough moments that life will provide.

I fear hubris but I do know that I have been aware in the past decades that strength breeds strength and that there are differences between the strong and weak. As liberals we should have compassion for the weak but we almost, at times, celebrate the weak without celebrating the strong.

You both are strong—alone and together—and you should take account of your strength. You should recognize it, feel it, shape it, talk about it, celebrate it.

One day, walking home from school, after Lee's death, she told me I had done all right—we had done all right.

Minnie Mae and I have both had many testings as you have had and each lays down a foundation for the next testing. And there will be more testings.

I don't think we talk enough about toughness and courage these days. I don't know if I want to go back to the Battle of Britain term when they talked about IMF fliers—Insufficient Moral Fibre—but I do know from my days in combat that there is a difference between the strong and the weak, between courage and cowardice. We don't like to talk about it but there is a difference.

Later that week, I had to write a poem for my poetry group. We meet twice a month and admission is by poem. I kept thinking about that line between fear and calm in medical situations. I have written many poems about my fifty-year-old and more war experience and did not want to write more about it, but when

I started writing, at the last moment, on the morning of the poetry meeting, I found myself writing what became, after five or six runs at it, the following draft of a poem.

My Last Virginity

My first time:
shells march across
the valley-bouquets
of flowering earth-
and up the ridge
to where I lie
waiting.

I ride earth
rising against me,
pulling away to rise
again, twisting up into me
then back, only to return
again and again until
one last shuddering
time.

Stone, steel, bone
clatter down.

Unexpected silence
and I rise to the sergeant's
barked command, step
across the edge of fear
into calm,

saunter down the ridge,
across the valley, between
the bullets that cannot
keep me from their woods.

Sudden flying bird,
quivering branch,
shadow soldier
who awaits our
rendezvous.

The poem isn't finished. I thought I was going to write a poem about the calm that comes after you cross the line separating it from terror. I was thinking of it in a medical situation, but the writing took it back to combat where the calm itself became terrifying, a coldness that allowed me to become a killer. That surprised, intrigued, and worried me. This is something I have to deal with. I will have to reread and rethink the poem, respecting what the poem itself wants to say, no matter how uncomfortable that is.

When I shared the poem with my poetry group, some thought it ended after the first three verses. One person thought I was describing a field of flowers in the first verse, not explosions that blossomed like flowers. Others liked the fourth verse, some did not get the last verse, one person thought it was a cliché, another thought it was brilliant, and still another thought it should become the first verse. I will consider all their concerns and mine.

Then, before the beginning of the next week, I had a column to write. Again the image of the sharp edge of shadow—dark to light—diagonally across a field, probably a battlefield, and the line "crossing the edge of fear." But when I started to write the column: "Let us celebrate the strong, the courageous, the responsible . . ." I found my mind jumping backward to a conversation we had had with a daughter weeks before when she reported on her oldest son's summer. I started the column again.

> This summer our six-year-old grandson, Joshua, learned to swim, even to swim underwater, ~~and to ride a two-wheeler, no training wheels.~~
>
> *I'd better focus on one challenge.*
>
> Time and again he had to step across the line between terror and confidence, to reach within himself and find that old-fashioned virtue, courage.
>
> *Now, I told myself, develop that idea, so the reader can understand what you mean.*
>
> It wasn't easy. I can remember the terror of the wobbly two-wheeler and the granite curb rising up so fast, so sure. And the getting up and trying again— and again. I was much older than Josh when I learned to swim. The terror of water over my head is still real to me.
>
> *I push on, knowing I'll write the complete draft of the column later. This is a rough sketch so I can get a feel for the voice and dimensions of the writing.*
>
> But I learned, as Josh has done, to step across the line of fear. I hope he will not have to step out of a plane, to advance against an enemy in a dark wood, but he will have to meet terror and advance.
>
> *Add a reminder of what I said in my note to my friends about celebrating the victim. I am not worried about this flatulent writing. They are just notes.*
>
> As a card carrying liberal, I usually focus on the victim. . . .
> I hope he will swim and ride a bike until he is a 110 years old. That is now a matter of choice. And courage will be a matter of choice all his life.
> Again and again he will come to a fork in the road where he has to choose the road of weakness or strength, the road of escape or responsibility.

Later, I wrote the column. Note how the line that ignited the writing appears in the final draft.

Age provides a panoramic view of life that allows us to see the significant in the commonplace. This summer our six-year-old grandson, Joshua, learned to swim, even to swim underwater.

It wasn't easy. I know because I was much older than Josh when I dared to go into water over my ankles, to say nothing of swimming in water over my head. I had almost "drownded," as I said then, three times.

Josh and I, each in our time, have learned to swim but, more important, we have learned to step across the edge of fear into calm, where we can do what has to be done.

Josh was building on that ability to pass from terror into confidence that he began to learn before he escaped the play pen, and he will continue to build on this foundation all his life.

We don't use the old-fashioned term *courage* much these days, but that is what Josh learned—again—this summer and what he will have to learn—again—all his life. He learned to do what has to be done.

It is also the summer he learned to ride a two-wheeler, and after this double triumph, he told his mother, "I can do anything." We laugh and celebrate with him and then grow quiet.

I remember, before my first training jump as a paratrooper, looking out of the open door of a dipping and rising, sideways sliding C-47 at the trees 1,400 feet below and reminding myself what I learned the summer I discovered I could dive from the float into water over my head and swim.

The memory of my learning to swim has served me well. I found I could step across the edge of fear, move out across the valley and up the hill where the Germans lay waiting.

I could, hardest of all, tell the doctors to let our daughter go.

I could, at the moment of my heart attack, as the nurses worked to the command of a doctor on the speaker phone, make my way from terror into that calm first made familiar at Lake Millen in Washington, New Hampshire.

I was reminded of the courage life takes when we received an e-mail message from our close friend Tom Romano in Ohio. We had spent the evening with the Romanos just the week before. Now his wife, Kathy, after a routine test that proved to be anything but routine, would have a mastectomy the following Monday.

They decided to be open about what was going on, their fears and their hopes, allowing their many friends to share as much as friends can share terror and hope.

We all know people, often in our families, who do not do what has to be done, who close down, retreat, break down—and we understand. The Romanos faced the fundamental issues of life itself. We would have understood if they had been weak. We did not know how we would have responded to their testing.

The surgery was successful. Kathy walked three-and-a-half miles two days afterward. The first tests were good.

I was astonished at how e-mail made it possible for Tom to keep so many of us informed and how each of us could instantly forward his reports to others.

Kathy and Tom also were amazed at how many people were able to reach out to them, each sending messages of comfort and love they found helpful.

I'm glad we have helped them, but I hope they know how they have helped us. Their openness, their courage, their sharing the intimacy of the decisions they had to make is a gift to us.

As we build on the lessons that Josh is learning as he swims further and further into deeper water, we also build on the examples of those who have allowed us to share their fears and their courage.

Before my triple bypass, I remember thinking of my good friend Hans Heilbronner and his courage before, during, and after his bypass. I took strength from him, and later others have said they took strength from me.

Each of us has to make that step across the edge of fear into calm alone, but we take it knowing that others we know and admire have done what we have to do.

I celebrate the good news with the Romanos, share the cautionary "so far" that all of us who have lived this long know to add, and offer thanks for their gift of openness and courage that will serve us well in what inevitably lies ahead in our own lives.

Some of the courage of Josh and the Romanos is stored away within me, and I will draw on it when I need to: make myself remember what Kathy and Tom said and imagine six-year-old Josh taking a deep-deep breath and hurling himself forward underwater.

I thought it was a good column, but my editor thought it went off the track in the middle, beginning with paragraph "They decided to be open . . ." through ". . . love they found helpful." I listened and let the column sit overnight, reread it the next morning and realized I had gone off track. There is a future column about the e-mail communities to which we belong. The next morning, saving what should be saved, cutting and adding, I think it made the column stronger—rewriting always does.

Age provides a panoramic view of life that allows us to see the significant in the commonplace. This summer our six-year-old grandson, Joshua, learned to swim in water over his head.

It wasn't easy. I know because I was much older than Josh when I dared to go into water over my ankles, to say nothing of swimming in water over my head. I had almost "drownded," as I said then, three times.

Josh and I, each in our time, have learned to swim but, more important, we have learned to step across the edge of fear into calm, where we can do what has to be done.

Josh was building on that ability to pass from terror into confidence that he began to learn before he escaped the play pen, and he will continue to build on this foundation all his life.

We don't use the old-fashioned term *courage* much these days, but that is what Josh learned—again—this summer and what he will have to learn—again—all his life. He learned to do what has to be done.

It is also the summer he learned to ride a two-wheeler, and after this double triumph, he told his mother, "I can do anything." We laugh and celebrate with him and then grow quiet.

I remember, before my first training jump as a paratrooper, looking out of the open door of a dipping and rising, sideways sliding C-47 at the trees 1,400 feet below and reminding myself what I learned the summer I discovered I could dive into water over my head and swim.

Later, I found I could step across the edge of fear, move out across the valley and up the hill where the Germans lay waiting.

I could, hardest of all, tell the doctors to let our daughter go.

I could, at the moment of my heart attack, as the nurses worked to the command of a doctor on the speaker phone, make my way from terror into that calm first made familiar at Lake Millen in Washington, New Hampshire.

I was reminded of the courage life takes when we received an e-mail message from our close friend Tom Romano in Ohio. We had spent the evening with the Romanos just the week before. Now his wife, Kathy, after a routine test that proved to be anything but routine, would have a mastectomy the following Monday.

Their friends would have understood if they had broken down. Who knows, we would tell each other, how we would respond to such news. We would have respected their privacy if they had decided to withdraw. We might do the same.

But the Romanos gave their friends an unexpected and invaluable gift. They invited us to share their anxiety and fears and hopes, and, yes, their courage. By e-mail we have been informed test by test, procedure by procedure, opinion by opinion. We could share, each of us in our own way, something of what they were going through. Not all, not much, but enough for us to store away for the day when we might need to draw on it.

Kathy's surgery was successful. She walked three-and-a-half miles two days afterward. The first tests were good. Further treatments are under discussion. We will hear of each decision ahead—and how they feel about it—as it is made. They say our responses by phone and e-mail and snail mail to their messages have helped them.

They do not realize how much they have helped us. The Romanos have given us a gift of courage. Of course, that is a term they would never use, but their behavior is nothing less than courageous. And courage is as contagious as fear.

As we build on the lessons that Josh is learning as he swims further and further into deeper water, we also build on the examples of those who have allowed us to share their terrors and their strength.

Before my coronary bypass I remember thinking of my good friend Hans Heilbronner and his courage before, during, and after his by-pass. I took strength from him, and later others have said they took strength from me.

Each of us has to make that step across the edge of fear into calm alone, but we take it knowing that others we know and admire have done what we have to do.

Some of the courage of Josh and the Romanos is stored away within me, and I will draw on it when I need to. Those lonely moments will be made less lonely as I force myself to remember how Kathy and Tom faced her cruel diagnosis and imagine how six-year-old Josh felt when he took a deep-deep breath and hurled himself into water over his head.

....

DRAW TO SEE

I believe I have learned almost as much about writing from art and photography as I have learned from reading. Artists and photographers have taught me ways to look at my world. They have shown me how specific detail reveals an enormous world. I have discovered how art and photography show complexity. They have taught me light and shadow, action and suspended action, what is done and what is not done, the significance of what is left out as well as what is included.

Some of the ways in which I use art to teach myself seeing and writing that you can use as well:

- I visit museums and pick out the works that attract and repel me the most. I pay more attention to the paintings, drawings, sculptures I need to see than to the ones celebrated by the critics. It is my response that guides me to the works of art that instruct me. Why do I like this painting so much? What has the artist done? How could I do that in writing? Why does this picture disturb me so much? What has the artist done? How could I do that in writing?

- I collect books on artists that stimulate me, especially reprints of artists' notebooks and sketches; I watch television shows about artists; I read art reviews and buy postcards and reproductions when I visit a museum; I put up art in my office where it catches the corner of my eye, and I have an impressionist screen saver collection on my computer.

- I have taken a few studio art courses in which I attempted to create art. I have watched television courses and read many textbooks on art that have told me how to see.

- I talk to artists, art students, and art teachers, discovering how they see their worlds. I have breakfast almost every morning with a sculptor, Michael McConnell, and watch him moving his head just a bit this way or that to see our familiar world anew. I do the same and am surprised at how my world arranges itself into a new meaning.

- I carry a sketchbook in the case I carry everywhere and sometimes try to catch a tree, a branch, a leaf, an old woman in a supermarket in a few lines. I may also draw from memory or from imagination, drawing a place, an animal, a plant, even a face I have never seen. I don't worry if I can draw well. The poorly drawn line reveals as well as the skillful one.

I just turned from the computer and made a quick pen-and-ink sketch of the tall, black-barked pines seen in silhouette with the morning sun behind them; then, with quick lines I suggested the oak and maple leaves that crowded around them. The observation required to do this drawing and the revelations of the lines themselves made me understand the woods better than I ever have. No museum will ever hang my sketch, but I have exercised my seeing muscles. When I see other trees, other woods, I will see them with more insight than I ever have before.

I do not think, then draw, but allow the pen to do the thinking. I do not worry if I know how to draw or how well I draw. These trees grow in fertile ignorance, from wonder and delight. My only ambition is to see each one as it grows under my hand. My hand moves quickly, easily, naturally, growing the tree organically from unseen root to seen branch and back. Some of these trees have grown from the ground up; others have begun in the sky and found the ground; still others have begun as outer horizons of trees, maps of trees, filled in as the pen explores.

Some of the trees have been carefully observed as the pen, brush, or crayon drew; others have been remembered; still more imagined: trees I had never seen until they appeared on the page. The act of drawing creates a tree that is not the one observed, but the one revealed by art, and the imagined tree may be more real than the one that grew at the edge of the field.

....

SEE ON A COMPUTER

I know that most people who think they cannot draw really can, but the computer allows everyone to learn how to see through art. There are many software programs designed to allow everyone to draw on screen. Geoffrey Chang, a young Toronto artist is aware of the connections between writing and art, and he uses the computer. He has written the following counsel for readers of this book who may use a computer drawing program:

> Visualizing is a very useful and important part of art work and also writing. This image appears in the "mind's eye" and should be complete with color, texture, and sometimes motion. If you want to apply your visualizations to your work, it is not only important that they are clear, but that they can be easily put into color, line, and/or words.
>
> Even though writing and drawing are quite different, you apply visualization to them in almost the same way. For some people, visualization comes more easily than for others. People who draw a lot often have more practice visualizing. But writers also visualize, just as much as artists. Writers think of the importance and the meaning of the visualization, whereas artists concentrate on the detail and color of the picture itself. But it is always important to be able to concentrate and analyze the visualization.

APPLYING VISUALIZATION TO WRITING

> There are many different parts of writing (of the writing process) where you can use visualization. To be able to describe and write a scene in a story properly, you must visualize. After visualizing the scene, you have a basis to continue the story. You should then try acting out the rest of the scene in your mind, making a realistic continuation to the story that fits in with the basic plot. Act out what you think your characters would say and do, and write how the people in your visualization feel. When you feel you should write this down, do so, but afterward it would be a good idea if you continued visualizing without interruption, keeping ideas fresh in your mind.
>
> Visualizing is also helpful in describing important objects, places, and people. When people who read this work visualize the story themselves, it is good for them to have a clear picture of the place or person you are writing about. You could even visualize things that you have seen yourself and use them in your story, so that you can describe them in more depth. Every now and then, read over your work, changing words to describe your visualization better.

APPLYING VISUALIZATION TO DRAWING

> Visualizations are somewhat easier to draw onto paper than to put into words, because drawing is much more direct. That is because your visualizations are

drawings drawn by your mind. Really, what you're trying to learn is how to help your hands draw as your mind does.

Before putting anything down on the computer screen, every artist has an idea in mind of how the picture will appear. It is not necessarily complex with many small details, but it has basic shapes, objects, and colors that the artist can identify. The first thing you draw is a starting point. This can be a large object like a mountain or a long line like the horizon or simply the ground line. It would be best if it had some distinctive curves or bumps to help you orient other things to it. This first, dominating shape is very important, because it determines the size and placement of all other objects in your drawing.

Continue drawing other shapes that you see in your mind's eye. If you feel that anything is out of place on your drawing, you should change it so that it fits in with your visualization. After all of the large objects have been drawn in place, continue putting down small details. Don't stick to one part of your drawing, filling it with tiny details; step back and look how you can uniformly draw the small details in each pan of the picture to give it balance. To make a realistic picture, color it the way your visualization is colored, and try using some three dimensional views.

Of course, when you're drawing one thing that does not take up the entire space, like a car, an airplane, a person, or any other single object, the process is slightly different. When starting, the first thing you draw is the frame. For something like a car or plane, the frame is not simple to draw. Draw it slowly. Pretend that your visualization is being superimposed on the screen and that you are tracing over it. Projecting your visualization like this can be very useful when drawing different objects that need to be certain distances apart. But don't try drawing from the lines you already have on the screen; it will change the proportions of the picture. Adjust the lines and placements of shapes by small amounts until you think they're right.

Never rush! If you're not satisfied with any part or all of the picture, start again; the beginning is always the most important part. Once the frame is complete, continue with large lines and shapes and then small details. Put down as many details as possible that do appear on that object, but don't make them too big. If you can't think of any more details to draw, go to a library and find a photograph of what you are drawing. Just one picture will give you many good ideas. Don't forget, if your picture is basically the same as your visualization, it will look great!

Whether using your computer or paper to draw or write, your visualization is a very good source of ideas, information, and creative inspiration. We all have visualizations, but not all of us realize how important and useful they are in all forms of art.

IN THE WRITER'S WORKSHOP

Ut pictura poesis. *[As in art, so in poetry.]* HORACE

I could keep myself busy for months without moving from one spot, just by leaning now to the right, now to the left. PAUL CEZANNE

First I must look, then I must learn. . . . Nothing seen, nothing said. THEODORE
ROETHKE

Make me see! CHARLES DICKENS

*I sat on the floor with the canvas propped against a chair—and with my house paint,
brushes and colours in little casseroles, I disappeared into that canvas.* D. H. LAWRENCE

*Try to forget what objects you have before you—a tree, a house, a field, or whatever.
Merely think, here is a little square of blue, here a streak of yellow, and paint it just as
it looks to you, the exact color and shape, until it gives you the impression of the scene
before you.* CLAUDE MONET

*No wonder writers, so many of them, have drawn and painted; the tools are allied,
the impulse is one.* JOHN UPDIKE

*You blank out whatever is in front of your eyes. That's why you see writers staring off
into space. They are not looking at "nothing," they're visualizing what they are thinking. I never visualize what a play will look like on stage, I visualize what it looks like
in life.* NEIL SIMON

I don't paint what I see, I see what I paint. PHILIP BAXTER

*Writing is important from the standpoint of presenting what one sees. No one else sees
the world exactly as I do, and I want to record what I see.* DIANA O'HEHIR

*The pictures in my head are fuzzy and out of focus. That's why I draw them—so I can
better see what they look like. If those images in my head were sharp and vivid, I'd
have no need to draw them.* DAVID MCPHAIL

··

QUESTIONS ABOUT SEEING

Some of the greatest books were written by writers who hardly
left their rooms! Everything they wanted to write about they already had in their heads. So why make such a big deal out of seeing, touching, and experiencing the world?

Because the image of the solitary writer in the garret, oblivious to life, is largely
a myth. Sure, some writers like to cultivate this image—it makes the rest of us
think they are geniuses, and it puts a romantic spin on the actual hard work of
planning, drafting, revising, and editing. These writers would like us to believe that
composing is purely a matter of inspiration, of becoming attuned to the world
through the mind's eye alone rather than through all seven of the writers' senses—
seeing, hearing, touching, tasting, smelling, imagining, and remembering.

But even these writers usually keep some sort of journal or notebook in
which they record their observations and jot down the details of everyday life. If
they don't, you can bet that they have perfected their writers' senses through years
of using them, of honing them through the experience of writing itself.

Don't be fooled by the myth. If you decide to isolate yourself and write
from the mind alone, you will cut yourself off from the richness of living, not to

mention writing. When you experience your environment through your senses, you are fully embodied; when you write through your senses, you embody the world.

If I want to write a poem or story, I can see where the craft of vision is useful, but if I want to write scholarly essays, how will "seeing" help?

Whether you are writing an analytical essay or a personal narrative, as you engage in the process of composing, you will find yourself using terms that refer repeatedly to seeing: Point of view, perspective, angle, focus, and revision are just a few of these terms. If you think of these words, they don't always literally mean using the eyes to see; they also mean envisioning or revising, seeing the world afresh through concepts and theories. Most of all, seeing through imagining.

Most of the world's greatest contributors to science, religion, and history were revolutionary "see-ers." When talking about people such as Albert Einstein, Marie Curie, Mahatma Ghandi, Martin Luther King, Susan B. Anthony, or Rosa Parks, we often use the term *visionaries*. We praise these figures for their "foresight" or their "fresh outlooks" on life. We discuss the ways in which they "opened our eyes" to new ideas and "revised" our ways of thinking. We refer to them as "far-seeing" people who refused to turn "a blind eye" on the world's injustices. We recognize them as people who argued ideas, took stances, and persuaded others through speaking and writing.

When you look deeply into concepts and theories, you become a visionary of a sort, an *insightful* writer who brings new perspectives to old ideas and issues—a thinker who sees in order that others may see.

But when I write a lab report or a report for work, I'm certainly not going to take a "fresh outlook" on life. I want to be straightforward.

Seeing well in order to write does not mean that you have to use flowery language. If you are writing a report or memo, you'll want to use concise verbs and clear sentences. But even with these direct and seemingly simple kinds of communication, the route you take is as important as your destination.

Seeing to write will enhance your presentation and the quality of your ideas, no matter what field you are in. Students preparing for careers in the sciences or business sometimes distinguish between creative and analytical tasks; experienced scientists, business people, and entrepreneurs know that writing and critical observation are linked. They have learned that observing, drafting, and revising (re-seeing, re-observing) result in creative approaches to new and old problems. Innovative changes and scientific breakthroughs are the direct products of the ability to see beneath, through, and beyond any given situation and to formulate solutions to problems through writing.

But how can research involve new ways of seeing? Doesn't re-search, by its very name, mean that someone else has already searched my topic and found all the answers?

That's one way to look at it, especially if you are writing a research paper that involves only gathering specific facts and figures about your topic. But if you want to write a paper that allows you to think through data and come up with your own opinions and ideas, you will understand research as a way of bringing new perspectives and insights to a particular issue or problem.

Think of the term *research* itself, a word that suggests re-seeing. When thinking innovatively about your subject, you will find yourself using words and terms that reinforce this idea of seeing. You'll want to *re-view* your topic and what has already been written about it. You'll begin to see the issues involved from different *perspectives* and perhaps develop a whole new *out-look* on the problem. As you discuss your topic with classmates or your teacher, you'll probably respond in terms implying sight: "Now I see . . . " "This author opened my eyes to the fact that . . . " "This writer over-looked an important idea." Research in this sense doesn't mean reporting. It means re-visioning through writing.

I'm visually impaired. I literally cannot see very well. Does this mean that my writing will lack a particular richness?

No. It means that your writing will be enriched, because you have learned to "see" through your other senses. Fully sighted people who are inexperienced writers often rely too much on their eyes at the expense of hearing, touching, and tasting. You, however, have probably learned to use all your senses: You hear the rise and fall of conversation, smell the fragrances of seasons, taste the nuances in flavors of food, and test surfaces with your hands. This too is seeing. This also is writing.

In fact, your "limited" or "distorted" sight may give you a personal and artistic vision of our world. I have a book by a famous British ophthalmologist, *The World through Blunted Sight,* by Patrick Trevor-Roper and Allan Lame (London: Penguin Press, 1970,1988) that documents how near-sightedness, far-sightedness, astigmatism, color blindness, cataracts, glaucoma, macular dystrophy, and degrees of blindness have affected great artists and, in effect, contributed to production of great art. These artists, because of "defects" in vision, have made it possible for us to see the world anew in their work.

....

SEEING ACTIVITIES

1. List songs that you love and that evoke a certain moment in your life. What memories do these songs bring back to you? Think of all the sensory details you associate with these songs and the events they represent—the

taste of fruit punch at the junior prom, the fragrance of your crumpled corsage, the smooth wooden pew at your friend's memorial service, the grief-stricken look on her mother's face, the feeling of cold water cascading over your body at the shore, the odor of hot dogs steaming on the vendors' carts. Come up with all the memories and sensory details you can for each song.

2. Join a group of classmates in choosing a campus issue to research. Conduct interviews and gather information, and then exchange topics and notes with another group. Research your new topic using the information you have been given. Find out at least three new things about your topic that the previous group missed. Practice seeing beyond the data for what is missing instead of what is there.

3. Look in a mirror and sketch a portrait of yourself. Then in your daybook describe your portrait and the process of drawing it. Did sketching your likeness help you see yourself differently? What details did you notice that you may not have noticed before?

4. Visit a room or spot you go to everyday and see it anew. List as many details as you can, from the unusual to the ordinary. Then circle the details that you noticed for the first time. Return the next day and notice what you didn't notice the last time.

5. Become a wall, floor, ceiling, door, or window expert. Starting in your classroom, join a small group of your classmates and choose one of those categories, then record all the details of the feature you have chosen. When you leave the classroom, continue to examine the feature wherever you go. If you choose windows, for example, observe windows inside and out, in dorm rooms and gymnasiums, on houses and churches. Note all the details you can. Join your group in reporting your findings to the class.

6. Try some intergenerational seeing. If you are a young student, think of an issue or topic that an older relative or friend might view differently from you; if you are older, choose a young friend or relative. Write your viewpoint in your daybook and then interview your friend to get his or her perspective. Describe how your ways of seeing are similar or different and why.

7. Go to a newsstand and examine the covers of one kind of magazine—news magazines, for example, or beauty, men's fitness, or home decorating magazines. List the various story titles and kinds of images the magazines feature on the front. What patterns do you see? What do they say about the particular genre of magazine? What do they say about our culture?

8. Pause at intervals and at different times of the day or night along your daily route home to your dorm, apartment, or house. Look and listen for what you have overlooked or never heard before. Note details in your daybook and describe how they change or remain the same.

9. Hone your sense of touch. Feel the textures of different cloths; run your hand along surfaces; immerse your fingers in liquids; hold objects and test their various weights and shapes. Record your observations in your daybook.

10. Go to a particular site with a writing partner and write about it separately, each from your own viewpoint. Compare notes and discuss the differences and similarities in the way each of you viewed the same space.

11. Describe in detail a feature from your family home. Call or write other family members and have them do the same. Have them choose a feature from memory or sight and describe it in a letter or over the phone. Compare their various perspectives and different ways of remembering and seeing with your own.

12. Interview someone who has access to a space that you don't normally enter, such as a teacher's lounge or private clubhouse. Have your informant describe the site from memory, then ask for permission to visit it. Record the features you see and compare them with what your interviewee remembered. How are they the same? How do they differ?

13. Visit the home of an historical figure and imagine how it looked when that person lived there. Stage a family scene in your daybook or write a story, using the details of a particular room. Later, research the figure and how he or she lived. Compare the details you find out with those of your imagination.

14. Sketch a house or building from different angles while viewing it from across the street, directly in front of it, or from an adjacent balcony. Don't concern yourself with being artistically talented or correct; just pick up as many details as you can. Then write an entry in your daybook comparing and contrasting the various perspectives and how they differ. Choose one of the pictures to revise and see how many more details you can include.

15. Visit an isolated or quiet spot, such as a church or wildlife sanctuary. Sit still and listen for at least fifteen minutes. Write down in your notebook everything you hear. Then add a layer of details by describing what you see and then what you smell. Finally, note everything you feel—cold, wind, snow, rain, sun, or heat on your skin. Then write a short descriptive essay about the spot using these details.

16. Go to the library and find two movie reviews in newspapers or magazines that offer different perspectives on the same film. Draw a line down a page in your daybook and record the main points of the first review on the left-hand side; record the second reviewer's arguments on the right-hand side. Finally, go see the movie yourself and write an entry in your daybook describing how your own perspective differs from or agrees with those of the reviewers.

17. Choose three campus sites and sketch them. Take your pictures to class and describe what details you observed as a result of drawing. Ask your classmates for suggestions that will improve your pictures. Then go back to the sites and describe them in your daybook drawing on the details you used in your pictures and the suggestions of your classmates.

18. Have your classmates bring in photos of their friends or families and gather them into a box at the front of the classroom. Then ask each person to choose a picture from the box and compose a poem or paragraph about it. When the whole class has finished writing, have them exchange pictures with others and write about different photos. Go around the class and read these aloud. Note the differences in your classmates' styles of seeing and describing the same photos.

19. Take a "smelling tour" of your neighborhood, jotting down odors and fragrances you encounter as you walk—food, flowers, garbage, rain, anything that you can detect by nose. Try to describe how these odors make you feel, what they remind you of, and what they say about your neighborhood.

20. See an argument from different cultural perspectives. With a group of classmates, choose a topic, such as affirmative action or immigration, and find one article each about the subject, making sure to include all perspectives, especially those of minority groups whose opinions may not be represented in mainstream publications. Be as objective as you can in your search, and when you have finished, list and compare the main points of each argument. Don't debate these points; discuss what they say about different cultural viewpoints and modes of seeing.

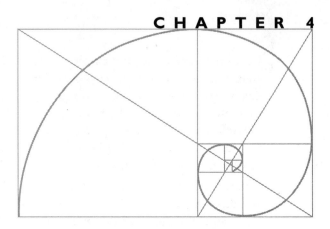

CHAPTER 4

FOCUS

All week long I know that I will sit down Monday morning and write a column for the *Boston Globe* that will resemble the personal essays I once wrote in freshman English. Readers often wonder how I can come up with new ideas, week after week, and so do I.

In trying to answer the question about how I find something to write about, I have examined my process and discovered three principal reasons.

1. I am constantly aware of my world and my reaction to it, as discussed in the last chapter.
2. I combine one, two, or three of the things I observe, think, and feel in a fragment of language I call a *focusing line.*
3. All I need is that line as a starting point. I don't need—or want—to know what I am going to say, because the adventure of the draft will reveal what I have to say and how I will say it.

The focus is the point at which writers concentrate their attention. When we take a picture, we focus on the spot where the most interesting or revealing detail may be captured in a photograph. It is the same with writing. The writer may focus on an event, a moment in a person's life, a decision, an act, a discovery, a cause or an effect, a problem or a solution, but it always defines a place where the writer expects to find significance by writing.

The primary focusing technique is the focusing line.

The focusing line is the words the writer uses to capture the focus, the starting point of the drafting process. It is more often a phrase—"an ordinary war"—than a sentence—"I write in my daybook that I had an ordinary war and think of the horrors that war makes ordinary." The sentence prematurely closes in on the subject, limiting what I may say; the phrase opens up the subject, stimulating me to think about unexpected connections and territories to explore.

The focusing line is often written in rather ordinary language, but it captures some tension, conflict, problem, irony, contradiction in the subject. This element gives the writer the energy to pursue the potential meaning that lies within the as-yet-unwritten draft.

The focusing line is often confused with a thesis statement; a lead, the first lines of a piece of writing; or an introduction. A thesis statement implies the final meaning of the writing to be written. A thesis statement may be helpful if the writer—and the instructor or editor—are willing to change it radically or abandon it when the draft contradicts it. Too often, a thesis statement implies that the thinking is done and the writer has agreed to a contract to deliver on the thesis statement. Writing is thinking; writing is discovery of new meaning. Therefore, I prefer the focusing line, which implies thinking during writing.

A lead, a journalistic term for the beginning or opening of a piece, often evolves from the focusing line but it doesn't need to. The focusing line inspires the piece of writing; the lead is designed to draw the reader into the text.

An introduction tells the reader what the text is going to say or why the writer has written the text or what methods the writer has used to research the subject. It places the cart before the horse for most readers, though. They will be put off by being given information they often do not know they need to know. The skillful writer weaves in the introductory information the reader needs to know at the moment in the text where the reader needs to know it.

The focusing line is where this writer's essays are born. The line ignites the draft. It is my primary focusing technique.

....

THE FOCUSING LINE

Progress toward the focusing line begins when I translate the images and the specific information I observe, read, or remember—as well as my feelings and thoughts in reaction to them—into words in my head or in my daybook. I walk around, as we all do, talking to myself.

> Those kids are teasing the golden retriever tied to a long chain. The chain yanks him back. That must hurt. His tail is wagging and he seems to be barking happily but I wonder. They run into his territory, then dash away, offer him a stick, then pull it out of reach, never let him get the stick. What did that ancient Greek, Bion, say, let's see, "Though boys throw stones at frogs in sport; the frogs do not die in sport, but in earnest." I'd like to give that to the dog. He could put it up on the wall of his doghouse. I remember the uncles teasing me at family dinners, giving me a drumstick, pulling back when I reached for it. And tickling. I hated tickling but everybody laughed. I didn't laugh. They thought it was funny when I fell off the dock and almost drowned. Don't want to be a little kid again.

Maybe that last sentence is a focusing line. No, not for me. Not this time. It doesn't itch enough. I don't need to pursue it. I allow my mind to run its strange course, as erratic as a dog following this scent and then another and another.

> Those kids teasing the dog are the same age as the kids I saw on the TV news last night. Was it the Middle East or Ireland? No matter. Their play is real. But childhood is tough. Learning about falling and the monsters in the closet at night and parents divorcing and pets dying and trying to figure out why people laugh at you when it isn't funny. Childhood—serious business.

There's a focusing line: Childhood—serious business.

> Learning to walk is cute for grandfather, not for the kid. Falling down isn't funny. I remember . . .

Surprise is what tells us we have a focusing line. We think of something that is different from what we expect: Childhood is not all play for the child. The focusing line—childhood is serious business—has tension, conflict, surprise imbedded in it. We think—or try to think—of childhood as a happy time, but often it is not. When we smile at children at play, they may not be playing but tasting real terror, rejection, fear. It is hard work being a kid. I do not know what I have to say about this subject. I will only discover what I have to say if I write a draft. But I have the focusing line: Childhood is serious business.

That focusing line may not appear in the final draft, but it is the starting point. It is something I need to think about, something that may produce more thought, more surprise, first for me, then for the reader.

The focusing line often appears in rather ordinary language, as this one did. It is the writing of the draft that reveals the extraordinary in the ordinary, but the line provides the energy that moves the writer and the writing toward meaning.

Consider some of the elements in an effective focusing line that reveal the energy necessary to drive a draft forward.

TENSION

A focusing line contains a conflict or problem that needs to be explored in writing. The quick note in my daybook reads "add/steele." Translation: "I must go back and read Addison and Steele to see how these eighteenth-century writers I once studied so carefully influenced me as a journalist. Might be a critical essay on how they relate to op-ed page pieces in papers like the *New York Times, Washington Post, St. Petersburg Times, Boston Globe.*"

MYSTERY

Usually there is a mystery in a focusing line, something I didn't understand and that I want—better yet, need—to understand. Line: "grdma tuff, kids weak."

Translation: "My grandmothers lost their husbands early. They were immigrants with small children, and they had to be strong, but somehow their necessary strength made their children weak."

INFORMATION

Specific information reveals an issue or situation that demands attention and is full of implication. Line: "Est Ger Secpol." Translation: "The East German secret police 'consisted of a force of 85,000 regular employees . . . 109,000 secret informers: that is, almost 1 of every 80 persons in the country. . . . The surveillance involved 1,052 full-time specialists who tapped telephones, 2,100 who steamed open letters, and 5,000 who followed suspects.'"

SIGNIFICANCE

A focusing line has to reveal a subject that is potentially important. Line: "artists teach writers." Translation: "I'm going to write a scholarly essay [or book?] on what artists have to teach writers. I go to the art museum to learn to write. [Another essay on music? Interview my son-in-law, Michael Starobin, composer?]"

FIND THE FOCUSING LINE

A focusing line is the product of all the observation and thinking that comes before writing: listing, brainstorming, mapping, free writing. If I plunge ahead and write before finding the focusing line, it is usually a waste of time; if I have the line, however, the process of exploring, planning, drafting, and revising usually goes well.

Of course, the focus of a piece changes as the writer gathers information and discovers its significance through writing. But without a draft focus, the writer wanders. I think the focusing line is one of the most important writing techniques I practice, and I learned it late in my life-long apprenticeship.

Here are some other focusing lines from my daybook that have produced pieces of writing. These lines are similar to brief artist's sketches, notes in a private language that will spark my imagination at my writing desk. Note that without explanation, they may not mean much to an outside reader. Each one is not the end—a thesis statement—but a beginning—an ignition statement.

> When we were first parents we knew nothing. We had doubts, questions, anxieties, fears, insecurities, ignorance.
> Now we have become grandparents, and we know everything.
> *This thought was scribbled in the car while I was doing errands after meeting my first grandchild; it led to a column exploring this new relationship. There is a tension between the sentences, and it led me, in part, to celebrate*

> *instinct. The new family does not need us, and that is just great. They have*
> *instinct.*

I always listened from the other room, learned the language of walls.

> *This line gave me a poem about the importance of stories in my childhood,*
> *how I lived by stories, trying to make sense of my world.*

Saw old movie with Clark Gable. He yells, "Get me Rewrite" so he could dictate his story. I was rewrite man who was got when I first worked for a newspaper.

> *This line could ignite an essay for college English on how dictation might*
> *help students to improve the effectiveness of their writing.*

As I look back on my life, I visit the geographies that contained my world.

> *I haven't written a piece based on this line. It may be a poem, an essay, a*
> *short story. I visited a neighborhood where I had lived when I was in elemen-*
> *tary school and became fascinated with the shrunken horizons of my world.*

Editor tells me, "Cut it in half." Piece better.

> *Study the manuscripts of famous writers and see what they cut. Is there a*
> *pattern that would help apprentice writers. Article for* **The Writer?**

Waking in the morning.

> *This private phrase has inspired a proposal for a book exploring the world*
> *of my aging, where waking in the morning is an exciting event.*

My father called in the middle of the night to ask, "How you doin'?" I expected more from this first call from the dead but all he wanted to know was
the ordinary.

> *Someday this thought will ripen into a poem.*

Looks—was I somebody?

> *This note scribbled on a piece of paper in a Washington, D.C. restaurant*
> *led to an essay about the whole business of celebrity and personal identity.*

WHAT THE FOCUSING LINE CAN GIVE THE WRITER

We are all terrified when we begin a first draft and step off into the unknown, but
the focusing line makes this step less terrifying. The focusing line solves a great
many of my writing problems in advance. Let's look at one of the lines above and
see how it helps as I begin a draft.

As I look back on my life, I visit the geographies that contained my world.

Possible Direction

I have a strong indication of where my mind might travel in writing a draft.

Research

I could choose to research my childhood neighborhood and examine the political, economic, and sociological changes in that area.

Reflection

I could think back upon my childhood and how that geography affected my life.

Description

I could map my childhood world in words and see how our vision of an area changes as we grow old: My first trip around the block was more exciting than my first trip to Norway.

Limitation

What I write will not be about my high school neighborhood, the battlefields on which I fought, the neighborhoods in which my children spent their childhoods. The line helpfully excludes.

Point of View

This can be thought of in two ways.

Angle of Vision. The point of view determines the place from which the writer and the reader observe the subject. The angle of vision includes everything that can be seen or known from that point. I may, for example, write from the point of view of an eight-year-old who has not yet questioned the prejudices of his parents, or I may write from the point of view of an adult critical of those prejudices. Sometimes *point of view* refers to first, second, and third person: I, you, he/she.

Opinion. Point of view also describes the opinion the writer has of the subject. It is important for the writer to have an opinion of the subject—my parents made the new neighborhood a fearful place because of their prejudices, an attitude that I as a child found unjustified.

Voice

Voice is the word music that reveals and supports the meaning of the piece. We all respond to what is said to us and, especially, how it is said. Voice is *the how*. In the focusing line, the writer's trained ear often hears the music of the piece: "The first lesson of my childhood was, 'Stay on your own side of the fence.'" This statement has a different music than, "My parents talked about a God of love, but the God they described disliked more than loved, never reaching across the backyard fence to our neighbors."

Form

Form is the type of writing: fiction, nonfiction, poetry, screenplay, argument, memo, lab report, book review. It includes the tradition of the type of writing; the reader knows what to expect from a story, a poem, an argument. In the line "The Good Book was, in my home, a Bad Book—full of what not to do" may ignite an autobiographical essay or to a memo to a textbook publisher arguing for more positive approaches in textbooks.

Structure

Structure is the way I anticipate getting from the first line to the last; it is the trail of meaning I will follow as I produce a draft. Structure may take many forms. In a narrative, the actions and reactions between the characters create a chronological structure that pulls the reader forward; in an argument, the logic of one point leading to another may drag the reader toward the writer's conclusion. The line "I read Hazlet before Orwell or E. B. White" implies a chronological survey of essay writing, going back to the nineteenth, and perhaps the seventeenth, century.

Opening

The focusing line often becomes the first sentence or paragraph of what I write. This lead leads—draws, entices—the reader into the writing. A focusing line like "my neighborhood had fences to keep out those who were different" might develop into the following lead: "Recently I visited the Land of Prejudice, the geography of my childhood where good fences did not make good neighbors."

Do I consciously march through all those elements when I develop a focusing line? Not always. But sometimes it helps to take apart what the cabinetmaker put together, to discover how she knew those pieces of burled wood could become a corner cabinet.

....

OTHER WAYS TO FOCUS

Here are some other ways in addition to the focusing line to find a focus.

THE STEINBECK STATEMENT

John Steinbeck used to write down what a book was about on a single three-by-five card. He might write a 500 page draft, but his focus would be on that sentence or two on the card. I have found it a valuable technique to do this when I have trouble with focus. That statement includes and excludes. It keeps my eye on target.

BUT—and don't forget this *but*—the statement will have to be revised as you write. You may know what you hope to write about when you start, but all writing is a voyage of discovery. You have to make course adjustments, refining and revising your initial statement as you discover what you have to say.

BEGIN BY ENDING

Many writers, including Truman Capote, Raymond Carver, John Gregory Dunne, William Gibson, Joseph Heller, John Irving, Eudora Welty, Toni Morrison, claim to know the end of a draft before they begin. They all have a destination that may be changed once they begin writing, but destination gives their first draft focus.

It may be helpful to write a dozen or two dozen last sentences. Once you choose one and know where you are headed, you may know where—and how—to begin.

FIND A CONTROLLING IMAGE

When you started to write as a child, you sometimes drew a picture first, sometimes wrote the caption first. You worked back and forth calling both drawing and writing *writing*. I think writers still work that way. I see what I write, and many times the focus of my writing is an image—my grandmother ruling the family from her sickbed, my first dead soldier and his look of surprise, the kitchen table that was always set at the end of a meal, ready for our next silent meal.

Pay attention to what you see with your mind's eye—or with your real eye—as you research or think about what you are going to write. The focus may lie in that vision. You may have a controlling image that will give a landmark to guide you through the writing.

ANTICIPATE THE READER'S NEED

The focus of a piece of writing may come from the reader. In writing memos to a dean when I was English department chairperson, I knew what the dean wanted to hear and how he wanted to hear it—documented with statistics. My job was to focus a wandering, discursive discussion of our department needs in a way that would lead the dean to "buy" our argument and give us the fiscal support we needed.

Put yourself in the reader's place to see if you can understand what a particular reader needs to learn from the text. That may be your focus.

MOVE THE ANGLE OF VISION

When writing, the writer invites the reader to stand at the writer's side so the writer can point out the view and comment upon it. The place where the writer stands gives focus to the draft. In writing for teachers, I often ask them to stand beside me when I was a high school drop-out. Many teachers were honor students and viewed school differently than I did, but if they want to reach all students, they need to see school as the less academically interested view it.

Often the writer moves the point of view or angle of vision, taking readers along as the view changes and their understanding of what they're seeing increases. It is where the writer and reader stop and what they pass by that keeps the writing in focus.

ADJUST THE DISTANCE

Distance is a key element in writing. Distance is how far the writer places the reader from the subject. Many writers always write close up; others always stand back at the same distance. Movies and television have made us all aware that the camera can put us on the mountain ridge watching the far-off cattle rustler and then move us in close to see one steer rolling its eyes in terror.

Move in close up, and you'll see in detail. The lens frames the revealing action, response, or object. You'll gain immediacy and intensity, but you can lose context, what the detail means. Stand way back and each detail is in context. Pun intended, you see the big picture. The frame extends so that you have a broad view, but you lose intensity.

The trick is to stand at a variety of distances, each appropriate to what is being said. The writer moves in close to increase intensity, then moves back to put what has been seen into context; the writer stands back to establish context, then moves in close to make the reader see, feel, think, care.

There is no ideal distance apart from subject. The craft is to always be at that distance that most effectively helps the reader see, feel, and understand. The skilled writer uses a zoom lens, adjusting the distance so that the reader experiences intensity without losing context, has enough detachment so that the reader has room to respond, is close enough so that the reader is forced to respond.

Play with distance as you focus and draft—describe your grandmother's hand as you held it in the nursing home, describe her in the group picture of the family arriving in America when she was the little girl in front—to see how it will help you explore your subject and communicate it.

ASK THE RESEARCH QUESTION

In the academic world, the focusing line becomes the research question. The sociologist, historian, physicist, economist, literary critic, health ethicist, philosopher, biochemist, and member of any other intellectual discipline needs to learn how to ask a good research question. The research question is central to the term paper, the master's thesis, the doctoral dissertation, the grant proposal, the paper at an academic meeting, the scholarly article and book.

The research question should:

- *Be significant.* Its answer should provide new insight or knowledge. *How does the brain affect learning to write?*

- *Be limited.* The answer should be accessible within the time available and other limits of the research—a semester, summer school term, thesis or dissertation year, sabbatical. *How did four stroke victims at the VA hospital relearn how to write?*

- *Demand a specific answer.* The question should bring forth an answer that is not vague and general, but specific and informative. *What were the three most important turning points experienced by the four stroke victims at the VA hospital as they relearned how to write?*

- *Be in a specific context.* The question should be connected to an existing strand of knowledge; someone should need to know the answer. *What are the implications for third-grade students with learning disabilities of the three most important turning points experienced by four stroke victims at the VA hospital as they relearned how to write?*

MAKE A THESIS STATEMENT

The thesis statement is a fully developed focusing line: "Toni Morrison reveals the tensions of small city, Midwestern life for everyone, not just African Americans."

The advantage is that the thesis statement provides focus for the research and the writing. Academic writing has historically favored argument in many disciplines, and the thesis statement in such a piece provides the writer and reader with a clear debating point. It encourages, for example, the reader to say, "Whoa! I'm not so sure Toni Morrison does that. Let's see your evidence."

Many teachers demand, for these reasons, that writers articulate thesis statements before researching or writing papers. The great danger is that the scholars will only look to document those statements when, in fact, they might discover different critical views.

In that case, a writer should submit the revised thesis statement to the instructor: "Toni Morrison's novels document how different the small city, Midwestern experience of African Americans is from that of their white neighbors."

START A NEW WRITING TASK

The writing process you are learning can be adapted to any writing task and to changing conditions. As you proceed through school and beyond, new classes and new jobs will demand new forms of writing: memos, reports, fund-raising letters, poems, case histories, theses or dissertations, sermons, police reports, book or literature reviews, grant applications, letters of sympathy, job or graduate school applications, screen plays, scientific or laboratory reports, legal briefs or judicial decisions, marketing plans.

A particular type of task will require a long text or a short one, straight text or text coordinated with a complex graphic design, writing alone or with a partner or a committee, completion in a day or less or a month or more.

In every case you will be able to adapt your experience with the writing process. I've adapted that process to write radio scripts; ghostwrite political and corporate publications; create short poems and long books; write memos, applications, reports, and all sorts of other writing tasks. You build on what you know how to do.

MAKE AN ASSIGNMENT YOUR OWN

The best strategy for dealing with any writing assignment effectively is to make it your own. The skilled writer shifts the ownership of the assigned piece of writing from the teacher or employer to the writer. There are guidelines for doing this:

Read the Assignment Carefully

Go over the assignment several times to make sure you know what is expected of you. If the assignment has been given orally, write it out and read it over. Make sure you understand the purpose of the assignment, not just *what* you are expected to do, but *why* you are expected to do it. The reason for the assignment will often help make the assignment clear. If you don't understand it, read what you have written back to the instructor.

Ask Questions

If you have studied the assignment carefully and still do not understand it, ask for clarification. It may be appropriate to ask to see good examples others have done in the past or samples of published writing that practice the lessons being taught by the assignment.

Stand Back

Once the assignment is clear, walk away from it. Study the assignment at a distance to see what comes to mind. The assignment should be given to your subconscious, which will play with it, making connections with what you know, have seen, experienced, thought about.

An assignment always increases my awareness. I'm told by an editor to do a story on street people, and I'm suddenly aware of the bag ladies, the young man mining the dumpsters in the alley, the woman talking to herself on the street corner, the late afternoon line at the mission or soup kitchen, the early morning turnout of drifters at the church dormitory for the poor. I note how they dress, I record the wary looks they give people, the way they make themselves invisible, the layers of clothing they wear, the bottles ineffectively hidden in small paper bags, the shaking hands, the shuffling steps. Little of this is conscious observation; I've just been made aware. I begin to see connections with experiences in my past—the refugees who clogged the roads leading from the battlefields they were fleeing and to which we were advancing—and with what I'm reading—perhaps Steinbeck's account of those fleeing the dust bowl for California during the Depression or John Berger's report on the guest workers imported to northern European countries from southern Europe.

It is often helpful to stimulate this essential circling of the subject by using the techniques in Chapter 1 such as brainstorming or free writing. Don't just attack the subject the way you've attacked similar subjects; collect and recollect information from which you can discover the most effective way to deal with this particular assignment.

Be Self-Centered

Look at the assignment from your own point of view. Don't begin writing from a point of weakness, saying to yourself that you know nothing about the topic. That is rarely true. Of course, you should do the academic work required by the assignment—read the book, survey the voters, perform the experiment, observe the patient—but go beyond that. Look at the assignment from a point of strength. Think about what you know that may connect with the subject. You may have job experience, for example, that will allow you to make a special connection with a character in a book who has moved to a new and alien place, discovered he or she is adopted, or is sent to a nursing home the way your grandmother was. A history assignment may connect with a novel you read in a literature course; a paper in business administration may make use of what you studied in a computer course. Look at the subject from your own point of view, so that you shift the position of authority from the teacher to yourself.

This principle does not mean that you have a license to be prejudiced, to present unsubstantiated opinions, to be unfair. It does mean that, in the process of thinking about the topic and writing about it, you should take advantage of what you know. If you are writing about the care of the elderly, you may use your experience in working as an aide in a nursing home, your family's guilt about sending a grandparent to such a home, your neighbor's reasons to stop working as a nurse for the elderly. Such information may give you a way to approach the subject or to document a point in your final draft.

Limit the Subject

Don't try to cover the history of medicine for the elderly in Western civilization since 1600 in five pages. Instead limit the subject—perhaps concentrating on one nursing home, one disease such as Alzheimer's, one day, or even one patient.

Limiting the subject allows it to be developed properly, so that one single point can be developed and documented in a way that satisfies the reader's hunger for meaning and information.

Remember the significant relationship between the words *author* and *authority*. Whenever possible, try to become an authority on the subject on which you are writing. You can do this by taking advantage of what you know, by researching the subject, and by exercising the muscle between your ears and thinking about the subject before you write. Thinking through your writing for each draft should be a way of discovering meaning.

FOCUS IN THE DAYBOOK

My daybook encourages the play that is essential in finding focus. It allows this process to happen when I'm waiting for my wife in a parking lot, watching the Celtics on TV, waiting for a friend to show up for lunch. I use these fragments of time to perform the brainstorming, mapping, listing, and other activities described in this chapter.

Here are some examples of focus-seeking play in my current daybook:

Poem?
in war he's at home
at home he's at war

> **This fooling around will become a poem.**

The toy I remember best from my childhood was an empty Quaker Oats box. I hated porridge but I loved my drum, my castle tower, my wheel, my echo box, my cave.

> **This note did become a column.**

When you age, your nose gets bigger—and your ears. We all become more of what we are.

> **This fragment became a television commentary.**

On the ten o'clock news
a soldier peers over the edge
of the TV screen . . .

> **This became a poem.**

FOCUS ON A COMPUTER

The computer allows me to write fast, and velocity is vital to me as I seek a focus for my subject. I can produce a flow of writing and then pluck from it the word, phrase, line, or paragraph that provides the focus. After that, it is easy to manipulate the other things I've written so that they line up and support the focus.

When I'm working on one thing that stimulates my thinking, and ideas for other subjects come to mind, I can easily make quick notes on my computer that I can file and read later. The computer also makes it easy to bring quotations, charts, figures, text, all sorts of information together and then to manipulate it so that it reveals a pattern of meaning.

HEAR THE UNWRITTEN VOICE

From the moment a subject occurs to me, I listen to the voices within the potential draft. I listen to the fragments—the lines—that pass through my mind and across my daybook page.

I have trained myself to hear the voice of the final draft in a fragment of language, the way an archeologist can examine a pottery shard and describe a civilization. The voice doesn't just lead to how the writing will be presented; it tells me what the as-yet-unwritten draft may be. It tells me what I think about the subject when I write about it. Voice leads to focus.

Let's take a simple topic—the house of my childhood—and read these fragments out loud to hear what they might tell me, the writer:

The house of my childhood

Secrets in the house of childhood

My escape from the lonely house of childhood

Brown—that was the color of my childhood

The lonely house of childhood

I miss the lonely house of childhood

We hurt with silence in the lonely house of childhood

I never thought I would escape the silence of my childhood

Silence made me hear the voices in the walls of my childhood home

We feared God, Grandma, Catholics, the Irish, scarlet fever, the bill collector, and funny foreign eyes in the house of my childhood

My house of childhood, so large when I lived there, seems tiny now

I am still the boy who could not ride a bike, was told not to play with Catholics, feared the silences that filled the house of childhood

Silence filled the house of my childhood

I always listened from other rooms, learned the language of walls . . .

The music I heard in that last line made me write the following lines in my daybook in June. They seemed to be looking for a poem:

I always listened from the other room,
learned the language of walls,
read silences, the shut door,
the dark. . . .

Later I wrote:

I learned the language of walls:
whispered argument, point
counterpoint, quiet.
I wove silence
into story. . . .

Different drafts appeared over time in the next daybook until I got to the one
I showed to my poetry group. It began:

Born onto a sea of narrative,
he thought stories were sound clouds.
shadows with voices . . .

The next day I wrote the poem through, beginning:

~~When~~ Night stories crept upstairs
~~he~~ where he captured them in the hall,
[he] hid them in his room . . .

During all that play I was listening to the voice of each bit of poem and looking for the focus—how stories were discovered by a child and how that influenced his life. I did it by play, ending up with the following poem:

The Storyteller's Childhood

When stories crept upstairs
he captured them in the hall,
hid them in his room, wove
them into dreams, watched

family stories travel
under the wallpaper, emerge
at the seams, found others escaping
faucets, chattering in water pipes.

Some stories exploded when he opened
the furnace door, others lay folded
in trunks, some had been framed
but could be heard if he was alone.
In winter, stories were etched
by frost on window pane; in summer
they came as shadows of bird wings
that woke him as they passed.

Some of the best stories were left
on morning pillows, others were told
by silence, escaped in a pause, grew
from the rich loam of never said.

Outside he found neighbor stories
caught in the privet hedge or played
out in pantomime against the drawn
shade. He stole stories humming

on telephone lines, trapped secrets
dogs shared in barking gossip, heard
confessions from the open windows
of passing cars, read stories

from faces, the way his father slowly
walked from the trolley car stop,
held the key before he turned
it in the lock. If he brought

bon bons that night their bed
would squeak. The boy crept out,
patrolled dark streets, stealing
neighbor's secrets before they woke.

It could also have been an essay:

My grandson lies quiet, attending to what I cannot see or hear. I wonder if he hears the voices in the walls I heard, joins the secret family that had a dog with a curling tail—we had no pets—escapes into a world of make-believe that was—and is—as real as the life I have lived.

As close as we are as a family, there is something private about the human condition. We may be the animal that most of all needs secrets. . . .

....

REVISE BEFORE WRITING

Don't think exclusively of revision as what you do *after* a draft is finished. Every idea you reject or accept is a demonstration of revision. Focus is an act of revision, as you choose what to focus on and what to ignore.

Each draft of the poem was revision, yet I was only trying to get to the beginning point of focus, to discover what the poem would focus on and reveal to the reader.

When you choose one subject over another; identify an angle of vision; select a genre; write a line, a paragraph, a page in your head or on the paper, you are revising, shaping what may be said, may be drafted.

IN THE WRITER'S WORKSHOP

. . . [I]f there is one gift more essential to a novelist than another it is the power of combination—the single vision. VIRGINIA WOOLF

I had a line—"I wonder will it strike us over here"—that I thought would be the last line of As If It Matters. *When I had that line, I knew the book was finished, but I hadn't got the poem to go with it. So I kept mulling that over, and then eventually I sat down and pushed around a poem. It works like that, by accretion. You turn yourself into some kind of magnetic field so that things stick, and then you sit down—and the hard part is—push it out, and then you revise it.* EAMON GRENNAN

I've always been highly energized and have written poems in spurts. From the god-given first line right through the poem. And I don't write two or three lines and then come back the next day and write two or three more; I write the whole poem at one sitting and then come back to it from time to time over the months or years and re-work it. A. R. AMMONS

What I do at the end of an afternoon's work is write two or three lines on what I think is the direction of the narrative, and where we might logically go the next day. CAMILO TOSE CELA

It was with that book [The Alleys of Eden] *that I finally figured out where a literary writer has to write from. That is, where I dream from, instead of where I think from. The hardest thing for me to learn as a writer was that I could not will my work into being. I learned I should not think about it. I should not abstract it and try to understand it in an intellectual way. I had to go to the dream place, into my unconscious, my artistic unconscious, and focus on the moment to moment flow of sensual experience to articulate my vision of the world. This was the fundamental thing and once I figured out how to go to that place consistently, everything else followed.* ROBERT OLEN BUTLER

You don't have to outline the play, it outlines itself. You go by sequential activity. One things follows the other. But it all starts with that first seed, conflict. NEIL SIMON

I understand only particles. I understand the characters, but the novel itself is not in focus. The focus comes at random moments which no one can understand, least of all the author. For me, they usually follow great effort. To me, these illuminations are the grace of labor. All of my work has happened this way. It is at once the hazard and the beauty that a writer has to depend on such illuminations.

After months of confusion and labor, when the idea has flowered, the collusion is Divine. It always comes from the subconscious and cannot be controlled. For a whole year I worked on The Heart Is a Lonely Hunter *without understanding it at all. Each character was talking to a central character, but why, I didn't know. I'd almost decided that the book was no novel, that I should chop it up into short stories. But I could feel the mutilation in my body when I had that idea, and I was in despair. I had been working for five hours and I went outside. Suddenly, as I walked across a road, it occurred to me that Harry Minowitz, the character all the other characters were talking to, was a different man, a deaf mute, and immediately the name was changed to John*

Singer. The whole focus of the novel was fixed and I was for the first time committed with my whole soul to The Heart Is a Lonely Hunter. CARSON MCCULLERS

The problem of creative writing is essentially one of concentration, and the supposed eccentricities of poets are usually due to mechanical habits or rituals developed in order to concentrate. Concentration, of course, for the purposes of writing poetry, is different from the kind of concentration required for working out a sum. It is a focusing of the attention in a special way, so that the poet is aware of all the implications and possible developments of his idea, just as one might say that a plant was not concentrating on developing mechanically in one direction, but in many directions, towards the warmth and light with its leaves, and towards the water with its roots, all at the same time. STEPHEN SPENDER

All I ever know is the first line, the first sentence, the first page. The work terminates itself with dictation from me. ERSKINE CALDWELL

I remember that I started writing Sleepless Nights *because of a single line. The line was: "Now I will start my novel, but I don't know whether to call myself I or she."* ELIZABETH HARDWICK

I wanted to quit my job writing promotional copy, but I had a wife and two kids to support. I wanted to do another novel but had no ideas. I was worried. Then two sentences came to me: "In the office in which I work, there are five people of whom I am afraid. Each of these five is afraid of four people." In a dream, a kind of controlled reverie, I quickly developed the characters, the mood of anxiety, the beginning, the end and most of the middle of Something Happened. *And I knew Bob Slocum, my protagonist, intimately. Eventually, a better opening line came to me: "I get the willies when I see closed doors," and I wrote the first chapter around that line. But I kept the original to lead off the second part.* JOSEPH HELLER

I replied that I could no more define poetry than a terrier can define a rat but that I thought we both recognized the object by the symptoms which it provokes in us. . . . Experience has taught me, when I am shaving of a morning, to keep watch over my thoughts, because, if a line of poetry strays into my memory, my skin bristles so that the razor ceases to act. A. E. HOUSMAN

QUESTIONS ABOUT FOCUSING

I went to a great concert this weekend, and I want to write about it from beginning to end so I can remember all of it. I don't want to leave anything out. So why should I try to focus?

One of the best things about writing is that it is something you can do by yourself and for yourself. That's why many of us keep diaries that list sequences of events and activities we don't want to forget. We want to look back on these entries years from now to remember an incident that seemed significant to us at the time of writing. And that's okay.

But writing for a class or group is always a negotiating process between making personal meaning and making meaning purposeful; while you will want to be true to your own experiences when you write, you will also want to convey those experiences in a way that will entice your reader, make him or her want to dive into your essay and follow it through to the end.

Just because your reader may not have been present at the event you describe doesn't mean that he or she craves a blow-by-blow account of the entire day. What your reader is looking for is something that makes your experience at the concert different from the experiences of the thousands of others who also attended.

Getting down every detail in your first draft is a great first step; you can always keep this draft as your own personal record of the event. But your next step should be to find a focusing line, something that will label the experience as your own and give your reader something to think through. You may, for example, choose to focus on a chance meeting with an old friend at the concert, or the interactions between particular groups of people, or even the outrageous clothing that many of them wore. Whatever your focus, it should convey a sense of your unique perspective and experience, the ingredients that make you different from other people and other writers.

What if I don't have a unique perspective? How can my focus possibly be interesting to other people?

New writers often think they have nothing different or important to say to an audience. They are afraid that their experiences are so insignificant that they will never fill up the number of pages required for any one writing assignment. So instead of narrowing their focus and going for depth, they broaden their focus and skip across the surface, filling up as many pages as they can.

Finding a focus doesn't mean writing about experiences no one else has had or ever will have; it doesn't mean being a genius or clever or breaking new ground. If you think in these terms, you will be afraid to write at all! What finding a focus means is locating a significant or provocative corner of your larger experience, then making yourself at home in it, furnishing it with vivid details, and inviting your readers to occupy that corner with you.

If a television or movie director were to film a single event in your life, he or she would certainly not film every single person you met, every meal you ate, your entire drive to or from the event, or every conversation you had. A good director would highlight only particular moments, scenes that convey a sense of who you are and how you relate to your world.

Let's take MTV's *The Real World* program as an example. A documentary about young adults living together, the show gives viewers glimpses into—not a panoramic view of—its characters' lives. While we see the young stars engaging in everyday activities, we view those activities through a very selective lens. The camera crews may very well film hours and hours of interactions and conversations among these people, but the directors edit the film so that we see only bits and pieces of it.

Include all the details you want about a day or an event when you write in your diary or when you draft an essay. Then go back and choose a handful of interesting images and try condensing them into one focusing image. If you want, arrange particular images, lines, or sentences from your draft into a poem that will help you focus. Use this focusing poem as a kind of outline for your draft.

What if what I want to focus on isn't what my readers think is most important?

Getting feedback from readers while you are drafting is an important step in writing. Reader feedback helps you see around corners and uncover blind spots in your essay; it lets you know when your writing is engaging and when it is just plain boring—when you could say more and when you've simply said enough!

But sometimes you can reach an impasse in your relationship with your readers. When you find yourself being tugged and pulled between your own ideas and theirs, you may have to clarify your focus so that your readers can understand it better, or you may need to gather more information and develop your own ideas.

At times like this, don't automatically dismiss the reactions of other readers. At the same time, feel free to take a risk and try out the focus you want. You may find that the tension between your readers' wishes and your own will forces you into a deeper exploration of your ideas.

What if my readers want me to focus on one thing only and I want to focus on several?

Don't be surprised if the more you explore, the more complicated your focus becomes; what may seem like a single focal point at the start of your draft may quickly turn into several. It's okay to write about two or three things that are equally important. But then you have to find a way of making the combination of them most important. For example, "Most law school professors agree that there are three qualities an effective courtroom lawyer needs," or "there are four equal forces that came together and led us into the Vietnam war."

FOCUSING ACTIVITIES

1. Brainstorm a list of subjects that entice you, confuse you, anger you, please you. When you finish your list, jot down one word next to each item that you feel sums it up. Choose three words from this list and

write them on the board. After all your classmates have done the same, choose six words from the entire list. There may be no rhyme or reason why you choose the words: They may remind you of something or you may simply like the way they sound. Beginning with the first word, free write on each. Then choose one free write you'd like to expand and with the help of a writing partner, list three more words about that topic. Repeat the process until you have narrowed your focus and gathered plenty of details.

2. Draw a map of a place you like or dislike. Be as creative as you wish, but don't worry if your map isn't artistically beautiful. When you have finished drawing, free write about your place, what it means to you, why you drew it the way you did, what memories you have of it. Then trade maps with a writing partner and free write about each other's maps. What do you think the space you see represents for your partner? What does it say about him or her? Brainstorm a list of questions about the maps and when you have finished, read your questions to one another. Using these questions, free write about your own place again, and read your free writes to one another.

3. Do a quick inventory of your clothes, starting with the garments you are wearing now. Don't worry about being thorough; just list rapidly what items come to mind, including shoes, coats, belts, and other accessories. Choosing five of these items from your list, brainstorm a list of associations for each: When did you buy them? Why? Why did you single them out in your list? Where have you worn them? When? Who were you with? What happened on the day you were wearing them? Do any of them have sentimental value? Select an item from the list and write a story about it, using the details you have jotted down.

4. Take a writing partner on a personalized "tour" of your hometown, city, or neighborhood. Begin by quickly listing in your notebook all of the "hot spots" or places that have meaning for you. Skip over the spots you consider dull and move from one hot spot to another. Jot down stories about each spot, and then read your list and stories to your partner. Ask your partner to draw a map of your hometown based on what you have read and then have your partner choose a spot on the map he or she would like to return to. Free write about that spot.

5. Start a round robin of storytelling and focusing. Begin by having one person in a group write about a significant personal experience. The writer then passes the story on to the next person, who reads it and circles one image, passage, or line that reminds him or her of an experience, about which he or she writes. Continue the chain of response and storytelling until the book comes full circle. Pass it around again.

6. Wander out into the hallway or situate yourself at the busy entrance of a building. Record the conversations of passers-by. Free write about these conversations, imagining what they mean to the participants, or write about similar conversations you have had with friends.

7. Solve a mystery. Join a group of classmates in ferreting out information about a local issue or problem. Focus solely on that issue. Interview people and read up on the problem in newspapers and other media. How did the labor dispute at the local factory begin? Why do coaches earn more than faculty at some schools? Who painted the classrooms in your buildings institutional green? Collaborate on a draft, and in your daybook keep track of who does what and your collective writing process.

8. Brainstorm a list of relatives and free write about each. Choose one or two whom you want to learn more about and focus on them, or choose a couple of relatives you know well and want to write about.

9. Visit the library reference room with a partner and split up. Browse through the many specialized encyclopedias, dictionaries, and bibliographies. Select those that interest you and record their titles in your daybook. Look through these books and select three entries or topics that you want to know more about, or that you already know something about, and write them down. When you get back to class, compare lists. Choose four of the topics—two from your list and two from your partner's—and free write about each.

10. Write down one question a day about something ordinary, strange, or disturbing. Who designed the engineering building? Why is the town cemetery in the center of the business district? How do hummingbirds mate? Who came up with the general education requirements? Then start a Book of Questions, passing it around weekly so that all members of the class can record their questions. Select five questions a week (at least three that aren't your own) and free write about them.

11. Make an authority inventory, listing all the things you're an expert on, that you have focused on: the jobs you can do, the things you can repair, the places you've lived or visited, the problems you can solve, the hobbies you enjoy, the people you know, your family background. Each of us is an authority on many things, and our best writing usually comes from what we know and care about.

12. Free write on any topic you want and read it aloud to the class. Ask your classmates to go to the board and write down one word, sentence, or fragment that they remember from the free write. Have them explain their choices and how these pieces of your essay can help you focus.

Then write about your topic again, choosing a focusing point from their suggestions.

13. Map, free write, list, or brainstorm on any subject or subjects. Look over what you've written and arrange the ideas and details you like best into sentences, combining some if necessary. Select one sentence from your list and begin a draft using it.

14. Enter an Internet chat room, and start a conversation about a narrow topic. If you enter a cooking chat room, for example, ask for advice about baking a very particular kind of food, such as popovers or cheese soufflés. As people respond, make a list of the details they use to describe the subject and how they approach it. Then write about what you've learned. Think about how different and less detailed your paper would be if your focus were more general—if you had asked about "cooking" instead of "popovers"!

15. Draw a line down the middle of a page in your daybook. While watching a suspenseful movie or television show, sum up on the left-hand side what happens in each scene. Record on the right-hand side all that you think is left out of the filming. What don't you see during the show? What does the director include or omit? When you finish, go back over your list and in a few sentences describe the focus of the show, trying to sum up the main point.

16. Choose a favorite sitcom or drama on television and videotape at least one scene. Returning to that scene as often as you need, jot down all the details of setting, dialog, and acting. Rethink the scene from the perspective of a writer and reader rather than as a viewer. Write it up in your daybook not as a script, but as a passage in an essay or story. Since your assumed reader cannot see the scene as it was shown on television, adjust your focus and flesh out the details.

17. Exchange a personal photo with a classmate and write about what you see in the picture. Then retake the photo from a different angle or proximity. Imagine how the photo might change if the camera were further away or if you were in a helicopter looking down. What might a close-up shot reveal? What would it omit? In your daybook, experiment with different angles, frames, and perspectives for the photo.

18. Sum up the main points of a famous family feud, an argument you remember having had with your parents or siblings. Draw a line down the middle of a page in your daybook, and on the left-hand side explain your own point of view in detail, examining it from every angle. On the right-hand side, explain the opposing viewpoint, that of your parents or siblings. Be as objective as possible. When you have finished, ask your

groupmates to review the arguments of both sides and serve as a mediating board. Have them write up an analysis of the situation. How is their perspective different or like the opposing perspectives? How does their focus compare to yours or those of your opponents?

19. Repeat Activity 18, but focus on a political or academic debate rather than a personal argument. Find an essay in a news magazine or scholarly journal and examine opposing perspectives.

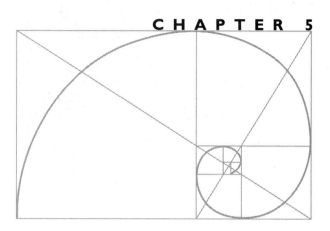

CHAPTER 5

EXPLORE

Writers are the explorers society sends out to describe our public and private worlds. They use language to capture in words the not-yet-thought, the not yet said. They make the unknown known through language; they make the unspoken heard through voice. They live at the far and close edges of our lives, revealing what others have not seen—or not understood—in the world around them and have not seen within them.

Writers work at this exploration all the time: It is their blessing and their curse. They examine what others overlook; they reflect on what they see—and their reactions to it. They are blessed in never being bored, always remaining aware of the drama of the ordinary and the internal drama of trying to accept and understand what they have seen. They are cursed in always being aware of what is painful in life and aware of their own pain in observing it. The novelist Somerset Maugham explains, "The author does not only write when he is at his desk, he writes all day long, when he is thinking, when he is reading, when he is experiencing; everything he sees and feels is significant to his purpose."

The explorer first seeks information. Writers write with information—the specific, accurate information that readers need. Readers read to satisfy their hunger for information—specific, accurate information they can use. The writing act begins with the accumulation of the raw material of writing. The act of writing gives that information meaning: Writing is thinking.

Chapter 4 showed how the writer explores the external and internal world to find a topic. This chapter shows the writer/explorer at work developing the information from which the topic will be understood by writer, then reader.

THE WRITER'S EYE

Central to exploration is the writer's eye. The writer's eye sees what is, what isn't, what was, what may be. An athlete's eye is inherited. I go to an eye doctor who treats many players on the Boston Celtics basketball team, and I asked him if their eyes, not just their height and jumping ability, differ from those of the rest of us. He held up a finger far out of my peripheral vision and explained that all the Celtics could see the finger that I could not.

The athlete's eye is genetic, but the writer's eye can be developed. You can train yourself to see revealing specifics. A revealing specific is a detail, fact, quotation, word, phrase that gives off extra meaning. The politician on the platform may pay close attention to a series of speakers, then look away, paying no attention, when the next speaker is a woman. It is an accurate detail that gives a clue to his attitude toward women. The screaming of the basketball coach that confuses his own players, the students who sit together at lunch and the ones who want to sit with them but don't, the trustees' decision to spend money for a hockey rink but not for faculty salaries are all revealing specifics.

The writer's eye collects the concrete information that readers like: a statistic, a fact, a direct quote, a specific act. Concrete details give a draft liveliness and authority—readers believe, often in error, that more specific detail makes a more authoritative author. Writing seems to ring with authority just because it is specific.

The writer's eye gathers information, using all the senses—the way the overhead light glints off the surgeon's scalpel, the eyes that reveal so much—and so little—above the surgical masks, the smell of medicine and sterilizing steam, the brass taste of fear, the feeling of helplessness a patient experiences when lashed down on a surgical table, the comfort of the nurse's touch.

Lying there, with part of your body asleep but your brain wide awake, you hear what isn't said, see what doctors don't do as well as what they do, the looks that pass from doctor to nurse to technician. You feel something of what it must have been like to have surgery before modern anesthesia, what surgery may be like with the further development of the laser. You see what is, what is not, what was, what may be.

The writer's eye sees patterns. Specifics have to add up, to lead the reader toward a conclusion, to answer the tough question, "So what?" You see the way the police stop the driver of a Lexus that goes through a red light but treat her with courtesy. Then you see the police stop a battered Chevy for the same offense, make the driver get out of the car and slam him up against the hood, while another officer calls in to see if the car is stolen or if the driver has a record. You are aware of the skin color of the second driver and begin to remember your father's prejudiced comments at the dinner table, how the teacher laughed when an African American showed up in an elective math class—"No special treatment here, Darius,"—what the history textbook said about the Holocaust. You connect all such specifics into a pattern of prejudice.

E. M. Forster said, "Only connect," wise instruction for the writer, who deals with context and implication. Specific details are not enough by themselves. The way the police handle a suspect must be connected with a pattern of police brutality, training, prejudice, whether or not the treatment is appropriate or excessive.

The writer sees past and future. My mind turned backward in a recent column, when I wrote of looking out at snowy woods and seeing snowball fights when I was a boy, and fire fights during the Battle of the Bulge in World War II when I was a young paratrooper; I recalled my first sled rides with Uncle Will and a snow hut I built as a boy. I walk by a new building on campus and see within it the memory of the old building on the same spot that was torn down. Cows turn into parked cars, and I see the future shopping mall destroying the farm. The writer is always looking backward and forward, studying the present to discover the causes of events and to imagine their effects. The writer lives in a changing world, seeing what is, what was, what may be. As Robert Cormier says,

> What if? What if? My mind raced, and my emotions kept pace at the sidelines, the way it always happens when a story idea arrives, like a small explosion of thought and feeling. What if? What if an incident like that in the park had been crucial to a relationship between father and daughter? What would make it crucial? Well, what if the father, say, was divorced from the child's mother and the incident happened during one of his visiting days? And what if . . .

The writer's eye instructs; it sees meaning where the writer did not see meaning. Writers write from what they don't know as much as from what they do know. In Chapter 1, I didn't start out knowing the meaning of that afternoon when I painted the back steps with water. I wrote to see what writing would teach me.

As I write about my war experience—how much distance there had to be between us when we dug in along the front line, how we kept from getting to know replacement soldiers because most of them would be wounded or die, how we could not admit our terror to those around us—I begin to remember how lonely infantry combat was, how little comradeship there was at the front lines. Language defines, develops, and changes my world.

The writer's eye provides the abundance the writer needs during writing. When you write about a person, place, or event important to you, you begin to remember details you didn't know you had stored in memory years before. I start to describe my first car and remember the high, crooked gear shift, the feel of the accelerator pedal; I hear the rasp when I apply the hand break; I smell the oil and gas and exhaust and the city smell in the wind that strikes my face. The more details I write, the more I have to write. This marvelous eye gives the writer a resource of revealing detail. What is most magical to me is that my writer's eye saw all sorts of specifics of which I was not aware until I wrote.

Stop reading, and take a piece of paper. Return in your mind to an important experience in your life, and list the details you remember using all your senses. Soon your writer's eye will reveal what you didn't know you saw at the accident scene, in the locker room, on the first day of school in a new town, last Saturday night.

....

SEARCH AND RESEARCH

THE INTERNAL SEARCH

School teaches us to look in the library, on a CD-ROM, in the laboratory, but the writer first looks inside at what is stored in memory. By writing, we make use of all that we have lived, felt, thought, know, if we respect and make use of what we have unconsciously stored in memory.

Remember

The first place from which to collect information is memory. You have recorded far more than you may realize on most subjects, or you can put a new subject in a context of memory. When I visit a new high school, I always remember North Quincy High School and failing and dropping out and, finally, flunking out. I collect information about the new school, first of all, in the context of my own autobiography.

Start your collecting process by listing in your daybook or journal, or on any piece of paper, code words and revealing specifics that remind you what you know about the topic. In remembering high school, I might list:

Mr. Collins, the principal

Bench outside his office

Day I goosed a teacher by accident

Miss Gooch, who had to jump to answer the phone on the wall

Teacher who took a swing at me because I was a Scot

Stack of forged hall passes I found when we moved

History report on Bismarck

Jobs more interesting than school

Class of 45+ students

Teachers condemned to teaching

Chicken game we played when writing in class

"Stardust" played last at ALL dances

Grade of 65, not a C or a D

I thought rich kids were born with slide rules

This is a private list as yours will be. It will give you notes to yourself that may start a chain of memories. The more specific the items, the more memory will be triggered.

THE EXTERNAL SEARCH

The external search extends the internal one, reaching out to library and computer online sources, authorities that can be reached in person, by mail, by phone, on the Internet. It combines all the normal techniques of the scholar with on-the-scene research and interview techniques of the journalist, sociologist, anthropologist.

Read

There are as many ways to read as there are to write, yet most people—prisoners of habit—usually read in the same way, at the same pace, no matter what the reading task. Never let school give you the impression that reading always has to be work, a purposeful job of collecting information. Reading can often be play: It is one of the best ways to leave the real world and escape to others.

Read Fast

Many people say that they read slowly but they remember what they read. The research I have read—and my own experience—denies this assertion. Of course, there are times when you have to—or want to—read slowly to savor or decode a text, but speed itself can be a benefit to reading. When you read fast, your effort concentrates the mind. You pay attention; your mind doesn't wander; you enter into the text and are carried along by the logic, the emotion, the music of language. Many times you have to read fast to allow the threads of the text to weave themselves into meaning. Read too slowly and you see only an individual thread or two, not the pattern evolving. Try it. Many schools teach speed reading, but you can do it yourself by forcing yourself to read fast at the point of discomfort.

Stop here if you are a slow reader. Don't read each word individually but make yourself read in groups of words or lines, not single words. Move right ahead. See what happens.

Afterward, you may have to go back and read a selection again or study one passage carefully, but then your attention will be concentrated on what you know you need to understand—and I suspect you will remember more than you expected to remember.

Skimming. To collect information efficiently, the reader has to get through many books, articles, and reports to discover what needs close attention. Here's a checklist that may help you organize your reading by skimming.

- The title should suggest just what the book or article covers.
- A book's table of contents and an article's abstract may reveal their subjects.
- An author's biography may help you discover the relationship of the writer to your topic, as well as the author's authority to write on the subject.
- The index will lead you to discover specific references.
- The bibliography will send you to other sources to explore.
- Scan the text itself to find revealing section headings or key words.

The reading writer needs to develop these techniques, which, of course, may be applied to scanning newspapers or microfilm or files the writer finds through computer online research.

Interpreting. Once your eye has caught a key word or a specific, revealing detail, interpret its meaning by putting it in the context of the piece you are reading or writing, or both. A college's brochure may boast, for example, that 60 percent of its student athletes actually graduate. One reader may be impressed by the statistic, while another may be appalled at the high percentage who fail to earn degrees.

Meaning never lies in isolated facts, but in context. It is the job of the reader to try to determine the information within the writer's context and then to use that information in a context that is appropriate and accurate.

Immersing. Fast reading can produce immersion in the text where you lose yourself in the mood, the poetry, the sweep of the account that puts you on a street in a strange city, in the hospital waiting room, in combat. By reading fast, you get the feel of a subject and the sense of the writing itself.

Connecting. Fast reading reveals information that connects with other information in the text, in other texts, in your notes and drafts, in your mind. Remember that you are writing to discover meaning, to allow specific pieces of information—represented by words—to arrange themselves in many patterns until one reveals significance.

Interview

The interview, in which you ask questions of an authority on your subject, is one of the basic tools for collecting significant information. Most people are shy about interviewing others. It helps to remember that the person who is being interviewed is being put in the position of an authority, and most people like to be authorities, to tell others what they know.

An interview can be informal—just a casual conversation—or formal—for which you make an appointment, prepare carefully, and probe deeply into the subject.

Prepare yourself for an interview by finding out as much as you can about the person you are going to interview. Prepare at least four or five principal questions you must ask in order to get the information you need. (Those are usually the questions the reader would like to ask if he or she were there.) Think of the reader; ask the reader's questions.

It's important to *listen* to what your interview subject has to say; don't go on asking the banker about interest rates after she has said the bank is closing. The interviewee may surprise you by what he or she says, and you have to decide on the spot which lead to follow.

Most interviewers take notes by hand, but it is more common to use a tape recorder. You should always ask permission to use a tape recorder on a telephone interview when the subject can't see the recorder. Face to face, when the recorder is visible, it is a courtesy, not a necessity, to ask permission to record. Most people prefer taped records to an interviewer's notes. Some even insist on the interviewer using a tape recorder—or make their own taped records of the interviews. You should, however, practice taking notes by hand, capturing the essence of what people say, even if you use a tape recorder. Sometimes the tape doesn't work, and if you're not taking notes yourself, you may become lazy and miss what's being said.

It's always best to interview a subject in person, so that you can see the expression on the face, the body language that emphasizes or contradicts what is being said, the environment in which the person lives or works, the way the person interacts with others. If you can't interview someone in person, then you may have to do so by telephone, or even by mail.

How the Interview Can Lead to Writing. When you are researching any topic, from criminal justice to World War II to urban blight to environmental hazards, don't forget to use live sources. Talk to the people who are involved. They will not tell you *the truth;* they will tell you *their own truths,* and then you will have the challenge of weaving all the contradictions together into a meaning.

Use the Telephone and the Mail

Organizations are also good sources of information. The library has directories of organizations that will help you find groups whose main function is distributing information on one side of a public issue; they are for or against abortion, distributing condoms to fight AIDS, allowing individuals to own hand guns, saving or developing wilderness areas. They will send pamphlets, brochures, or reports and answer your questions.

Governments—local, county, state, federal, and even international organizations such as NATO and the United Nations—have many groups that will provide you with reports, speeches, laws, regulations, proposals. Your local members of Congress can help you find the right agency and the office within the agency to contact.

Use the Library

One of the greatest sources of material is the "attics" in almost every town, city, and state in the country, as well as in schools, universities, and the nation's capital itself. These attics collect books, magazines, newspapers, pamphlets, phonograph records, films, TV and audio tapes, photographs, maps, letters, journals—all the kinds of documents that record our past. We call these attics *libraries.*

Every library has a card catalog and/or computer file that identifies resources available there and gives their locations. Frequent more than one library, if you can. When I was free lancing, I found it a good investment to pay for cards in four library systems. Libraries are elemental sources for a writer, as important as wind is to a sailor.

If you are not yet familiar with your library, most have tours that will show you how they work. Take the tour. Most libraries also have pamphlets that help you find what you need to know. Study such materials. Most of all, use the library. Browse. Wander. Let the library reveal its resources to you. If you need help, ask for it. Cultivate a good working relationship with your librarian. Librarians are trained to be of service, and all of us who write are indebted to their patience and skills in finding information for us.

It's important when you find a reference in the library to make a note of all the essential information about it so that you can use the library easily the next time, and so that you can list the source in footnotes or a bibliography. Even if you write something that doesn't have footnotes or a bibliography, you should know exactly where you got the material so that you can respond to questions from editors or readers.

Usually you should record the author's last name first, then first name, then the middle initial, the title of the work (underlined if it is a book, or within quotation marks if it is an article), the publisher, the place of publication, the date, the number of pages, and, for your own use, the library reference number together with the name of the library.

Such notes tell you where the information is. It's important to keep a record of the books and other sources you found worthless, so you won't go over them again, as well as the ones that are particularly valuable. Most research doesn't result in big breakthroughs, but a slowly growing understanding of the subject.

The Internet

The Internet today gives access to almost instantaneous contact with libraries around the world, as well as sources we can interview, organizations, government agencies, corporations, universities. I am continually astonished by the fact that I can enter a topic, a detail, a name, a category and have instant access to all sorts of references about it from all over the world.

As I read these days, watch TV, use e-mail, I keep seeing Web sites and addresses that I record to investigate. Most sites have links with many other sites which, in turn, connect with others.

Observe

Don't overlook one of the writer's primary sources of information: first-hand observation. See how many of your five senses you can use to capture information—and to communicate that information to your reader.

Go to a place that is important to your topic. It may not be the place where you write. You may be writing about the Continental Congress in which our nation was born; you can't visit it, but you will understand that process better if you visit a legislature, a city council session, a town meeting.

Awareness Increases Awareness

As you train your writer's eye, you will discover how much you notice: the way an old lady dresses for her weekly trip out to the supermarket, how the candy and gum is placed so it can be grabbed by children riding high in their seats in supermarket carts, how the dignified, well-dressed man palms a candy bar and the look of shame on the face of the young boy who is with him. I am never bored because my eye makes the world interesting, exposes the extraordinary in the ordinary, the significant in the trivial.

··

EXPLORE USING THE DAYBOOK

I explore my world in the daybook that is always with me. I note revealing specifics, quotations, references, facts, thoughts of my own on the piece I am researching, but more important, on whatever passes by that interests me.

I make notes in the margin—"col?" "WTL, Ch. 3," "Poem," "Novel," "Ohio talk"—that allow me to find these chronologically recorded fragments. I am amazed at how material accumulates. I paste in news stories, notes and drafts I have written on the computer and printed out, references to books I must look up or sources I should write or call, leads and outlines and rehearsal drafts that may reveal voice.

The more I write down, the more I remember. The act of writing something down reinforces memory, and many times I do not have to look up what I have written. It also stimulates my observing/recording skills, making me more aware than I was before I adopted the daybook custom.

EXPLORE USING A COMPUTER

The computer has changed the entire world of international research. The problem used to be, "Where can I get the information I need?" Now it is, "How can I handle the abundance of information that lies just behind my keyboard."

Libraries are now computerized, with computerized connections to other libraries and with data sources that may be in other cities or countries but just seconds away by a modem that can send information over telephone lines. Librarians, media center experts, and computer specialists can help you tap into these services, and you should make these methods a part of your education.

I have developed my own files of information—for example, writers' quotes—that I can draw on right in the middle of a paragraph, since I work on a hard disk. I have past notes as well as other pieces of writing all stored away so that they can be retrieved in seconds. My research notes go into the file, usually placed where they may appear in a draft so that the text is written between them and they become a sort of pre-outline. Each day I use my computer to record and recover information.

HEAR THE VOICE

During exploration, the writer is alert for the voice of the material that may become the voice of the text. There is music in every piece of research you discover. Listen for the dancing avoidance in the presidential statement, the ponderous cadence of the scholarly tome, the rage in the voice of the dispossessed, the smug song from the fortunate, the drumbeat of damnation in the legal brief. Quotations from live interviews, phone calls, books, articles, memos, reports, papers help tell you of the significance of what you are hearing.

Voice is a clue to meaning the way movie music underlines the action on the screen. Often in writing you pick up the voice that is appropriate to the text from what is said by the research sources. Also, don't forget to listen to the voice of your own notes. You may, for example, make notes on how animals are tortured to test cosmetics and hear anger in your voice that will be tamed and made effective in your final written argument.

Never forget that writing is music. The melodies you hear rising from the page are vital to earning the reader's trust and to communicating the meaning of what you have to say. The music of your drafts—your voice—also helps to instruct you in the early stages of writing, telling you what you feel and think about the subject.

....

REVISE AND RESEARCH

Don't wait until a draft is completed to revise. As you explore and find more material—substantiation, contradiction, doubt, qualification, new meanings—you will keep changing the first vision of what you will eventually write.

I had a clear focus all thought out for one piece. I planned to write about a beautiful, clear September morning and about going sketching with my son-in-law. But on the morning I planned to do my research, the sun was hidden, leading me to revise my topic and write the following column:

> My son-in-law Karl Nestelberger and I tip toe out of the house in the lightening dark just before dawn, whispering so we will not wake anyone else in the family.
>
> Other early morning companions go fishing or hunting, but we intend to catch what can't be caught. We are going sketching, trying to capture the world in line, form, and color.
>
> We drive to Wagon Hill in Durham, New Hampshire, and hike around the closed gate to a spot Karl had found the day before. He says it is an ideal place to sketch.
>
> I am disappointed. It is not near the water. It is just fields and trees and woods edge, but he is a landscape painter who finds wonder in the ordinary, magic in subdued shapes and colors.
>
> I say nothing. I know the excitement of sketching and the drama at the beginning or the end of the day when the sun is low in the sky and the shadows are long. Then the most ordinary field develops a special texture.
>
> There is light, but this morning there is no sun. The sky is gray. There are no dramatic shadows. All the greens and browns and yellows are muted.
>
> We grump mildly at the lack of the predicted sun, but know that his brush and watercolors, my pen and crayons will show us what we do not yet see. We set up, hesitate in respectful fear before the blank page, then have the courage of the first line.
>
> The magic never fades. I'm not talking about museum drawings or paintings. I'm not even talking about failed works of art. I'm talking about sketches, the quick lines and wash that place on our sketchbook pages not what is in the world, not what we see with our eyes, but what is seen by brush or pen.
>
> I have jumped out of planes and had enemy soldiers make little flowers of earth dance around me but those moments are no more exciting to me than what happens when a line reveals.
>
> In silent companionship, we look across the same fields and then steal glances at each other's sketchbooks. We inhabit different geographies.
>
> Partly this is due to pen or brush, watercolor or crayon; partly due to the fact he is a trained artist while I am amateur; partly due to who we are since we each draw our autobiography; but mostly the differences are too dramatic

to be explained. We are practicing, experiencing the astonishment of what craft sees.

Then nature plays its own trick. Fog suddenly hides the woods, makes the fields grow small, the now familiar clumps of tree and bush mysterious. The muted colors are made light and pass into degrees of white and gray.

Still Karl and I look, each in our own way, trying to see when there appears less to see and discover shapes we have never paused to see before, shades of gray we have not known. We remain where we are, practicing our companion crafts, but I have the image that we are children again, dashing wildly down the fields gathering armloads of fog—graygreen and greengray, yellowgray, and browngray. The sky has fallen and we can, if we pay attention, see our familiar world changed by the visiting clouds.

And then the gate to Wagon Hill has opened and we are surrounded by circling, sniffing packs of dogs and dog owners, who let the animals off their chains. Following their noses, the dogs race into the fog, become gray, blurred fastmoving ghosts of dogs.

The next morning we again sneak out early to sketch. This time we set up shop at the near end of Great Bay. The tide is out and the world once more muffled in fog, but this morning we do not complain. We have learned to respect the quiet mystery of the fallen sky.

We remark on the quiet of the morning. All sounds are muffled. Even the seagulls seem subdued. I notice how, this second morning, our pens and brushes grow more courageous. We let them run, as the dogs, let off the leash, ran free yesterday, chasing what we could not sniff.

Our hands move faster, trying to keep up with the line and our sketches, in the way of art, grow both simpler and more revealing at the same time.

Four young women come by, watch us draw and paint, say nice things about what they see on our pages, then descend to a float. Suddenly we hear, rising from the float, four women's voices softly humming what we think are hymns.

It seems right, appropriate to the natural world that is always the same and never the same, always full of secret lines and shapes and colors and understandings available to those who are quiet, observe, and wait.

Much of the excitement in writing comes from having an opportunity to research and explore subjects you want—or need—to find out more about. Exploring both satisfies and stimulates your curiosity: The more you find out about a subject, the more you realize there is to explore. You will have a rich inventory of material that will make your writing easy and will also satisfy the reader.

IN THE WRITER'S WORKSHOP

The writer . . . sees what he did not expect to see. . . . Inattentive learner in the schoolroom of life, he keeps some faculty free to hear and wonder. His is the roving eye.

By that roving eye is his subject found. The glance, at first only vaguely caught, goes on to concentrate, deepen; becomes the vision.   ELIZABETH BOWEN

If you knew where you were going why would you bother writing? There'd be nothing to discover.   JOHN GUARE

In Time Will Darken It *I couldn't decide whether the hero went to bed with the young woman from Mississippi or not, so I wrote it both ways, and continued to write it both ways, chapter after chapter after chapter. It was like a fork in the road. I finally faced the issue and decided that in the year 1912, he wouldn't have. So I threw away all the rest of it. It was a wasteful way of going about it, but I had to discover the form from the material. I didn't have a clear idea, usually, of what I was up to.*
WILLIAM MAXWELL

As great architects and others have said, God lies in the details. I would say that Art lies in the details and that the best skill that a writer can develop is an openness, a receptivity to life, at its most basic level, its most intricate details. There's almost nothing that can go wrong in a book that you can't fix with fascinating, riveting details of one sort or another. That's what life is; life isn't general. Life is texture, process, complexity. The intimate, sometimes terrifying, details of life are to my mind what make life so unexpected and breathtaking. If you can convey a scene in sensory detail, not only can you enter that scene yourself in your imagination or memory, but you can allow readers to walk into that scene also at the level of their senses.   DIANE ACKERMAN

The law of particularity forces fiction writers, poets, and dramatists to obsess over details, instances, and concrete images, while treating the experience of one or two characters as if it matters as much as the sum total experience of the entire human race. To writers, a moment in time, properly rendered, is worth all time—a single, vividly imagined place is worth the cosmos. History is the record of the causal link between human choice and consequence, and as the very word implies, history in that sense is the ground of story itself.   JAMES CARROLL

The more particular, the more specific you are, the more universal you are.   NANCY HALE

. . . [A]s you continue writing and rewriting, you begin to see possibilities you hadn't seen before. Writing a poem is always a process of discovery. You discover things about yourself as a poet, about language, about the nature of poetry. I think it was W. H. Auden who once said to me that writing a poem is like solving for X in an equation.
ROBERT HAYDEN

That's not what writing is—writing what you know. You write in order to find things out. . . . It's an act of discovery.   GARRISON KEILLOR

To be a writer does not mean to present a truth, it means to discover a truth.   MILAN KUNDERA

For me, writing poetry is a series of bewildering discoveries, a search for something that remains largely unknown even when you find it.   DAVID WAGONER

What discoveries I've made in the course of writing stories all begin with the particular, never the general.   EUDORA WELTY

In travel you discover something and then go home and write about it. In fiction the discovery comes at the moment of writing. Halfway down the page you suddenly meet something unexpected. It's the surprise in writing that is the sustaining factor. PAUL THEROUX

....

QUESTIONS ABOUT EXPLORING

I'm okay with exploring my own life. That's no problem. But what about someone else's life? What right do I have to barge into their world asking questions?

Just thinking about this issue means that you have all your writer's senses attuned to the people around you, that you are being *sensitive* in the truest sense of the word! You are also feeling the full ethical weight of what it means to be a writer.

It's true. You certainly don't want to trample on someone else's privacy in search of material. But you don't want to look at people as completely isolated beings either. Lives bump up against one another. We make sense of our own lives by comparing them with others—by watching people live, solve problems, celebrate successes, and survive tragedies. Just because we observe, interview, and write about people doesn't mean that we are voyeurs or have a sadistic urge to see others exposed or in tears. It only means that we seek a common ground between our world and theirs, that we tread the terrain between one life and the next in search of what's similar and what's different.

Besides, writing is thinking, and thinking means asking questions. That's why good writing requires barging around a bit. Be sensitive. But also be inquisitive.

What if I don't get other people's lives right when I write about them?

There are no right or wrong ways to portray people; there are only different perspectives. Certainly, you don't want to be vicious or uncaring in the way you gather information or write about others. As long as you are not consciously harming people, you shouldn't worry about asking questions or examining how other people live and what they think.

What if people won't give me information?

Give them a reason to give you the information. Flattery is a good reason. If that doesn't work, then you have to find another good reason: Do they want to help educate you? Do they want to persuade? Do they want revenge? Do they want to raise money for their cause? Do they want to defend themselves?

Some people simply want to talk. Many people go through their lives unheard. This is often true of the elderly or people whose jobs or positions in society don't generally put them in the limelight. People like this are often thrilled that you consider their input significant, and they are usually happy to help you out.

There are many reasons why people will give out information; you just have to find the one that will unlock the information you need.

How do you know who's an authority and that what they tell you is true?

If you are interviewing people face to face, it's a good idea to find at least three sources for any important data. It's not so much that people lie as that they're uninformed; they believe what they're telling you, but it may not be true. As a researcher, you have to keep your common sense in good working order. When you are suspicious about a statement or a detail, pay attention to that hunch and check it out.

If you are getting your data from the Internet, checking sources may not be so easy. Web pages, chat rooms, bulletin boards—all of these sources may contain interesting information, but there is usually no single way of judging its accuracy. Always question what you read over the Internet (or for that matter in any printed text!). If you can, find information about the same issue from several different sources. You may also need to qualify your sources as you write up your data; let your reader know which you think are accurate and which you question.

So I should stick with only official sources, right? I should always go straight to the top for information?

If you want an expert on a particular subject, the best way to find the authority is to ask the people in that business who's the best. Ask nurses in the hospital, police officers on the force, teachers in the school, scientists in the lab whom you should talk to find out about your subject. They work with all the authorities.

They are also authorities themselves, and this is an important point. Never underestimate the value of information you can get from those who are not "top dogs." These people have perspectives that may very well differ from those of official sources, and if you want to get a complete picture of an organization or site, you shouldn't forget these "everyday" people. They keep things running, and they also operate in the thick of activity instead of shutting themselves away in offices. While they may not be able to give you official documentation about your topic, they will certainly have an abundance of personal experiences to add to your information. Combined with other sources, interviews with these people will help you round out your research.

What if there are no books written on my topic?

That doesn't mean that your topic is not worth writing about or exploring. It may mean that you have a unique perspective on your topic.

Writers who are just beginning to explore often become discouraged when they find that no single "authority" has written about what interests them. They forget that exploring means searching and synthesizing clues and information. It means going on an adventure of discovery rather than a package tour of a well-known land. It means being a detective rather than a collector of facts and figures.

Rather than finding a single book that will cover your topic, find many different sources that refer to the subject you want to write about. You might check out data in magazines or newspapers, on the Internet, or in government documents, for example. You might interview people and send away for information from certain organizations.

Okay. I've gathered different sources and interviewed lots of people, but none of them agree on anything! Now what?

Don't be discouraged if all your sources don't say the same thing. Gather as many different perspectives as you can on your topic, and arrive at your own conclusions. That's the whole purpose of exploring. It's also one of the main reasons we write.

But first you will want to organize all your data so you can be clear about the issues and points of disagreement. To do this, draw a line down the middle of a page in your daybook. On the left, sum up very briefly all of the arguments of your various sources. Next to each argument on the right-hand side of the page, sum up in one word or sentence the main issue it addresses.

Now go back and organize your sources according to issues, making sure to note just how each agrees or disagrees with other sources. When it comes time to write your paper, you will have a clearer idea about the issues and the points of disagreement, and you will probably have formulated your own opinion from reviewing the issues and arguments.

....

EXPLORING ACTIVITIES

1. Go to the library and use Infotrac or a similar computerized database to track a story in newspapers and magazines. Use other databases to see what has been written about the story in literary and academic journals. Listen to various news broadcasts on the radio. Watch national news programs to see how they report the story. Gather as much information from as many different sources as possible, and keep track of which sources yield the most, and which the least. Pay particular attention to the different angles and perspectives each source takes.

2. Look in the class Book of Questions (created for Activity 10 in Chapter 4) and select one that intrigues you. Gather all the information you can to answer that question. Interview people, read city documents, check out library sources, and use your own eyes and other senses. Then with your partner or group, scan the information you have gathered and generate even more questions. Return to your sources or find new ones in order to answer those questions. Repeat the process until you have narrowed your focus and gathered all the information you will need to write about your topic.

3. Think of a famous or historical local figure you want to find out more about. Begin at the library with biographies about the person, and look in the online database or card catalog for general information on your subject. Ask reference librarians what related materials are available. Then contact your local historical society and ask them where the personal papers and diaries of the person you have chosen are located and whether you can gain access to them. Such papers, called *primary sources,* are often housed in university or local town libraries or special museum houses. Sometimes you need official permission to read them, but most institutions will cooperate with you if you are doing research.

4. If you have older students in your class, explore an event or events that happened during their lives (such as the Vietnam war, the peace movement, the Kennedy assassinations). First write down in your daybook everything you think you know about the event, and then come up with a list of questions to ask your older classmates. Pay special attention to the language they use, listening for the slang or jargon of the period you are studying. Ask questions about things you don't understand, but also let your interviewees focus on whatever they want.

5. Access an Internet search engine, and type a word or words that sum up your topic. Browse at your leisure, moving from Web site to Web site according to your interests. Print out or keep a list of information that interests you and the addresses of the Web sites you consult.

6. With a group of classmates, take a sensory tour of a site—a favorite spot in the mountains, a beach, a town, a neighborhood, or perhaps a place of historical significance. Ask each person in the group to be responsible for one sense—seeing, hearing, tasting, smelling, or touching—and to record as many sensory details as possible. Reconvene as a group, and write up a portrait of the site.

7. Pick up a local newspaper, and focus on an issue being debated in your town. Research the issue by visiting government offices, Web sites, and local libraries. You might also want to check with the office of deeds,

wills, and other records. Town libraries often keep extensive records on civic debates. Call the town or city hall and get a list of public offices, or look in the phone book under the listings for your town government. These sources will give you a better idea of where to start.

8. Visit a nursing home or senior citizen's apartment and ask to meet residents who want company. Meet them individually or invite them to gather as a group. Tell them that you are interested in hearing about their lives and the eras in which they lived. As you listen to their stories, jot down all the facts and details you can, asking questions as you go along. When your interviewees are comfortable with you, ask them if they would mind allowing you to see personal snapshots, letters, or diaries. Make a commitment to visit them once a week over a semester and offer them services in exchange for their time and stories, such as rides to church or the hairdresser, or a steady arm for a walk around the block.

9. Treat "invisible" people as significant sources of information. Such folks include custodians, food-service workers, clerical help in university offices, homeless people on the street—people we often tend to dismiss as insignificant. Ask them questions about their lives, and invite them to tell stories about what they see, hear, and experience around them every day.

10. Explore your local or school government. Attend city council or student senate meetings, and keep up on the issues by looking in newspapers and listening to reports on local radio and television. Tune in to the local talk shows, and interview officials and citizens. Keep a log of issues that interest you and the details that pertain to them. Use your writer's eye and other senses to take in the whole scene and to analyze the people and debates involved.

11. Walk through a cemetery and observe and record as many details as possible: names and dates, sizes and condition of headstones, genders of the deceased, relationships, years lived, the vaults, statues, and tombstones, the cemetery landscape itself. Write a history of the cemetery just from what you observe. Do you think some "residents" were richer than others? Later, go to the church or public office that keeps the cemetery's records and read them for more information. Visit your local library, and check out newspaper stories and other printed sources about the cemetery and the deceased. Then revise your history according to the new details you gather.

12. Browse through bibliographies. These are lists of books and magazines by other authors whom writers consult when exploring and gathering information about their topics. Go to the library, and select a book about your topic; copy the bibliography (usually located in the back of

the book or at the end of each chapter). Exchange bibliographies with a classmate and discuss the different angles and perspectives writers listed in the bibliographies have taken on your topic. Circle a few of the books or periodicals on the bibliographies you want to look at. Locate these materials and consult *their* bibliographies.

13. Choose three of the most helpful or unusual sources you have found, and write them on the board in class. When your classmates have done the same, go around the room and describe your sources and how you have used them. Choose six sources from the board that you have not yet used but would like to try.

14. Take your daybook to a public space, such as a restaurant or cafe. Write down as accurately as possible the conversations of people who pass by or converse at tables in your vicinity. Pay attention to the sound and rhythm of speech, and record as many comments and dialogues as you can. Don't worry about following any one conversation through from beginning to end. Just try to catch the gist of what people are saying.

15. Go to yard sales, and list interesting or unusual items you see for sale. Find out as much as you can about the histories of the objects, who they have belonged to and the people who are selling them. Observe the people who buy the objects, and listen in on the comments they make about them. Between sales, sit down somewhere and write about the most interesting items, people, and conversations you've observed and listened to. Be on the lookout for humorous remarks, surprise purchases, and odd or interesting characters. List or write about as many of them as you can.

16. Visit the special collections departments, rare book rooms, or archives in your school or town library. These departments often house books and other materials pertaining to local or university history. Some include first editions of local authors' works or the letters and diaries of local literary and historical figures. Explore these collections by listing in your daybook as many of the resources they offer as you can and the possible topics for writing and research they suggest.

17. Paste interesting newspaper articles or personal artifacts in your daybook. Share your daybook with a writing partner, and ask him or her to choose at least three items from it and to interview you about their significance and what prompted you to choose them. Ask your partner to take notes while you talk, and get a copy for your daybook.

18. Write an exploratory draft on your topic and pass out copies in a small group. Ask your classmates to comment about the quality of information they find in your piece and where they want to see more. Have them suggest sources that might be useful to you.

19. Explore a topic through different genres of writing. If you are interested in football, for example, find novels, poems, movies, plays, essays, songs, newspaper columns, editorials, television shows, or public records that pertain to the game. Select three pieces written in three different genres, and report to the class about how they are different from or similar to each other.

20. Draft a family history. Interview relatives and family friends. Use the Internet to look up genealogies and Web pages of relatives, or go to the library's genealogy section. Make a family tree or start a family newsletter that focuses on a different aspect or branch of the family every month.

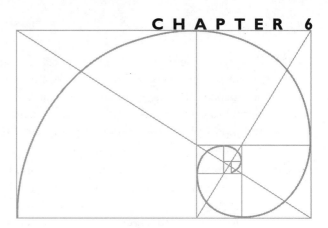

PLAN

At a few wonderful—always unexpected—times the writing flows so fast the draft seems to unroll ahead of you like a highway at night. If this happens to you, keep driving at top speed; follow the highway, and allow the writing to write itself.

Most of the time, however, it is hard to decide which highway to take; or the car won't start; or, after starting, it bucks and stalls. You have a focus, a destination, an idea of what you want to say but . . .

It is time to plan.

A writing plan is an artist's sketch, a carpenter's plan scratched on a board, a cook's recipe that will be changed in the cooking. A writing plan is not a work order or a binding contract. It is an educated guess, a hunch, a suggestion—"Hey, let's head for the beach." When you actually write, you may not get to the beach; you may stop along the way, decide to go to the mountains, run into some interesting people and spend time with them. The picnic may be eaten in a restaurant or the restaurant food taken out to the rocks. But you would not achieve the surprise without the plan.

START WITH A BASIC PLAN

When I feel the need to make a plan, my favorite one has the following elements:

Title

Lead

Trail

End

TITLE

During my apprentice years I drafted as many as 150 titles while I researched and thought about an article I planned to write. I scribbled titles in my daybook during commercials on TV, when a friend was late for lunch, while taking a break from another writing project.

Each title helps me:

- Refine the focus.
- Establish the voice.
- Target a reader.

I might, for example, work on an essay on football, a game I both enjoy and despise. Notice how my draft titles refine the focus, contain a voice, appeal to a reader:

To Hurt Is the Name of the Game
Football: America's War Game
Symbol of U.S. Militarism: Football
What I Learned by Playing Football
Hurt or Be Hurt
The Maim Game
Balance the University Budget: Junk Football
How to Exploit Students
Have You Ever Met a Scholar/Athlete?
My Knee Fifty Years after the Kick-off
Do You Want Your Leg Straight or Bent?
Play with Pain
Hours of Commercials; Seconds of Action
Why I Love/Hate Football

None of these choices quite work, but you can see how each is a predraft of the text, and each demands a *different* text.

LEAD

The lead—the beginning or the promise of the opening—is the single most important element in my planning. I always begin with a lead—the first sentence, paragraph, or page that will lead the reader into the piece. Here are some leads that pass through my mind or appear on my daybook page:

I was hit by an illegal, blindside clip on a kick-off in 1942, and my knee still hurts.

I do not approve of football—a violent, militaristic game—but I have a season ticket.

Historians may see football as a metaphor for what America became at the end of the twentieth century—a violent, militaristic society.

Football taught me to hit first, to hit hard, to play with pain, to get ahead in my career.

I like watching football, because it is metaphor for the macho, corporate society in which we live.

On the football field I learned to swell up so I looked bigger than I was; to grunt, to hit someone I was not mad at, to shower with dozens of strangers, to become an American male.

I spent a few years learning to play football; I spent the rest of my life trying to unlearn what it taught me.

Football prepared me for combat. My coaches were like infantry officers: loud, confident, and often dangerously wrong.

Let's choose that last one. You can see how much is established in a line or two.

Genre

It is an essay—perhaps an argument against the militarism and violence of football—in which the author will explore the world of football in the context of his wartime experience. It is *not* a poem, play, short story, or news story about a football game, although I might explore this subject in those forms of writing another time.

Focus

The essay will focus on the relationship between football player and coach.

Context

The essay piece will be placed in the context of the beginning of another football season.

Voice

The voice is cynical, ironic, antiauthority, critical with a strong flavor of bitter humor.

Audience

Football fans who are not aware of how players are treated and what is wrong about a sport that encourages that treatment.

The Writer's Authority

The lead establishes the authority of the writer to speak as a former football player and combat veteran.

Angle of Vision

Coaches will be seen from the perspective of a player who later served in combat.

Opinion

The critical opinion of the essay will allow the possibility that the writing will make the writer see the issue in a different way.

Material

The lead makes the writer aware of the material in mental inventory for the task: I was a scholarship player kept on the field with injuries that bother me more than fifty years later. I also have a mental file full of wartime experiences—the lieutenant who caused his unit to mutiny, the stupid before-battle speech, the colonel who commanded U.S. troops to attack other U.S. troops.

Length

It's shaping up as a strong opinion piece based on autobiographical evidence, not a take-out or exposé. I'd better keep it to 800 to 1,200 words if it is to be published and read.

Pace

Pace is the speed of the writing, which may accelerate when action is described and slow down when the writer reflects on the action. The voice of my first line tells me that the piece should move quickly to keep the reader involved and support the cynical, antiauthority voice. The beat is established in the voice. It should move rather quickly—a guerrilla attack, not a long campaign.

Proportion

Proportion is the effective balance between the parts in a piece of writing: pro as well as con, dialogue and description, action and reaction, statement and documentation, humor and seriousness. In this case, there had better be some objective, contemporary evidence to balance the autobiographical views of an old man.

Evidence Required

Play the devil's advocate to your own prose, doubting, questioning to discover the evidence you would need to believe and trust the writer. At some points as I read my draft, I hear myself responding, "Yeah? Who Says?" I then insert who says into the text, attributing the quote, citing the study, documenting the authority for what I have said.

Potential End

The closing will probably echo the lead and suggest that the writer was prepared for combat by football but not in the way expected.

I am surprised in spelling all of this detail out for you. I do my lead writing instinctively, and I am newly impressed by how much I depend on the lead, the key part of my basic writing plan.

TRAIL

Sometimes the lead is enough planning for me, but usually I mark a trail through the material. I rarely make an outline because it restricts discovery. The sketch of the trail ahead usually incorporates the three to five points I may cover. I always remember, however, that writing is thinking, and the writing may take me where I do not expect to go. The plan does not deny discovery but stimulates it.

In this case my trail might read:

Football practice

Combat practice

Reality

That list would be enough to get me through the draft. I would show the confidence of the football coach and the game plan; the confidence of the infantry officer and military tactics—and then the reality: game confusion and combat confusion.

END

Many writers—Toni Morrison, John McPhee, Katherine Anne Porter, John Irving—claim they begin writing knowing the end of a piece. I didn't believe them until I found in my daybook a lot of *K*s, for kicker, my code word for an ending. I, too, began with a destination, a place where I thought I would end.

In this case my ending or kicker might read:

K—echo back to coach, was prepared

Implied in that line is the idea that I was not inspired in the way the propaganda about football predicts—heroic deeds and exalted patriotism. Football prepared me for the stupidity of war and those who conduct wars.

This quick outline prepares me to write a draft. Many of the problems I will face in its writing have been solved by my basic plan. I also gain another advantage in planning: Once the plan is written, it doesn't matter if I am kept from writing for a few days or a week. I can go back to the plan at any time and begin a draft.

PLAN THE PROMISING OPENING

Effective writing opens with a promise to the reader. A writer usually thinks of the opening—beginning or lead—of a piece of writing in terms of the reader. Readers are in a hurry, they have many distractions; a writer has seconds—no more—in which to catch and hold the reader's attention.

The opening does this by promising information that the reader wants or needs. It promises clarity and grace; it hopes to surprise. The lead promises to satisfy the reader's expectations: A narrative tells a story; an argument argues. The opening establishes a tension that produces the energy that drives the story forward. The beginning promises a closing, a sense of completion.

The writer must be aware of the promises made in the opening if they are to be fulfilled. Joan Didion reports, "What's so hard about the first sentence is that you're stuck with it. Everything else is going to flow out of that sentence. And by the time you've laid down the first *two* sentences, your options are all gone." Elie Wiesel adds, "With novels it's the first line that's important. If I have that, the novel comes easily. The first line determines the form of the whole novel. The first line sets the tone, the melody. If I hear the tone, the melody, then I have the book."

As established in the basic plan, an effective opening solves most of the problems the writer would face in the first draft, and it solves them efficiently, ahead of time, when the writer is not trapped in a tangle of prose.

HOW TO WRITE AN EFFECTIVE OPENING

I *never* proceed with an opening unless I think it will produce a good piece of writing. That's the only *never* in my personal toolbox. An opening may not produce a piece of writing that works, and I may have to start over; what I discover in the writing may require a new opening; but I know only one place to start: at the beginning.

The search for the opening begins when I receive the assignment or when I realize I have a piece of writing that must be brought to paper. Sometimes the idea for a piece of writing comes to me in the form of the line or sentence or paragraph that becomes the opening.

In every case, I play with potential openings all during the research and planning process. I note possible openings in my head, in my daybook, in my file on the computer for that topic. When it is time to write, I play with openings. Play is important. I must be free to make discoveries, free enough to allow what I am writing to tell me what I need to say and how I need to say it. I used to write at least fifty to seventy-five openings for every article or book I wrote. After fifty years of writing, I am not that compulsive, and I don't keep count. Once every couple of years an opening will come to me that seems just right the first time, but most of my openings are products of word—and sentence and paragraph—play.

When I write an opening, I am consciously trying to get at the essence of the story. I keep standing back and saying to myself: What is the central tension? What's new? What is changed? How is the reader affected? What do I or the reader need to know? What is the key problem? What surprises me? What question does the story answer? What do I expect the reader to think, feel, do after reading it? I have been involved in researching the details of the topic; now I have to stand back and see its significance.

Use the checklist that follows to find some effective ways to play with your own possible beginnings.

OPENING CHECKLIST

After you have written your final opening, read it again. Make sure your opening is:

- *Quick.* The reader will decide to read on—or not to read on—in a matter of seconds.
- *Accurate.* The reader who spots even a tiny error will refuse to believe anything you write.
- *Honest.* Don't hype an opening to tease the reader, because you must deliver what you promise.
- *Simple.* Cut back the underbrush. Use proper nouns, active verbs, and concrete details whenever possible.
- *Packed with information.* The effective opening gives the reader information, and that information makes the reader want to read on.
- *Heard.* The reader should hear an individual writer speaking directly to the reader.

CATEGORIES OF EFFECTIVE OPENINGS

It may be helpful to take a piece of paper and list the kinds of openings you have in your writer's toolbox. Most writers have many more ways of beginning a piece of writing than they realize. Some of the openings in my toolbox are familiar ones.

News

Begin by telling what the reader needs to know in the order she or he needs to know it. Cover the five *W*s—who, what, when, where, why—especially why.

> The computer system at Western State University crashed when 2,500 students signed up for the same section of freshman English yesterday. They did it to protest new, adviser-free computer registration procedures.

Anecdote

This opening tells a brief story that captures the essence of what you will be dealing with in the piece. It is the most popular magazine article opening, but watch out—if it's a good story but doesn't aim the reader in the direction you want to go, the whole piece may be lost.

> When Lorraine B. Well, registrar at Western State University, turned on her computer yesterday morning, she was surprised by a message in huge letters on her screen: "Tidal Wave."
>
> She didn't know what it meant until the university computer system crashed. More than 2,500 students had registered for the same section of freshman English to protest the adviser-free, computer registration program designed by Registrar Well.

Quotation

A quote is a good opening device, for it gives additional authority and an extra voice to the piece. Like the anecdotal opening, however, it must be right on target.

> "This human being heard the students," said Lorraine B. Well, Western State University registrar who developed adviser-free computer registration procedures. A student protest shut down all university computers.
>
> More than 2,500 students registered . . .

Umbrella

This opening covers several equal, or almost equal, elements in the story.

> Registration procedures at Western State University are being reconsidered in an emergency meeting this morning after students—by computer—protested new adviser-free computer registration procedures.

Description

The writer may open by setting the scene for the story. Use specifics.

> Students at Western State University went online last night at the school's computer centers, from dorm rooms, from work stations, from their homes, from the library, even from bars and students hang-outs where they could plug their laptops into phone lines.
>
> They all—more than 2,500 of them—registered for Section 13 of freshman English to protest new adviser-free, computer registration . . .

Voice

Voice establishes the tone for communication between reader and writer. Read aloud and make sure that the voice of your opening is communicating information in the tone appropriate to that information.

> Civil war broke out on the campus of Western State University when computer fought computer.
>
> Angry at a new, adviser-free computer registration system, students mobilized 2,500 computers and commanded them to attack.

Announcement

This lead simply tells the reader what you are going to say.

> Registration will be delayed at Western State University until a traditional faculty advising system is recreated. It will take the place of a computer registration system attacked by students armed with their own computers.

Tension

This opening reveals the forces of the story in action. They are coming together on a collision course or pulling against each other. The opening contains the forces, and makes the reader feel the tension between them.

> "Human Beings 2,500; Computer 0." That was the headline in the Western State University newspaper today when a protest shut down a new computer registration system.
>
> Philosophy Professor Owen Scanlan was not sure it was a victory for human beings. "They had to use computers to attack the university computer," Scanlan pointed out.

Problem

This kind of opening establishes the problem that will be solved, or not solved, in the piece.

> How could students protest an impersonal, computer-based registration system at Western State University? By computer.

Background

The writer first gives the reader the background of an event, argument, conflict, issue, or action.

> Students at Western State University have complained for years about their difficulties in making appointments with their faculty advisers. When Lorraine B. Well was appointed registrar last year, she was told to solve that problem.
>
> Registrar Well designed an adviser-free computer system that made students demand a return to the bad old days. More than 2,500 . . .

Narrative

This opening establishes that the story will be told in narrative form. Be careful not to start too early. Start as near to the end as possible to involve the reader in the story. Background information should not be delivered ahead of the story itself. The reader needs to be involved in the story first to know what information is needed—then the experienced writer delivers it.

When Lorraine B. Well was a student at Western State University twenty years ago, she had to stand in line from 7 a.m. until after 4 p.m. one day each year to register for courses.

In the years since then, she has been a graduate student, a corporate executive, a college professor. When she was appointed as registrar last year, Dr. Well believed that since all students had access to computers, she could design a humane, human-being-free registration system that would eliminate standing in line.

Question

This opening sounds like it should work, but it rarely does. The writer usually knows the answer to the question, and so it sounds patronizing, like the nurse who says, "Now we would like to take our medicine, wouldn't we?"

How can registration lines at Western State University be eliminated? Not by computer, not yet.

Point of View

The writer establishes the position from which the reader will be shown the subject.

I am a computer major, a hacker to be honest. I love computers, but I am writing this letter to protest the new computer registration system at Western State. I need a human being, not a computer, to give me advice on the courses I should take to study computers.

Reader Identification

The writer anticipates the reader's concerns and responds to them immediately.

Western State University computerized registration advising, saying that all students today are used to computers. The administrators did not consider that students still would like to be advised by a human being. "Students won't use the computer advising system," predicted junior Minnie Mahler. "I'm a computer major and I'm going to talk to my professors face to face about what courses to take."

Face

A character is revealed in action. The reader becomes interested in the person and then the issue.

Stanley Hunan was the first to hear the beeps and notice the blinking screens that signaled a major attack on the new Western State University computer advising system.

A work study student at the computer center, his job was to monitor a registration system he resented.

Scene

The writer establishes a scene that is central to the meaning of the piece.

> A Western State University student with a baseball hat on backward rushed into Harry's bar last night, looking around wildly, "Need the men's room?" Harry asked.
> "No. A telephone," the student said, waving a laptop at the puzzled barkeep.

Dialogue

The reader hears one person speak and another react. It's not often you can use this opening, but when it's appropriate, it is dramatic and provides a lot of energy.

> "I wanted to eliminate lines," Registrar Lorraine B. Well told a Western State University sophomore yesterday.
> "You did," answered the student. "But you eliminated a human being, as well. I need a conversation, not 'if you are a liberal arts student, select Option 5.' I'm a dual biochem and forestry major, and the computer doesn't recognize that."

Process

A process central to the story is shown in action, and the reader is carried forward into the story.

> Students at Western State University who want registration advice have to boot a computer, click on "Regist" and hope they have a problem or conflict that has been programmed into the system.
> The following commands—a student pointed out that the word seems to contradict the principle of offering advice—reveal what it feels like to be a Western State student in need of registration counsel.

These are not all the possible ways to write openings. They are samples from my own toolbox. Make a list of the openings you like to write, and then look through periodicals and books to see other ways of writing them. Then steal the technique. Create your own museum of openings.

My museum of leads has an obvious one right inside the front door: "In the beginning God created Heaven and earth" (Genesis 1:1). I learn from leads by expert writers that I have collected. Here, for example, are many leads that introduce the same subject: New York City.

> *At the height of Harlem's nighttime fury a white police officer stood in the litter of glass and garbage that had come crashing down from the darkened rooftops and raised a bullhorn to his mouth. "Go home," he pleaded with the glowering Negro mobs that clustered along Seventh Avenue and atop the shabby tenements. "Go home," "Go home." From a man in the mob came a shout: "We are home, Baby."*
> *TIME,* JULY 31, 1964

I often feel drawn to the Hudson River, and I have spent a lot of time through the years poking around the part of it that flows past the city. I never get tired of looking at it; it hypnotizes me. I like to look at it in midsummer, when it is warm and dirty and drowsy, and I like to look at it when it is stirred up, when a northeast wind is blowing and a strong tide is running—a new-moon tide or a full-moon tide—and I like to look at it when it is slack. It is exciting to me on weekdays, when it is crowded with ocean craft, harbor craft, and river craft, but it is the river itself that draws me, and not the shipping, and I guess I like it best on Sundays, when there are lulls that sometimes last as long as half an hour, during which, all the way from the Battery to the George Washington Bridge, nothing moves upon it, not even a ferry, not even a tug, and it becomes as hushed and dark and secret and remote and unreal as a river in a dream. JOSEPH MITCHELL, "THE RIVER MEN," *THE NEW YORKER,* APRIL 4, 1959

For more than half an hour thirty-eight respectable, law-abiding citizens in Queens watched a killer stalk and stab a woman in three separate attacks in Kew Gardens. Twice the sound of their voices and the sudden glow of their bedroom lights interrupted him and frightened him off. Each time he returned, sought her out, and stabbed her again. Not one person telephoned the police during the assault; one witness called after the woman was dead. MARTIN GANSBERG, *THE NEW YORK TIMES,* MARCH 27, 1964

The New York Giants, who overwhelmed two opponents at football last year, underwhelmed ten and whelmed two . . . RED SMITH, *NEW YORK HERALD TRIBUNE*

On any person who desires such queer prizes, New York will bestow the gift of loneliness and the gift of privacy. It is this largest that accounts for the presence within the city's walls of a considerable section of the population; for the residents of Manhattan are to a large extent strangers who have pulled up stakes somewhere and come to town, seeking sanctuary or fulfillment or some greater or lesser grail. The capacity to make such dubious gifts is a mysterious quality of New York. It can destroy an individual, or it can fulfill him, depending a good deal on luck. No one should come to New York to live unless he is willing to be lucky. E. B. WHITE, "HERE IS NEW YORK," *HOLIDAY,* APRIL 1949

All of these writers deal with the same subject, but what a variety of approaches—and voices. Create your own museum for inspiration and instruction.

....

ALTERNATIVE WAYS TO PLAN

Many times the way I planned the last piece of writing doesn't work on the next one. I have developed many other planning techniques. The following sections cover some of them.

ANSWERING THE READER'S QUESTIONS

There's a myth that popular writers write down to the reader, that the reader is a slob with a fifth-grade education who picks his teeth with a beer can. Not so.

The reader is an intelligent person who may not know the subject but is no dope. The reader will ask intelligent questions of any piece of writing, and they must be heard and answered by the writer.

Sometimes it helps me to imagine the reader sitting across from my desk, sprawled in an armchair, a skeptical, surly doubting Thomas. I make a statement, and my reader snarls, "Who says?" I stick in an attribution. I say something else, and the reader asks, "How come?" I stop and tell the reader how come. I write another paragraph, and the reader says, "What's that mean?" I tell the reader what it means. The reader snarls, "Who cares?" I make sure the reader knows the importance of what I'm saying. Other times I imagine a specific person, an individual who is not at all impressed by me or what I know about the subject. By writing to that person, I make my draft clear.

Sometimes I have to write for several very different readers. In that case, I pick one of them and write for that person. In the revision process, I read and revise for each of the other readers. But I must focus on a single reader at a time.

Good writing is a conversation between an individual writer and an individual reader. The writer has to anticipate where the reader is in that conversation and deliver the information the reader needs when the reader needs it.

Sometimes the reader asks so many nasty questions I can no longer write. I get mad at this surly, overly critical baboon who makes me feel dumb and inadequate. When that happens I send him out of the room. I'll deal with him later, after the draft is done, during the last stage of the writing process, when I have to invite him in anyway. He isn't polite about leaving. Sometimes he even makes obscene gestures and wears that all-knowing sneer that says, "I'll get you later." Fair enough. I'll have to deal with him later, but when I do there will be a text we can read together. If I don't get him out of the room, there will be no text at all.

After I have drafted the questions the reader will ask, I put them in the order the reader will ask them. That's always predictable and I have begun to outline my article.

OUTLINES

Outline is a nasty word to many students, and I was one of them, for this method is often taught in such a rigid manner that it doesn't work. An outline is not a formal blueprint that has to be followed precisely; it is not a contract, and you can't be sued if you break it. An outline is a sketch, a guess, a scribbled map that may lead to a treasure. Writers may create outlines and then not refer to them during the writing, for what they learned by making the outlines allows them to get on with the writing. Sometimes it is also helpful to make outlines in the middle of the writing to see where you've gone and where you might go, and at the end of the draft to see what you have discovered through the writing and how you have organized your material.

There are many ways to outline. This section shows eleven possible types. None of them is *the* way to outline. Develop your own system of outlining. Outline only if it helps you, and then outline in a way that provides that help.

I will demonstrate each outline on an assignment given by several freshman English instructors at the University of New Hampshire: Describe your home town. The work of a student, Sarah Hansen, who did an excellent job of describing her home town, is reprinted in Chapter 10.

Outline 1

This one is my favorite form of outline; it was described on pages 138 through 142.

Title
Lead
Trail
End

Demonstration of Outline 1

(TITLE)	My Home Town Was a City
(LEAD)	When other people talk of their home towns, they mention lawns, trees that arch over streets, and backyard swimming pools.
	My home town was a city. I remember alleys, boarded up stores, and vacant lots.
(TRAIL)	• But where I lived was neighborhood.
	• Geography of neighborhood.
	• Who lived there.
	• Games we played.
(END)	When I visited my roommate's home town, it was like a movie set. I thought I'd be envious, but the streets were empty, I never saw his neighbors, I wondered how he could stand the quiet that kept me awake half the night.

Outline 2

My next favorite form of outlining is the one I use in my textbooks. It is the one I would most likely adapt in writing an academic research or term paper.

1. I write the chapter or section titles, playing with them until I get the wording right, until I see a clear line through the material.
2. I write the major headings for each section within the chapter, playing with them until I see a trail through the chapter or section.
3. I write the subheads for each section within the major section, ordering and re-ordering them.
4. I draft the text for each section, changing heads as the material dictates. Writing is thinking, and the order will change in the writing.

This procedure is a good technique for outlining a research paper, grant proposal, corporate annual report, brochure, any sort of writing that must communicate an abundance of information in an orderly fashion.

Demonstration of Outline 2

1. The title of my sociology paper will be "The Urban Neighborhood as Home Town."

2. The main sections will be:
   - Expanding Horizons
   - Worlds within Worlds [ethnic diversity]
   - Neighborhood Games
   - Neighborhood Ethics
   - Neighborhood Inheritance [Beliefs taken to suburbs]

3. The subsections within the section on Expanding Horizons will be:
   - Apartment
   - Stairway
   - Front stoop
   - Block
   - Back alley
   - Across the street and away

4. Draft a section within a section at a time. If one doesn't go easily, skip to the next. When you go back, many sections will not be needed, and the rest will be easy to write.

Outline 3

This formal outline style may be appropriate for a formal, very structured subject. It uses Arabic and Roman numerals and capital and small letters to break a subject down into categories and subcategories in a logical sequence. Numerical outlines are also popular in some disciplines, and many computer software programs have a formal outline pattern built in.

The most formal outline style requires a full and complete sentence for each entry, but most writers just use fragments as signals for what will be said. Be careful in using the formal outline, because it may inhibit the search for and discovery of meaning that should come during the writing.

Demonstration of Outline 3

[One section of a sociology paper on urban neighborhoods]

III. Neighborhood games
  1. Importance of games
    A. Aldrich study
      a. LePage response
    B. History of games
  2. Nature of games
    A. Hiding
      a. Hide and Go Seek
      b. Ring-a-lievo
    B. Sports
      a. Stick ball
      b. Basketball
      c. Street hockey
      d. Soccer
    C. Gender differences
      a. Boys' games
      b. Girls' games
      c. Cross-overs
        1) Boys playing girls' games [rare]
        2) Girls playing boys' games [often]
    D. Ethnic differences
      a. White neighborhoods
      b. African American
      c. Latin American
      d. Asian

Outline 4

A writer friend of mine, Donald H. Graves, uses this outline form. He lists everything that might be included in the piece of writing in the left-hand column; then he moves items to the columns marked Beginning, Middle, End.

Some of the things don't get moved, of course, and others come to mind as the outline is being made and go right into the appropriate columns. Some things in the left-hand column are not used. It's a brainstorming list, and it becomes an inventory of material that may be used. Some items that are not on the list come to mind when the writer is working on the right-hand columns. The items are ordered—by number—within the columns after the writer has finished. Then the writer is ready to write.

Demonstration of Outline 4

Beginning	Middle	End	Brainstorming List
Home town urban	Qualities of neighborhood life:	How urban attitudes influence	Stick ball
Neighborhood urban unit	Ethnic comfort/ discomfort	How see suburban world through urban values	Latins played soccer
You are defined by your neighborhood	Diversity comfort/ discomfort		Blacks played basketball
	Fears		Whites played hockey
	Pleasures		Don't date X
	Games		Girls' games
	Family		Dress
	Dating + mating		Mixed families
			Loyalty to your own
			Food
			Racial myths
			My values today
			Alleys, loved alleys

Outline 5

A way to use the outline to dramatize the importance of certain parts of the piece of writing to the reader is to make a box outline in which the size of each box represents the importance of each part. The first paragraph, for example, is much more important to the reader than the pages that follow and might be two inches by four. The subject of the next four pages might be indicated in a phrase contained in a box only one-quarter of an inch by two inches. A main turning point might be in a box one inch by three, and then the rest of the piece might appear in another tiny box. Finally the closing might be in a box as large as—or larger than—the first paragraph. This can best be done with boxes, but it can also be done with typefaces.

This outline style really forces me to face up to the importance of the opening and the ending—to the importance of what I'm going to say and how I'm going to say it. It also forces me to see the structure of the piece in stark, efficient terms.

Demonstration of Outline 5

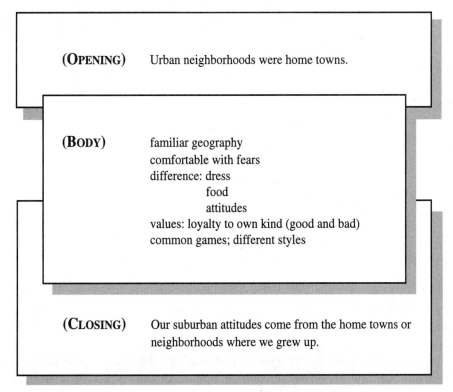

(**OPENING**) Urban neighborhoods were home towns.

(**BODY**) familiar geography
comfortable with fears
difference: dress
food
attitudes
values: loyalty to own kind (good and bad)
common games; different styles

(**CLOSING**) Our suburban attitudes come from the home towns or neighborhoods where we grew up.

(Continued)

(OPENING)	Urban neighborhoods were home towns.

(BODY)	familiar geography
	comfortable with fears
	difference: dress
	                food
	                attitudes
	values: loyalty to own kind
	(good and bad)
	common games; different styles

(CLOSING)	Our suburban attitudes come from the home towns or neighborhoods where we grew up.

Outline 6

A fine way to outline, especially on a complicated subject, is to brainstorm the questions the reader will ask and then put them in the order the reader will ask them.

There will usually be five questions—sometimes three or four, sometimes six or seven, but most likely five. You don't want to use the questions in the draft, but simply give the answers. The questions are in the reader's mind; the writer anticipates and answers them.

Demonstration of Outline 6

The questions are brainstormed, written down as they come to mind:

- Who were your neighbors? Did you get along with them?
- How can you have a home town when you lived in a city?
- How is a neighborhood like a small town?
- How does your home town, your urban neighborhood, influence your life today?
- What attitudes and beliefs did you take away from the neighborhood?
- What was life like in your home town [neighborhood]?

Now the questions are put in the order the reader will ask them and sharpened:

- How is a neighborhood like a small town?
- What was daily life like in your city neighborhood?
- Who were your neighbors?
- How did you get along with them?
- What attitudes and beliefs did you take away from the neighborhood?

Outline 7

The writer can adapt outline forms from other disciplines. I often find it helpful to use a flow chart, similar to those used in systems engineering and business organization study. These charts are designed to show how a factory works, how materials flow from a natural resource to a manufactured product, how power flows in a corporation. Using this device, I can often spot a movement or force that can order my piece.

Demonstration of Outline 7

When we moved to city I discovered neighborhood was home town ⟶

Geography of neighborhood ⟶ Streets and blocks ⟶ Ethnic

boundaries ⟶ Playing and living within boundaries ⟶ Attitudes

and beliefs neighborhood taught me

Outline 8

A related outline form I find useful I've borrowed from computers. Computer users have developed a number of different forms of outlining that break down complicated subjects into their sequential parts. Most of these outlines flow from left to right.

At the left I state an issue: "The home town in the city is the neighborhood." Then I give two extreme responses, one above the question and over to the right—"physical boundaries"—another below and over to the right—"ethical boundaries." I break down every answer this way until I see a pattern of potential meaning emerging.

Demonstration of Outline 8

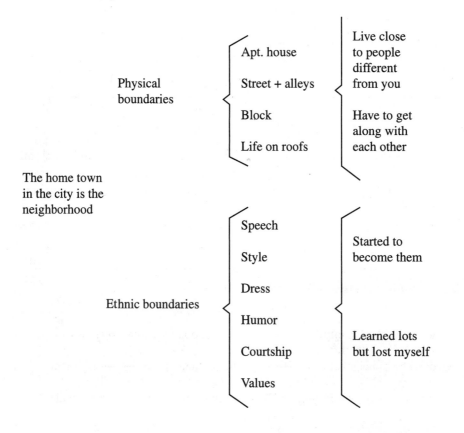

Outline 9

In many effective pieces of writing, fiction as well as nonfiction, each chunk of writing—a paragraph, a page, a scene—answers a question and asks a new question. For example, will they get married? Yes, but will they be happy? Will the product sell? Yes, but will it bring a profit? You can create an outline by anticipating and listing these questions.

Demonstration of Outline 9

Q. How is neighborhood like a small town?
A. People know you, you know people.

↓

Q. How well do you know each other?
A. We live on the street.

↓

Q. What is that like?
A. A big stage, everyone watching.

↓

Q. What do they see?
A. In my neighborhood, people of different backgrounds playing/fighting together.

↓

Q. Against each other?
A. No, against other neighborhoods.

Outline 10

Many fine writers, such as John McPhee and John Gregory Dunne, use a card technique to outline. This is the most popular technique for movie script writers.

Each scene or key topic in the writing gets its own card, sometimes using cards of different colors for different characters, or different kinds of material in nonfiction. Then the cards are pinned to a cork board and moved around so the writer can see the pattern of the entire piece—book, movie, or article.

Demonstration of Outline 10

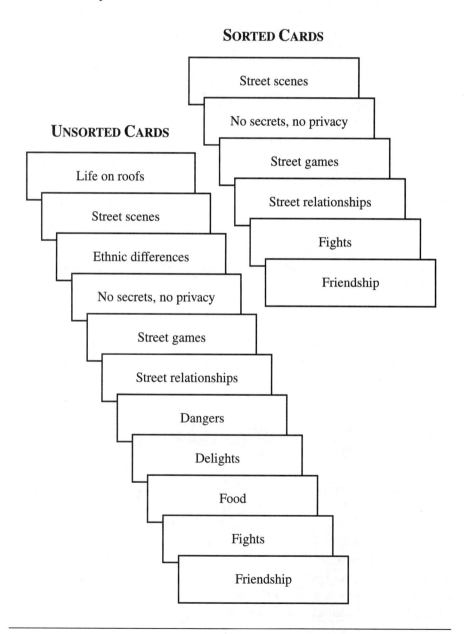

SORTED CARDS

Street scenes

No secrets, no privacy

Street games

Street relationships

Fights

Friendship

UNSORTED CARDS

Life on roofs

Street scenes

Ethnic differences

No secrets, no privacy

Street games

Street relationships

Dangers

Delights

Food

Fights

Friendship

Outline 11

Make a separate file folder for each topic within the piece of writing, a method that is helpful on a large project. You can renumber and move the file folders around, and you can put all your raw material—clips, photocopied articles, notes, photographs—right into a folder. When a folder is full, it may have to be divided. When it has nothing in it, you may have to drop that topic or do more research.

Demonstration of Outline 11

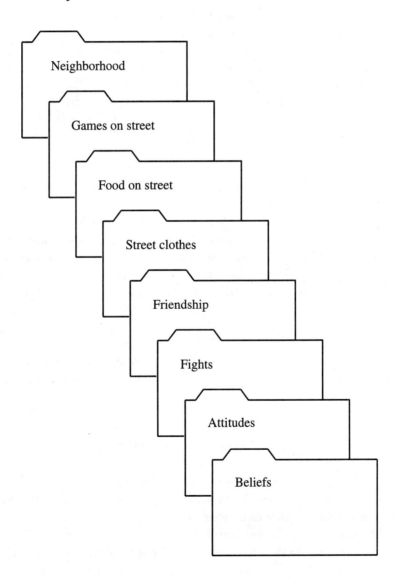

Try out these outline forms, and then make up others that fit the way your mind works. There's no one way to outline, and no eleven ways to outline. But you should find some way of pre-seeing what you may write.

Yes, there are writers who say that they do not outline. But if you interview them, as I have, you find that most of them have outlined in their minds, sometimes without being aware they were doing it. That happens to me sometimes; I just know where the writing is going and how it is going to get there. It seems like a feeling, even though it's probably a very organized intellectual act. When this happens to me, I write. I don't outline unless I feel the need to outline. But I do find that most of the time, my drafts collapse unless I have outlines in my mind or on paper.

Of course, when you outline, you may realize that you need more information or that you need a different focus; you may have to go back through one or more of the earlier stages of the writing process. That isn't failure. You haven't made a mistake. That's one of the main reasons to outline, so that you will see the information you need to have before you write the draft. You will see, by outlining, if you have the information to develop the focus.

PLAN IN THE DAYBOOK

My daybook could be called my *planning book.* In this notebook I record ideas, draft lines and leads, make the sketches I call *outlines,* note what I will write the next day. This talking to myself in the daybook stimulates the subconscious and keeps a project working during the majority of hours in the day when I am not at my computer. My daybook is always nearby when I am walking, in the car, on an airplane, attending a meeting. If an idea surfaces from my subconscious, I can catch it in my daybook.

The daybook is the place where I perform the play that leads to writing, capturing ideas, connecting them to other ideas, studying the created pattern, rearranging it into another meaning and also playing with language that reveals the surprises essential to writing.

PLAN ON A COMPUTER

The computer is a wonderful place to play with pattern and language. There are outlining programs, but I prefer to make my own lists, charts, outlines of all forms so that I can see a sketch of what I may write.

When I use Outline 2, the seams between exploring and planning and drafting blur. I may move raw research right into place in a plan, and I may also write at any place in the plan, if the writing is ready to be placed on the page.

I used to write magazine articles in sections, and my study floor would be covered with slips of paper of varying sizes along with heaps of raw research material. Now I do all that on the screen as I perform the task of the writer: making order from chaos.

PLAN THE VOICE

Voice is what I am; voice is the person in the writing; voice is what persuades the reader to listen and draws the reader on. We can train ourselves to hear the voice of the finished draft in the fragments with which we plan; we can decide, in advance of the first draft, how we will tune voice to support and communicate the meaning of the writing.

THE PERSONAL VOICE

Each writer has a personal voice. I can recognize family and friends from another room and on the telephone. People have their own music made up of genes and hormones, regional and ethnic influences, professional training and daily exercise in speaking. Natural tendencies in speech are influenced by other voices and by what draws the best response from those to whom a person speaks. How speech is paced, its pauses and underlined phrases, sense of humor, anger, irony, despair, joy are all communicated by voice. People relate to each other through speech: As the father of daughters, I once read their relationships by how they spoke on the phone to young men.

We can hear those qualities of our personal voice in the lines we write as we plan and decide which ones should be emphasized and which should be de-emphasized.

THE DRAFT'S VOICE

Just as I have a voice, so does my draft and so do the fragments that will lead to the complete draft. Planning involves listening to possible voices in your head and your daybook, then choosing the voice appropriate to the subject and the audience. You draft a statement for a scholarship application in your head, but you continue listening and hear a whining voice that would turn anyone off; you discard the language. Then you hear the voice of a person so humble and lacking in confidence that the money would be wasted—that person doesn't have enough confidence to graduate. You try another, with confidence, but with so much confidence that the voice sounds arrogant. Then you tone it down and hear the kind of confident but not cocky person the committee would like to support, and you write the application in that voice.

THE REVEALING VOICE

As we plan, we hear ourselves speak from the page. How we say what we say often reveals the meaning of the draft. The voice tells us what is important—and that often surprises us. You write a psychology paper on alcoholism and its voice helps you realize how angry you are about your friend's drinking and how scared you are for him. Voice is a significant element in learning by writing.

REVISE THE PLAN

Planning is revision as its purest. The process allows you to abstract many possibilities and describe them simply so that they can be compared and evaluated.

As you make each plan, you are revising potential drafts, solving problems efficiently before they stop the writing of the draft. Many times the revised plan reveals that you need to go back and recast the whole piece—the subject, the genre, the audience are not what you thought they would be. When that happens, you usually have to check with the teacher or employer before you go on. The revised plan allows you to avoid a finished draft that does not meet the teacher or employer's assignment.

After consulting with your teacher or employer, you may produce a newly revised plan. That process is central to the process of writing. Writing is discovery, and each discovery modifies or develops a plan.

IN THE WRITER'S WORKSHOP

Has a drinking song ever been written by a drunken man? It is wrong to think that feeling is everything. In the arts, it is nothing without form. GUSTAVE FLAUBERT

By the time I sat down at the typewriter, I was writing a book quite unlike the one I had at first planned to write, because I was quite unlike the person who had first considered writing it. INGRID BENGIS

Planning to write is not writing. Outlining . . . researching, talking to people about what you're doing, none of that is writing. Writing is writing. E. L. DOCTOROW

I have a plan in my head, but I never write it down and I often diverge from it. Some writers put down a chapter by chapter analysis, but for me a novel is a kind of exploration of an unknown goal, so I allow myself to change direction quite frequently. There is usually a point about halfway through when I can see the rest of the plan. That's a really satisfying moment for me. I suspect one of the advantages of my method is the feeling of exhilaration towards the end. Those who plan in detail can become bored halfway through, because they know where everything is going. MARGARET DRABBLE

I think it is important to make a detailed plan before you write the first sentence. Some people think one should write—"George woke up and knew that something

terrible had happened yesterday"—and then see what happens. I plan the whole thing in detail before I begin. I have a general scheme and lots of notes. Every chapter is planned. Every conversation is planned. This is, of course, a primary stage, and very frightening because you've committed yourself at this point. I mean, a novel is a long job, and if you get it wrong at the start you are going to be very unhappy later on. The second stage is that one should sit quietly and let the thing invent itself. One piece of imagination leads to another. You think about a certain situation and then some quite extraordinary aspect of it suddenly appears. The deep things that the work is about declare themselves and connect. Somehow things fly together and generate other things, and characters invent other characters, as if they were all doing it themselves. One should be patient and extend this period as far as possible. IRIS MURDOCH

If you enter into language hopefully, trustfully, your faith will be rewarded. Language is always helping you, suggesting resources for the emergencies you meet. But you have to be ready to welcome the distortions of your original plan that language presents along the way. In that sense I'm a happy venturer into the distortions, if you like, of what language gives us. WILLIAM STAFFORD

As Nabakov said about Gogol: "He built the firm foundations for his books after he finished them." This is what I do. I pour it out and then organize it, then outline it, then structure it. After I've finished it. The structure's got to be there already. A bridge can't be held up by paint but you may discover the underlying structure worthwhile, as you go along. HERBERT GOLD

There are a number of established mystery writers who prefer not to use outlines. For someone starting out, however, I think the key to writing effectively (meaning salably) is having a good plot, and I think the key to a good plot is a good outline. I start thinking about a story the same way I used to conceptualize a lawsuit—by deciding where I wanted to be at the end of the case and backtracking from there. At the end of a lawsuit, I want the jury to come back in my client's favor. For that to happen, I have to present, in some coherent form, a sequence of events through witnesses and documents that will persuade the judge that the jury should get to decide the case. That means I have to backtrack conceptually from where the case will end to where it began (the intersection accident, the signing of the contract, whatever), recognizing along the way which people, places, and events I will need and want (there is a difference) to include.

I believe that it is best to structure a mystery novel the same way: Decide on your ending, then backtrack to decide who and what you include where, so that the story, run forward, will make sense and be entertaining. The beauty of this system is that your "backwards" outline forces you to think through each essential element of the puzzle in its logical place, so that you can then vary its position as deflection and masking of your mystery require. That same process will also save you substantial time overall, as you'll be wasting less effort creating well-wrought scenes that just don't "fit" your story. Also, if you have to squeeze your writing around full-time job or family commitments, the backtrack, elaborate outline, once completed, allows you to write the story forward in little segments, which will tend to be consistent with each other even though actually written some days or weeks apart. I know that some writers *believe that excessive outlining stultifies the imagination. I believe that a certain amount of imposed discipline allows one to have freedom.* JEREMIAH HEALY

After I've outlined a chapter and decided pretty much what material I want to go into it, what notes I want to refer to, I do a rough draft of it, and then I write and rewrite the same page over and over until I've got it as nearly right as I can get it. On a really good day I can turn out two pages at most. When I finish a chapter I scrub that up before I go on. It's a feeling of not wanting to build on shaky foundations. JUSTIN KAPLAN

I do not begin my novel at the beginning. I do not reach Chapter 3 before I reach Chapter 4. I do not go dutifully from one page to the next, in consecutive order; no, I pick out a bit here and a bit there, till I have filled all the gaps on paper. That is why I like writing my stories and novels on index cards, numbering them later, when my whole set is complete. Every card is rewritten many times. About three cards make one typewritten page, and when finally I feel that the conceived picture has been copied by me as faithfully as physically possible—a few vacant lots always remain, alas— then I dictate the novel. VLADIMIR NABOKOV

The work is with me when I wake up in the morning; it is with me while I eat my breakfast in bed and run through the newspaper, while I shave and bathe and dress. It is the coming day's work which is occupying my thoughts; the undemanding routine activities permit—encourage—my mind to work on the approaching difficulties, to solve the tactical problems which arise in the execution of the strategic plan. So, the day's work is clear, usually, in my mind as I stand screwing up my resolution to begin again. Then I find myself in my workroom, uncapping my fountain pen and pulling my pad towards me and glancing down the paragraphs written yesterday, and instantly I am swept away into composition. C. S. FORESTER

. . . [P]lanning it. That's ninety percent of the work—pacing the floor, thinking it out, the plot and the structure. The actual writing just takes two to three weeks. Writing it down for me is the easiest part. WOODY ALLEN

Follow the accident, fear the fixed plan—that is the rule. JOHN FOWLES

....

QUESTIONS ABOUT PLANNING

Doesn't planning take all the creativity out of writing? You talk about writing as an adventure! How about good old inspiration?

The idea of planning often brings to mind drudgery instead of play. But if you think about it, even child's play is planned: Hopscotch has an outline, a formula to it, and so does hide and seek. That doesn't mean that the game itself has to be dreary, or that there is no room for departure from plans or rules.

You get tricked into thinking that the planning stage is the ultimate bore if you see it as a rigid part of a lockstep process. But if you think of it as a stage you can always return to, then you won't get backed into a corner with your plan.

Planning is a way of exploring. Choose from the many different outline styles in this chapter or combine them. Make up your own outline. Draw pictures or cut out pieces of information and paste them on your plan. Do whatever you think is necessary to help you envision your final paper. If the plan doesn't work, go back and change it.

And don't be surprised if the plan inspires you to get going on your draft!

`Forget it; I can't write using an outline. Never could and never will. I freeze when I see one.`

If you can organize your paper without an outline, don't make one. Some people never use outlines, and others only do when they're faced with an unfamiliar writing task. Many writers let their pieces shape themselves and then impose structures on them. Do what you feel is best for you, but don't be afraid to experiment either.

`What if I have a teacher who wants me to stick to an outline when I want to change it after I begin writing?`

You may want to talk to your teacher about your new ideas. Have your new outline on hand for him or her to look at. If your teacher still insists that you stick to your original outline, then you will have to explore your topic within certain perimeters; these perimeters may not be what you would like, but they will still allow you to think and write critically about your topic.

Some teachers fear that if their students deviate from outlines, they will write papers that are disorganized and hard to read. These instructors are concerned that their students will not learn enough about their topics by writing this way. Another teacher might want you to discover very specific information about a topic and so ask you to adhere to a specific outline.

Whatever reasons your teacher has for requiring a strict outline, you can still explore within those restrictions. You can draw information from a variety of sources, experiment with point of view and angle, and choose a focus within the perimeters of the outline.

`How can I do all this planning when I've got to write the paper tonight?`

If you have an hour, take five or ten minutes to collect the information you will need to write. Take a few more minutes to be sure you have a focus, and then a few minutes to put the information in order. If you take ten minutes for each of those tasks, you'll only have invested half an hour. You'll have twenty minutes to write and ten minutes to check over what you've written. The planning will make your draft quicker, often longer, and better.

This kind of quick planning will come in handy when you have to write an essay answer to an exam question or fill out an application that requires long answers. If you have only a limited amount of time, don't give up on planning. Condense your writing process and put the time you have to good use.

```
I don't have any problem writing my paper once I get started, but
it takes me hours to come up with a good lead or opening. How can
I get beyond this?
```

By getting beyond it. Don't be a perfectionist with your openings. The process of writing will allow you to return to them later. Do what you need now to get going, even if you write an impossibly sappy, dry, or silly opening. Just plunge in and start to write. Put someone's name on it and start it as a letter, or write the closing before the beginning. Go with what works.

....

PLANNING ACTIVITIES

1. Jog, walk, swim. As you fall into the rhythm of your body's movements, think about the rhythm of your piece. Let words and lines unfold as you go. When you have finished, write your ideas down in your daybook. Don't be discouraged if they are incomplete concepts or half-finished leads and sentences; arrange them as potential headings for your paper's outline, and begin gathering information and details for each heading.

2. Draw a picture of your essay. Make it any shape you want, adding width where you want plenty of details and condensing where you want fewer details. Try drawing dark or jagged lines where you want your essay to reflect anger or other volatile feelings or soft, thin lines for more benign emotions. When you complete your drawing, write one sentence in each part of the sketch that sums up what you want each section of your essay to do.

3. Ask each member of a small group to adopt one of the outline plans in this chapter and begin to plan and draft an essay. Make sure no two students adopt the same one. Have each person distribute copies of his or her outline to the group and report on the successes or failures of following it. Ask each to select another outline form and repeat the activity.

4. Write a first draft without an outline. Give a copy of your draft to your writing partner and ask him or her to outline it in whatever fashion he or she wants. Then decide together what needs to be added to or omitted from the outline. Come up with a list of questions that you and your partner want your draft to answer, and then adjust your outline using these questions.

5. Brainstorm catchy subtitles and order them according to how you want to present information in your paper. When you have finished writing

your draft, keep your subtitles or remove them and insert sentences that connect the different sections of your essay.

6. Ask your writing partner or group to brainstorm questions about your topic and then select at least ten questions they want answered in order of importance or interest. Make an outline for your draft using these questions as major headings.

7. Before you go to bed, meditate quietly on your topic and envision the arrangement of your essay. Make sure you have a pad and pencil nearby, and when you have a flash of inspiration, scribble down a sentence or two to jog your memory in the morning. Allow yourself to sleep on your ideas, and then take fifteen minutes when you wake up to flesh out the details. Later, arrange your meditations in outline form.

8. Brainstorm sentences, fragments, and lines about your topic. Gather them together in your daybook in the form of a poem. Arrange and re-arrange them according to length, rhythm, kind of information they convey, tone, or voice. Then rearrange your poem into an outline, with each line functioning as a major heading.

9. Do a brainstorming map. Discuss with a writing partner the most inter-esting clusters that emerge on your map and circle them. Then think of a sentence that states the central topic or focus of each cluster. Under each sentence list as many related details as you can think of. Then arrange the sentences according to the order you want them to appear in your paper.

10. Make each member of your writing group responsible for gathering at least five titles from a particular kind of publication—a tabloid newspa-per, a regular daily newspaper, a popular magazine, a scholarly journal, or a literary magazine. Read your titles aloud to the group and explain to the class why they caught your eye and the kinds of stories or articles they announced. Discuss how the various titles change in mood and tone according to type of publication.

11. Gather with a group of classmates in a coffee shop or cafe that encour-ages hanging out. Talk shop. Discuss how each of you is planning to write a particular essay and offer suggestions or ask for help. "Steal" ideas liberally and contribute what you can. Ask questions, order more coffee, and talk some more. Don't underestimate the value of talk and commu-nication when you get stuck planning.

12. Watch a documentary on PBS, The Learning Channel, or The Discov-ery Channel. In your daybook sum up the major issues the documen-tary covers, and list as quickly as possible the information the director uses to illustrate each point. Notice how the show moves, in what order

the director addresses issues, how the documentary opens, how it segues from scene to scene, issue to issue, how it ends. When the show is over, make an outline of the documentary as you imagine the director planned it. What was the effect of this plan on the viewer? How would the documentary have changed if the director's plan had changed?

13. Use an e-mail partner or class pen pal as your planning board. Explain to your partner in as much detail as possible what you hope to achieve in your story or essay and how you are thinking of going about it. Ask your partner to suggest an outline for your story.

14. Think of the effect you want each section of your paper to have on your reader, then make a checklist of each part. Start with the words: "With this title I want my reader to . . ." ("become interested in what I have to say," "laugh," "expect to be surprised," "expect a serious piece," "take me seriously," etc.). Move through each section of the piece as you envision it, and anticipate the reader's response.

15. Go to a writer's bulletin board on the Internet. Scan the postings for advice on planning and outlining. Post a message asking for help in planning your piece, and explain what you want to do with it. Print out replies from other writers and paste them in your daybook. Refer to them as you draft and plan.

16. Pass out a draft to the class, and ask everyone to write a lead for it. Collect the leads and paste them into your daybook. Circle five styles you want to try, and write a paragraph telling why. You may choose one lead because it sets a reflective tone, or another because it introduces humor or irony to your paper. Being able to explain why you want to try a particular lead will help you plan the tone and voice of your essay and the angle you want to take. Return to your list later and experiment with other leads.

17. Most computers will let you locate a particular word as it is repeated throughout your text. As you enter bits and pieces of information and details for your draft, listen and look for words that repeat or that strike you as being important to your topic. Then run a word search, and when you find the pieces of text with the keywords in them, cut and paste to move these pieces around until they are organized under each keyword. Let these keywords be your outline headings. Organize the keywords and text according to the order you want them to appear in your draft.

18. Think of your paper as a tour route with each paragraph or section a stop along the way. You are the tour guide, and your readers are the tourists. Draw a picture of the route, and then write down what your

tourists can expect as they travel through your essay. Field questions from them about the details of each stop.

19. Write a story about a personally significant moment that begins in one of two ways: "It was the worst moment of my life," or "It was the best moment of my life." Then write ten different endings to the story that don't repeat or paraphrase the beginning. Let your readers walk away moved, provoked, or questioning. But don't placate them with a statement that ties things up neatly.

20. Write an unruly draft and go through it paragraph by paragraph, jotting a sentence or two in the margins of the paper summing up what each paragraph says. Read through your marginalia and see what points are repeated or rephrased in the paper. Use these as your major points for planning your paper.

21. Have an outlining fest. Choose an essay or story to read together as a class, and then have each class member draw up an outline for it, being as creative as he or she wishes. You may decide to use the outlining ideas in this chapter. Gather all outlines into a class binder for ideas on planning future essays.

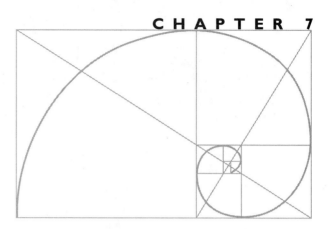

CHAPTER 7

DRAFT

Now—at last—write!

Begin to explore your topic with a discovery draft.

No matter how familiar you are with the subject, no matter how well you have thought about and researched the topic, no matter how well you have planned solutions to the problems in the draft, you will be surprised by what appears on the screen or the page.

The draft does not say what you expected. The first draft makes your argument stronger or weaker; it reveals a different problem or solution; it contradicts or deepens your previous beliefs; it reveals a new meaning or changes an old one; it speaks in an unexpected voice or grows into an unintended form. In these ways and others, the draft betrays the writer's intentions, and the inexperienced writer often believes that these surprises are failures.

Just the opposite. Writing is not thinking thunk, thought completed before the draft and transcribed to the page. Writing is thinking. As we think, our thoughts change. We use language to discover what we know, what it means, and how we feel about it.

A writer writes to see what the blank page reveals. Writers welcome—encourage, cultivate, even force—surprise, contradiction, the unexpected.

Wallace Stevens said, "The tongue is an eye." We speak, and we see what we did not see before. Words hold meaning still, sentences clarify and connect, paragraphs develop and place in context, all revealing an evolving meaning that is more than we planned. In writing, two and two add up to seven, eleven, twenty-three.

CULTIVATE SURPRISE

The three primary surprises you can hope to experience while writing a discovery draft are contraction, expansion, and connection.

CONTRACTION

Writing is, first of all, a narrowing down. Before we write, our ideas float like untethered balloons filled with possible meaning. Then we choose a word, connect it with another word and the meaning is captured and limited. We take the broad, horizonless, not-yet-thought and contract it so that it begins to have a specific meaning.

> It was a ~~beautiful, bright, sunny and warm~~ Saturday morning.
>
> It was a back-to-schooldays Saturday morning.
>
> *The rolling barrage of vague adjectives contracts to one evocative detail that should make readers remember lazy Saturdays when there was no school and they could lie abed.*

Written language—including the language of mathematics—is the most disciplined form of thinking. Words define. Words give thinking precision. Words connected with other words fence in a specific meaning.

In speech we can use words that are not quite on target but still convey meaning by qualifying them with tone, inflection, facial expression, gesture. The single words *school days* can mean happy, boring, childish, nostalgic, fearful, silly, hateful depending on the speaker's inflection, facial expression, gesture.

Writing is more difficult. You have to be understood across time and distance. The meaning has to be clear. "School days are happy memories to some, not to me. They were humiliating. We had to hold up one finger or two to indicate why we needed to go to the 'basement.' I can remember the long time before the hand on the clock clicked one minute. I remember failure in the classroom and being beaten up on the playground—'Wanta knuckle sandwich?'"

We write to capture meaning, to limit and qualify, to surprise ourselves by what happens when we control possibility.

EXPANSION

At the same time, writing expands meaning. We see possibilities we have not seen before. The defined examples above resonate with potential meaning the moment their meaning is limited. This seems a contradiction but it is not: The more specific we are, the more possibilities occur. The narrowed concept of a Saturday morning expands.

> It was a back-to-schooldays Saturday morning. Mr. Walsh was pushing the whirring lawn mower back and forth, back and forth. He watched the shadow of a maple leaf, the size of monster's hand, lazily wave back and forth across the wall. It was a kite flying day.

We begin to enter the Saturday world of the child in bed and his unexpected joy at a day of loneliness without having to deal with playmates. He will be free to wander the alleys and vacant lots with his imagination his only companion. He will be Long John Silver, a Native American chief, Robin Hood, King Arthur, Buck Rogers zooming around space with his shoulder rockets.

This is the view from the writer's desk. Each word, phrase, sentence, paragraph reveals potential. This assertion is just as true if the writer is publishing military history, ecological studies, merchandising programs, medical research, music criticism, screenplays. Writing leads to meaning.

CONNECTION

As you draft, especially if you write fast, you will create unexpected connections. The draft reveals surprising meanings.

> It was a back-to-schooldays Saturday morning. Mr. Walsh was pushing the whirring lawn mower back and forth, back and forth. He watched the shadow of a maple leaf, the size of monster's hand, lazily wave back and forth across the wall. It was a kite flying day.
>
> But he wouldn't be flying a kite. The grounding sound was not a lawn mower but his breathing machine, and the shadow was from his father, pacing back and forth by the hospital window.

Patterns of significant meaning develop from the connections of details that may come together accidentally in the flood of a first draft. The lazy weekend morning becomes something the writer and then the reader do not expect but the details make it true. Writing is thinking, and we think in patterns of meaning by making connections we did not see until we began to draft.

Those are just a few examples of the types of surprises you may experience if you are lucky enough to create a discovery draft in which you write more than you expect.

THE WRITE ATTITUDE

In sports, at work, in personal life, attitude controls what we do. If we expect failure, we experience failure; if we expect rejection, we receive rejection; if we think we will strike out, we will strike out. The attitude of the writer is a major factor in determining how well he or she writes.

In addition to a life attitude, each craft has its own peculiar required attitudes.

LOWER YOUR STANDARDS

Politicians and parents constantly call for higher standards in school, but in writing students have to lower their standards in the beginning. It is important to repeat the advice I carry with me every day, the counsel I have to remember every time I write a first draft, comes from poet William Stafford:

I believe that the so-called "writing block" is a product of some kind of dispro-portion between your standards and your performance. . . . One should lower his standards until there is no felt threshold to go over in writing. It's *easy* to write. You just shouldn't have standards that inhibit you from writing.

• • •

I can imagine a person beginning to feel he's not able to write up to that standard he imagines the world has set for him. But to me that's surrealistic. The only standard I can rationally have is the standard I'm meeting right now. . . . You should be more willing to forgive yourself. It doesn't make any difference if you are good or bad today. The assessment of the product is something that happens after you've done it.

Copy this quote. Put it over your desk, as I have. Add to it the wisdom of the master nonfiction writer, John Jerome: "Perfect is the enemy of good."

WRITE BADLY TO WRITE WELL

The only truly failed draft is a blank page. My closest writing friend, Chip Scan-lan, to whom I always turn when I'm stuck, reminds me that we have to "write badly to write well." When I start to write, I want a final draft first, but that isn't possible; it isn't even desirable. It would mean I was trying to pawn off a preowned piece of thinking as an original. Slick, glib writing should not be the goal; I should be seeking writing that is turning up unexpected, undeveloped meanings. My early drafts should be filled with accident, awkwardness, possibility, potential.

When building, reconstructing, or painting a house, the workers have to erect a jumble of ladders and levels on which they can stand. This scaffolding is essential to the building of the house, but it is not the house itself.

As I writer I have to construct drafts that are not the final draft. They help me build the house of prose or poetry. They are essential tools, but after I am through I take them down and the reader never sees them. As I work on the scaffolding, I have to remind myself that the false starts, clumsy sentences, undeveloped para-graphs, false trails, wrong words, mistakes in syntax and spelling are all scaffold-ing that will be taken down in the revision and editing process. Now I have to build the house.

REMEMBER THAT A DRAFT IS AN EXPLORATION

You do not know what you want to say when you begin a first draft, and therefore you do not know how to say it. Content predicts technique. In a first draft I write to discover what I have to say. There will be other drafts before the final one. I will have time to re-develop, refine, shape, revise, edit. All writing is an experiment in meaning—and most experiments fail.

Study what attitudes you had when writing went well. Hold to those atti-tudes and develop them so that it becomes easy to write.

....

TECHNIQUES TO WRITE A DISCOVERY DRAFT

The draft will lead you toward meaning—if you let your prose run.

WRITE TOO FAST

There's no highway speed limit on writing. To make a baseball curve, to balance on a bicycle, to a save a person suffering a heart attack, speed is essential. Velocity is vital also for discovery draft writing.

It is speed that enables the writer to outrun the internal censor and write what the writer does not expect; it is speed that causes the instructive failures essential to effective writing. Each failure shows what it may be possible to say and how it may be possible to say it. As in scientific discoveries, laboratory errors lead us forward.

WRITE TOO MUCH

Most beginning writers underwrite. They assume the reader will have the same amount of knowledge about a subject—and the same concern for the subject—they do. It is better to overwrite, to turn out a draft that has an abundance of revealing detail. Effective writing is built from concrete, accurate information. Too many beginning writers think that writing is made with words and literary flourishes that are detached from meaning. Good writing is not a collection of colorful balloons that bob aimlessly against the ceiling. Good writing—poetry as much as nonfiction—delivers information to the reader.

While drafting, the writer should be conscious of the information that is being delivered to the reader, and the writer should try to make that information as abundant and specific as possible. Words, after all, are symbols for information. Words that have no information behind them are as valuable as checks drawn on an account with no money in it. Readers hunger for information, and the writer should satisfy this hunger by constructing a piece of writing with solid chunks of information.

DEVELOP

Don't jam all the information you have into a short paper. That produces the garbage compactor draft. All the information is jammed together into a tiny, unreadable block.

Brevity is achieved not by compression so much as by selection. The writer has to select the information the reader needs and then develop it properly. Each anecdote, definition, argument, description—whatever needs to be said—has to be set up and developed adequately so that the reader can experience that part of the story at an appropriate pace, a pace that will allow the reader to absorb the information.

DOCUMENT

Document each point you make. The reader needs evidence to support each point. Sometimes a statement can be so specific that it carries its own evidence within it, but most times a statement needs to be backed up with an example, a statistic, a quotation, a reference to authority that will convince the reader.

Unfortunately, most people write with the evidence they feel most comfortable using. One writer always reinforces a point with a quotation from an authority; another salts the page with statistics; a third backs up each assertion with an anecdote; still another writer will walk on stage and use an *I* to speak directly to the audience. Watch out that you don't always choose the same form of evidence; instead, use the form of documentation that will most effectively persuade the reader.

WRITE INSIDE THE DRAFT

Each writer comes to the writing desk full of myth and legend, instruction and admonition, tradition and rules crowding the brain. The writer has to put all that aside and enter into the draft. Of course, a writer's experiential history and scholarly knowledge of tradition exists, but it must be drawn on subconsciously, in response to the problems of the draft.

People who do not write believe that writing flows magically from some inherited skill called *talent,* or, at the other extreme, they imagine that a piece of writing is constructed, brick by brick, from some blueprint. The truth is, the writer's craft is different. The draft grows organically from within itself. The author writes a few words and that leads to a sentence. The writer listens to the sentence, and it demands another sentence to define the meaning of the first one. Then the defining sentence needs one that clarifies it, and soon the writer has a paragraph, a block of meaning, that has to be placed in context. The writer listens and responds to the instruction of the draft, line by line. This process sounds complicated but it is usually quite easy, a natural process.

The writing of the draft proceeds paragraph by paragraph, each unit of writing telling the writer what must come next, if the writer listens to the draft. Let me show you what I mean by revealing the instruction from the draft I received when writing an essay published in the *Boston Globe.* I began with description:

> August is the month when ~~many of us~~ we receive our children and grandchildren back from summer camp tanned, ~~scraped~~ scabbed [?], and ~~strange~~ a bit unfamiliar.
>
> > *I changed "many of us" to "we" because it was shorter; I saved two words. I kept "receive" because it had an echo of the ceremonial and "grandchildren" because the column I write is primarily for those over sixty years old. I changed "scraped" to "scabbed" because it is more accurate, but I stuck in a*

question mark so I'll consider whether it is too strong a word on a second reading.

"Strange" gave me the important idea at the end of the paragraph but it seemed too strong, as if the camper returned from Mars, so I spent the two words I had saved earlier and made it "a bit unfamiliar." The surprise of unfamiliar comes at the end of the paragraph, the point of greatest emphasis.

My instruction from the draft came here: Write the next paragraph to find out what was unfamiliar and what that idea implied. I wrote within the draft, concentrating on that single issue of unfamiliarity.

We wanted them to begin the exodus from the nest—and we may have wanted some privacy in the nest—but we know they have lived a life we will never really know and that in surviving homesickness they may even suffer a bit of return-homesickness.

The next paragraph will grow from my reading of this one. Why did we send them off, and what might it mean? What if they like life away from home better? I am simply following meaning, picking up the clues in one paragraph and developing them in the next. I like the clause "and we may have . . ." that runs against the grain of the text. Now the reader asks, "What do you mean 'return-homesickness?'" and I answer, because a draft is a conversation with the reader. I have to anticipate and answer the reader's questions during the draft.

I did. After nine weeks at Camp Morgan in Washington, New Hampshire, I dreaded the return from the woods to my city home, to a family I did not understand, ~~and~~ to school [?].

After a quick transition, in the third paragraph—maybe I should have done it earlier but I have to do it here—I anchor the piece to a specific place and then answer the reader's question: Why did you dread the return home? I dropped the "and" because of the music of the paragraph, but I wondered if the last words would seem too abrupt so I bracketed the question mark, a reminder to answer that question later.

Camp was not easy, in fact my experiences at summer camp ~~made~~ prepared me for basic training and paratroop school not so many years in the future. But camp made me realize I could survive on my own in an alien and often terrifying world.

A new idea: Camp was not easy. The expected view is that all campers are happy. Here I tell what summer camp prepared me for—another unexpected answer—war. The next paragraph must answer the question: What terrified me?

~~There were~~ I entered a world of strange boys, spiders, snakes, weird food, woods in which I could get lost, a lake in which I could drown.

I did not want to begin with those dead words "there were," so I find another way to start. I use specifics, and in putting the most terrifying element at the point of emphasis—the end—I create a sketch map or out-line of the next part of the essay, although I do not realize it at the time. The list proceeds from the relatively trivial "strange boys" to the possibility of death, "drown."

[An only child,] I learned to survive in the cruel world of boys, to commit [the] sins of omission, to laugh at what I did not understand, to wear masks that hid my feelings, to become a boy-man.

I started without "an only child" but I go back and add these words, be-cause they set up the situation as it was in my life. I was generally more comfortable with grown-ups than with kids my own age. But now I am surprised, and I write in the hope of such surprises. Remember, I write without knowing what I am going to say—I am thinking in writing. A new thought has arrived on the page: that part of growing up, of losing inno-cence, is hiding your feelings, a sad but necessary stage of maturity. Such surprises of thought keep me writing. I did not know until I wrote this essay that I had received an education at camp in corporate male behavior.

My graduate degree in the hiding of feelings came ~~when~~ the summer I found I would be in the same tent with a boy who kept snakes. I was—and am—terri-fied of snakes (Freudians may make whatever they want of that), but I slept on the cot next to him [and his tangle of snakes] for sixty-three nights and he never knew ~~it~~ my fear.

I hear the reader asking for more documentation, and I provide it. I tell the anecdote of the snakes, but now it is in a context that makes it signifi-cant—I do not let the snake-boy know my fear, just as I will not let my boss know that I think his new organizational plan will replace confusion with chaos.

I also know the liveliness that results from specifics—sixty-three nights is more dramatic than nine weeks. I also feel free to interrupt the text with the Freudian remark, which reminds the reader that an old man is looking back at his camp experience. The reader's point of view is at the side of the old man.

In all such articles, I am trying to write with the ease of a real conver-sation and the efficiency of an imagined one. The meaning of the piece is in the reflective voice of the writer, who is looking back from a distance with good humor and some surprise.

In the last reading I change the rather free floating "it" at the end of the paragraph to the more specific "my fear."

~~Scholarship boy and had a small taste. . . .~~

When something occurs to me as I draft that I may want to mention, I make an immediate note within the draft, the way an explorer marks a map, recording a hill or a bay that may be visited later. In writing this column, I was aware that many children cannot afford to go to camp, and I want to

tell everyone I was at camp on scholarship. I cross out this information, be-
cause it does not move the essay forward.

Before I went to camp I had three times almost drownded, as we said, could
not swim, and was terrified of water above my ankles. Family home movies
celebrated my shame each Christmas.

> *I'm a bad typist, and many times my typos lead to good writing. I mistyped*
> *"drowned" as "drownded"; I realize this was just the word I would have*
> *used at camp, so I kept it.*
>
> *In writing this paragraph, I'm following the map created earlier, when*
> *drowning was at the point of emphasis in the paragraph and I set up my*
> *fear of the water. My embarrassment or shame is introduced by the men-*
> *tion of home movies. These things are not thought up; they arrive on their*
> *own energy.*

One of my ~~most powerful~~ strongest memories of camp was ~~sitting high in the~~
~~woods~~ hiding in the KYBO—Keep Your Bowels Open—during Beginner's
Swim and hearing the hated, cheery sounds of boys having fun echoing off
the lake.

> *"Strongest" saves a word; "hiding" saves several. "KYBO" and its transla-*
> *tion help establish the male, juvenile, bathroom humor of the environment*
> *where no one would be sympathetic to a kid scared of the water. My alien-*
> *ation and loneliness is, of course, a subtheme that is flowing strongly*
> *through the piece.*

But I did learn to swim ~~over my head~~ IN WATER OVER MY HEAD, to mess
funny food around on my plate so it looked eaten, to accept the punishments
I then thought painful and now think cruel and perverse—knuckle punches on
the arms from college football players, naked parades in front of camp administrators—and survive.

> *I change the original to "IN WATER OVER MY HEAD" in caps to capture a*
> *hint of how a young boy would say it. I skip by all the difficulty I had learn-*
> *ing to swim, ease off with the food, then find myself mentioning the pun-*
> *ishments that were "cruel and perverse."*
>
> *Chekhov said, "If in the first chapter you say that a gun hung on the wall,*
> *in the second or third chapter it must without fail be discharged." If I mention*
> *"cruel and perverse" punishments, I must document such a strong charge im-*
> *mediately. I insert examples of each right in the middle of the sentence where*
> *the reader needs the information. At this point, I stop and do a word count*
> *on my computer: 389. Like the explorer, I need to know how far I have come*
> *and how much further I have to go within the target limit of 800 words.*

My memories of summer camp after more than fifty years [end? wonder
about kids coming home this month] surprise me. I am nostalgic for those
four summers on Melon [check] Pond~~, grateful~~.

> *It was NOT Melon Pond but Millen Pond.*

I look back with a longing for evening on the lake, the feel of a canoe riding in the water, the lone bugle playing taps at lights out, waking before the others in blankets ~~pinned~~ held together with giant safety pins on Blueberry Hill and seeing the valleys hidden by rivers of mist.

> *I describe what I remember and then, in the next paragraph, return to what I would have expected. In a final reading, I add "for another" before "evening."*

I would have expected memories of companionship, stories around a campfire, even memories of practical jokes, perhaps the morning I woke ~~to find myself~~ nose to nose with the camp goat my tent mates had tucked into bed with me.

> *I catalogue what I learned and, in writing that list, I categorize them at the end. I also like to inject a little humor in a text that's growing serious. It gives the reader a little room and makes the texture of the essay a bit richer. I also find I put a touch of the serious into humorous columns for the same reasons.*

I was an only child who learned to live with boys my own age, to think of others than myself, to accept a world that was not designed to my needs, to make friends of strangers, but my best memories are of those times when I was alone.

> *The last paragraph tells me what the next one will be—my best memories. I am struck in reading these notes made during writing how easy the writing is, one paragraph grows simply and naturally out of the other. Now I must describe the best memories.*

Those were the magic moments when I scouted far ahead in the woods, was allowed to take out a canoe alone, when I spent a day exploring the Asheulot River, when I fell behind the pack and accepted my need for the loneliness I had always been made to feel was wrong, somehow un-American by the parents, teachers, and ministers I tried so hard to please.

> *Specifics usually reveal meaning. I have discovered—in the fourteenth paragraph—the meaning of the essay in the words "accepted my need for the loneliness." But in discussing this acceptance, I have to put the need into the context of a culture that resists aloneness, denies the solitary life. In the last reading, I add "blueberrying" before "pack" to make it more specific.*
> *Now I wind up the essay with a statement of what camp taught me:*

Summer camp gave me the ability to swim underwater, ~~the skill of hiding my true feelings, and the acceptance of a strange secret,~~ taught me how to get along with others—live a public life—but it also allowed me to accept my secret—that I often was my own best companion.

> *Then I have to tie the ending back to the beginning. I struggle a bit, cut out lines that don't work for me, are not pointed enough, have been said before. In the last reading I add "too" before "public life" for musical reasons—it seemed to sound better.*

I watch today's campers return lugging strangely sewn leather billfolds, bent hawk feathers, bags of ~~dirty filthy~~ stinky laundry and wonder what they will remember—and treasure—when they are over sixty.

> *I saw children returning from summer camp and felt powerful emotions I could not name or describe. I wrote to name and understand them, and, traveling within the landscape of the draft, I found those emotions and what they meant. In going back through this piece for you, I was struck by how easy and natural the trip was. One thing—literally—did lead to another. Each paragraph predicted the next paragraph.*

I need to know the traditions of my craft, need to hear what other writers, my teachers, and my editors tell me, but I need to shut all that off at the moment of drafting and concentrate all my attention on what is happening at this moment in the draft, solving the problem of the following sentence. I travel light, making the journey a step at a time, rarely looking far ahead or behind, dealing with the situation underfoot. The traditions of language and rhetoric are implied, and all the work is performed in the unraveling context. I don't want to see in this landscape what has been seen in others but to see it anew, with little prediction or intent.

....

DRAFT LAYER BY LAYER

A writer may fear saying too much or know the subject so well that he or she imagines a few general words will give the reader the same full vision they spark in the writer; that person will end up producing copy that is superficial, thin, and undeveloped. Another reason for undeveloped writing is that writing doesn't usually come all at once. It often comes in spurts: Writing produces more writing. I do not know what I will write or how I will write it until I draft. Then the evolving draft instructs me, telling me what I have to say and hinting at how I may say it. With this developing insight comes an increasing awareness of audience; I write in the beginning for myself and later for others.

One technique I use to avoid undeveloped pieces is to layer my writing. Once I did quite a bit of oil painting, and my pictures were built up, layer after layer of paint, until the scene was revealed to me and a viewer. I've been writing each chapter of some of my books, articles, and poems the same way, starting each day at the beginning of yesterday's draft, reading and writing until my daily stint is finished. Each day I lay down a new layer of writing, and when I read it the next day, the new layer reveals more possibility.

There is no one way for writing to develop. As I layer, I may start with a sketch, other times the first writing feels complete. (The next day's reading usually shows it is not.) Sometimes I race ahead through the draft; other times each paragraph is honed before I go on to the next one. I try to allow the draft to tell me what it needs.

I start reading, and when I see—or, more likely, hear—something that needs doing, I do it. One day I'll read through all the written text and move it forward from the last day's writing; another time I'll find myself working on dialogue; the next day I may begin to construct a new scene or argument; one time I'll stumble into a new discovery and later have to set it up or weave references to it through the text; I may build up background description, develop the conflict, make the reader see a character more clearly; I may present more documentation, evidence, or exposition or hide it in a character's dialogue or action.

Layering is ideally suited for writing on the computer, as it is easy to write over what you have written, but it can be done with typewriter or pen and paper as well. Part of the technique involves developing inserts that can be written or pasted within sentences or paragraphs, between paragraphs or sections, at the end, in the middle, or even before the beginning. Remember there are no rules; the draft leads and you follow.

The best way I know to get the feel of layering is to write a paragraph—perhaps of description—then to start again on a new page and write it again without reading the first one or, at least, only reading it loosely. Write easily. Relax. Let the draft lead. Then do it a third time, a fourth, perhaps a fifth. Does that mean you should always do it five times? No. The draft may call for three layers—or seventeen. Let me demonstrate and comment as I do:

Layer 1

When I think of North Quincy High School, I think of corridors more than classrooms. I expect to think of classrooms. Say elementary school, and I think of the huge classroom clocks with roman numerals and waiting for the last clicks in the afternoon. Three minutes. Two. One. Escape.

I start by writing down my first thoughts about high school.

Layer 2

North Quincy High School. Not classrooms but corridors jammed with the hourly flood of teenagers. Beer jackets and saddle shoes, letter sweaters and girls with mysterious blooming sweaters. Sweater girls. Shouts and laughter, "swell" and "neat," the harsh, ugly south-of-Boston accent and the fastracingyankeetalk, the slamming of locker doors and the bells summoning the prisoners for lock up.

I try to get into the text faster and, most of all, to develop the scene in my mind, to flesh it out with detail.

Layer 3

I heard myself say, "Everybody's alienated in high school" and was surprised I saw North Quincy High School and long, empty corridors.

I got into it slower so I could put it in context.

I would have expected to remember classrooms, hours that felt like whole lifetimes, clocks with huge roman numerals with hours between the click of the minute hand, teacher voices that used sarcasm like the flicking end of a bull whip.

> *I transposed the material from elementary school. We had the same clocks in high school, and I waited for their clicks with the same desperation.*

Or the flood of students between classes, beer jackets and sweater girls, "swell" and "neat," the slam of locker doors, peanut butter and jelly sandwiches, the perfume of sneakers and gym shorts.

> *I added detail, paced it a bit differently. All this detail I hoped would take me back to high school and lead me to meaning.*

But what I remember, with something close to nostalgia, is the long, empty corridors with the classroom doors closed.

> *I develop the key image, the picture that haunts my memory.*

Layer 4

We were talking about high school the other night, and I heard myself say, "Everybody's alienated in high school." I was surprised I saw North Quincy High School—long, empty corridors—and felt something that felt like nostalgia. High school was not a good time for me. I dropped out twice and flunked out at the end. I would have expected anger, perhaps bitterness, even embarrassment, not nostalgia.

> *In the previous paragraph and the following one, I continue to develop with more detail, setting up the situation in the first paragraph, revealing the world of the school in the second.*

I would have expected to remember classrooms, hours that felt like whole lifetimes, lectures on physics or algebra in which I lost any sense of meaning, clocks with huge roman numerals with hours passing between the click of the minute hand, teacher voices that used sarcasm like the flicking end of a bull whip. Or the flood of students between classes, beer jackets and sweater girls, "swell" and "neat," the slam of locker doors, peanut butter and jelly sandwiches, the perfume of sneakers and gym shorts. But what I remember, with something close to nostalgia, is the long, empty corridors with the classroom doors closed.

The floors gleamed with wax and the green locker doors were silent. The walls, I think, were stucco, and light fixtures hung from the ceiling. Inside the glass doors of the classrooms, I saw the tired gestures of the teachers and numbed faces of the students, faces that seemed drugged by information they did not want to know and would never understand.

> *Now I have placed myself—and, therefore, the reader—in the lonely corridor. As I distance myself from those locked into the classrooms, teachers*

and students alike, I am unknowingly taking a big step toward the meaning the next layer of text will reveal.

Layer 5

My wife and daughters and I were talking about high school the other evening—none of us wanted to return—and we laughed at someone who was still angry at being unappreciated and alienated in high school. I heard myself say, "Everybody's alienated in high school." As I spoke, I was carried back to North Quincy High School, with its long, empty corridors, and something that felt like nostalgia.

> *In the first paragraph I am extending the context a bit, setting the scene more completely. In these first paragraphs I am instinctively establishing mood, tone, pace; tuning my language to the evolving voice of the piece that will reveal meaning to me and will reveal and support meaning to the reader.*

I was surprised. I have never felt nostalgic about high school before. It was not a good time for me. I won no letters, retained a virtue I desperately wanted to lose, dropped out twice, and flunked out at the end. I would have expected anger, perhaps bitterness, even shame, not nostalgia.

And I would have expected to remember classrooms, those educational cells to which I had been sentenced for hours that felt like whole lifetimes, lectures on physics or algebra in which I lost any sense of meaning, clocks with huge roman numerals with hours passing between clicks of the minute hand, teacher voices that used sarcasm like the flicking end of a bull whip. Or the flood of students between classes, beer jackets and sweater girls, "swell" and "neat," the slam of locker doors, peanut butter and jelly sandwiches, the perfume of sneakers and gym shorts. But what I remember, with something close to nostalgia, is the long, empty corridors with the classroom doors closed.

The floors gleamed with wax, and the green locker doors were silent. The walls, I think, were stucco, and orange-bulbed light fixtures hung from the ceiling. Inside the glass doors of the classrooms, I saw the tired gestures of the teachers and numbed faces of the students, faces that seemed drugged by information they did not want to know and would never understand. And I was alone in the corridor. I had escaped.

With the word escape, the text has revealed its meaning to me.

Of course, I remember those corridors with nostalgia. Just the other day I found stacks of forged corridor passes, stored away in case I returned to high school. I worked on the newspaper and the yearbook; I learned the system and then how to work it. I escaped home room and study hall, sometimes even class. I possessed the loneliness I had learned at home and the delicious egotism of alienation. I was an outsider, a writer before I knew I would become a writer, an almost man with forged corridor passes, documentation that I could escape high school, learn new systems and how, as a loner, to manipulate them. Those aged slips of paper were, I now realize, my diploma, and oh how I have used that education in the years since, walking so many corridors by myself, alienated and smug.

In the last paragraph I have explored, developed, examined, and extended the meaning I discovered, playing with it, turning it over, moving back to the slips, seeing their significance, delighting myself with the surprise of "smug," which gives me an insight about my lifetime of proud alienation. I have maintained the private illusion and arrogance of alienation even when I have earned awards, promotions, titles, tenure. I suppose that I am smugly alienated, secretly feeling superior to those around me. Too true, at times, but not all the time, I hope. This writing I did just to document a point has put me on the analyst's couch, revealed myself, and made me squirm; it has made me feel that I deserve a couple of good squirms.

In reading over all this, I am struck by my patience. Once, I would have wanted to know the meaning right away—or even thought I should have known the meaning before I wrote the first word. I would have sought meaning, panted after it. Now I am patient—and confident. Experience has taught me that if I keep writing, meaning will come. I will not think meaning. I will watch meaning arise from my page. The painter William de Kooning once said, "I can't paint a tree but I can find a tree in my work," and Pablo Picasso testified, "To know what you want to draw, you have to begin drawing. If it turns out to be a man, I draw a man. If it turns out to be a woman, I draw a woman." They are patient, and I have learned patience as well. I have learned that I have learned it by rereading these drafts.

That was fun—and totally unexpected. The conversation took place and the image of the empty corridors came to mind, but I didn't begin to understand them until I completed this hour of layering, putting down text on top of text, revising to produce a first draft.

You will see other things I have done—good or bad—or should have done. You may make your own discoveries, comfortable and uncomfortable, as you live through my drafts. Mark them all down on my draft; try the same thing on yours.

What will I do with Layer 5? I don't know. Play with it perhaps. See if it grows into a column or a short story. It may pop up in the novel I'm drafting or turn into an academic article on layering, maybe even shrink to become a poem. Most likely it will remain what it is, a piece of writing that was fun to do because it captured an important part of my life and allowed me to examine it and come to some understanding I did not have before.

DRAFT UNIT BY UNIT

The third principal way that I draft is by units. This is the best way for me to write long reports, term papers, or nonfiction books that are not narratives or single, long stories.

As I mentioned in the last chapter during the discussion on outlines, when I'm writing a book, I write the chapter heads first, then the primary subheads for each section, then the heads for the sections within the sections. Then I draft individual subsections, either in sequence or as they're ready to be written, creating the book as you would create a mosaic, block by block.

Of course, I may move the blocks around, leave some out and add new ones as I write the draft and discover what the reader needs.

TWENTY-SIX TREATMENTS
FOR WRITER'S BLOCK

It never gets easier to write. All writers are masters of avoidance. If interruptions don't occur, writers create them. They make phone calls, travel far on unnecessary errands, cut wood in July, buy snow shovels in August. When it is time to write, writers read, attack the correspondence and the filing, sharpen pencils, buy new pens, change typewriter ribbons, shop for word processors, make coffee, make tea, rearrange the furniture in the office. When writers get together, they share, often shamefaced, new ways to avoid writing.

But some of that avoidance is good. E. B. White reminds us, "Delay is natural to a writer. He is like a surfer—he bides his time, waits for the perfect wave on which to ride in. Delay is instinctive with him." This waiting is purposeful, for most writers discover that starting a draft prematurely causes a total collapse three, five, or seven pages along, and it's harder to repair a train wreck of a draft than to start one along the right track.

Writers, of course, being writers, are never sure whether they are allowing their subjects to ripen properly or are just being lazy. This waiting is often the worst part of writing. It is filled with guilt and doubt, yet it is essential.

Then comes the time—often commanded by the deadline—when there can be no more delay, when the writing must be done. Here are some ways to overcome inertia and start writing:

1. *Nulla dies sine linea.* "Never a day without a line." Make writing a habit. Sit in the same place with the same tools every day and write until it becomes uncomfortable *not* to write. Then writing will come as a matter of course.

2. *Make believe you are writing a letter to a friend.* Put "Dear _____" at the top of the page and start writing. Tom Wolfe did this on one of his first New Journalism pieces. He wrote the editor a letter saying why he couldn't write the piece he'd been assigned. The letter flowed along in such a wonderful, easy fashion that the editor took the salutation off and ran it. It established a new style for contemporary journalism.

3. *Switch your writing tools.* If you normally type, write by hand. If you write by hand, type. Switch from pen to pencil or pencil to pen. Switch from unlined paper to lined paper, or vice versa. Try larger paper or smaller, colored paper or white paper. Use a bound notebook or spiral notebook, a legal pad or a clipboard. Tools are a writer's toys, and effective, easy writing is the product of play.

4. *Talk about the piece of writing with another writer, and pay close attention to what you say.* You may be telling yourself how to write the piece. You may even want to make notes as you talk on the telephone or in person. Pay attention to words or combinations of words that may become a voice and spark a piece of writing.

5. *Write down the reasons you are not writing.* Often when you see the problem you will be able to avoid it. You may realize that your standards are too high, or that you're thinking excessively of how one person will respond to your piece, or that you're trying to include too much. Once you have defined the problem, you may be able to dispose of it.

6. *Describe the process you went through when a piece of writing went well.* You may be able to read such an account in your journal. We need to reinforce the writing procedures that produce good writing. A description of what worked before may tell you that you need to delay at this moment, or it may reveal a trick that got you going another time. Keep a careful record of your work habits and the tricks of your trade, so that you have a positive resource to fall back on.

7. *Interview other writers to find out how they get started.* Try your classmates' tricks and see if they work for you.

8. *Switch the time of day.* Sometimes writing at night when you are tired lowers your critical sense in a positive way, and other times you can jump out of bed in the morning and get a start on the writing before your internal critic catches up with you.

9. *Call the draft an experiment or an exercise.* Good writing is always an experiment. Make a run at it. See if it will work. The poet Mekeel McBride is always writing "exercises" in her journals. Since they are just exercises and not poems, she doesn't get uptight about them, but of course if an exercise turns into a poem, she accepts it.

10. *Dictate a draft.* Use a tape recorder, and then transcribe the draft from it. You may want to transcribe it carefully, or just catch the gist of what you had to say. No matter how experienced you are as a writer, you are a million times more experienced as a speaker, and it's often easier to get started writing by talking than by simply writing.

11. *Quit.* Come back later and try again. You can't force writing. You have to keep making runs at it. Come back ten minutes later, or later that day,

or the next day. Keep trying until the writing flows so fast you have to run along behind it trying to keep up.

12. *Read.* Some writers read over what they've written, and they may even edit it or recopy it as a way of sliding into the day's writing. I can't do that; I despair too much, and when I read my own writing I feel I have to start over again; it's worthless, hopeless. If you don't feel that way, however, it may be a good device to go over the previous day's work and then push on to the new writing, the way a house painter paints back into the last brush stroke and then draw the new paint forward.

13. *Write directly to a specific reader.* The too-critical reader can keep you from writing, but you can also get writing by imagining an especially apprecia-tive reader, or a reader who needs the information you have to convey. If you can feel that reader's hunger for what you have to say, it will draw you into the text. Sometimes when I write, I imagine the enjoyment I expect Don Graves, Chip Scanlan, or Nancie Atwell to feel at an unexpected turn of phrase, a new insight, or a different approach. I read their faces as I write the way you read a friend's face during a conversation.

14. *Take a walk, lift weights, jog, run, dance, swim.* Many writers have found that the best way to get started writing is by getting the blood coursing through the body and the brain. As they get the physical body tuned up, the brain moves into high gear. Exercise is also the kind of private activ-ity that allows the mind to free itself of stress and interruption and re-hearse what may be written when the exercise is done. Running, walking, bicycling, or swimming are great ways to let the mind wander while the body is working.

15. *Change the place where you write.* I write in my office at home, but I also write on a lap desk in the living room or on the porch. I like to take the car and drive down by Great Bay, where I can look up from my lap desk and watch a heron stalk fish or a seagull soar—the way I would like to write, without effort. Some writers cover their windows and write to a wall. I like to write to a different scene. Right now, for example, I'm looking at the green ocean of Indiana farmland and a marvelously angry gray sky as I drive west and write by dictation. In the 1920s writers thought the cafes of Paris were the best places to write. I don't think I could work on those silly little tables, but my ideal writing place would be in a booth in a busy lunchroom where nobody knows me. Yesterday morning I started writing in a Denny's in a city in Michigan; it was a fine place to write. When my writing doesn't go well, I move around. I imag-ine that the muse is looking for me, and if she can't find me at home I'll go out somewhere where I may be more visible.

16. *Draw a picture, in your mind or on paper.* Take a photograph. Cut a pic-ture from a magazine and put it on your bulletin board. When small

children start writing, they usually first draw pictures. They do on paper what writers usually do in their minds—they visualize their subjects. Last summer I started my writing sessions by making a sketch of a rubber tree that stands on our porch. I wasn't writing about the rubber tree, but the activity of drawing seemed to help me get started and stimulate the flow of writing.

17. *Free write.* Write as hard and as fast and as free as you can. See if language will lead you toward a meaning. As I have said before, free writing isn't very free, for the draft starts to develop its own form and direction. But the act of writing freely is one of the techniques that can unleash your mind.

18. *Stop in the middle of a sentence.* This is a good trick when the writing is going well and you are interrupted or come to the end of the day's writing during a long project. Many well-known writers have done this, and I've found that it really helps me at times. If I can pick up the draft and finish an ordinary sentence, then I am immediately back into the writing. If I've stopped at the end of a sentence or a paragraph it's much harder to get going. If I've stopped at the end of a chapter, it may take days or weeks to get the next one started.

19. *Write the easy parts first.* If you're stuck on a section or a beginning, skip over it and write the parts of the draft that you are ready to write. Once you've got those easy, strong pieces of writing done, then you'll be able to build a complete draft by connecting those parts. A variation on this technique is to write the end first, or to plunge in and grab the beast wherever you can get hold of it. Once you have a working draft, you can extend it backward or forward as it requires.

20. *Be silly.* You're not writing anyway, so you might as well make a fool of yourself. I've numbered the day's quota of pages and then filled them in. One of my writer neighbors loves cigars, but he won't let himself have a cigar until he has finished his daily quota. Reward yourself with a cup of coffee or a dish of ice cream or a handful of nuts. It is no accident that some writers are fat; they keep rewarding themselves with food. Do whatever you have to do to keep yourself writing. Jessamyn West writes in bed the first thing in the morning. If the doorbell rings she can't answer it; she isn't up and dressed. Use timers, count pages, count words. (You may not be able to say the writing went well, but you'll be able to say "I did 512 words," or "I completed two pages.") Play music, or write standing up. (Thomas Wolfe wrote on top of an icebox, and Ernest Hemingway put his typewriter on a bureau.) Start the day writing in the bathtub as Nabokov did. Nothing is too silly if it gets you started writing.

21. *Start the writing day by reading writing that inspires you.* This is dangerous for me, because I may get so interested in the reading I'll never write,

or I'll pick up the voice of another writer. I can't, for example, read William Faulkner when I'm writing fiction: a poor, New Hampshire imitation of that famous Mississippian is not a good way to go. The other day, however, when I couldn't get started writing, I read a short story by Mary Gordon, one of my favorite authors. Reading a really good writer's work should make you pack up your pen and quit the field, but most of us find reading other writers inspiring. I put down Mary Gordon's short story and was inspired to write.

22. *Read what other writers have written about writing.* I may not write as well as they do, but we work at the same trade, and it helps me to sit around and chat with them. You may want to start a "commonplace book," an eighteenth-century form of self-education in which people made their personal collections of wise or witty sayings. I've collected what writers have said about writing in my own commonplace book, selections from which are now published in my book *Shoptalk* (Boynton/Cook/Heinemann, Portsmouth, New Hampshire, 1990). Some of my favorite quotes from that collection appear in the section *In the Writer's Workshop* sections in this book as well as throughout the text. I find it comforting to hear that the best writers have many of the same problems I do, and I often browse through these quotes as a way of starting.

23. *Break down the writing task into reasonable goals.* A few years ago I watched on TV as the first woman to climb a spectacular rock face in California made it to the top. It had taken her days, and as soon as she got over the edge, a TV reporter stuck a microphone in her face and asked her what she'd thought of as she kept working her way up the cliff. She said she kept reminding herself that you eat an elephant one bite at a time. You also write a long piece of writing one page, or one paragraph, at a time. John Steinbeck said, "When I face the desolate impossibility of writing 500 pages a sick sense of failure falls on me and I know I can never do it. Then I gradually write one page and then another. One day's work is all I can permit myself to contemplate." If you contemplate a book, you'll never write it, but if you write just a page a day you'll have a 365-page draft at the end of a year. If you're stuck, you may be trying to eat an entire elephant at one gulp. It may be wiser to tell yourself that you'll just get the first page, or perhaps just the lead done that day. That may seem possible, and you'll start writing.

24. *Put someone else's name on it.* I've been hired as a ghostwriter to create texts for politicians and industrialists. I've had little trouble writing when the work will carry someone else's name. Most of the time when I can't write I'm excessively self-conscious. Sometimes I've put a pseudonym on a piece of work, and the writing has taken off.

25. *Delegate the writing to your subconscious.* Often I will tell my subconscious what I'm working on, and then I'll do something that doesn't take intense concentration and allows my subconscious mind to work. I walk around bookstores or a library, watch a dull baseball game or movie on TV, take a nap, go for a walk or a drive. Some people putter around the house or work in the garden. Whatever you do, you're allowing your mind to work on the problem. Every once in a while a thought, an approach, a lead, a phrase, a line, or a structure will float up to the conscious mind. If it looks workable, then go to your writing desk; if it doesn't, shove it back down underwater and continue whatever you're doing until something new surfaces.

26. *Listen.* Alice Walker says, "If you're silent for a long time, people just arrive in your mind." As Americans we are afraid of silence, and I'm guilty too. I tend to turn on the car radio if I'm moving the car twenty feet from the end of the driveway to into the garage. One of the best ways to get started writing is to do nothing. Waste time. Stare out the window. Try to let your mind go blank. This isn't easy, as those who have tried meditation know. But many times your mind, distracted by trivia, is too busy to write. Good writing comes out of silence, as Charles Simic says. "In the end, I'm always at the beginning. Silence—an endless mythical condition. I think of explorers setting out over an unknown ocean . . ." Cultivate a quietness, resist the panic that the writing won't come, and allow yourself to sink back into the emptiness. If you don't fight the silence, but accept it, then usually, without being aware of it, the writing will start to come.

These are some ways to get writing. You will come up with others if you make a list of techniques from other parts of your life that may apply here. A theater major may know all sorts of exercises and theater games that can spark writing. A scientist will be able to apply experimental techniques to writing. Art majors know how to attack a white canvas, and ski team members know how to shove off at the top of a steep slope. Keep a record of methods of starting writing that work for you.

DRAFT IN THE DAYBOOK

My daybook is a secret place where I can write badly to write well, be silly, attempt crazy experiments, play with words and ideas. When this play is completed and I go to my writing desk, the draft always goes more easily.

I also print out predrafts from my computer so that I carry them with me. When I have a fragment of time, I can pick up the draft and fiddle around with it, noting what might be added, cut out, moved around. Again, this makes the next day's writing go easily.

....

DRAFT ON THE COMPUTER

The computer and the daybook overlap. I have a laptop computer that sits by my chair in the living room. Often I use that computer while I am watching television or listening to music, to try new drafts or to keep a draft going. I have traveled to Greece, Scotland, twice to England, to each corner of the United States, and over much of Canada with different versions of a laptop—I'm now on my fourth. It allows me to write a draft wherever I am—in a car or bus, on a train or plane, on a ferry or a boat, in a hotel room or a stateroom.

The computer forgives. More than that, the computer doesn't give a damn if I write well or not. It doesn't care if I spell properly, have them double negatives, syntax up the mix, tipe stoopuityly sos i kanhrkdlee reda itt. You think I'm kidding? Seventy-five per cent of my misspelled words cannot be recognized by my spell check function. I'm not proud of that, but the computer allows me to achieve a draft.

The computer allows me to write fast; it allows me to write faster than my internal censor can read and faster than my critical mind can think. I can draft what I do not yet know I have to say. I can draw in background material, move parts of the draft all over the book, write trial drafts, predrafts, sketches, experiments in language and meaning that are central to creativity.

I can write a draft on the left and another on the right of the screen. I can make a copy and tear it apart. I can use all sorts of typographical adjustments and other design changes to let me see how the text can be clarified. The computer is the basic drafting tool of writers today.

....

HEAR THE DRAFT'S VOICE

I have drafted pages with the computer screen turned off. I look at the keys when I draft—or out the window into the woods at the squirrel circus that never ends. I hear the evolving text, and the music of the draft often tells me what I feel about the subject—hate, nostalgia, sadness, rage, anger, detachment, concern. I draft with my ear to understand the meaning of what I am saying. I want to recreate the music that will support that meaning as well as reveal it.

I also write with my ear because I have had much more experience with oral language than with written language even if I am a writer. I may write a thousand words or more a day and read many times that much, but I speak 10,000 words a day or more and hear even more than that. I want the language experience of my ear involved in the making of the draft.

Good writing is not speech written down, but it creates, in the reader's mind, the illusion of speech. The writing that readers most enjoy reading has the sound of a good conversation, the one you wish you had created at the party.

....

REVISE WHILE DRAFTING

Drafting implies revision; each line, each word, each space between words is an experiment in meaning. As I draft I write the word I do not expect to write, keep it, qualify it, change it, revise it.

Often this revision is almost instantaneous. Brain delivers message, and hand changes message. Words qualify what I have said before and predict what I may say in the future. The draft is an evolution of that process: What I write, then read, changes what I will say next. It is a dynamic process, never static, constantly undergoing change as vision and word try to come together.

These days I often revise and even edit as I write, stopping after four paragraphs or more to revise before going on. Layering combines an immediate revision technique with drafting.

IN THE WRITER'S WORKSHOP

How do I know what I think until I see what I say? E. M. FORSTER

I write in longhand. That machine on my desk [a word processor] is for typing out, not composing. For years I had my portable typewriter on which I typed the final draft, so that others could read it. Now I do the same on the word processor. I don't even edit on it, but rewrite and rewrite in longhand. After many drafts I finally type it out. The word processor is, for me, nothing but a typewriter, only you don't have to use Typex to erase or correct a mistake. AMOS OZ

Let's say the first draft occurs in my head. Because I think about these things for a year or so before I start writing them down, and I know fairly well what I'm going to do. I don't know the specific words that I'm going to use, but that isn't usually the problem. The problem is finding the correct organic shape and the emotional shape for a piece. The choice of words is a secondary matter. EDWARD ALBEE

Of The House of Five Talents, *I wrote the first draft in longhand, with a pencil, on Saturdays, Sundays, and vacations; had it typed, triple spaced; and then carried it around in a briefcase. Thus I was able to work on it very easily not only evenings but on the subway or any other time when I had a few minutes to spare. You have to be fresh for the first draft of a book, but I find that once I get to work on the second or third draft; it's like knitting.* LOUIS AUCHINCLOSS

I write the first draft quickly, as I said. This is most often done in longhand. I simply fill up the pages as rapidly as I can. In some cases, there's a kind of personal shorthand, notes to myself for what I will do later when I come back to it. Some scenes I have to

leave unfinished, unwritten in some cases; the scenes that will require meticulous care later. I mean all of it requires meticulous care—but some scenes I save until the second or third draft, because to do them and do them right would take too much time on the first draft. With the first draft it's a question of getting down the outline, the scaffolding of the story. RAYMOND CARVER

(1) Do not wait until you have gathered all your material before starting to write. Nothing adds to inertia like a mass of notes, the earliest of which recede in the mists of forgone time. On the contrary, begin drafting your ideas as soon as some portion of the topic appears to hang together in your mind. (2) Do not be afraid of writing down something that you think may have to be changed. Paper is not granite, and in a first draft you are not carving eternal words in stone. Rather, you are creating substance to be molded and remolded in successive drafts. (3) Do not hesitate to write up in any order those sections of your total work that seem to have grown ripe in your mind. There is a moment in any stretch of research when all the details come together in natural cohesion, despite small gaps and doubts. Learn to recognize that moment and seize it by composing in harmony with your inward feeling of unity. Never mind whether the portions that come out are consecutive. (4) Once you start writing, keep going. Resist the temptation to get up and verify a fact. Leave it blank. The same holds true for the word or phrase that refuses to come to mind. It will arise much more easily on revision, and the economy in time and momentum *is incalculable.* JACQUES BARZUN

My "first draft" is IT. I can't rewrite to any extent: I've tried once or twice, but I haven't the mental stamina and I feel all the time that although what I'm attempting may be different, it won't be better *and may very well be worse, because my heart isn't in it.* DICK FRANCIS

My first draft was 700 pages not because I had so much to say, but because I had so much to find out. EDWARD HANNIBEL

I normally do three drafts, never more and seldom less. The first draft is long and kind of an exploratory draft, with a lot of guesswork involved in it, some of it unsuccessful guesswork. Frequently in the first draft of a book there will be an element of redundancy, and you will write the same scene several times, an important scene in the novel, and you won't recognize perhaps you're doing that. The second draft is basically a cutting draft, in which you eliminate the bad guesses, pure mistakes, redundancies, and overwriting of all kinds. In the first draft when you're trying to develop a character, you let conversations run on for pages if you want to. In the second draft you tighten that. The third draft is stylistic basically. I don't pay much attention to style in the first two drafts; I write fairly rapidly, and I'm trying to visualize the scenes I'm describing as intensely as possible. The third draft is the stylist draft. I may get down to two eventually. I never want to go above three, because in a sense you participate in the emotions of the book every time you do a draft, and I think three times is about as many times as you can participate in those emotions and keep them alive. It goes cold. LARRY MCMURTRY

Writing the first draft is the hard part, when you're actually trying to think of what happens next. That's quite painful but the rest is fun. JOYCE CAROL OATES

Writing a first draft is like ice fishing and building an igloo, as well as groping one's way into a pitch-dark room or overhearing a faint conversation, or having prepared for the wrong exam or telling a joke whose punch line you've forgotten . . . TED SOLOTAROFF

The first draft is always scary to me. I can't risk interrupting it for long or I may lose it. The momentum is important; there's a sense of pushing off from one side. It's like building the Verrazano Bridge from one side, hoping it won't fall in on the way. You don't know if you're going to make it. MARGE PIERCY

....

QUESTIONS ABOUT DRAFTING

I don't write drafts; I just sit down and my writing flows. When I'm through, I've said all I want about my subject. So why should I change?

Because you have probably never found out how much more you have to say. If you never draft and revise, you won't ever see the complexities of the topics you write about. You won't know how much more depth you can bring to your subject. If you're still not a believer, try writing an exploratory draft anyway. See where it takes you. Go about it earnestly and record your progress in your daybook.

What if I have the opposite problem? I have a hard time getting anything down on paper. I worry before I even begin a writing project, and then I get knots in my stomach when I sit down to do it.

No deadline, assignment, or piece of writing is worth getting sick over. But sometimes it's worth getting mad over! I knew a writer once who used to get paralyzed when she sat down to write in front of an empty computer screen. She'd get sick to her stomach before she had written a word; then she'd get angry for getting sick! By that time she'd march back to her computer and chew it out. Then she'd just write.

But it's easy for other people to say "just write!" If I want to write something really good, it takes a lot of effort. Besides, my grade point average depends on how well I write.

These are valid concerns. Most writers want to write something good, and all writers have to take the consequences for writing well or poorly: Students know that good writing usually results in good grades. Professionals know that good writing results in paychecks.

The problem comes when you let the consequences of writing overshadow the process itself. It's the process of writing that will help you get beyond what is often a paralyzing perfectionism. As you sit down to that blank screen or paper, say to yourself: "This is just an exploratory draft; no one else has to read it. I can do what I want with it, and I can always change it later."

At this point in your process, expect to write badly if you need to. Write quickly, just get something down.

But what if there's absolutely nothing in my head when I want to write?

If you draw a total blank, it doesn't necessarily mean you are paralyzed from fear or an overdeveloped sense of perfectionism; it may mean that you need to go back and do more brainstorming, mapping, focusing, or planning. You may need more information to get you going or a solid angle from which to start. In these cases, you might want to return to some of the activities and suggestions in earlier chapters of this book and use them to jump-start your draft. If you still can't write, it could be that the conditions for writing are simply not good for you. Get up and walk away for awhile.

When I get stuck, I don't try to force the writing. I back up, stop, do something else, and try again, perhaps in ten minutes, perhaps the next morning. I'm a morning writer, and I find that if the writing doesn't come one time, it will come the next. But be assured that it will come.

But what if I have a paper due the next day? I don't have time to wait for the writing!

Then you will have to force the writing. Even the most well-organized professional at one time or another encounters a deadline bind. At those times, if the writing does not come easily, the writer works to get something, anything, on paper.

Look at some of the adjoining activities for ideas about drafting. In one of them I suggest setting your clock for a sustained period of time and making yourself write until the alarm goes off. Disciplining yourself like this doesn't mean producing gobbledygook. It means getting said what needs to be said within a given period of time, then going back to revise it. That's what all writers need to do when they are face-to-face with a deadline.

I'm more afraid of losing control of my paper than of having nothing to say.

The planning and focusing you do before beginning your draft will give you a certain amount of control over what you write. But it's not at all unusual for an exploratory draft to take on a life all its own. This may be frightening, but it's also good. When the draft starts leading you instead of you leading it, it probably means there is some real thinking going on. Since writing allows you to try on new ideas and perspectives, you may have to change your strategy as you articulate your thoughts. You can always go back and fiddle with your focus or outline so that it accommodates your new way of seeing and thinking.

But what if the draft is literally all over the place and doesn't
make any sense?

This is still not a bad thing. It's the draft leading you back through a thinking process, getting you to clarify what you want to say. Use some of the suggestions and activities for focusing listed in Chapter 3. A writing partner or group will also be helpful here; other readers can sum up your major points for you, or you can jot down in the margins of your paper what you want to do with each section. That will give you a sense of direction. Then go back and make an outline for your draft and try to stick with it. You can always go back later and develop or pare down areas of your paper as you see fit.

DRAFTING ACTIVITIES

1. Power through a draft. Read through all of the information, interviews, details, and facts you have collected for it, but don't consult them while drafting. Do as much as you can from memory, and leave a space or asterisk in the text wherever you think you want to insert more details. For the time being, don't get hung up on particulars.

2. Get a draft down, then write another draft without looking at the original. Include only what you remember or want to remember. Allow the draft to lead you into new areas. Do this again. Then go back to your drafts and select the one you like best, or revise by combining the best elements of each.

3. When construction workers build a new skyscraper, they erect boards and railings and elevators around it so that they can do their work without falling off. When getting through a draft seems as challenging as building a skyscraper, let your process become your scaffolding. Analyze your process in the draft itself: "I'm not sure what lead I want here, but I need to start with something, so how about this? . . ." "I thought I knew what to do at this point, but now I'm stuck." "This part of the paper is the suspenseful turning point, so I want it to be good." And so on and so on. When you are through, take down your scaffolding and let your draft stand by itself.

4. Compose your draft in vignettes rather than paragraphs. A vignette is a short sketch or portrait that stands on its own. Writing vignettes instead of connecting paragraphs will help you focus on details and get a sense of your major points; this method allows you to dip in and out of your story as you plan. Sketch out a list of scenes or incidents that you want to include in your paper. Take one "corner" of each scene or

incident, and explore it in detail: a description of your uncle's garden, for example, or the kind gesture of a stranger on the street. Then read your vignettes with an eye toward coherence and connection.

5. Cut up your draft according to ideas or major points and arrange them in "thought piles" on the floor, ordering information according to each idea or thought. Then use these piles to write another draft and to keep it under control.

6. During your most productive period of the day, set your alarm and write for a sustained amount of time, anywhere from one hour to three. Make sure that you are not interrupted during this period. Think of this time as a business or academic appointment and keep it!

7. Break up your writing time: Fifteen minutes before breakfast, a half-hour after lunch, an hour at night, or fifteen minutes before you go to bed. Make sure to write fast and furiously, filling up every minute you have.

8. Think of your classmates as business colleagues, and schedule meetings with them twice a week to discuss your draft. Always have a new or revised chunk of writing to show them at the appointed time.

9. Start in *medias res,* which is Latin for "in the middle of things." Don't get hung up on finding a perfect lead, but jump in anywhere. Write a piece of description, a chunk of dialogue, or even the conclusion to your story. Develop an idea for the middle of the piece, or select one image or concept you know you can write about comfortably and start with that.

10. Write by ear. Compose sentences that have the right sound to them, the perfect rhythm and voice for the effect you want on your reader. Drum out a rhythm on your desk or daybook before drafting. Imagine what a reflective, inspirational, argumentative, persuasive, sarcastic, honest, or upbeat piece might sound like, and don't worry yet about how much information or sense your sentences convey. Let the sound guide your writing.

11. Experiment with genres if you get stuck. Write a poem instead of an essay; then turn your poem into a complicated recipe. Write up instructions for writing your essay. Make a "grocery" list of pertinent points. Write a letter to your friends telling them the story you are about to write. Turn your intended story into a play. Then turn your play into a story. Get writing.

12. Go ahead, break the rule: Tell, don't show! For the time being at least, forget about details, description, dialogue, and development. Write your draft in summary form as though it were an encyclopedia entry or an abstract. Then go back and fill in the details, showing rather than telling.

13. Draft directly to other writers on the Internet. Set a schedule to e-mail each new section of your draft to someone you meet in a writer's chat room, or post your draft in installments to a writer's bulletin board.

14. Set up a writers' Web page on the Internet as a class, or get one of your computer whiz friends to do it for you. Publish a schedule on the page that advertises the "publication" dates of parts or whole drafts. Then take turns as a class or in groups "publishing" pieces of your drafts.

15. Pretend that you're writing in your diary rather than composing a story or assigned essay. Don't try to be deep or complicated. Just get your draft going. Use plenty of time references and words that imply sequence, just as you might in a diary: "That morning . . ." "Later . . ." "After a while . . ." "Then . . ." Let these time words propel you forward; you can always remove them later.

16. Put on your favorite classical music—a waltz, prelude, concerto, or symphony—or any kind of music that takes you out of the moment and puts you into a reflective mood. Take a deep breath and "fall" into the music. Vow to write for the length of time it takes for the piece to play, and when it ends, leave your last sentence unfinished. Take a break. When you return, put on a new piece or repeat a melody that worked for you before. Pick up where you left off by finishing the last sentence you wrote.

17. Arrange with your teacher to set aside a drafting period in class, a half-hour or so of writing time once or twice a week. Write sections of your draft by hand during this time as quickly as possible. Commit yourself to having a substantial chunk of text to read aloud to your classmates when the period ends.

18. Make drafting part of a larger ritual of physical and intellectual well-being. If you're a morning person, meet the sunrise with t'ai chi, a cup of herbal tea, and a half-hour or more at your computer. If you work best at night, combine your drafting time with deep breathing exercises and meditation. Visualize productivity, and say no to anxiety.

19. If you have writer's block, get a change of scenery; take your draft and work somewhere other than your usual writing space. Move from space to space if you need to, making yourself comfortable in each and vowing to write a chunk of draft before moving on.

20. Commit yourself to a certain number of pages each day—whatever seems reasonable. Meet your daily quota and revise what you have at the end of each week.

21. Meet a daily paragraph quota. Determine to write a certain number of paragraphs each day, perhaps five or ten. If you finish quickly, write more or go back and hone your paragraphs. If you are having difficulty

writing, push yourself to meet the quota anyway, knowing that you can revise later.

22. Take a significant piece of information from the writing you're working on and list all of the ways it can be documented: quotations, statistics, descriptions, anecdotes, and so on. Then develop it, using some or all of these elements.

23. Go back through activities for previous chapters and use any—or many—of the suggestions for collecting, focusing, or ordering to see if they will help you get a draft flowing.

24. Get an opening paragraph down, and have your partner or group brainstorm questions about what should follow. Write out detailed answers to these questions on your draft, and then decide what parts of these answers you want to keep. If particular questions get you rolling, go with them.

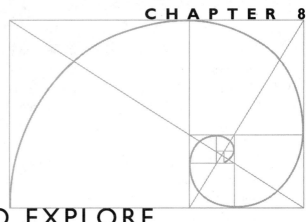

CHAPTER 8

REVISE TO EXPLORE MEANING

Beginning writers sometimes believe that the first draft of a piece is the last; experienced writers know the first draft is the beginning. Writing is rewriting. Writers write to think and rethink, to discover and rediscover, to explore and reexplore, to clarify and reclarify.

Beginning writers sometimes think revision is punishment; experienced writers see revision as opportunity. The writer has found a subject with possibility, a subject that has the potential of new meaning, a subject that may be worth a reader's attention—if it is explored and clarified with revision.

Beginning writers—and sometimes their teachers—think revision and editing are the same. Neaten up the first draft, correct the spelling, punctuation, grammar, and you're done. But experienced writers know what Ernest Hemingway, Nobel-Prize winning novelist, meant when he said, "Prose is architecture not interior decoration."

Through revision, the writer discovers meaning, explores and develops it, then designs and constructs a piece of writing that will carry the meaning to readers. After the building of meaning is completed, the writer "decorates" by editing, cleaning up the prose, arranging it so the meaning is clearly and attractively displayed.

Re-vision is re-seeing the topic so the writer can discover meaning.

Editing is making the meaning clear so a reader can understand meaning.

I am going to produce a rough first draft in response to a real writing assignment I have been given, then introduce a strategy for revising it—a logical, easy to understand, and easy to use method of revising—that can be applied to any writing task, a term paper or critical essay, lab report or office memo, thesis or letter of sympathy, case history or poem, scholarship application or take-home exam. Poets and screen writers, historians and Supreme Court justices, marketing executives and clinical psychologists, novelists and engineers all have to think by writing and rewriting—and then rewriting again.

This piece of writing starts with an assignment from Diane Koski of the University of New Hampshire Foundation, a fund-raising organization for the college where I am both an alumnus and a retired faculty member. She asked me to write a letter telling how the university has changed in the past fifty years that might inspire financial support from my classmates. This is exactly the sort of assignment that might be given to an engineer, lawyer, sales manager, grant-seeking scientist, hospital administrator, minister, priest or rabbi, anyone who has to produce a piece of writing designed to attract money. I've done this sort of writing professionally, and I am doing this one as a volunteer—a reluctantly drafted volunteer. Out of guilt and a sense of duty, I agreed to a task I did not relish but I nevertheless plunged in.

I always start the same way, talking to myself in my head and in my daybook. I'm a visual person, as most writers are, and I see in images or pictures: myself as a soldier climbing down from the train that no longer runs, marching down Main Street, coming back to Durham after the war, twenty-one and a steak of white in my hair, particular classrooms in Murkland Hall, teachers such as Gwynne Daggett and Carroll Towle and Sylvester Bingham and Bill Hennessey and their offices, and my first wife. I walk around with that movie running through my head, and then I begin to hear fragments of language—proper names such as *T-Hall* and phrases— "an educated man can sit alone in a room and be happy." Finally, I start to write a discovery draft, beginning with description. In this case I am trying to discover what I find special about my educational experience as a student and a teacher at the University of New Hampshire.

> The troop train pulled into the train station in Durham, New Hampshire, the one that is now an ice cream parlor, and we were marched up Main Street where GIRLS! lined the streets. I didn't know then that my first wife was among them, and I did not know that Durham would be my home—with my second wife and our three daughters, one of whom would be carried to the Durham Cemetery when she was only twenty. I wanted to be going overseas, not to school. My father wanted me to have my war, and I did too. So did my church. "Onward Christian Soldiers, Marching as to War." I didn't know I would become a paratrooper and survive combat. That I would return to school, marry the co-ed. If we had lived together, as my daughters and their husbands did, before marriage, we would never have married. I was insulted when someone suggested I should become a teacher. I didn't know I'd be a professor at this campus. I don't remember the classes so much as the professors' offices, conferences with Carroll Towle, his corncob pipe and his enthusiasm as he attacked my drafts. [And my conferences with his son years later.]

Gwynne Daggett, his sleeves rolled up above his knotty biceps, his hands clasped behind his head, and his delight in ideas, attacking and defending, questioning, doubting, caring. When I was a teacher years later, I don't remember the classroom as much as my office and meeting all my students every week. One on one. I remember my learning as much as theirs. My teachers, I realized then and now, were still learning with me.

Now I have a first draft, one page, 272 words. It is a jumble that jumps around in time and topic, an example of free writing that isn't close to a polished letter to alumni, but I sense there is something there I can build on. I am an experienced detective. Sometimes the topic or approach is obvious. I see it immediately and that is it. Other times it is not obvious, and I follow an organized search plan I call a *strategy for revision*. It was, at first, instinctive, but now I have made it into a chart so I can share it with others. It provides a logical approach to revision. If you study the chart you will see that the writer first looks within the draft itself, then looks ahead to new drafts, finally looks back to the original assignment. Revision is, after all, thinking, a process of discovering new meaning.

....

THE STRATEGY OF REVISION

1. Look Within for the Surprising	2. Look Forward for the Changing	3. Look Back for the Expected
Word	Purpose	Purpose
Line	Meaning	Meaning
Distance	Distance	Distance
Voice	Genre	Genre
Focus	Audience	Audience
Details	Evidence	Documentation
Sequence	Order	Logic
Purpose	Pace	Pace
Meaning	Proportions	Proportions
Genre	Development	Development
Audience	Voice	Voice

I move quickly through the strategy of revision, skimming over some points, lingering over others, moving back and forth between the three forms of revision, as you will when you are experienced with the entire process. But to understand the strategy, you should, at least once, examine an early draft, point by point, to see the full potential the strategy can reveal in a draft. That is what I will do to see if my discovery draft has the potential for me to fulfill the assignment of a fund-raising letter.

I scan the text, reading quickly.

I. LOOK WITHIN FOR THE SURPRISING

Word

I hesitate over "GIRLS!" I realize, now that my consciousness has been raised, that the word *girls* hearkens back to an era I could remember and explore in a column. No other word really sparks my interest.

Line

"Onward Christian Soldiers" catches me, because it was one of my favorite hymns when I was young. I didn't hear the irony of a killing, militaristic Christianity until I saw my first dead German soldier and his belt buckle, which proclaimed that God was with the Whermacht, Hitler's army. "I don't remember classes as much as the professors' offices" also catches my eye. That may lead to something.

Distance

I'm remembering my first view of the campus reflected through the many lives I would live in Durham. Should I stay at that distance—the assignment would seem to demand that—or would it be more effective move in close, put the reader with me on campus in 1943?

Voice

"I remember my learning as much as theirs" has a certain melody or music I can imagine developing as I write.

Focus

The focus is on the meetings, one-on-one, with my professors. That may be the focus of the next draft.

Details

I need more details like Towle's corncob pipe and Daggett's pride in his biceps.

Sequence

I sense a sequence or implied narrative that could run through the piece: discovery that my teachers were learning with me and later discovery that I was learning with my students.

Purpose

To get alumni to see what is special about this intimate form of education, to encourage them to celebrate and support it—with cash.

Meaning

At a university, faculty and students learn together.

Genre

This piece looks like an essay, more than a letter, a personal reflective essay that puts our alumni experience in a positive educational context.

Audience

I could target a different audience—the readers of my column, teachers who read my articles and textbooks, but here the audience will be alumni.

It took me a few minutes to zero in on this draft and find the approach I can use to produce a fund-raising alumni letter. Writing is always a matter of selection, choosing the road to go down and making choices all along the way. Today I have found, within my discovery draft, my approach to the assignment—I will write about students and teachers learning together—but I must, to avoid problems as I write this piece, at least check the other two strategies of revision.

Next, I look ahead to see what may need to be changed.

2. LOOK FORWARD FOR THE CHANGING

Purpose

In reading these 272 words, I might have decided to write about the relationship of men and women (girls) in the 1940s or a militaristic Christianity or the importance and techniques of conference teaching of writing.

Meaning

Any of these issues may have a new meaning that I might feel the need to explore. In fact, I think I will celebrate—in a column—the benefits of feminism for an old man who now has women friends.

In fact, I am going to start next week's column right now, while the words are eager to flow:

> The other morning I marched down Durham's Main Street, which runs through the middle of the University of New Hampshire, and was both a retired professor taking his constitutional and an eighteen-year-old soldier marching down the same street in 1943.

What I remember is not the itchy winter uniform, the green lawns and brick buildings but the GIRLS! that lined the sidewalk.

Today I do not see girls but women.

The girls were mysterious, alluring, threatening, different. The women to whom I nod or wave, with whom I stop to chat today are colleagues and friends.

Once I have this much written, I can go back and finish it when I have time.

Distance

As I get back to thinking about my fund-raising letter, I might zoom back and forth, almost line by line, from present to past and back, making a virtue of one of the weaknesses of the discovery draft.

Genre

I see poems and short stories in this draft that I may develop later.

Audience

There could be a general audience—old timers who would be nostalgic, young people who would be astonished, feminists who might be pleased, old fogies who might realize the benefits—to them—of the feminism they have attacked.

Evidence

I could go to school records which might document curriculum arguments for or against conference teaching or rules and regulations that would document the very different treatment of men and women at UNH then and now. I might interview women who have lived these changes.

Order

I might not start with my parade down Main Street but with the scene, after I returned, of the Military Arts Ball, which no longer takes place in Durham.

Pace

I might saunter through the past or speed from present to past and back.

Proportions

I will always have the question of how much past and how much present.

Development

I must have enough information—descriptive details, facts, documentation—to make the past clear to the young, the present clear to the old.

Voice

My voice must, as always, be appropriate to the subject, the audience, and myself. I must be aware of language—girls, dates, balls, curfews.

Again, let me remind you that these lists are just quick checklists to protect you from wasting your time on fruitless revision, allowing you to concentrate your energy where revision will be rewarded. Finally, it is important to look back to what was expected. If you are rewriting a novel, you may want to betray your expectations, but if you are revising a screenplay for a Hollywood producer, a marketing report for a corporate vice president, a thesis for an academic committee, or a fund-raising letter for an alumni officer, you'd better be sure you can fit your discoveries to their expectations.

3. LOOK BACK FOR THE EXPECTED

Purpose

My focus on individual education can fit the purpose of showing alumni a consistent strand that deserves their pride and their funds despite all the changes at their university.

Meaning

It is significant that university faculty continue to learn and share their learning with their students.

Distance

It is appropriate for me to move back and forth in time, as long as the time shifts clarify the meaning I am communicating for my readers.

Genre

The essay format of the letter will work, I think.

Audience

My audience is clear. Men and women who graduated fifty years ago.

Documentation

My documentation is personal and anecdotal, which is appropriate for this piece of writing.

Logic

The emphasis on individual learning is logical, it makes sense.

Pace

I shall have to make sure the readers are kept moving forward fast enough so they will continue to read, slow enough so they will absorb what I have to say.

Proportions

I will have to make sure there is little—but enough—of a fund-raising appeal, surrounded by mostly informative material. I will also have to make sure there is enough reflection to recreate the past but much more on what is going on at UNH today. That is what we hope they will support.

Development

I will have to develop each part well enough that the reader can re-live or live it.

Voice

My voice should not be pushy. I should simply recount what I have experienced at UNH in a way that encourages them to support the school. (Fifty-two alumni responded with $5,265.)

Here is the revision I submitted:

> I first came to Durham in 1943 when an Army sergeant counted cadence as we marched down Main Street. I returned from Europe in 1946, surprised to have survived combat, and experienced an unexpected intimacy of learning with Carroll Towle, Gwynne Daggett, Bill Hennessey, and others who met with us in class, in their offices, in their homes and ours, in the corridors of Murkland, and on the sidewalks of Durham.
>
> I lived the glorious triangle of university learning:
>
> An individual teacher,
> a senior learner
>
> > A test to be understood,
> > a question to be asked,
> > a problem to be researched
>
> An individual student,
> a junior learning
>
> In 1963 I was invited to return to the university to set up a journalism program, and I reentered the triangle of learning as the senior learner, meeting with each individual student every week in the method of Carroll Towle and the pattern of freshman English which is still taught by class and conference.
>
> Since retiring from the faculty nine years ago, I have continued to live in Durham, observing the evolving university first hand. I have cheered the hockey and football teams, applauded the academic honors won by faculty and

students, watched the new buildings rise on a campus I still find beautiful, but most of all, I have celebrated the evidence I have found that the triangle of learning goes on: An individual professor and an individual student learn from each other as they confront a specific intellectual question.

This individual learning is expensive but central to the university. It is the way that faculty continue to learn, that students discover how to learn, and that society benefits from their combined learning.

Visit the campus and you see buildings, but if you are fortunate enough to live here you may catch a glimpse of what goes on in the seminar room, faculty office, laboratory: a belief doubted, an answer that finds a question, a principle challenged, a theory tested, a pattern explained, a problem solved that gives birth to a new question.

In room _____ at the Whittemore School of Business and Economics, Dr. _____ _____ meets with_____ _____. They are fascinated with _____ and study the puzzling results of a survey that contradicts expectations. Now they have a problem to solve that may change the way _____ look at _____.

In a laboratory in_____, _____ _____ uses a _____ to test and retest a _____ taken from Great Bay the day before. She calls over Dr. _____ _____ who runs his own tests, and then they sit down to study computer printouts that may some day lead to_____.

[And so on for the School of Health Studies and Human Services and the College of Liberal Arts]

Four individual students and four individual faculty members focusing on four significant questions. Radiating out from them are the intellectual interactions of _____ full-time and part-time faculty members with _____ undergraduate and graduate students.

Of course there are large classes, but the center of what goes on at the University of New Hampshire is that grand triangle of individual learning. I give to support what happens when an individual instructor and student learn from each other, and I hope you will join me.

The alumni office did the research that changed, developed, and filled in my blanks, and the letter was published pretty much as I had drafted it. But it was not a first draft; it was a revision constructed after exploring a discovery draft.

Notice that I passed up many topics in that discovery draft: my desire to go to war and what happened when I did; marriage, divorce, remarriage; the births of three children and the loss of one; what I studied in school and how it affected my life; what it was like to return and teach where I had been a student; teaching my teacher's son; profiles of Towle or Daggett; an essay on what makes a good teacher—all those topics and more embedded in 272 words. But I had an assignment, and so I concentrated on what might help me fulfill that assignment.

....

TWO KEY QUESTIONS

Another approach to revision is built on two key questions:

WHAT WORKS?
WHAT NEEDS WORK?

Years ago, before I had a computer, I would write at least three drafts for a magazine article and revise each by hand at least ten times. To discover what I was doing so I could teach it to my students, I pasted each typed draft on a much larger piece of paper, revised, then wrote in these large margins what I was doing, why I was doing it, and how. I surprised myself. I thought I was fixing failure and correcting error but discovered that, most of the time, I was strengthening success. I was building on the elements in the draft that worked, making them stronger, rather than correcting error.

Once I found what worked and developed those elements, I went on to what needed work. I found that many of the errors, problems, or failures in early drafts disappeared as I revised by focusing on developing the strengths of the article. Those that hadn't disappeared could then be addressed.

Let's see how this system of revision works. I will write a brief freewrite or discovery draft:

> I am going to a football game—UNH versus Delaware—opening game of the season. We will sit on the fifty yard line, twenty rows up. Beside the Drouins who we sit with at hockey games. I've been going I went to my first football game in this stadium fifty-one years ago. It is named for a classmate of mine, Andy Mooradian, who was athletic director. He died of cancer, and one of his daughters was one of the best friends of my daughter's. I don't approve of football—it is a violent and militaristic game—but I love it. I played it and got to college on a football scholarship. My right knee still hurts from an illegal block on a kick-off, no substitutes then. That was fifty-four years ago. When I watch the game, I'll be on the field. The fat old grad will sit in the stands, and the eighteen-year-old will go in at right tackle.
>
> Actually I'd like to play right defensive end. I feel I could. The illusion is worse than my wife believes. I know I could sack the quarterback. I'd be cool. Not jump around, simply point down with the first finger of my right hand. Cool. Cold. Tough. Mean. All the virtues.

A jumble—a badly written jumble, but what works for me is the illusion of the old man that he could play a young man's game—and the tension that he doesn't approve of the game and still loves it. Teachers and editors might see the contradictions as a failure, something that needed to be fixed—or abandoned. I see the contradictions as what works, what has potential.

What is failure to one writer is opportunity to another; what doesn't work for one writer may work for another. I am reminded of what novelist Fay Weldon said:

> What others say are your faults, your weaknesses, may if carried to extremes be your virtues, your strengths. I don't like too many adjectives or adverbs—I say if a noun or a verb is worth describing, do it properly, take a sentence to do it. There's no hurry. Don't say "the quick brown fox jumped over the lazy dog." Say, "it was at this moment that the fox jumped over the dog. The fox was brown as the hazelnuts in the tree hedgerows, and quick as the small stream that ran beside, and the dog too lazy to so much as turn his head." Or something. Writing is more than just the making of a series of comprehensible statements: It is the gathering in of connotations; the harvesting of them, like blackberries in a good season, ripe and heavy, snatched from among the thorns of logic.
>
> Having thus discouraged the apprentice writer from overuse of adjectives, I turn at once to Iris Murdoch and find she will use eighteen of them in a row. It works. What is weakness in small quantities is style in overdose. So be wary of anyone who tries to teach you to write. Do it yourself. Stand alone. You will never be better than your own judgment, and you will never be satisfied with what you do. Ambition will, and should, always outstrip achievement.

Remember Fay Weldon: Ask "What works—for you?" Ask "What needs work—from you?" Then ask what the reader needs.

THE REVISION CHECKLIST

Revision is not editing. They are two separate activities, and keeping them apart makes the task of preparing a final draft much easier.

The following diagram shows how the emphasis changes from revision to editing:

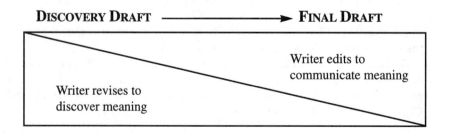

Revision is re-seeing the entire draft so that the writer can deal with the large issues that must be resolved before she or he deals with line-by-line, word-by-word issues involved in editing.

In reading for revision, it is important to step back and scan the draft so that you can see it as a whole. In this way, you will notice such things as the relationships between the sections of the draft that you cannot see when you are concentrating on the relationship between a particular verb and an individual noun.

Make your own revision checklist. Mine is in the list below. The list is long, but many of the questions can be answered in an instant. Because you have focused, explored, planned, and drafted, you have solved most of these problems in advance. This is a checklist to see if any problems remain that must be solved before the editing that produces the final draft:

CHECKLIST FOR REVISING

Subject

- Do I have something I need to say?
- Are there readers who need to hear what I have to say?

Focus

- Does the draft make a clear, dominant point?
- Are there clear, appropriate limits to the draft that include what needs to be included, exclude what is unnecessary?
- Do writer and reader stand at the appropriate distance from the material?

Authority

- Are the writer's credentials to write this draft established and clear?

Context

- Is the context of the draft, the world in which the story exists, clear?

Voice

- Does the draft have an individual voice?
- Is the voice appropriate to the subject?
- Does the voice support and extend the meaning of the draft?

Reader

- Can you identify a reader who will need to read the draft?
- Can you see a reader who will want to read the draft?
- Are the reader's questions answered where they will be asked?

Genre

- Is the form of the story the best one to carry the meaning to the reader?
- Does the draft fulfill the reader's expectations of that form?

Structure

- Will the lead attract and hold a reader?
- Does the ending resolve the issues raised in the draft?
- Is there a clear trail through the draft?
- Does each point lead to the next point?
- Does each section support and advance the meaning?

Information

- Is the reader's hunger for specific information satisfied?

Documentation

- Does the reader have enough evidence to believe each point in the draft?

Pace

- Is the reader carried forward toward the intended meaning by the flow of the draft?
- Are there points where the draft needs to be speeded up to keep the reader from abandoning it?
- Are there points where the draft needs to be slowed down so the reader has time to comprehend the meaning of what is being written?

Proportion

- Are the sections in appropriate proportion to one another to advance and support the meaning of the draft?

Quantity

- Where does the draft need to be developed?
- Where does it need to be cut?

Move through the checklist quickly, scanning the draft and then revising part or all of it as necessary until you have done all you can do—or until the deadline is upon you. Then begin editing the final draft.

REVISE IN THE DAYBOOK

Even when I have discovered an appropriate revision strategy, even when I know what works and what needs work, I often have to stand back from the draft, to get distance from what I have written and sketch what I may try in the next draft. That is when I return to my daybook.

I have learned to stand back the way an artist stands back from a painting. I do not look at the draft; I do not try to remember it. I simply play around with words, phrases, lists, diagrams, beginning paragraphs, fragmentary outlines. All are revisions, although they are only single words or selections a few lines long. Each shows me how the piece might be reworked.

I have to keep reminding myself not to get too serious, not to strain, but to play with the ideas in the draft, so that I can catch sight of the one that works out of the corner of my eye. The daybook allows me to do this in the traffic jam, on the bench at the front of the supermarket while once again waiting for my wife, while there are commercials on the television, in the doctor's waiting room. The daybook allows me a few moments of constructive play, and often, looking back, I find that it only took a minute, three, five to sketch out a revision I can complete the next morning—one that works.

REVISE ON A COMPUTER

The computer has improved writing, primarily because it makes revision easy. When I first began to write magazine articles, I typed a draft and literally cut it apart, writing inserts that I glued, taped, or stapled into the text, marking it up until I—or my wife—typed the mess up. Then I attacked the clean, new draft, messing it up until I couldn't read it and had to start the process again.

On the computer, you can save each draft, then write the new text right over a copy of the old one. The computer allows you to save text, cut it, move it around, fit it in a new place, try new drafts, revise old drafts—and it can be done with ease.

LISTEN TO TEST READERS

Watch out. The longer I write, the more care I take with who I allow to see my work. We all need good test readers, but they are rare. The writer has to search for friends, coworkers, classmates, teachers, editors who can test what you have written. Good test readers usually share similar qualities:

- They write themselves. They know the territory emotionally and intellectually and can appreciate how the writer is thinking and feeling.
- They listen to what the draft is saying without preconceptions about what the writer should say and how the writer should say it. I once had a

well-known poet read my short poems and tell me that since I was a big guy, I should write big poems. He didn't seem to understand that the poet in me is a short, secretive little guy. The criticism wasn't helpful. The effective test reader is a colleague who helps you, the writer, see what is evolving in a draft that is unexpected and worth keeping. This reader delights in surprises, in variation, in diversity, and helps evaluate the text on its own terms.

- They are honest. The effective test reader is able, because of the his or her own accomplishments, to admit to envy and admiration and to deliver disagreement and doubt. The critic does not withhold comments from both ends of the spectrum, but tries to deal not so much in general praise or criticism as in specific comments on what works, and why; what doesn't work, and why; what may work, and why.

- Most importantly, the test reader makes you want to write. The test reader may deliver bad news, but you should always leave the effective test reader eager to get back to the writing desk, to attack and solve your writing problems. Cultivate this kind of test reader. How do you find such readers? By sticking your neck out. You show your drafts to those who you think will help you, and you return to those who do.

You say you have to deal with a teacher or an editor who isn't helpful? Of course you do; of course I do. But I also have a few test readers from whom I learn. They are my secret editors and teachers. I turn to them to find out how to deal with the others. Some of them actually are editors and teachers, for if you are a writer you never stop going to school.

IN THE WRITER'S WORKSHOP

I've done as many as twenty or thirty drafts of a story. Never less than ten or twelve drafts. It's instructive, and heartening both, to look at the early drafts of great writers. I'm thinking of the photographs of galleys belonging to Tolstoy, to name one writer who loved to revise. I mean, I don't know if he loved it or not, but he did a great deal of it. He was always revising, right down to the time of page proofs. He went through and rewrote War and Peace *eight times and was still making corrections in the galleys. Things like this should hearten every writer whose first drafts are dreadful, like mine are.* RAYMOND CARVER

It takes an awful lot of time for me to write anything. I have endless drafts, one after another; and I try out fifty, seventy-five, or a hundred variations on a single line sometimes. I work on the process of refining low-grade ore. . . . No. I am not inspired. JAMES DICKEY

. . . I began to write essays, one a month for Esquire *magazine, and I am not exaggerating when I say that in the course of writing a short essay—1,500 words, that's*

only six double-spaced typewritten pages—I often used 300 or 400 pieces of typing paper, so often did I type and retype and catapult and recatapult myself, sometimes on each retyping moving not even a sentence farther from the spot I had reached the last time through. At the same time, though, I was polishing what I had already written; as I struggled with the middle of the article, I kept putting the beginning through the typewriter; as I approached the ending the middle got its turn. (This is a kind of polishing that the word processor all but eliminates, which is why I don't use one. Word processors make it possible for a writer to change the sentences that clearly need changing without having to retype the rest, but I believe that you can't always tell whether a sentence needs work until it rises up in revolt against your fingers as you retype it.) By the time I had produced what you might call a first draft—an entire article with a beginning, middle, and end—the beginning was in more like forty-fifth draft, the middle in twentieth, and the end was almost newborn. For this reason the beginnings of my essays are considerably better written than the ends, although I like to think no one ever notices this but me. NORA EPHRON

What makes me happy is rewriting. In the first draft you get your ideas and your theme clear, if you are using some kind of metaphor you get that established, and certainly you have to know where you're coming out. But the next time through it's like cleaning house, getting rid of all the junk, getting things in the right order, tightening things up. I like the process of making writing neat. ELLEN GOODMAN

I work not by writing but by rewriting. Each sentence has many drafts. Eventually there is a paragraph. This gets many drafts. Eventually there is a page. This gets many drafts. WILLIAM GASS

I write very impulsively, so terribly fast only I can decipher my scrawl. But only one-quarter of this first outpouring, at the most, is usable, so actually I work very slowly. It's mostly pacing, researching, brewing endless cups of herb tea while I think of how to annotate these terrible earlier drafts. Hours are spent figuring how to rewrite one single sentence—I've never managed to write anything, even a book review, in fewer than three or four drafts. FRANCIS DE PLEXIS GREY

I love revision. Where else can spilled milk be turned into ice cream. KATHERINE PATTERSON

Language is where you live, it's a real place, more important than geography. JONATHAN RABAN

We think only through the medium of words. . . . [T]he art of reasoning is nothing more than language well arranged. CONDILLAC

There is a sort of basic law about everything for me, and that is that you have to pay attention. You've got to pay attention, as a writer, to the structure of language. You've got to pay attention to the sounds. BARRY LOPEZ

You have to keep working to find your voice, then have the grace or good sense to recognize it as your voice and then learn how to use it. JOHN GUARE

Write it out as verbose as you want. Have verbal Diarrhea. Then cut the unnecessary words, but keep the plot. Then rewrite and cut again. Then rewrite and cut again. After three times, you have something. DAVID MAMET

....

QUESTIONS ABOUT REVISING

When I write a paper, I'm usually pretty satisfied with it the first time around. I figure that what I've written down is what I want to say. So why revise?

Writing well is thinking deeply. Real thinking, like thoughtful writing, happens in layers. We think on the surface, and then we dip below. Surface thinking helps us get done what needs to get done everyday. This kind of thinking is perfectly fine for routine writing tasks, such as making lists or composing notes to our siblings or roommates. This is superficial writing and there's no need to revise it.

But thoughtful writing requires a more complex analysis of ideas, images, and concepts. That's why we layer writing through drafting and revising, to get below the surface to the core of analysis. That's where the surprises and insights are; that's when and where we really start to see. Until you explore layers of thinking through writing and rewriting, you will never know exactly what it is you want to say or are capable of saying.

In the past when teachers asked me to revise, they just wanted me to clean up a few sentences and check my grammar and spelling. Why can't I do that now?

You can. Go ahead and fix mistakes, correct your grammar, be conscious of your spelling. A note of caution, though: Cleaning up and correcting are proofreading; they are cosmetic remedies rather than methods of thinking. They do not constitute revision, at least not in the way I use the term. Revision is just what it says: re-vision, or seeing again through rewriting. Seeing deeply means writing deeply, and to write deeply means to think deeply. This is what revision is all about.

Correct grammar and spelling are important, but it's probably no use fixing up what you've written in a first draft if your ideas and how you write about them are likely to change during the process of revising. While it doesn't really matter if you "clean up" earlier or later, it may make more sense to save this step until the end.

How do I know what needs to be revised in my paper? Where do I start?

If you are not used to revising, it is a good idea to roll up your sleeves and plunge right in. Move things around, change your focus, write from another perspective or angle. Experiment. As you transform your draft, you begin to see the various possibilities of each piece of writing. You also demystify your writing so that you aren't afraid to mess with it. This kind of mucking around with what once seemed solid and fixed will help make the revision process seem less daunting.

As you look for different ways to revise, you also want to work closely with a writing partner in class or read your drafts aloud in a group workshop. Ask for feedback, and practice giving feedback to other writers. This exposure will help you become a more apt critic of writing, not to mention a better revisionist.

`What if I gather too much feedback? How do I revise?`

Learning how to cull through comments and suggestions is an essential writer's skill. Different readers read differently. While there is often a consensus in writers' workshops about what needs to be done with a paper, it is just as likely that your readers will disagree in their suggestions. You will never be able to satisfy all of them. But you will have a sense of what you like or don't like about the suggestions you receive. Pick and choose from them; don't try to incorporate all of them into a revision. You'll only get muddled and end up confusing your readers.

Try to weigh feedback and suggestions against your own intentions as a writer. Trust your own intuitions about your writing and how your draft speaks to you. Ask specific questions of your readers about what you've accomplished and hope to accomplish in your draft. That way you will be sure to get feedback that is useful to you. You will also remain in charge of your writing.

`What if I have a teacher who won't let me revise my papers?`

I know of no teacher who would be disappointed to receive writing that is well-thought-out and thoroughly revised. No instructor in his or her right mind would out-and-out ban revision. Whether or not a teacher allows you to revise papers that have already been graded, however, might be a different issue.

You will probably be given many opportunities to revise in your writing class. You will be asked to take your work through a process of brainstorming, focusing, planning, drafting, rewriting, and editing. The goal of this process is to enable you to turn in your finest work at the end of the semester.

In other classes, teachers may expect you to revise on your own. When you turn in a paper they will expect you to submit a polished product that has already been rewritten and proofread. This does not mean that you have to give up the process that worked for you in your writing classroom. It only means that you will have to follow up your process on your own.

Develop a schedule of deadlines for each step in the procedure from brainstorming to planning, drafting to revising, focusing to editing. Give yourself time to go back and revisit steps as needed. Then when your deadline arrives, turn in your best revised work.

REVISING ACTIVITIES

1. If you keep a diary or a journal, go back to entries that describe a significant period in your life. When you originally wrote these entries, you wrote them for yourself alone; now envision a readership—your

classmates or the readers of a newspaper column you might write. How would you change these entries for your readers? What would you keep and what would you omit? Consider how your own perspective on the events or period you wrote about may have changed with time: What do you know now that you didn't know then? What experiences have you had that allow you to read these entries differently than before?

2. Go to a favorite outdoor site and write about it, double spacing and keeping wide margins. Put the piece away for two weeks and then return to the site, changing your perspective by sitting in a new place to write. Look again at your surroundings, jotting down any extra details that you may have missed the first time. Then note in the margins and between the lines of your paper what you would want to develop or change. As you re-see your environment, how might you revise your paper? How might your focus change according to your new perspective?

3. Give copies of the second half of your draft to the class. Ask them to write a couple of paragraphs each describing what they imagine the first part of the draft to be like. Then pass out copies of the entire draft and discuss ways that their readings of the draft's conclusion may help you revise the first part.

4. Pass out copies of a complete draft. Read it in chunks from beginning to end, pausing after each reading to allow your classmates to write a response. Make sure they do not read ahead in the draft; have them anticipate what will follow. Note what they hope or hope not to see in your draft as it progresses. Record their emotions and thoughts as the story advances. Hear the draft as it unfolds. When you have finished reading the entire paper aloud, ask the class what disappointed them, surprised them, disturbed them, satisfied them about the draft as it progressed.

5. Hand out copies of your paper and read it aloud to your class. Then pass around a piece of paper and ask your classmates to compile a "What if?" list: "What if you dropped this opening paragraph and began here?" "What if you forgot this part about your aunt and wrote just about your grandmother instead?" "What if you took the wonderful sentence in the middle of paragraph five and made that your focal point?" Choose one or more of these "what ifs" and use them to revise your paper.

6. List at the top of a draft at least three of the seven writer's senses—seeing, hearing, touching, tasting, smelling, imagining, and remembering. Then go back through your paper and expand the areas that bring these senses into play, incorporating into your draft the details that pertain to each sense. As your paper expands, you may want to go back and pare down other sections where you summarize or tell instead of describe and show.

7. Select one sentence or paragraph that your draft could not be without. Use that sentence or paragraph as your introduction and see where it takes you.

8. Put your draft away for two or three days after you write it. Then take it to a spot where you can reflect quietly. (I know of at least one writer who sits in an empty church to do this.) Read your draft twice and "listen" deeply to your own responses. During your first reading, jot down a word or two in the margins of your paper that sum up gut reactions to what you read, moments of sudden revelation, joy, or dismay; moments when your writing seems either exquisitely honest or woodenly false. ("I didn't know until I read this sentence now how bitter I still am about this incident." "That neat ending sounds like a fairy tale and just isn't true.") As you go over your paper a second time, read with an eye toward change, and expand your marginal comments into suggestions for revision. ("I think I'll start my paper by talking about my lingering bitterness." "I want to open up my ending so it sounds not so happy-ever-after.")

9. Ask a writing partner to pinpoint three or more techniques you might use to improve your paper. He or she might, for example, suggest that you use more dialogue, details, or documentation. Then layer your revisions, concentrating on one technique at a time. Don't try to incorporate everything at once. Pause between each revision and note how your draft changes with each layer.

10. Start with the first full paragraph on your second page, and drop your entire first page altogether. You may have to revise the opening sentence of this paragraph a bit, but use it as the start of your revision. If you wish, incorporate bits and pieces of your original first page into the rest of your story. Then reread your draft to see how it changes. Does your new beginning confuse the reader, or does it invite her with an interesting lead? Do you still need what preceded your new beginning, or can the revised paper stand on its own without that material? What changes in the body and conclusion of the draft will you have to make in order to accommodate your new beginning?

11. Choose a significant scene or idea in your draft and copy it onto a new piece of paper. Expand that particular moment in your essay by examining it from every perspective and angle you can think of. Embody it with details. When you have finished, reincorporate the expanded scene or idea back into your paper and see how it changes the draft's focus. Try another scene or idea.

12. Read your paper aloud in a small group, and have your classmates note where you pause, stumble, or otherwise revise your wording as you read.

Reading aloud like this lets the draft speak and teases out areas of your paper that want more attention. Go back to these spots and figure out what you intended to say but never said, what you should have omitted but kept, what the draft itself wants you to hear.

13. E-mail a draft to an Internet writers' group and ask them to schedule an online workshop session. This is a good way to widen your reading audience and to get feedback from experienced writers. Listen to the advice these writers give you, and ask questions. Apply suggestions you like toward your revision.

14. Have a classmate interview you and write up your biography. Revise the biography from your own perspective, highlighting and expanding what you want, and downplaying or omitting sections that seem unimportant to you. Perhaps you could select just one scene or incident from the biography that you want to write about and let that be your focus.

15. Work with a partner to re-see (re-vise) selected portions of your draft. Read aloud passages that are meant to convey specific images, and ask your partner to listen without reading along. Pause between selections and have your partner describe to you what he or she sees, or doesn't see from your reading (I see . . . ;" "I wish I could see . . .;" "I don't see enough of . . .;" "I don't get a full picture of . . . "). Have your partner jot down specific questions that will help you re-see portions of your draft. ("What color hair did your friend Tom have?" "What kind of furniture did the scary room have?" "How did the girl move when he was scared?")

16. Find an op-ed, persuasive, or argumentative piece in a newspaper or magazine that you disagree with, and then revise it from your own point of view. Incorporate parts of the original piece into your own paper as a way of accounting for the opposing perspective, but rework the article so that your own opinions become the focal point.

17. Copy your draft onto a computer disk or hard drive, or photocopy it for safekeeping. Then take your original copy and drop a bomb on it! Demystify it. Break it up, fragment it, "discombobulate" it. Try a bit of dialogue here, expand description there, cut paragraphs or sentences in the middle, rewrite the conclusion as the lead, or the lead as the conclusion. Try different fonts. Incorporate poetry into the story. Rewrite whole scenes or incidents from another person's viewpoint. Take risks and have fun with your draft. (Remember: you still have a copy of your original version!) When you finally have a working draft—a fragmented piece in progress—share it with a group. Have each person pinpoint at least three new areas of your draft that intrigue him or her. Choose from these to find a basis for a more coherent revision.

18. Start a group revision binder. With three or four classmates, choose a notebook that will hold a semester's worth of your collective drafts and responses. Keep the binder in a public area at the reserve desk of the library, for example, or outside your instructor's office. Divide the binder into two parts: Part I: Drafts, Part II: Suggestions for Revision. Collect your drafts in Part I, and have plenty of blank paper on hand in Part II. Each week, select a classmate's draft from Part I and write a detailed response to it in Part II. Make sure that each group member receives a response from at least one other member weekly.

19. Divide your draft into sections, leaving ample room between each. Write in the blank spaces between each section, answering the following questions: "What do I want to achieve in this section of my draft?" "What have I achieved?" "What more do I have to do to this section in order to reach my goal?"

20. Follow the same procedure above, but list only what you hope to achieve in each section. Then pass the draft on to a partner, and let him or her decide whether or not you've achieved your goal. Have your partner suggest ways of revising your draft to better accomplish what you want.

21. During the first week of class, write an essay about your impressions of college. Exchange the essay with a classmate to keep until later in the semester. Before the semester ends, have your partner read your essay aloud to you. As you listen, note what changes in perspective you have now as a seasoned college student as opposed to someone who is brand new to campus. What things would you want to develop, downplay, or change in your original essay? How do time and space help you revise what you wrote earlier?

22. Start a writer's exchange with other students in your major or area of interest. By campus mail or e-mail, exchange drafts of essays you are writing in your chosen discipline and ask for feedback. You might get together as a group for scheduled meetings. Pay special attention to the details that make writing for your major different from the writing you may be doing for your English class, and use these as you go about revising. Once a month, report to your writing class on the progress of your other academic writing.

23. Collect simplistic endings from television sitcoms and dramas. See how many endings you can find that resolve all the characters' issues and problems within thirty or sixty minutes. Then rewrite the endings to make them more complicated.

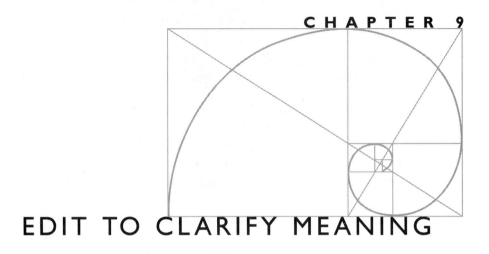

CHAPTER 9

EDIT TO CLARIFY MEANING

There are few satisfactions—and you know which ones they are—that are greater than editing a final draft—word by word, space by space, line by line. As Diane Ackerman says,

> Most of a writer's life is just work. It happens to be a kind of work that the writer finds fulfilling in the same way that a watchmaker can happily spend countless hours fiddling over tiny cogs and bits of wire. Poets also love to fiddle with a word here, a word there—small spaces for hours. And when I'm working on a poem, I'm working harder than I've ever worked at anything in my life—I'm concentrating harder. But it's enjoyable. Not something I would describe as fun—it's more like rapture, a kind of transcendent play.

Fiddling around with a piece of writing is fun because the subject comes clear. I like to make my copy simple, easy—like the flight of the seagull. Each editing makes the writing more natural. Editing—ironically—makes each draft more spontaneous.

I'm going to write a few lines about a cliché topic—Father's Day—and then see if I can edit in the meaning.

> I never expected to be a father. My own father was at work or church most of the time. Even when he was home, he seemed at a distance, another, stranger male in a house dominated by women—his grandmother and her daughter. I didn't really know what a father was supposed to do. Then I had a daughter, and I found I knew what to do.

Editing is simply a matter of adding, taking away, moving around, and making sure the result was clear. Do I have something to say? I can't edit until I have specified a topic, since all editing is aimed at developing and clarifying the topic. No topic, and editing is a waste of time. In my sample, I do have a topic—discovering how to be a father.

I also need a structure, a design and order. I have that. I have an embedded narrative—how I passed from not knowing a father's role to knowing. Now I can edit.

I move some of it around:

> My own father was at work or church most of the time. Even when he was home, he seemed at a distance, another, stranger male in a house dominated by women—his grandmother and her daughter. I never expected to be a father. I didn't really know what a father was supposed to do. Then I had a daughter, and I found I knew what to do.

I put in and take out:

> My ~~own~~ father was ~~at work~~ on the road buying silk stockings, women's corsets, or ladies gloves or at the department store making sure they were sold at a profit. If he wasn't on the road ~~or~~ he was at church, a deacon trying to fulfill the orders of the prophets. When I was young, I didn't know the difference between profits and prophets. Both ruled our life. ~~most of the time.~~ Even when he was home, he seemed at a distance, another, stranger male in a house dominated by women—my mother and her mother. ~~grandmother and her daughter.~~ I never expected to be a father; I didn't ~~really~~ know what a father was supposed to do. Then a nurse handed me Anne, my first daughter, wrinkly red and howling. ~~Then I had a daughter and I found~~ I knew what to do. No thinking, just instinct. I held her against my shoulder and rubbed circles around her tiny back. Her howls became sobs, her sobs moans, her moans, silence. She slept, and I became a father.

That's all. In most cases, editing means putting in more than taking out, moving around, simply clarifying.

I have worked for the past few years with editors on some of the best newspapers in the country, and I've found that these editors make the same mistake most teachers—and their students—make. The mistake is to plunge in and start editing language first, working from the written line back to form and then to meaning. It simply doesn't work.

PROOFREADING AND EDITING

Proofreading is what most people think of when editing is mentioned, but it is only a small part of editing. It is important to correct spelling, to check facts and names and quotations, to conform to certain stylistic standards of mechanics and usage, to clean up typographical errors. But editing is that and much more.

Editing is the honing of thinking, making meaning rational and clear, accurate and graceful. Editing is the final clarification of meaning. You choose one word and reject another word in relation to meaning. If the meaning isn't clear, the choice will be arbitrary and often wrong. There are no rules for word choice unrelated to meaning. Also, when you choose to write a short sentence or paragraph, it is usually for emphasis, and unless you know what you want to emphasize you won't know whether to make the sentence or the paragraph long or short.

When you edit, you repeat steps from the revision checklist, but your reading is different. When you revise, you read to see what needs to be done in the next draft; when you edit, you are the reader's advocate, preparing the final draft for your readers.

EDITING PRIORITIES

Effective editing is usually the result of three separate and distinct readings, each with its own pace, strategies, and techniques. The highly skillful editor or writer may be able to perform all three readings simultaneously, moving from the large global questions of meaning to structural questions of order, and to line-by-line questions of voice. But those interrelated skills are best developed by separating the reading—reading first for meaning, next for order, and third for voice.

Of course in each case the writer has to keep an eye open for the audience, standing back and making sure that what is being said and resaid on the page is clear to the reader.

This seems to be a slow process, but the first reading is usually a very fast one—a quick flyover of the territory to make sure that there is a single dominant meaning and an abundant inventory of information to support that meaning.

If there is no subject, no dominant meaning, no inventory of information, it is a waste of time to do more revising and editing. Stop immediately. Find a subject. Find its meaning. Find the facts to support that meaning.

The second reading looks for form and structure. It is a bit slower, but not much. The piece is still read in chunks to see if the sections support the main point and appear when the reader needs them.

If there is no form to the writing, no order within that form that leads the reader to meaning, read no further. It will be a waste of time. Stop. Choose a form and establish an order within that form.

At the end there is the third reading, a slow, careful, line-by-line editing of the draft to be sure that it is ready for a final proofreading. Here the writer cuts, adds, and reorders, paragraph by paragraph, sentence by sentence, word by word.

The process of three readings may sound tedious, but it shouldn't be. In each case you'll have the excitement of discovery, of finding a meaning that you did not expect to find and defining a change to make it become clear. Writing gives you the satisfaction of craft, the feeling you have when you lean your weight into the corner and make your bicycle swing gracefully where you want it to go. Writing is similar to hitting a tennis ball, baking bread, building a sturdy shelf, sewing a dress, planting a garden. It is a process of making, and it is fun to make something well, to handcraft a piece of prose that will carry meaning and feeling to another person.

EDITING MARKS

Most computer editing is invisible, but those who work with typewriter and pen or pencil will find it helpful to mark up the copy according to the traditions of the editor's trade:

During the first two readings I sit away from the desk, if I am not using a computer, in an easy chair and use a clipboard or a bean bag lap desk. I read the draft quickly, as a reader will, and do not mark anything within the text. I do not correct spelling or typos, change words, revise, or edit. Instead, I make marks in the left margin:

✓ A check for something that works,

✳ a star for something that works well,

C a C for something that needs cutting,

⌐→ an arrow that suggests movement,

⋎ a two-headed arrow to indicate the need for expansion,

—▶◀— two arrows pointing at each other to show what needs to be tightened,

? and a question mark for further consideration.

These marks allow me to move through the text quickly.

In the following list are some of the most helpful editing marks for the third, careful, line-by-line reading. If you are reading "hard copy" (manuscript pages, not a computer screen) you will find these marks helpful in editing your drafts or the drafts of a classmate in a peer-editing session:

paragraph	The craft of editing depends on reading aloud.
capital	the craft of editing depends on reading aloud.
lowercase	The craft of editing depends on reading aloud.
close	The craft of edit ing depends on reading aloud.
separate	The craft of editing depends on reading aloud.
transpose	The editing craft of depends on reading aloud.
punctuate	The craft of editing depends on reading aloud.
insert	The craft of editing depends on reading aloud.
take out	The craft of editing depends on reading aloud.
cut	The craft of editing depends on reading aloud.
restore	The craft of editing depends on reading aloud.
move	Insert A The craft of editing depends on reading aloud.

Large inserts should be numbered or lettered and an

arrow should be marked in the margin of the text

where it is to be placed.
move Insert A here

EDITING CHECKLISTS

The following checklists are built on the editing system that uses three readings— one for the topic, one for development of the topic, and one for language that communicates the topic. Of course the actual process of revising and editing will not be so neatly contained. Change of focus leads to change of language, and change of language can change the topic; still, the master list is a way of proceeding logically and efficiently through a series of confusing writing problems.

Each writer has his or her own strengths and weaknesses. Eventually you should adapt my checklist to your own style, problems, and solutions.

Many times writers edit against deadlines, without time to carefully revise and edit. Remember that you have to deal with the first item before going on to the second and the second before the third. Here is a checklist for that situation:

THE QUICK EDIT CHECKLIST

- State the single, most important message you have for the reader in one sentence.
- List the points that support the message in the order the reader needs to receive them.
- Read the draft aloud to be sure the text is accurate and fair, and that the music of the language supports the message you are sending to the reader.

When you learn that the first draft is not the end result of the writing process, you will plan to allow time—at least as much as comes before the first draft—for reading, revising, and editing. The quick checklist is designed to help in the three readings for subject, structure, and language, but don't be surprised when you have to move back and forth through the checklist as solutions breed problems, and new problems demand new solutions.

THE EXPANDED EDIT CHECKLIST

The list is long, but remember that many of your answers will come rapidly, in a second or less. You are scanning the text to catch the problems that have survived the writing process and must be solved before the draft is final, ready to face a reader.

- *State the single, most important message you have for the reader in one sentence.*
  - Does the draft deliver on the promise of the title and lead?
  - Does your message have significant meaning you can make clear to the reader?
  - Is the message important, worth the reader's time?
  - Does your message contain the tension that will provide the energy to drive the reader forward?
  - Is your message focused? Do you have a clear point of view toward the subject?

- Is the message placed in a significant context? Will that context be clear to the reader?
- Does the message have limitations that help you control and deliver the information?
- Do you have an abundance of information upon which to build the draft? Can you answer the questions the reader will certainly ask?
- Is that information accurate and fair?
- *List the points that support the message in the order the reader needs to receive them.*
  - Is the form, the genre, of the draft appropriate to deliver the message to the reader? Will it contain and support the meaning of the draft?
  - Does the structure within the draft support and advance the principal message?
  - Does the order in the piece make the reader move forward, anticipating and answering questions as they arise?
  - Is the structure logical? Does each point lead to the next in a sensible sequence? Is there a narrative thread that carries the reader forward? Will the sequence or narrative stand up to a doubting reader?
  - Is the draft too long? Too short?
  - Are the proportions of sections within the draft appropriate to the information they deliver? Are there sections that are too long? Too short?
  - Is the draft effectively paced? Does it move fast enough to keep the reader reading, slow enough to allow the reader to absorb what is being read?
  - Does the draft go off on tangents that take the reader away from its principal message? Does it include elements of good pieces of writing that do not support the current message but may be developed on their own later?
  - Is each point supported with evidence that will convince the reader?
  - Is the draft written at a distance that will involve the reader but also allow the reader to consider the significance of the message?
- *Read the draft aloud to be sure it is accurate and fair, and that the music of the language supports the message you are sending to the reader.*
  - Does the title catch the reader's attention, and does it make a promise to the reader that can be fulfilled by the draft?
  - Does the opening accomplish the same thing?
  - Is each piece of information accurate and fair and presented in context?
  - Does the reader need more information? Less? Can anything be cut? Must anything be added?

- Does the reader finish each sentence having gained information?
- Can the draft be heard by the reader? Does the music of the draft support and advance the meaning of the message?
- Does the draft reveal rather than tell whenever possible? Does the draft call attention to the message rather than the reader?
- Does each paragraph and each sentence emphasize the appropriate information?
- Does the sentence length vary in relation to the meaning being communicated, with shorter sentences at the most important points?
- Does the draft depend, at important points, on the subject–verb–object sentence?
- Is the draft written in the active voice whenever possible? Is each word the right word?
- Have all sexist and racist language and stereotypes been eliminated?
- Has private language—jargon—been replaced with public language the reader can understand?
- Has worn-out language—clichés and stereotypes—been replaced with language that carries specific meaning to the reader?
- Is the draft primarily constructed with verbs and nouns rather than adverbs and adjectives?
- Has the verb *to be* in all its forms been eliminated whenever possible? Excess *would*s, *what*s, and *ing*s?
- Is the simplest tense possible used?
- Are the tenses consistent?
- Are any words misspelled?
- Are the traditions of language and mechanics followed, except when they produce ungraceful language or change the meaning of the draft?
- Is the draft attractively presented, so that nothing gets between the reader and the message?
- Does the closing give the reader a feeling of closure and completeness, yet stimulate the reader to continue to think about the message that has been delivered?

Develop your own editing checklist, building on your own strengths and weaknesses in writing. Do not forget that this final stage of writing is still focused on discovery of meaning; as you edit, you learn more about your topic and make what you have to say come clear to the reader—so clear and easy to read that the reader may believe the writing was spontaneous.

CLARIFY IN THE DAYBOOK

My daybook becomes, in this last stage of the writing process, a lab book in which I make note of references and facts I have to check in the library, illustrations and charts I have to locate and reproduce, reprint permissions I have to obtain. I also note problems that should be added to my personal checklist.

Most importantly, I make notes of questions, problems, conflicts that have arisen during the writing of a draft that may lead to new pieces of writing.

The computer is of enormous help in editing, making it possible to read the draft and fix problems with spelling, punctuation, diction, usage as you read.

EDIT ON THE COMPUTER

Most software programs check the spelling in a document, but they will pass any correctly spelled word. If I mistype *top* for *to,* the program does not recognize the incorrect word. It will say OK to any real word. Other programs identify problems in mechanics and usage, but be careful with those as well. No software program can institutionalize George Orwell's wise advice in "Politics and the English Language":

(i) Never use a metaphor, simile, or other figure of speech which you are used to seeing in print.

(ii) Never use a long word where a short one will do.

(iii) If it is possible to cut a word out, always cut it out.

(iv) Never use the passive where you can use the active.

(v) Never use a foreign phrase, a scientific word, or jargon word if you can think of an everyday English equivalent.

(vi) Break any of these rules sooner than say anything barbarous.

Pay special attention to that last rule.

TUNE THE VOICE

Edit out loud. Listen to the music of the draft, and tune it so that each paragraph, each line, each word, each space between words creates a beat and melody that supports and advances the meaning of the draft.

Your ear has been trained since early childhood to listen to language and to use language to be heard. Your ear knows when the voice is honest or dishonest, graceful or clumsy, true or false.

IN THE WRITER'S WORKSHOP

Vigorous writing is concise. A sentence should contain no unnecessary words, a paragraph no unnecessary sentences, for the same reason that a drawing should have no unnecessary lines and a machine no unnecessary parts. This requires not that the writer make all his sentences short, or that he avoid all detail and treat his subjects only in outline, but that every word tell. WILL STRUNK

The American oral language is very musical, and if you read a lot and get involved with language, you can get a feeling for how the lines wish to proceed, how the words wish to follow each other, how the sounds work together in a kind of music. LUCILLE CLIFTON

A writer's independence and interdependence depend on his language. For a writer embodies a terrible paradox. He works alone, but he works with the most socialized of tools: language. The fullness of the collective expression. He cannot exist as a writer without a collectively wrought, preexistent reality: the reality of language. But his work cannot die if he adds to that reality a significant voice that is actually a contribution to the life of a language that will outlive him. In this process he gives up his ego in order to feed that reality, and so writing is always a sacrificial act. But his language will endure because a people cannot be deprived of language, for language is like air: it belongs to all or none, it cannot be caged, murdered, or stripped, no matter how many books are burned, forbidden, or persecuted: for language to die, the whole human race would have to perish along with it. Thus Thomas Mann outlives Hitler, Osip Mandelstam outlives Stalin, Pablo Neruda will outlive the Chilean junta. CARLOS FUENTES

The voice is the element over which you have no control: It's the sound of the person behind the work. I suppose there are some more or less conscious elements in voice; that is to say, a self-conscious manipulation of rhythm that may become habitual. But even the rhythms, it seems to me, stem from personality rather than from something acquired or mechanical. They're the tremblings of individuality. A person whose mind blurts will blurt in prose, and a person whose mind flows will flow in prose. JOHN HERSEY

Just to write a good sentence—that's the postulate I go by. I guess I've always felt that if you could keep a kind of fidelity toward the individual sentence, that you could work toward the rest. RICHARD FORD

I work with language. I love the flowers of afterthought. BERNARD MALAMUD

The language must be careful and must appear effortless. It must not sweat. It must suggest and be provocative at the same time. TONI MORRISON

English usage is something more than mere taste, judgement, and education—sometimes it's sheer luck, like getting across a street. E. B. WHITE

Working at sentences and rhythms is probably the most satisfying thing I do as a writer. I think after a while a writer can begin to know himself through his language. He sees someone or something reflected back at him from these constructions. Over the years it's possible for a writer to shape himself as a human being through the language he uses. I think written language, fiction, goes that deep. He not only sees himself but begins to make himself or remake himself. DON DELILLO

When it comes to language, nothing is more satisfying than to write a good sentence. It is no fun to write lumpishly, dully, in prose the reader must plod through like wet sand. But it is a pleasure to achieve, if one can, a clear running prose that is simple yet full of surprises. This does not just happen. It requires skill, hard work, a good ear, and continued practice . . . . BARBARA TUCHMAN

There are, of course, basic principles to be observed: Adjectives are to be avoided unless they are strictly necessary; adverbs too, which is even more important. When I open a book and find that so and so has "answered sharply" or "spoken tenderly," I shut it again: It's the dialogue itself which should express the sharpness or the tenderness without any need to use adverbs to underline them. GRAHAM GREENE

The language leads, and we continue to follow where it leads. WRIGHT MORRIS

....

QUESTIONS ON EDITING

My writing partner or classmates tell me that I don't have to change a thing, that everything is clear and makes sense to them. So I guess I don't have to edit, do I?

That depends. If you have edited thoroughly before asking your classmates to look at your work, it could be that your writing is ready to go. It might seem like an empty task to edit once more. Maybe you simply don't need to.

Or it could be that you need to imagine a wider audience for your work, a readership more varied than the one composed of your classmates. Imagine a magazine or newspaper that might publish your work, and think of the audience you might have. Is your piece ready for publication without further editing? Would your main images and ideas be absolutely clear to all of your readers?

Sometimes your classmates will understand what you write about because you share similar experiences with many of them: You may all be close in age, or live and work within the same school environment. For this reason, they may not need images or ideas clarified. They can simply "relate" to what you write. But someone who does not occupy the same realm of experience as you and your classmates may require more clarification. Keep these readers in mind as you edit.

I always edit right on the computer, but when I print out my work and ask other people to read it, they still find spots that need clarification. Should I always edit by hand?

The computer or word processor is a great tool for editing and revising. You can easily delete, add, move around, or insert material. With many computer programs you can also check your spelling, look up definitions of words, and use a thesaurus to find just the right word.

Still, the experience of reading on the computer, while useful, is no match for reading printed copy you can hold in your hand. Most of us are more experienced in reading printed material this way. Most of us learned to read this way. So reading a final revision solely on the computer can be somewhat artificial.

You will also want to imagine how your readers will receive your final piece. Unless you are transmitting your piece by e-mail, they will most likely be sitting down, holding it in their hands—at a desk, the breakfast table, or the library or on the subway.

Edit and revise on your computer as you compose. But when you are preparing your final manuscript, print out a copy that you can read at least three times, layer by layer—for meaning, form, and presentation. Take your copy into some quiet corner and mark it up. Make your changes on the computer and then print out your copy again; repeat this sequence as many times as you need to read it to complete a thorough editing.

Why can't I just run a grammar and spell checker on my computer?

Go ahead. These tools are useful. But they are no substitute for reading a draft for meaning. Your computer cannot do that. Sometimes it will even give you the wrong grammar suggestion for the meaning you want. You may purposely use long sentences to imply seriousness or formality, and your grammar checking software will advise you to cut them in half. At other times you might want short, concise sentences or purposeful fragments, and your program will tell you to correct or lengthen your sentences.

Since you edit as much for the voice of the draft as for meaning and correctness, you will want to listen to your writing rather than depend on your computer to tell you if it's right or wrong. Spell check final revisions, but don't count too much on grammar checkers and other writer's programs to edit your piece. They make assumptions about what is standard writing and who are standard writers. You have your own voice, and your writing reflects that voice. There is nothing standard about it.

How do I know when I'm done editing?

When the deadline arrives. I once took a survey of all the people in my department at the university who had written books. They had all revised or edited their books after their manuscripts had been accepted. There is no natural end to the editing process. As Paul Valery said, "Writing is never finished, only abandoned."

What if I don't have time to edit?

Sometimes when you have to turn in writing that you do on the spot, you won't have time for extensive editing or revising. This possibility is particularly likely when you're writing answers to essay questions on exams. The trick in situations like this is to plan before writing.

With essay answers and other kinds of on-the-spot writing, you should take a few minutes to sketch out an outline or structure for your answer before you begin, since you will not be able to go back and reorganize when you finish. You will probably also want to edit as you write, or schedule a few minutes at the end of your available time to go back and make whatever changes you can while keeping your paper reasonably legible.

If you are in the habit of editing your work anyway, you will develop an eye and ear for what's right or out of place in your writing. Reading and editing closely while you have time will sharpen your editing skills for those occasions when you don't.

EDITING ACTIVITIES

1. Have an editing fair. Break the class into groups, and make each responsible for a common writing problem. One group might become experts on avoiding the passive voice; another on comma splices. Still another might concentrate on eliminating wordiness or finding active verbs. Have two groups at a time set up separate "booths" in class so that everyone else can stop by with their drafts and work on specific issues. Hold a fair at least once a week, rotating groups and assigning new topics as needed.

2. Collect troublesome sentences from your own work. As your writing partner, group, or teacher helps you recognize wordy, unclear, or grammatically weak sentences, add them to your list. Select one or two sentences from the list daily, and work with a partner to rewrite them.

3. Take a piece of writing, your own or someone else's, and cut it in half. Replace multiple words with one when one will do. Make war on needless adjectives. Cut back on prepositional phrases. Pare to the bone.

4. Choose a descriptive piece of writing with vivid and specific imagery and make it vague. Replace concrete adjectives *(limp, sallow, square, sharp)* with abstract adjectives *(awesome, beautiful, boring, ugly)*. Then read the passages aloud to see how they change. Close your eyes and try to picture the images. Which adjectives work? Which don't?

5. Exchange papers and circle all the descriptive adjectives. Which are vague, abstract? Which convey specific images? Help your partner substitute concrete adjectives for vague ones. Eliminate adjectives where your partner uses too many.

6. As a class, list on the board as many vague or abstract sentences you can: "It was sure a bright day." "The room was really nice." "The poem was

pretty boring." "It was the most exciting moment of my life." With a partner select five of these vague sentences, and make them vivid and descriptive. Read them aloud to one another to see if you get the picture.

7. Choose five sentences from any of your drafts, and rewrite them in at least five different ways: Make them concise, vague, descriptive, awkward, short, ungrammatical, whatever. After each rewrite, incorporate the sentences back into the drafts they came from, and discuss with a partner or group how they change the original paragraphs.

8. Examine with a group how a published writer uses a combination of long and short sentences to set the pace and tone of a piece or to keep it interesting. Then rewrite a portion of the piece so that all of the sentences are the same length. Read the paragraphs aloud and compare them to the original. What happens to the piece of writing when the sentences don't vary?

9. Exchange papers with a partner and edit each other's drafts. Make sure that you give your partner a clean, working copy so that he or she will feel free to mark it up. Read carefully, but edit boldly; don't be afraid to cross out words, pare down or clarify sentences, correct spelling, or identify grammatical errors.

10. As you read each others' papers in a group or class, write down striking or boring adjectives on individual slips of paper and drop them into a box. Every other week have an adjective fest. Draw at least ten adjectives out of the box and, in a group, compose a short paragraph in which you incorporate them. Use them sparingly in concise sentences, or sprinkle them liberally through ornate sentences. Discuss how the different uses of these adjectives adds or detracts from a piece of writing.

11. Keep two verb lists in your daybook, one for strong, active verbs (*yank, scoop, sweep, hurl*), and the other for passive verb forms (*was yelled at, is made clear, was held by*). As you read textbooks, stories, poems, signs, essays, instructions, novels, drafts, or e-mail messages, write down strong, interesting verbs on the active verb list, and then write a sentence next to each using the verb in the passive voice. Jot down passive constructions on the passive verb list, and write a sentence for each changing the passive voice to active. Once a week, select two verbs from both lists and discuss them with your group. Explain how the active and passive voices convey different tones and meanings.

12. Internet bulletin board posts and e-mail messages are often notorious for bad grammar and poor writing. Download some of these messages into your computer, print them out, and bring them to class for an editing spree. Work by yourself or in a group to clarify and weed out wordiness.

13. Challenge another writing class or group to a cliché collecting contest. (Some examples of clichés: "Blind as a bat," "loose as a goose," "under the weather," "butterflies in my stomach.") Through the course of a week, scan newspapers, magazines, and other reading material for clichéd or worn-out phrases. Listen to conversations, news broadcasts, and talk shows for more clichés. Write down the date, time, and source of each "cliché sighting." The group with the fewest sightings has to compile a list of all clichés to hand out to both groups.

14. Brainstorm a list of clichés in class, and write them on the board. Then exchange papers with a writing partner and go through line by line in search of clichés. Add more to the list on the board as you find them. Circle them and have the authors write replacement phrases or sentences.

15. Have a partner check off or circle awkward or vague sentences in your draft and hand your paper back to you. Rewrite each marked sentence at least three times on another piece of paper. First copy the original sentence. Then begin each subsequent sentence with the phrase, "In other words." Work toward increasing clarity with each sentence.

16. Have a partner read through a couple pages of your draft and then write one sentence in the left margin next to each paragraph briefly summing up what the paragraph is saying. If your partner has trouble summarizing a paragraph or misreads your meaning, rewrite the troublesome passage, working to clarify each sentence.

17. Pass out copies of your final revision to the class and read aloud. Ask the class to put a check next to sentences that need clarifying or grammar that needs correcting. Keep the workshop focused on editing and clarification rather than major revisions.

18. Read your paper backward, sentence by sentence, starting with the very last one. This technique allows you to pick out mistakes you might normally gloss over when reading logically from beginning to end, front to back.

19. Find an example of bureaucratic writing on the memo board of your city hall or in notices published in the local newspaper, or find parts of a politician's speech in a magazine, newspaper, or public document that you think use particularly flabby language. Such pieces of writing are often packed with passive verbs, cluttered with abstract adjectives, and jam-packed with "learned" words. Unclutter them. Rewrite these pieces as simply and clearly as possible, using the active voice, eliminating meaningless adjectives, and replacing show-off vocabulary with simpler words.

20. Read your draft line by line, making the changes necessary to clarify your meaning. If you can't read the text after you've made a number of changes, retype it, incorporating the editing you've done, and then attack it again. Have some of your classmates edit your paper while you edit theirs.

21. Refer to the editing checklist in this chapter, and personalize it with some editing tips of your own. Then go through each item one by one and scan your paper closely for errors. If you want, go through the first five or so points on your own, then pass it on to a classmate who can look at the next group on the checklist with fresh eyes. If necessary, keep passing it on.

22. Rewrite your title for different genres or different markets. Pretend that your piece is a newspaper column, and write an appropriate title. Make it an essay in a scholarly journal, and rewrite the title. Come up with a list of different kinds of publications and their markets, and rework your title for each market, making it as catchy to the reader's eye as possible.

23. Contact a local newspaper editor, and ask him or her to save drafts for you from a single published column or editorial. Tell the editor you are mainly interested in seeing how final drafts are proofread for publication. Compare the writer's draft with the editor's proofread copy, and discuss how they differ. Does the writer make any "mistakes" that are similar to yours? Do you see any patterns of errors in the writer's drafts that the editor picks up on and corrects? Do you agree with the editor's changes?

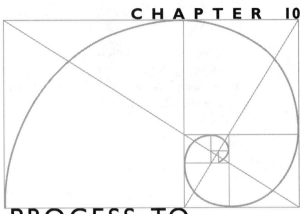

FIT YOUR PROCESS TO YOUR TASK

When you know how to write and revise, you are prepared to accept and complete a great many different writing tasks—some you never expected to perform.

A research paper, annual sales report, book report, scholarship application, poem, essay of literary analysis may look different when they are printed, but they are constructed of common elements and with similar skills.

When you have come this far in the study of writing, you have experienced all the essential skills you need to write effectively. If you now learn the basic elements from which writing forms are constructed, you can prepare yourself when a professor asks for a critical essay, a science teacher assigns a lab report, a history instructor demands a term paper, experience inspires a poem, the concert committee assigns you to write a press release, a foundation invites a grant proposal, an employer asks for a marketing memo, or a supervisor wants an analytical report on a manufacturing process.

The ability to adapt your writing process to new writing tasks will serve you well after college. One study revealed that electrical engineers do far more writing after college than English majors do. As you live and work in an increasingly complex and shrinking world, you will find yourself communicating in writing with supervisors, subordinates, colleagues, clients, customers around the globe.

Specific writing tasks may change, and the messages they produce may, in your lifetime, be sent and received by technological devices we cannot yet imagine—I never imagined a fax or modem—but the demand for clear writing will increase as we work with people over great distances.

HOW TO RESPOND TO A NEW WRITING TASK

There are logical steps to follow when faced with a new writing task. First, listen to the instructions, and ask questions if you do not understand the purpose of the assignment or what the person giving the assignment expects. It is helpful to study examples of similar assignments. Each writing form has its own traditions, but you may depart from them for reason; if you do not know the tradition the reader expects, however, you cannot depart from it in a way the reader will accept.

If you give yourself a writing task—a letter applying for a job, a note of sympathy, a journal narrative of an important event in your life, a memo redefining your job, a poem—you need to listen to yourself and then, playing the reader, question yourself to determine your expectations.

Writing forms or structures may appear arbitrary, but they have all been constructed, as houses are constructed, in response to logical, predictable demands. Houses need roofs and walls, doors and windows, rooms and hallways to satisfy the needs of people who live in them. The design of the house will change if is to be built in northern Maine or southern Arizona, if it is in Manhattan or on a farm in North Dakota twenty miles from town. But each house is a variation on a common need.

The same elements occur in every writing. Traditions are simply the records of how writing has been constructed in the past to solve special problems, the way a house in Minnesota may have a peaked roof so snow will not collapse it, and one in Arizona will have thick walls and extended eaves to make it cool and keep out the noonday sun. If you look at the problems a writing tradition attempts to solve, you will understand the tradition and be able to adopt or adapt it to solve your writing problems.

The following sections review the questions to ask when you confront a new writing task.

WHY WRITE?

The writer needs to answer that TOUGH question. To choose, adapt or develop a form, the writer needs to know the purpose of the writing to be done.

There are important, general reasons to write. Writing is the most disciplined form of thinking. Writers have to make the writing clear to themselves if they are to make it clear to readers. The act of writing demands content that is accurate, documented, authoritative, persuasive.

A written text can be read and understood over distances of time and place. It can be read and reread, shared, examined, revised, edited, considered, and reconsidered by many people. It provides a continuous point of reference.

In most literary works the purpose for writing is less clear to the reader, sometimes even to the writer in the beginning—to celebrate an experience, to explore an event, to understand a character, to examine an emotion, to tell a story, to entertain—but most writing does not produce literary works; it usually has a clear purpose—to persuade, to inform, to explain.

The reasons people write vary greatly. The writer may want to get a passing grade in history or share her historical research with other historians; the writer may want to report on families who have multiple social problems for a course in social work or persuade the government to concentrate all its services on a few problem families; the writer may want to recruit students for a junior-year-abroad program or to persuade an employer to adopt a new sales approach.

A good way to understand the purpose of a piece of writing is to define what you expect the reader to think, feel, or do after reading it: "I want the reader to respect our Franco-American heritage;" "I want our government to concentrate on those few families in town who are the breeding ground for most of our social problems;" "I want students to sign up for a junior year in Siberia;" "I want my boss to try a new sales technique."

A clear purpose helps the writer define, limit, and focus what the writer has to say and often predicts the form that will fulfill the writer's purpose.

WHAT IS MY MESSAGE?

Writing is thinking, and writers discover what they have to say by saying it. The message cannot be entirely predicted, and so the writer not only chooses the form of writing according to the message, but adapts that form to fit the evolving meaning.

Some writing tasks, such as poetry, are highly inventive, with the message discovered during the line-by-line drafts. But most writing tasks in the academic and working world have a clear purpose: to identify, define, and develop an historical trend; to report on the results of a biological experiment; to analyze a piece of literature; to explain a new software program; to suggest solutions that may solve a traffic problem at the supermarket checkout counter.

Sometimes a word will reveal my message to me in the private way of a writer's language—"advantaged"; or more likely a phrase, "the disadvantages of being an advantaged student," occasionally a sentence, "I came to realize my disadvantaged students had an advantage." Too often an editor, early in a project, will demand a clear, specific, conclusive statement of intent. Sometimes this is called a *thesis statement,* but I do not like the term; teachers held me to statements that I had to make before I had completed my research and before I had thought about the topics by writing drafts.

The message statement is not a contract. It is a goal, a possibility, a target, a starting place. Some such statements might be:

- To document the role of French Canadian priests in the exploration and mapping of North America
- To argue that social services should concentrate on the families in a community that have the most physical, emotional, social, educational, and financial problems
- To recruit students for a junior-year-in-Siberia program sponsored by the Russian department
- To propose that an automobile dealer consider the no-salesperson approach, where each car has the final price posted and there is no negotiation

WHO IS MY READER?

The message statement usually implies the audience: The first message above implies a history instructor or an audience of American historians; the next a sociology professor or a legislative group or agency that controls a budget; the third, college students who have enough money to spend a year abroad; the fourth, the owner or manager of an automobile dealership.

It is important, as you can see, to limit or target a specific audience. A sociology professor teaching an undergraduate course would require a different form and voice from a professor of social work in a graduate program. If the professor is in political science, still another form might be required. If the writer is appealing for a change in the law or a change in agency policy, the form of the appeal will again be different.

WHAT EVIDENCE WILL PERSUADE MY READER?

When you have decided on the purpose, the message, and the reader, you can anticipate the reader's needs.

Readers are hungry for information. Specific, accurate information gives your writing authority. The reader says, "This guy's done his homework; this guy knows his stuff." Readers need documentation; they need evidence to be persuaded.

Writers need to remember to write with information, no matter the writing task. Readers read, above all, to be informed.

WHAT VOICE WILL KEEP THE READER INTERESTED AND MAKE THE READER BELIEVE WHAT I HAVE TO SAY?

The reader responds, above all, to voice, to the individual who stands behind the page. We each have our natural voices that are reproduced in our writing, and we need to develop and control those natural elements that are composed from ethnic and family heritage, environment, and practice in speaking and listening. Voice is also a matter of intellectual, social, and emotional style. Your challenge as a writer is to hear your voice then tune it to the topic and the audience.

As you plan to write, you should compose fragments, perhaps sentences and paragraphs, in your mind and on your journal pages, listening to make sure that the music of the language supports your meaning and communicates to a stranger.

Effective writers hear, then see, their language appear on page or screen. They tune the language—word choice, pace, rhythm, manner or style to what is being said and to whom it is being said.

WHAT FORM WILL CARRY MY MESSAGE AND ITS DOCUMENTATION TO MY READER?

Finally the writer chooses the form, the vehicle that will carry meaning to the reader, or adapts the assigned form to the particular writing task.

To write this section, I looked in memory for the basic writing tasks I have done and came up with four tasks that have their own basic structures. You can do the same thing when faced with a writing task: Look within your experience and the demands of the job, then decide how to do it. Of course my "inventions" were discovered by the Greeks centuries ago, but we have to keep creating a rhetoric that serves our task, our audience, our time.

These are the basic writing tasks or problems the writer has to solve. The writer's purpose defines, in part, the solution or form, and these forms lie behind the writing in other genres—screen writing, poetry, science writing, historical writing, business and political writing. The writer begins with the tasks writers most frequently face:

To describe

To analyze

To inform

To persuade

Of course, these forms overlap. Description may be necessary to persuade, informing may involve analysis, and so on. The writer creates the form that fits the task, adapting the formal elements to the immediate task, inventing each time from the materials that have been invented before.

Most writing tasks are not so neat that you can run into the warehouse and grab a pretested, prepared writing form. Each task is different, and you need to adapt traditional forms to the new task and sometimes design a new form. It is really a simple task.

KNOW THE MESSAGE YOU HAVE TO DELIVER ⟶

⟵ KNOW THE PERSON TO WHOM IT IS TO BE DELIVERED

DESIGN A LANGUAGE VEHICLE
THAT WILL DELIVER
THAT MESSAGE TO THAT READER

WRITE TO DESCRIBE

Description is the basic form of writing, but when I first taught freshman English it was outlawed in our program as being too simple for academic discourse. Simple? That was the opinion of those who did not write. Description is not simple, but it is fundamental and the best way, I believe, to lay the foundation of the writer's craft. At first, you use description to capture a place or a person, then places with people, then people interacting with others, and you end up describing ideas, theories, concepts, thoughts and feelings, propositions and conclusions, speculations and facts. All forms of writing contain descriptive elements that make readers see, think, feel, react.

Writing description can introduce you to the discipline of recording information, ordering it into meaning, and communicating that meaning to readers. All the elements of effective writing—accuracy, concreteness, meaningfulness, context, development, form and order within a piece, emphasis, documentation, flow, grace, style, reader awareness, proportion, pace, voice—may be called upon when you write description.

TIPS ON WRITING EFFECTIVE DESCRIPTION

- *Be accurate.* The writer has to earn the reader's trust. A single error in fact or an accurate fact in the wrong context can cause the writer to lose the reader's trust.

- *Be specific.* Readers hunger for concrete details. The specific carries authority with it. Don't use words such as *beautiful* and *ugly* that carry no meanings out of context. What is beautiful or ugly to one person is the opposite to someone else. Give the reader specifics, and the reader will feel or think the reaction to it. Don't tell the reader what to think or how to feel; make the reader think and feel by using specific images.

- *Create a dominant impression.* Establish a focal point, and relate all your details to that point, developing and supporting it. If you walk into a trauma center, your eye goes to a stretcher or to a team of people working on someone or to parents sitting and waiting. Everything in your description must flesh out the dominant impression.

- *Establish an angle of vision.* The reader should see the trauma center from a particular angle: from the waiting room or the swinging doors of the ambulance bay, from the patient's bed looking up, from a nurse or doctor's eyes looking down. This position can move, but it should move slowly. Think of how a professional moves the movie camera and how the amateur blurs the screen by panning too quickly.

- *Determine the correct distance.* Stand at an appropriate distance to reveal what you want to say. Zoom in close for intimacy and immediacy; draw back to put the subject in context; move back and forth so that the topic is revealed effectively.

THE NARRATIVE ESSAY

Narrative—storytelling—is the most important form of description. Narrative allows the writer to describe historical and current events, processes and travels, searches and researches, biographies and autobiographies, reflections and investigations, actions and reactions that take place in the river of time.

We think of narrative as primarily a fiction technique, and when I first started teaching, narrative was not allowed in freshman English. Yet writing narrative is an essential skill for a nonfiction writer, too. In fact, all effective writing has an embedded narrative; the reader may not be aware of it, but the implied story keeps the reader's interest and moves the reader forward, toward the writer's meaning.

Narrative also satisfies the reader's fundamental hunger for story, chaos ordered into meaning. Readers who would not read about a subject on their own, will make the effort if it is told in the form of story: The boring financial or scientific story is unbored if you read the account of a fiscal battle or a scientist's struggle to make a breakthrough.

TIPS ON WRITING NARRATIVE

- *Time in a story is not a clock.* The second hand does not move evenly, click by click, toward the minute; the minute hand does not move evenly, click by click, toward the hour. Time in a story is distorted, as it is in life. We spend a great deal of time telling of a moment in great detail then skip to the next moment that is important to the story. When I was in the infantry, we used to say that combat was days of boredom with minutes of terror. That comment also describes the use of time in a narrative.

- *Show, don't tell.* This fundamental rule of dramatic writing applies to any narrative, whether it is fiction or nonfiction. The reader likes to have the story revealed, and it takes a while for an inexperienced writer to show what is happening rather than telling the reader what is happening—and what to think and feel. Narrative makes the reader think and feel for himself or herself. I write fiction, and when I make the transition to narrative, I find myself seeing the event I am describing as a movie. I do not say the character is scared; I show his hand shaking, his eyes open wide and looking around, his hesitant step and quick retreat back through the door.

- *Build with scenes.* The basic narrative unit is the scene, just as in a play or movie. The scene includes character, action and reaction, and setting. At the end, at least one of the characters is changed.

- *Characters interact.* Character, not plot, makes the story go. One person says or does something—or says or does nothing. "I love you," she says. He stands up, nods to the people at the next table and leaves the restaurant. There is an action and a reaction, and now the story will grow as she acts or he returns and she leaves and so on. Story is built on character.

- *Dialogue is easy.* Beginning writers are often afraid of dialogue. I remember what Elizabeth Bowen wrote: Dialogue is action. It is what people do to each other. The only exercise I assign is one to teach dialogue. Here is the situation: She is meeting him to tell him she is pregnant; he is meeting her to tell her that he does not want to see her anymore. Write that scene entirely in dialogue. Not names, no he saids or she saids. Just speech in quotation marks, one speaker to a paragraph.

This is still description, the revealing of the world. All of the issues of description exist in other forms of writing, but they are especially clear in the writing of description. Read descriptions that help you understand a subject, make notes on the techniques the writer uses. Try them yourself.

WRITE TO ANALYZE

As we describe, we analyze. We cannot help but evaluate what we have seen, taking it apart to see what makes it work. Analysis is as important to the writer's tool box as the wrench is to the mechanic. Analysis helps you understand an idea, an event, a feeling, a text. Analysis is a work of the mind more than the emotions.

Graham Greene once asked a profound question: "Isn't disloyalty as much the writer's virtue as loyalty is the soldier's?" Writers are blessed and cursed with this disloyalty. Disloyalty allows them to stand back from themselves—and their families, friends, churches, jobs, organizations—dissect what is happening to see what forces are at work. Writers suffer from this distancing, always standing back and questioning their motives, what they do and do not do, how they and their families, friends, neighbors, colleagues act and react. Writers question the world; nothing is sacred.

Writers are take-aparters. They x-ray, analyze, and look for causes and effects, theories, patterns, systems. The only defense of the writer's lonely trade is that writers are also put-togetherers. They construct their own analyses, new buildings of meaning that bring order, sense, and reason. These new constructions will face analysis from others as the intellectual world struggles to understand.

The principle elements of effective analysis include a clear and *fair* statement or description of what is to be taken apart, a logical process of dissection complete with evidence at each step of the way, a tone or voice that is appropriate and convincing, and a conclusion that constructs a new meaning.

TIPS ON WRITING ANALYSIS

- *Read the text.* The text may be a novel, documentation of a new personnel procedure, a sociological report, the film of a football game, a marketing plan, an environmental report. Read it quickly all the way through, then read slowly, step by step, to make sure you understand what you are analyzing—or what you don't understand.

- *Respond.* Respond to what you are analyzing—an essay, a manufacturing procedure, an historical theory, a medical treatment, an engineering report, a political speech, a movie—by taking into account your personal reaction. Too often, analysts stand back, not allowing themselves to connect what they are analyzing to their own experience, not realizing that emotion and personal thoughts are appropriate factors in analysis. When I analyze an historical account of a military event, I make use of my experience in combat; when I analyze a news story, I make use of my experience as a newspaper reporter.

- *Discover the focus.* To begin analysis, the writer should understand the central meaning of the process, event, discovery, law, theory, text to be analyzed. The writer works backward from the meaning or point of focus to see all that leads up to it.

- *Look for patterns.* Meaning is constructed of relationships. One thing leads to another. Look for those connections, the map of meaning the writer has drawn.

- *Be skeptical.* Use your common sense. Question. Doubt. Check the evidence the writer uses to support the meaning. Double-check the sources.

Examine the author's chain of logic for weak links. Remember what Ernest Hemingway said: "The most important essential gift for a good writer is a built-in, shock-proof shit detector."

- *Look at the context.* A piece of writing does not float free like a birthday balloon. Study what is written against the context in which it is written, the world in which the writing exists.

- *Write in an appropriate voice.* In most cases of analysis this means a professional, somewhat detached voice. The voice of a fair judge who is looking at the subject with a stern impartiality and analyzing in a way that is speaking to the subject, not the person or people behind the subject.

ANALYSIS IN THE BOOK REPORT

The book report is a common form of analytical writing, and the biggest mistake students make is to leave out the analysis. They limit their book reports to simply informing the reader that the book exists while the real purpose of the book—or article or short story—review is critical analysis. The reader wants an informed opinion of the information in the book, and the writer's success depends on presenting that information.

TIPS ON WRITING A BOOK REPORT

- *Include publication information.* The reader may want to buy the book or order it from the library. List the title and subtitle if there is one, the author, the publisher with principal city of publication, and the year of publication.

- *Be critical.* That does NOT mean being negative. It means evaluating the content and the presentation within the book.

- *Document each point with quotations.* The reader wants evidence to support what the reviewer says.

- *Compare.* Look at the book in the context of other books that have been published on the same subject, evaluating their strong and weak points.

- *Include biographical information about the author.* This background is helpful if it will help the reader to understand the basis of the writer's authority—or question it.

THE REFLECTIVE ESSAY

The reflective essay is a more sophisticated form of analysis. It often begins with a personal experience—the death of loved one, the coach's instructions to cheat to win a game, the decision to get—or not get—an abortion. The essay finds meaning in its subject.

It is a common misconception that analysis is a cold, detached, scientific process in which the writer analyzes the thoughts, experiences, writing of others. Of course, this assumption often holds true, but in reflective essays the writers analyze their own thoughts, feelings, reactions. A classic case of such an essay is George Orwell's "A Hanging" in which the real subject is Orwell's reflection upon his reaction to the event.

The personal experience is analyzed in much the same way as it is in the academic paper, but that experience is written about in a much more reflective manner as the writer focuses on a personal experience and finds meaning in it. The finding of meaning or significance is important. People who tell stories often just ramble on. The writer of an effective essay reflects, ruminates, considers, reconsiders, and takes the reader along on the adventure of thought.

That meaning may be thought out in considerable detail before the first draft is written. This is likely to happen when the writer attempts to explore a traumatic subject, such as the death of a loved one, because that topic has been rehearsed, thought over and over in the writer's mind.

The meaning, however, may be discovered entirely in the writing. The writer may be obsessed with a subject and have no understanding of it until the shape of the draft, what is in the act of being said, and how it is in the act of being said, reveals the meaning to the reader. This often happens to me. I plunge in, hoping that meaning lies on the blank page—or the blank screen—and it usually does, revealed in the words I do not expect to write. Most times meaning comes in a combination of pre-thinking and drafting. I have a hint, a clue, a sense of what I may discover, and then the writing defines and redefines, qualifies and clarifies that idea, gives it fullness and meaning.

In writing the reflective essay, you discover and develop the skills of critical thinking. You move in close and then stand back. There is immediacy and detachment, close examination and the placing of an event in perspective. There is compassion and judgment, feeling and thought.

An effective reflective essay is often personal, but it is not private. The reflective essay allows the reader to discover the subject—and the meaning of the subject—with the writer. The reader is invited to think along with the writer and to think against the writer, discovering in the act of reading the reader's own meaning in the essay.

TIPS ON WRITING THE REFLECTIVE ESSAY

- *Be personal.* The more personal you are, the more universal your readership. You should speak to the human condition—in specific terms. Your strength is your difference, your own peculiar vision of the world.
- *Allow your mind to run free.* Write fast so that you will discover what you didn't know you remembered, what you didn't know you thought and felt, what patterns and connections lay hidden in the experience.

- *Be critical.* The function of writing the personal or reflective essay is to find meaning in experience, not just to record experience. Be skeptical and critical, challenge your own prejudices, beliefs, your own knowing.
- *Put your vision in context.* Describe your vision of the world then place it in a context—historical, scientific, sociological, psychological, political. The personal experience should connect with a larger meaning.
- *Take the reader along.* Invite the reader to accompany you as you reflect upon experience. Allow the experience and the meaning that arises from it to unfold at a pace that encourages the reader to follow.

WRITE TO INFORM

One of the reasons to write is to report, to make others understand our knowing and our living, to explain. As the old hunter came back to the cave and described the mastodon, where it could be found, how it could be trapped, so we as citizens and scholars report back to the community so that what we each learn is shared with others, and the community knowing exceeds the knowledge of each individual.

To inform, you have to attract listeners by quickly showing them how what you have to say affects them. You have to make a connection with the reader, so that person has a personal stake in hearing what you have to say.

This is a tricky business. If you are too sure of yourself, too full of your own knowing, you will offend and put off potential listeners. You will call attention to yourself, not to what you have to say. On the other hand, if you are too modest, too shy, too unsure of what you have to say, no one will pay attention.

The best way to steer a middle course is not to say too much about oneself and not to say too much directly to the reader, telling the reader how valuable one's information may be for him or her. Instead, deliver the message, focus on the material itself, allowing its importance to grow in the reader's mind as he or she is informed by the facts.

Humans enjoy learning—and perhaps as much enjoy being authorities and informing others. You will be well read if you give the reader information the reader can put to use—and can share with others.

TIPS ON WRITING TO INFORM

- *Write with information.* Give specific, revealing details, concrete facts, accurate information. Build the piece of writing from information not language. Be direct, informative.
- *Anticipate your reader's questions.* Role play your reader and imagine what you would need and want to know—and when you would want to know

it. Good writing is a conversation with the reader in which the writer hears the reader's unspoken questions: "How come?" "What do you mean?" "So what?"

- *Answer your reader's questions.* In writing, the reader has no stupid questions. The reader must be accepted where the reader is. It is the task of the informing writer to serve the reader who does not know.

- *Connect the information with the readers' experience.* Give readers information in a form and context they can use in their thinking, in their lives, in their work.

- *Write in an inviting voice.* Do not preach, condescend, patronize, talk up or down to the reader. Just share your delight in the information with the reader in a voice that focuses on the information to be shared.

THE RESEARCH PAPER

One common way of informing is to write a research paper. In writing, revising, and editing the research paper, you must conform to the style in which research is reported in your discipline. Each scholarly discipline has its own form for the research paper. Not only are there significant differences in the way the physicists, literary scholars, sociologists, historians, botanists report their findings, but a single discipline such as psychology may have different styles within the field with clinical psychologists, social psychologists, and laboratory psychologists all conforming to different traditions. Discover the traditions and forms of the research paper appropriate to the discipline in which you write a research paper.

There are, however, important similarities in all research papers.

THE RESEARCH QUESTION

Good research is usually the product of a well-focused question. The experienced researcher spends time narrowing that question until it is one that can be answered within the limited time of a course or a grant and with the resources available to the researcher. Research is a discipline of accumulation, with each researcher adding to the increasing knowledge within a field of study.

RESEARCH NOTE TAKING

The researcher must have a consistent system of note taking appropriate to the discipline. Note cards—3×5, 4×6, 5×8—are still popular because each card can be ordered and reordered during research as the scholar explores the subject.

The biggest problem for the inexperienced researcher is knowing the difference between a direct quote and a paraphrase. A direct quote is precisely what it said or written. It is enclosed in "quotation marks." Paraphrasing is the technique of putting what you have read or heard in your own words; a paraphrase can never be put in quotation marks, but it should have an attribution so the reader can follow the quotation back to the source.

As the note cards are reordered, the information on the source of the information travels with the note. Write down *ALL* the details on where you found the information. For example, the title of the book, the author's name, the person quoted, the publisher of the book and the city where it was published, the edition or printing, the year of publication, the library where the material is stored, the chapter, page, paragraph, and line so that you can check the source, and so that other scholars can go to the source of your information.

PLAGIARISM

If you use another writer's words as your own, you have committed a major—perhaps *the* major—intellectual crime. I have been plagiarized, and I know what it feels like. A high school student won a national writing contest with a short story of mine until someone recognized it; a nun who ran workshops for writing teachers used almost 100 pages of one of my books, distributing it as her own text, until another nun read it and identified it as mine. In both cases, the plagiarists had not changed a word. I felt as though they had broken into my mind and stolen my ideas and my language.

Plagiarism is a felony. Where I taught, students who plagiarized were given Fs and made to take the courses over. I thought they should have been driven from the campus and banned from ever returning; or hung by their writing hands from the university flagpole for a month; or put in stocks in front of a dining hall so students could pelt them with old salad parts; or used as human football tackling dummies; or charged with theft in a court of law, as they would have been if they had stolen the computers or typewriters on which they had plagiarized.

The responsible writer—student or professional—gives credit for the specific words, information, and ideas that belong to someone else.

THE FORM OF THE RESEARCH PAPER

As I said at the beginning of this section, you must conform to the style required by your discipline. This is not a time for creativity. The form is designed to serve readers; they expect to find the information they need in a familiar form and place.

Footnotes

The research paper serves other researchers, and so you provide the sources of specific information *at the time you use that information* through a footnote system. A footnote tells the reader where you discovered the fact or quote you are using at the moment the reader reads it. This is easy if your notes are in order.

Bibliography

At the end of a research paper, you should provide other scholars with a list of your sources according to the style of the field in which you are working. Your note cards, if properly kept, make this a simple task.

Follow the golden rule: Serve your reader as you would want to be served yourself.

TIPS ON WRITING THE RESEARCH PAPER

- *Attribute.* Attribute. Attribute. The reader of a research paper not only wants to know the evidence you have to back up each point, but also where it came from. You should have a system of footnotes and bibliography that the reader can use to research the same area.

- *Define your terms.* Each discipline or profession has its own language or jargon that others may not understand. It is important to define any term that the reader may not understand, that others in a different branch of the same discipline may not understand, or that has a different meaning in normal, nonprofessional speech.

- *Use graphics.* Make charts, maps, illustrations that will clarify your research. Use typographical designs and type styles that emphasize what you have to say. If you have a list format, you may want to use a list, as I have here, rather than running information entirely in normal sentences.

- *Explain your methods.* Other researchers will want to know the procedures you followed to get your results. This part of the presentation may incorporate a review of the literature, or that review may be a separate section of the paper in which you reveal what you read and comment on how helpful particular articles or books were.

There are many forms of writing we use to inform: speeches and presentations, letters and brochures, advertisements and book reports. Each form has a similar purpose: to teach the reader the subject.

WRITE TO PERSUADE

One of the principal reasons we write is to persuade. In the academic world, this form of writing is often called *argument,* but most students hear that tone and imagine a fight. I use the term *persuasion,* which more accurately describes the form—and voice—of appropriate intellectual discourse in which writers attempt to persuade readers through a process of reason to reconsider their views on a topic.

In fact, I believe, academic argument is a term and a process left over from the days when the academic world was exclusively male. The training I received from my male professors—and all my professors were men—was similar to the training I received on the football field and in the paratroops. Truth was found by two men taking completely opposite sides and each trying to destroy the other. It must be a direct descendant from the tournament practice of two knights trying to knock each other off their horses.

When I taught a course in argument, I found the male students comfortable with this term to describe a form of writing that is designed to cause the reader to rethink a position. They had been socialized on the playground or hockey rink to appear as if they enjoyed battle: hurt and do not reveal your own hurt.

But the majority of students in the class were women, most of them far brighter than the males in the class (and the male who taught the class). They hated *argument.* I think we need far more development of forms of persuasion which are not built on the concept of the knights with lances hurtling toward each other on horseback. I reject the term *argument* and use *persuasion* to describe the form of writing in which the writer attempts to make readers reconsider their views on a topic.

Persuasion is the basic form of intellectual discourse; it is the way that new ideas are introduced, that old ideas are discarded, and old ideas are adapted to new trends of thought.

TIPS ON WRITING PERSUASION

- *State your position.* This is no place for suspense. Make it clear what you intend to advocate. Define and establish your own issues and the context in which they are to be discussed.

- *Establish your credentials.* Let the reader know up front what experience you have had, what research you have done that should convince the reader to listen to your position.

- *Anticipate your reader's points.* You should be able to empathize with your opponent. Read that person's mind by imagining you are taking the other side, then make the best persuasive points you can.

- *Counter your opponent's points.* Now that you know your opponent's views, you can counter them right away, answering them before presenting your own views.

- *Appeal to reason.* Readers are rarely persuaded—at the least in the intellectual world—by emotion. Appeal to reason, base your position on documented evidence presented in a logical order.

There are many other forms of persuasion. A letter applying for a job or a grant tries to persuade others that you should be given a job or financial support. Again, you should role play those people so that you will know what appeals to them, what questions they will ask, what information they will want to know, what tone of voice will persuade them.

TIPS ON WRITING A LETTER APPLYING FOR A JOB

- *Research the application process.* Talk to your college placement office for counsel in writing job-seeking letters. Study books and articles that describe the strategies and techniques of successful job seekers.

- *Research the company.* Look up the company at which you are applying in the business references in the library. Read the company's annual report and brochures, interview people who work and have worked there, who supply the company and are supplied by the company. Make sure you know what the firm does—provide advertising services or manufacture ball bearings—and how it does that job—specializing in mail-order advertising or selling ball bearings in the international market.

- *Say specifically what skills you offer a potential employer.* "I'm willing to do anything" doesn't entice an employer, but "I learned to get along with a great variety of people working as a waiter, then the head waiter, at a resort that attracted many tourists from overseas" or "I tested my courses in accounting against my experience in summer jobs, in serving as treasurer of the student union, and in spending a semester internship with the Internal Revenue Service."

- *Be specific about your goals.* Tell the employer what you hope to learn from the job, what additional skills you hope to develop, so that you may better serve your employer.

- *Anticipate and answer the prospective employer's questions.* Remember that the reader is looking for someone who fills the company's needs. Read the advertisement or job announcement carefully and respond to the specifics of the position.

- *Sound professional.* Write in a professional manner that demonstrates that you are someone who will do a good job and represent the company well.

You will discover in using your experience with the writing process that you know how to define the writing job to be done. You can adapt or design a form of writing that will communicate your meaning to your reader with graceful efficiency.

QUESTIONS ABOUT FITTING YOUR PROCESS TO YOUR TASK

I'm not planning on getting a job where I have to write. Besides, I'll probably have a secretary who can write for me. Why should I think of adapting my process to other writing tasks?

Many jobs do not require writing. But just as many do. Because so many companies are in the process of downsizing and reorganizing, you may find yourself performing a variety of tasks, including writing.

Keep in mind too that the personal computer has replaced support staff in many organizations. Because it is so easy and quick to compose, revise, and edit on computers, employers have cut back on clerical help who take dictation and write up reports and letters. Usually one person does it all. That means you.

Won't I only have to worry about the forms of writing for my particular position?

You might want to consider the advantage of good writing skills if you decide to change jobs or seek a promotion. Most people no longer stay in one job for life, but change careers several times before retirement. The more multiskilled you are, the better prepared you are to meet any job demand. If you end up starting your own business, your writing skills will be all the more valuable. As your own employer, you may need to write grant requests, issue publicity statements, and correspond with clients all at one time.

If you learn now to adapt your process to various writing tasks, you will be prepared for whatever employment opportunity comes your way.

Why don't we learn how to write memos and reports in college instead of critical essays or personal narratives? It seems to me that learning these forms would prepare us more effectively for the "real" world.

You very well may write reports, memos, applications, letters, and other kinds of business forms in a business communications class or another writing class. But it's important not to lose sight of what writing's all about; it helps us communicate, and it helps us think.

Many top companies do not necessarily recruit students who come equipped with specific skills such as report or memo writing. They hope instead to find students who have learned how to think critically in college and can transfer their analytical skills to the work arena. They want workers who can analyze and solve problems as well as communicate. Your writing process will help you develop the analytical skills these employers seek.

You've stressed the importance of finding your own voice and topics when you write. Yet now you're saying that I have to fit my voice and ideas into a particular form or genre. How can I write like that and still be original?

It's true that certain academic disciplines or fields of work have established accepted forms of writing. But this does not mean that you have to give up hope of working creatively. Scientists have always written their findings in a strict format. First they state a problem and a hypothesis for solving the problem; then they describe the methodology they intend to use in their study; finally they write about their findings and conclusions. But no one accuses them of being unoriginal. In fact, we are most likely to classify scientists as creative problem solvers.

Besides, no matter what form you use when you write, and no matter what your task, you will decide what details and information you will include in your piece. Your word choice and style of composing will enhance a sense of your own voice and perspective in whatever you write.

Don't give up on originality when you must write within the perimeters of a particular genre. Make the genre work for you.

`You haven't talked about length. Isn't that part of form?`

It is. As you study the traditional forms used to solve specific writing tasks, you will get a sense of the expected length, but that doesn't mean you have to meet it. You should give the reader all the information the reader needs and no more.

In general, remember: Shorter is better. I have never had to cut a piece of writing without making it better. One famous writer said to "kill all your darlings." I don't entirely agree. Some of the writing you especially like may be effective, but there is a danger that many of the paragraphs we like really don't carry their weight of meaning to the reader. When that occurs, cut them. If you have writing that you really like, you can always save it for another piece.

This is just as true of literary writing as business writing. Poetry is the highest form of literary art, in part, because it says the most with the fewest words.

Peter de Vries said, "When I see a paragraph shrinking under my eyes like a strip of bacon in a skillet, I know I'm on the right track."

`What if I mix forms? Can't you write reflectively and still do research? Or be persuasive and still write reflectively?`

Absolutely. It's good to be aware of the different features of each form, but you certainly can mix them if the draft leads you in that direction.

If you are writing formal reports for another class, check with your teacher first to see if it's okay to mix forms. Some teachers will want you to follow a particular genre in order to learn certain things about a topic.

ACTIVITIES TO FIT YOUR PROCESS TO YOUR TASK

1. Ask a professor to suggest a journal in your field of interest, or go to the library and ask the reference librarians to direct you to one. Copy an essay, study, or report from the journal and then outline it in your daybook.

Notice how the author moves through the piece, what kinds of information he or she uses, and how it is arranged.

2. Collect at least three editorials, opinion pieces, or other kinds of persuasive writing from magazines or newspapers. Read each piece twice. After the first reading, write down your immediate responses: Did the piece persuade you? Did it help you change your mind about a particular issue or topic? During your second reading, jot down the author's major points. How does the writer establish himself or herself as an authority? How does he or she use evidence and information? In what ways does the writer account for opposing viewpoints? Decide from this reading which of the three pieces you found most persuasive and why.

3. Split up in groups of three or four and visit different offices on campus. Have each group member interview an employee in the office about the kinds of writing he or she is expected to do at work. Ask if you can get copies of various reports, letters, or memos that the employee is likely to write. Then come back together as groups and discuss the main features of the different forms or genres. Do some of them have standard openings, use formal language? Do any include pictures or graphics? How do they begin and end? Who is the audience for each piece of writing?

4. Have each member of your group select a piece of writing that represents a particular genre, and imagine the process the writer went through. Pretend you are that writer and plan the piece—what information you'll need, the kind of readership you anticipate, how you intend to focus, when you expect to have a draft, what kind of feedback you will get, how you will revise and edit it.

5. Compare and contrast two pieces of writing in different forms—a researched essay with a persuasive essay, for example; or a reflective essay with an analytical essay. Draw a line down a page in your daybook and outline the main features of the first essay on the left, the second on the right. Discuss your findings in class.

6. Select a piece of writing, and rewrite the opening in a form suitable for at least three of the following genres—the reflective, persuasive, analytical, research, or narrative essay. Then write a couple of paragraphs describing the differences between the openings, the tone of voice you established, and what information you included in each. How do your different openings foretell the kind of writing that will follow?

7. Think of a career you might like to enter after college, and brainstorm a list of the forms of writing you think you would do in that field. Then arrange an interview with employees in the field, and ask them to

describe in detail their writing tasks. Ask to see copies, and note down the main features of particular genres.

8. Brainstorm a list of all the writing tasks you've had to do over the past two to four weeks. Don't leave anything out; include application essays, exam essay answers, school excuse notes for children or siblings, memos, reports, lab observations, and so on. Then with a partner, talk about the context or setting for each form of writing. Where or why did you compose each? Who did you expect your readers to be? In what ways did the forms differ from one another? What might be appropriate to one form of writing and not to another? Did you feel that you were a novice with some forms and an expert with others?

9. If you had to write a college application essay, pull it out and review it. Recall the process of writing it and the kind of advice parents, teachers, friends, school counselors, or writing tutors gave you. What specific details did they want you to concentrate on? What did they think was appropriate to include or omit? What difference did the perceived readers of the piece make in the way you wrote it? How did you revise it? What features characterize this kind of essay as a particular genre?

10. Try your hand at a writing form you are unfamiliar with. If you have never written an analytical essay, for example, plan one from beginning to end, and take it through the steps of your writing process. Keep track of your progress in your daybook, and make sure to note what you had to do differently with this piece of writing than with others you have done. Refer to the tips in this chapter on writing the form of essay you have chosen.

11. Keep a notebook of writing you do for other classes. Include whatever instructions your teachers may give you, the pieces of writing themselves, and any notes and drafts. Insert a blank sheet of paper after each piece and write a short but detailed analysis of how you approached the assignment and wrote it.

12. Think of a writing assignment that proved to be particularly challenging to you. Pretend that your writing partner must complete the same assignment. Define the assignment, the form of writing it required, and how you completed it. Then write up a list of tips, similar to the ones in this chapter, that will help your partner.

13. Gather sample essay questions from exams you have taken or that other students in similar classes may have taken. Determine the amount of time you are allowed to answer each question and then practice planning, writing, and editing the answers. In the margins of the text sheet or on a separate piece of paper, give yourself time to sketch out a thoughtful outline

before you begin. Then write your answer and edit it. Work to complete all steps in the process within the allotted time. Keep practicing until you feel comfortable with the process and meet your time goal.

14. Join a group of classmates to study three or four genres of television shows (a sit-com, a drama, a detective or cops show, a documentary, a mystery, a made-for-TV suspense film, a magazine news program, etc.). Assign one kind of show to each person. Take notes as you watch. Think of the writer's role and what features of the genre he or she must emphasize. What kinds of elements characterize certain kinds of shows? Get together as a group and write up an analysis comparing and contrasting the different features of particular television genres.

15. Choose one of the essay forms featured in this chapter, and find a published essay that is most like that form. Using the writing tips I've given for each form, analyze the essay and describe how the writer incorporates these steps into his or her piece. Note also where the writer deviates from the "tips" or combines different forms.

16. Write a persuasive essay that's not so persuasive. In other words, disregard the tips for writing such an essay. Ignore your opponent's arguments, and don't back up your points with evidence. Ignore reason, and make only emotional appeals. Then read your essay aloud to a group and have them "workshop" the essay to make it better. Ask the group to give you specific details and to talk about their responses to the essay as you read it.

17. Choose a letter to the editor from your school or local newspaper. Analyze the letter and discuss why you think it is or is not effective. Make a list of suggestions for the writer that might help him or her write a more effective piece.

18. Ask a teacher in your major or field of interest what constitutes good student writing in that discipline. Have him or her give examples from successful student papers, or ask if you may have copies. What details of writing did the successful student writer pay attention to? Why are these details particular to that field or discipline?

19. Talk with someone who has created a home page on the Internet. Study other home pages, and note the features of this particular genre. What kind of writing is expected on a home page? What kind of writing would not be expected? How much of the writing is dictated by the technical perimeters of the home page itself? How does text interact with pictures or graphics in these pages? What other forms of writing does home page text resemble? Design your own home page.

20. Take a piece of writing, and draw up a plan for turning it into a research paper. You might, for example, study a letter to the editor in the school

newspaper to determine sources of information you would want to consult, how you would document the paper, and how you would prepare it for presentation. Then write a research proposal to your partner in which you outline your plan. Note the different features you want to include in your paper and your process for writing it, including deadlines for drafts, revisions, and editing.

21. Find five different kinds of writing—book review, editorial, lab report, office memo, and so on—and write up a reader profile for each, specifying age range, occupation, and interests. Explain what features from the piece of writing tell you about the kind of person who is most likely to read it. Is it the writer's formal or informal voice? The kinds of information he or she uses? The format of the piece? Think of other ways that each piece is "pitched" to a particular readership.

22. Write a multigenre essay or research paper. Consciously mix forms and shape your writing process to various writing tasks—all in one piece. Write in the style of a newspaper reporter, a poet, an essayist, or a scholar. Use subheadings or transitional paragraphs to connect the various pieces or styles, or let them stand alone as vignettes. Then write a few paragraphs reflecting on your multigenre process.

23. Take a task that you are familiar with on the job, in a sport, or in another course, and list the steps in the process you use to complete the task. Compare that with how you write to see if there are ways you can apply those familiar, successful methods to the writing task.

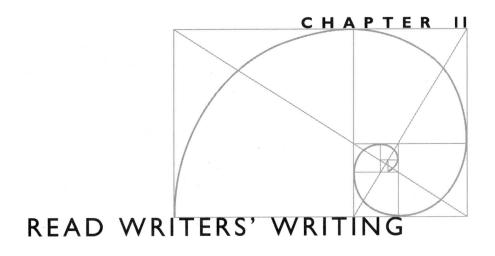

CHAPTER II

READ WRITERS' WRITING

When writers read something, they are aware of other writers at work behind the pages.

They share the same craft and therefore understand the problems the published writer faced and applaud when they read a skillful, perhaps unexpected solution. Of course, writers learn from the authors they read, but, even more, they experience a joy in reading writing that is well crafted, that clarifies meaning with grace and the illusion of ease.

The reading writer sees the author's choices underneath the page and learns from them: This problem was solved, this one was not, another was avoided. When reading, the writer scans the landscape of the subject and notices how the fellow writer chose to focus; the writer imagines the scaffolding the author erected to organize the draft and then took down so it would not get in the reader's way; the writer, when reading, hears the language that might have been used as well as what was actually used.

When I am served a dinner with each course hot or cold, every dish ready on time, I applaud, because I understand, firsthand, how difficult it is to do that. I sketch landscapes when I travel and so have a special appreciation of Rembrandt's sketchbooks, where so few lines reveal so much. I played right tackle, and when I watch a football game, I take pleasure in the quick, well-timed brush back block that gently neutralizes a linebacker's charge.

When I hear a writer extend the horizon of language, leaving out an abundance of detail, but revealing more with less, when I see someone shape a worn vision so it becomes new, I cheer and I learn. Ironically, I often learn more easily from bad writing. When a great writer, such as Shakespeare, captures a human emotion in a phrase, it is magic, all the craft hidden by grace. But with a poor writer, the workings are all exposed. I see what not to do, and, more often than you would think, what to do with more skill.

But I do not use other writers as conscious models, carefully imitating them. Rather I absorb the lessons of other writers by reading. They tune my instinct so that what I do "naturally" or because of "talent" I often learned subconsciously when I was reading.

In this chapter we will read together as writers, taking delight in what other writers have done and perhaps tuning our instincts so that when we face a similar writing problem, we will solve it, not knowing where we learned the solution.

ANNIE DILLARD

I read Annie Dillard's essay "Schedules" because I am schedule-obsessive and want to see what this wonderful writer has to say about her working habits. I am particularly interested when she describes her workplace from where so much writing that has given me pleasure has come.

> *I write these words in my most recent of many studies—a pine shed on Cape Cod. The pine lumber is unfinished inside the study, the pines outside are finished trees. I see the pines from my two windows. Nuthatches spiral around their long, coarse trunks. Sometimes in June a feeding colony of mixed warblers flies through the pines; the warblers make a racket that draws me out the door. The warblers drift loosely through the stiff pine branches, and I follow through the thin long grass between the trunks.*
>
> *The study—sold as a prefabricated toolshed—is eight feet by ten feet. Like a plane's cockpit, it is crammed with high-tech equipment. There is no quill pen in sight. There is a computer, a printer, and a photocopying machine. My backless chair, a prie-dieu on which I kneel, slides under the desk; I give it a little kick when I leave. There is an air conditioner, a heater, and an electric kettle. There is a low-tech bookshelf, a shelf of gull and whale bones, and a bed. Under the bed I stow paints—a one-pint can of yellow to touch up the window's trim, and five or six tubes of artists' oils. The study affords ample room for one. One who is supposed to be writing books. You can read in the space of a coffin, and you can write in the space of a toolshed meant for mowers and spades. . . . Appealing workplaces are to be avoided. One wants a room with no view, so imagination can dance with memory in the dark. When I furnished this study seven years ago, I pushed the long desk against a blank wall, so I could not see from either window.*

> **I do not agree with the author's rejection of a view. My desk faces one view, and when I am at my computer I face another. But then I don't see as Annie Dillard does and I delight in the simple, graceful way the birds pass through her world and am respectively amused by the difference between her romantic view of nature and the sleeves rolled up, practical attitude she has toward her workplace.**

ROGER C. PARKER AND DAVID A. HOLZGANG

Too much writing in the computer software manuals on which we all depend obscures and confuses when we need clarification. One exception to the rule is Roger C. Parker, a nationally recognized expert on computer graphic design. With David A. Holzgang, he has written *WordPerfect 6 Secrets* (IDG Books, 1993) in which they argue for simplicity and clarity and then—miracle of miracles—practice what they preach. Here is an example I admire. The writers' problem was to demonstrate the simplicity they recommend. They achieve George Orwell's goal: "Good writing is like a window pane." Parker and Holzgang do not strut like peacocks, telling us how much they know about computers; they call attention to the subject, and I greatly admire such transparent writing, knowing very well how hard it is to be simple.

> *Simplicity is preferable to complexity. The thousands of typefaces available and the numerous page layout and typographic features in WordPerfect can actually hinder, rather than enhance, your ability to create good-looking, easy-to-read documents. You may have noticed, too, that pages, like products, that pass the test of time are often characterized by a deceptive simplicity. The trendy, the gaudy, and the attention-getting publications often quickly become passé.*

> The New Yorker *magazine, for example, has remained virtually unchanged for over fifty years, as has Strunk and White's* The Elements of Style. *The simplicity of their designs allows the message—the ideas expressed in the writing—to emerge unscathed. Trendy magazines like* Rolling Stone, *regional magazines like* Texas Monthly *or* New York, *and the Sunday supplements of most metropolitan newspapers, however, often rely upon short-lived redesigns to maintain reader (and advertiser) enthusiasm. Trendy publications often sacrifice the ease with which readers can understand their articles in a continuing search for impact and novelty.*

> *The issue of efficiency also plays a role in design. A complex document is usually harder and more time-consuming to produce than a simple one and often opens the door to more opportunity for you to make mistakes. Good-looking design often reflects a deceptive simplicity, a transparency that allows the message, not the medium, to emerge.*

> *Simplicity is also preferable to complexity because complexity often has unwanted side effects. . . . Text wraps tend to create narrow columns of type, which are frequently characterized by irregular word spacing and excessive hyphenation, creating a problem where no problem previously existed.*

> **Although Parker and Holzgang are not writing for professionals but beginners, they do not write down to their audience. They also clarify and document each point as they make it so their meaning is clear.**

SEI SHŌNAGON

Writing crosses barriers of culture and time. Sei Shōnagon was a member of the aristocracy; I came from a working-class neighborhood. She was Chinese; I am American. She wrote in the tenth century; I write a millennium, a thousand years, later. Yet I delight in—and share—her views of our world in the journal she called "Hateful Things."

> *One is in a hurry to leave, but one's visitor keeps chattering away. If it is someone of no importance, one can get rid of him by saying, "You must tell me all about it next time"; but, should it be the sort of visitor whose presence commands one's best behavior, the situation is hateful indeed.*

> • • •

> *Someone has suddenly fallen ill and one summons the exorcist. Since he is not at home, one has to send messengers to look for him. After one has had a long fretful wait, the exorcist finally arrives, and with a sigh of relief one asks him to start his incantations. But perhaps he has been exorcising too many evil spirits recently; for hardly has he installed himself and begun praying when his voice becomes drowsy. Oh, how hateful!*

> • • •

> *A man who has nothing in particular to recommend him discusses all sorts of subjects at random as though he knew everything.*

> • • •

> *I hate the sight of men in their cups who shout, poke their fingers in their mouths, stroke their beards, and pass on the wine to their neighbours with great cries of "Have some more! Drink up!" They tremble, shake their heads, twist their faces, and gesticulate like children who are singing, "We're off to see the Governor."*
> *I have seen really well-bred people behave like this and I find it most distasteful.*

> • • •

> *One has gone to bed and is about to doze off when a mosquito appears, announcing himself in a reedy voice. One can actually feel the wind made by his wings and, slight though it is, one finds it hateful in the extreme.*

For exorcist read neurologist—or the ologist of your choice, perhaps a resident who has been on duty for ninety-seven hours. I am struck—again—in reading these simple observations how important it is to capture and examine the ordinariness of life. In the small there is the large—the disinterest of some who care for us when we face life-threatening situations and how much it can hurt those who are suffering, all told in a few simple words.

ANNA QUINDLEN

Anna Quindlen has given up her column in the *New York Times* to write novels but here, in one of her last columns, she shows how much she can say within the limitations of journalism—or perhaps because of journalistic training which makes it possible for the reporter/writer to get to the essentials immediately and communicate human events and the emotional reaction to them with short words in brief sentences.

> *My great journalistic contribution to my family is that I write obituaries. First my mother's, twenty-two years ago, listing her accomplishments: two daughters, three sons. Then that of my father's second wife, dead of the same disease that killed his first one.*
>
> *Last week it was my sister-in-law. "Sherry Quindlen, 41," I tapped out on the keyboard, and then it was real, like a last breath. "When you write about me," she said one day in the hospital, "be nice."*
>
> *For the obit I could only be accurate. The limitations of the form eliminate the more subjective truths: a good heart, a generous soul, who made her living taking care of other people's children. My brother's wife, the mother of a teenager and a toddler, who went from a bad cough to what was mistakenly said to be pneumonia to what was correctly diagnosed as lung and liver cancer, from fall to spring, from the day she threw a surprise fortieth birthday party for her husband to the day he chose her casket.*

> **I reread each sentence, amazed at how this craftsperson, whose trade I share, can accomplish so much so quickly—and yet I never feel rushed. I have time to reflect, to see my own memories in what she has said of hers. Reread these sentences aloud. For example, read the series of clauses in the not-so-simple last sentence to see how much chronological, medical, and emotional territory she covered in forty-seven words: "who went from a bad cough to what was mistakenly said to be pneumonia to what was correctly diagnosed as lung and liver cancer, from fall to spring, from the day she threw a surprise fortieth birthday party for her husband to the day he chose her casket."**
>
> **If you want to know how to write with specifics, study these lines.**

ED LINN

In writing about Ted Williams, the famous baseball player, in his book *Hitter* (Harcourt Brace, 1993), Ed Linn sets up Williams as an instinctive genius, comparing him to Mozart and others who supposedly had talents that did not have to be learned. He then allows Williams to respond to that concept. This writer is always impressed when a writer can get out of the way and let the subject do the writing. It gives the book liveliness, a change of voice, and a special authority.

When Williams is told he has a natural talent, he answers: "I can tell you exactly when it started:" he says. "It wasn't when I was ten or eleven. It happened when I was twelve. I had never followed major league baseball. The only players I had ever heard of were Ruth and Gehrig. And then I read that Bill Terry had hit .400, and that really excited me. Four hundred! I don't think I even knew what you had to do to hit .400, but I could tell that it was something wonderful. I knew I wanted to do that, too. Hit .400. I was so excited that even though it was dark out—I've never told this to anybody before—I got my little bat, ran out to our little backyard, and began to swing."

And continued to swing every night. Hour after hour, the little boy, alone at home, out in the tiny backyard, swinging by the light of the moon . . . Over and over and over. Whoooosh . . . whoooosh . . . whooooosh. "There were two things I concentrated on. First, I wanted to have a great-looking swing. That was important to me, everybody wants to look good. Second, I wanted to visualize what I was doing. And I always visualized myself in the Polo Grounds, because that's where Bill Terry played." Men on first and second, two out, high inside fast ball. See the ball, see the swing, see the bat hitting the ball, see the long, high fly arcing out toward the right-field bleachers. Whoooosh . . . whoooosh . . . whoooosh. Whoooosh.

"I was playing in a sandlot game, and I heard a man say, 'Gee, that kid has quick wrists.' And I thought, If you think I'm quick with my wrists now, just wait awhile."

I enjoy the way Linn allows Williams to talk and how Williams, interviewed and edited by Linn, recreates himself as a boy. Linn is a master interviewer, someone you want to talk to, and I imagine how long it took for Williams to tell this story he has never told before to Linn.

DOROTHY ALLISON

I remember getting goose bumps the first time I read these lines, the beginning of the Preface to *Trash,* a collection of stories by Dorothy Allison, a writer I had never heard of. I still get goose bumps.

There was a day in my life when I decided to live.

After my childhood, after all that long terrible struggle to simply survive, to escape my stepfather, uncles, speeding Pontiacs, broken glass and rotten floorboards, or that inevitable death by misadventure that claimed so many of my cousins; after watching so many die around me, I had not imagined that I would ever need to make such a choice. I had imagined the hunger for life in me was insatiable, endless, unshakable.

I became an escapee—one of the ones others talked about. I became the one who got away, who got glasses from the Lions Club, a job from Lyndon Johnson's War on Poverty, and finally went to college on a scholarship. There I met the people I had always read about: girls whose fathers loved them—innocently; boys who drove cars they had not stolen; whole armies of the middle and upper classes I had not truly believed to be real; the children to whom I could not help but compare myself. I matched their innocence, their confidence, their capacity to trust, to love, to be gener-ous against the bitterness, the rage, the pure and terrible hatred that consumed me. Like many others who had gone before me, I began to dream longingly of my own death.

I began to court it. Cowardly, traditionally—that is, in the tradition of all those oth-ers like me, through drugs and drinking and stubbornly putting myself in the way of other people's violence. Even now, I cannot believe how it was that everything I sur-vived became one more reason to want to die.

> **Whew! With enormous authority, with extraordinary control of specific in-formation, without anger and without a single whine, she takes us to the center of life. The one-line first paragraph presents us with the human dilemma to live or not.**
>
> **The next paragraph gives you her life before she escaped; the next the life after, allowing you to see the scholarship winners from the other side of the tracks or the trailer park as they see themselves and how they compare themselves to those who "belong"; and then the life of self-destruction, which we all have observed if not experienced.**
>
> **Accomplished in four paragraphs, 273 words. It is interesting to study these sentences to see how the writer has established a distance that allows her to take the reader into her world yet allows her to comment on it: dis-tance and voice, demonstrated by an enormously skillful writer.**

THOMAS FRENCH

Thomas French spent a year in a Florida high school—where he saw many in Dorothy Allison's situation—and wrote a superb book, *South of Heaven* (Double-day, 1993), that captures the world of the high school. An editor once said that a good reporter is "forever astonished by the obvious," and French is a great re-porter who sees the drama in the ordinary and reveals the true human condition. He is also a skillful writer who is able to describe what he reports with perception and grace. As a writer, I delight in how he dramatizes a significant situation that a less perceptive reporter would overlook.

Day after day, Karin sits in that class—she sits right in front of Bret Harper, the kid on the quiz team, the one known as Elvis—and listens to Ms. Fish talk on and on about synthetic division and inverse variation and negative reciprocals. She barely understands a word of it.

"Where are we? Wait," she says, frantically trying to keep up. "Please."

Karin might have a chance if only she weren't stuck in the middle of the pack, jammed into crowded rooms like this one. That's the problem. If she were a wonder-ful student like YY and the others, she'd be in those honor courses, where the classes are usually kept to a reasonable size. And if she were a failing student, she'd probably be down in the pod, where the classes are also small and where individualized attention is always the specialty of the day. But Karin doesn't fit either category. She's average, so she's forced to fight for air inside regular classes, where the rest of teen humanity is assigned. Sometimes, there are more than thirty-five kids jammed into one room, which means that the teacher hardly has time to take the roll, much less answer individual questions. In those classes, it's survival of the fittest.

Lots of times, if Karin has trouble understanding something, she doesn't even bother raising her hand. What's the point? She knows what happens to kids who are lost and try to take up too much class time with questions.

"If you don't get it," some teachers say, "we'll just have to move on."

> **As Ms. Fish talks "on and on about synthetic division and inverse variation and negative reciprocals. She barely understands a word of it." I am back in the classroom. French writes specifics that put me there.**
>
> **As a fellow writer, I want to stand up and shout—perhaps I did when I read "She's average, so she's forced to fight for air inside regular classes." Look how much he does with the verb, with the image: "fight for air inside regular classes."**

···

JOAN DIDION

The writer's mission is to articulate the experiences, thoughts, feelings of the inarticulate. I keep returning to Joan Didion's "In Bed," because I suffered migraines for years and first read this essay when I was having a migraine. She expressed the feelings I had not been able to express, and there was comfort in that—and I could give it to family and friends and say, "You wanta know how it is, read Didion. Here." Didion is the only person I have read who describes the relief and euphoria you feel when you return to life.

> *At first every small apprehension is magnified, every anxiety a pounding terror. Then the pain comes, and I concentrate only on that. Right there is the usefulness of migraine, there in that imposed yoga, the concentration on the pain. For when the pain recedes, ten or twelve hours later, everything goes with it, all the hidden resentments, all the vain anxieties. The migraine has acted as a circuit breaker, and the fuses have emerged intact.*
>
> *There is a pleasant convalescent euphoria. I open the windows and feel the air, eat gratefully, sleep well. I notice the particular nature of a flower in a glass on the stair landing. I count my blessings.*

> **Didion speaks for me, and there is therapy in that as when I write of my own anxieties, fears, problems. The naming of the dragon often makes him retreat if not disappear.**

MICHAEL KELLY

The best book to come out of the Gulf War, in my opinion, is Michael Kelly's *Martyr's Day—Chronicle of a Small War* (Random House, 1993). In the few paragraphs that follow he is able to reveal the robbing of individual personality that is one of the costs of combat. In this brief anecdote, we can feel, if not experience, the terror and inhumanity of war.

> *I remember one sharp, small scene. Several prisoners signaled to one of the Egyptian officers that they had to urinate. With a beckoning wave of his pistol, he moved them forward to the edge of the trench that had been theirs to defend. Motioning downward with the pistol he had them kneel in the mud. I thought for a horrible moment that he was going to execute them so that their bodies would tumble into the trench, but the Iraqis knew what he wanted. Together on their knees in line, they unzipped their pants and sent their streams into the ditch.*
>
> *Behind them, the others of their unit were now, as the Egyptians directed, taking off their boots. It is a difficult thing to take off a shoe with one hand remaining on your head. Some managed to balance on one leg, but most fell into a clumsy sit when they tried it. They pitched their boots into a pile, and the guards motioned them up again and herded them into two groups, the enlisted men in one, the officers in another, and they all sat down in the mud. A few feet away a .50-caliber machine gun had been set up on a tripod to guard them, and the young soldier who manned it watched with eager intent for the first sign of trouble, but he might have been assigned to cover a group of nuns for all the need there was of his services. The prisoners sat silent and unmoving.*

> **Kelly puts us beside him, as the expert writer always does, so that we see this scene and share his apprehension. Then we have the details, the revealing details. Notice how he lets us see them—and therefore makes us imagine we are them: "It is a difficult thing to take off a shoe with one hand remaining on your head. Some managed to balance on one leg, but most fell into a clumsy sit when they tried it."**

VIRGINIA WOOLF

In her essay "Street Haunting," novelist Virginia Woolf expresses a feeling I have as a city boy. These days it is politically correct to romanticize the country, but when I went to college after World War II we all dreamt of the city.

> *How beautiful a London street is then, with its islands of light, and its long groves of darkness, and on one side of it perhaps some tree-sprinkled, grass-grown space where night is folding herself to sleep naturally and, as one passes the iron railing, one hears those little cracklings and stirrings of leaf and twig, which seem to suppose the silence*

of fields all round them, an owl hooting, and far away the rattle of a train in the valley. But this is London, we are reminded; high among the bare trees are hung oblong frames of reddish yellow light—windows; there are points of brilliance burning steadily like low stars—lamps; this empty ground which holds the country in it and its peace, is only a London square, set about by offices and houses where at this hour fierce lights burn over maps, over documents, over desks where clerks sit turning with wetted forefinger the files of endless correspondences; or more suffusedly the firelight wavers and the lamplight falls upon the privacy of some drawing-room, its easy chairs, its papers, its china, its inlaid table, and the figure of a woman, accurately measuring out the precise number of spoons of tea which—She looks at the door as if she heard a ring downstairs and somebody asking, is she in?

> **It is the eye that writes, and Virginia Woolf's observations of city make me see the familiar as if I had never seen it before. At the end of this excerpt from an essay, I see the novelist as she captures the world of people. I have reproductions of paintings by the Dutch master Vermeer, who captured an action—a woman opening a letter—that somehow contains all the drama of life.**
>
> **At the end of this paragraph by Woolf, we feel the drama and mystery in the life of the woman, and I wish that Woolf would step through the window, enter into that life, and tell me if someone is at the door, or is it a memory or an apprehension; if there is someone at the door, who is, and what will happen as they face each other. The force of narrative that we talked about on pages 246 through 247 lies coiled in that last sentence.**

JOSEPH MITCHELL

Voice is the most magical and important quality in writing, and an example of voice I return to hear again and again is the master writer Joseph Mitchell—another celebrant of the city—as he begins the reportage that also provides the title of his most recent collection, *Up in the Old Hotel* (Pantheon, 1992).

Mitchell is an individual writer speaking to an individual reader. He reveals something of himself in the first lines. The pace is deceptively casual, reflective. He is going to report, and he quickly demonstrates his ability to report with startling specifics, but the important thing will be his thoughts, his commentary on what he finds. His voice promises that his conversation in type will be interesting and that he will invite readers to have their own thoughts in response to his.

Read this aloud to hear the music of Mitchell's written voice:

Every now and then, seeking to rid my mind of thoughts of death and doom, I get up early and go down to Fulton Fish Market. I usually arrive around five-thirty, and take a walk through the two huge open-fronted market sheds, the Old Market and the New Market, whose fronts rest on South Street and whose backs rest on piles in the

East River. At that time, a little while before the trading begins, the stands in the sheds are heaped high and spilling over with forty to sixty kinds of finfish and shellfish from the East Coast, the West Coast, the Gulf Coast, and half a dozen foreign countries. The smoky riverbank dawn, the racket the fishmongers make, the seaweed's smell, and the sight of this plentifulness always give me a feeling of well-being, and sometimes they elate me. I wander among the stands for an hour or so. Then I go into a cheerful market restaurant named Sloppy Louie's and eat a big, inexpensive, invigorating breakfast—kippered herring and scrambled eggs, or a shad-roe omelet, or split sea scallops and bacon, or some other breakfast specialty of the place.

I am always struck by that beginning followed by the glorious litany of fish, none a cliché, all familiar and at the same time somehow exotic and different.

NATALIE GINZBURG

Natalie Ginzburg (who died in 1991) was a major Italian writer whose "He and I" is a deceptively simple celebration of love. When I read it again and again, I am impressed by how much it reveals of human relationships—and I have a rare desire to imitate and write a column about my wife Minnie Mae and myself. Perhaps I will, giving full credit to Natalie Ginzburg.

He always feels hot. I always feel cold. In the summer when it really is hot he does nothing but complain about how hot he feels. He is irritated if he sees me put a jumper on in the evening.

He speaks several languages well; I do not speak any well. He manages—in his own way—to speak even the languages that he doesn't know.

He has an excellent sense of direction, I have none at all. After one day in a foreign city he can move about in it as thoughtlessly as a butterfly. I get lost in my own city; I have to ask directions so that I can get back home again. He hates asking directions; when we go by car to a town we don't know he doesn't want to ask directions and tells me to look at the map. I don't know how to read maps and I get confused by all the little red circles and he loses his temper.

He loves the theater, painting, music, especially music. I do not understand music at all, painting doesn't mean much to me and I get bored at the theater. I love and understand one thing in the world and that is poetry.

He loves museums, and I will go if I am forced to but with an unpleasant sense of effort and duty. He loves libraries and I hate them.

He loves travelling, unfamiliar foreign cities, restaurants. I would like to stay at home all the time and never move.

All the same I follow him on his many journeys. I follow him to museums, to churches, to the opera. I even follow him to concerts, where I fall asleep.

It is easier to have a clever idea than to carry it off, but she does, all the way through to the end. Note the word choice and the voice that doesn't complain or gripe or grouse or attack but simply celebrates their loving differences.

....

PETER D. KRAMER

The writer has the ability to recover significance from the river of experience and put it in context. Peter D. Kramer did that well in his best-selling book about an antidepressant drug, *Listening to Prozac* (Viking, 1993). In these few lines he exposes a central problem of mind-altering drugs: Is the real person the one without or with a drug?

> *An indication of the power of medication to reshape a person's identity is contained in the sentence Tess used when, eight months after first stopping Prozac, she telephoned me to ask whether she might resume the medication. She said, "I am not myself."*
>
> *I found this statement remarkable. After all, Tess had existed in one mental state for twenty or thirty years; she then briefly felt different on medication. Now that the old mental state was threatening to re-emerge—the one she had experienced almost all her adult life—her response was "I am not myself." But who had she been all those years if not herself? Had medication somehow removed a false self and replaced it with a true one? Might Tess, absent the invention of the modern antidepressant, have lived her whole life—a successful life, perhaps, by external standards—and never been herself?*
>
> *When I asked her to expand on what she meant, Tess said she no longer felt like herself when certain aspects of her ailment—lack of confidence, feelings of vulnerability—returned, even to a small degree. Ordinarily, if we ask a person why she holds back socially, she may say, "That's just who I am" meaning shy or hesitant or melancholy or overly cautious. These characteristics often persist throughout life, and they have a strong influence on career, friendships, marriage, self-image. . . .*
>
> *On imipramine, no longer depressed but still inhibited and subdued, Tess felt "myself again." But while on Prozac, she underwent a redefinition of self. Off Prozac, when she again became inhibited and subdued—perhaps the identical sensations she had experienced while on imipramine—she now felt "not myself." Prozac redefined Tess's understanding of what was essential to her and what was intrusive and pathological.*

Kramer is able to write with the authority of a physician without playing God. He is speculating, and he makes contact with the reader, allowing us to speculate along with him. He doesn't suggest an easy answer, perhaps there is no answer, but there certainly is an issue that we should consider for society—and for ourselves.

BERNARD CHAET

I always enjoy seeing how different writers approach the same subject: two well-written art books—so well-written you do not need the illustrations to which the authors refer. Each are writing about the line. In the first, Bernard Chaet discusses the line in his *The Art of Drawing* (Holt, Rinehart and Winston, 1983).

> *By traditional definition, a line is the product of a dot moving across the surface of a support, such as paper. Once put down, the line can establish boundaries and separate areas. It can, by its direction and weight on the page, generate a sense of movement. By applying lines in patterns of parallel and cross-hatched marks, the draftsman can simulate texture on a perfectly smooth paper surface with line alone. Indeed, using line—that simplest and most subtle of graphic means—exclusively, the artist can realize any visual effect desired.*

CLINT BROWN AND CHERYL MCLEAN

Writers know there is no one right way to say anything but many ways that work and many that do not. Chaet worked for me and so do Clint Brown and Cheryl McLean in their *Drawing from Life* (Holt, Rinehart and Winston, 1992).

> *The power of line lies in its versatility, the myriad ways in which the artist can express personal views or characterize the human figure. In twentieth-century artist Alberto Giacometti's drawing, Walking Man, Figure 1.2, the line itself is a metaphor for the body of the man. Giacometti's line abbreviates the form and concept of a man in motion, recognizing the power line has to imply so much beyond itself. In a more complete narrative, the Oriental master Hokusai uses a brisk, chisel-like line to suggest the tension and action of combative wrestlers, Figure 1.3. Honore Daumier lavishly applies line to build up volumes through a kind of sketchy layering, Figure 1.4. His lines are loaded with energy. Rather than give a clear sense of the body's contour, these lines collectively create an impression of the body as an undulating mass. Each line adds a bit more momentum and synergy to the overall impression of the drawing.*

JONATHAN SHAY

Jonathan Shay, a psychiatrist who works with combat veterans, saw a connection between the great Greek epics and the combat experience of Vietnam veterans. In his *Achilles in Vietnam* (Athenaeum, 1994) he argues for a different form of treatment for veterans. I always appreciate a clearly wrought thesis that tells the reader what the writer will argue for. After allowing the reader to hear testimony from a veteran, Shay says:

> *We shall hear this man's voice and the voices of other combat veterans many times in these pages. I shall argue throughout this book that healing from trauma depends upon communalization of the trauma—being able safely to tell the story to someone who is listening and who can be trusted to retell it truthfully to others in the community. So before analyzing, before classifying, before thinking, before trying to do anything—we should listen. Categories and classifications play a large role in the institutions of mental health care for veterans, in the education of mental health professionals, and as tentative guides to perception. All too often, however, our mode of listening deteriorates into intellectual sorting, with the professional grabbing the veterans' words from the air and sticking them in mental bins. To some degree that is institutionally and educationally necessary, but listening this way destroys trust.*

....

ANNE TYLER

Anne Tyler, one of our best novelists, has written brilliantly of being a writer, saying, "I hated childhood, and spent it sitting behind a book waiting for adulthood to arrive. When I ran out of books I made up my own. At night, when I couldn't sleep, I made up stories in the dark. . . . I guess I work from a combination of curiosity and distance. . . . Mostly, it's lies, writing novels. You set out to tell an untrue story and you try to make it believable, even to yourself. Which calls for details; any good lie does. I'm quicker to believe I was once a circus aerialist if I remember that just before every performance, I used to dip my hands in a box of chalk powder that smelled like clean, dry cloth being torn."

> *After his wife left him, Macon had thought the house would seem larger.*
>
> *Instead, he felt more crowded. The windows shrank. The ceilings lowered. There was something insistent about the furniture, as if it were pressing in on him. . . . The house itself was medium-sized, unexceptional to look at, standing on a street of such houses in an older part of Baltimore. Heavy oak trees hung over it, shading it from the hot summer sun but also blocking breezes. The rooms inside were square and dim. All that remained in Sarah's closet was a brown silk sash hanging on a hook; in her bureau drawers, lint balls and empty perfume bottles. Their son's old room was neatly made up, as sleek as a room in a Holiday Inn. Some places, the walls gave off a kind of echo. Still, Macon noticed he had a tendency to hold his arms close to his body, to walk past furniture sideways as if he imagined the house could barely accommodate him. He felt too tall. His long, clumsy feet seemed unusually distant. He ducked his head in doorways.*

(*From* The Accidental Tourist)

I have always been interested in the beginnings of books, especially novels, because the writer has to do so much without the reader becoming aware of him sawing and drilling, planing and shaping, hammering away.

Think how much a novelist has to establish:

- *A central tension or conflict that will carry an entire book forward when it is released*
- *A character that is believable, complex, interesting, and sympathetic enough for the reader to care what happens to that character*
- *A place where the story occurs*
- *A voice that supports its telling with an appropriate and attractive music*

All this in a few pages.

....

E. ANNIE PROULX

I have read and reread the beginning of E. Annie Proulx's *Postcards* (Collier, 1993). Read it to see if she grabs you as she grabbed me. To a writer, she accomplishes the impossible.

Even before he got up he knew he was on his way. Even in the midst of the involuntary orgasmic jerking he knew. Knew she was dead, knew he was on his way. Even standing there on shaking legs, trying to push the copper buttons through the stiff buttonholes he knew that everything he had done or thought in his life had to be started over again. Even if he got away.

What craft and what unusual and yet appropriate music she makes—how personal and yet accurate. In the very first line the world has changed and he—before we know who "he" is—is on his way. He is the one we soon discover who wanted to stay on the land, and his wife, whom he has just murdered, is the one who wanted to go. Talk about a central tension. He is on his way. Seventy-two words and we see his problems with the buttons of her coat as he tries to hide her. And the suspense: Even if he got away.

....

JOHN LE CARRÉ

John Le Carré also immediately draws me into *A Perfect Spy* (Bantam, 1987). Read and reread it to see how much he is doing line by line.

In the small hours of a blustery October morning in a south Devon coastal town that seemed to have been deserted by its inhabitants, Magnus Pym got out of his elderly country taxi-cab and, having paid the driver and waited till he had left, struck out across the church square. His destination was a terrace of ill-lit Victorian boardinghouses with names like Bella-Vista, The Commodore and Eureka. In build he was powerful but stately, a representative of something. His stride was agile, his body forward-sloping in the best tradition of the Anglo-Saxon administrative class. In the same attitude, whether static or in motion, Englishmen have hoisted flags over distant colonies, discovered the sources of great rivers, stood on the decks of sinking ships. He had been travelling in one way or another for sixteen hours but he wore no overcoat or hat. He carried a fat black briefcase of the official kind and in the other hand a green Harrods bag. A strong sea wind lashed at his city suit, salt rain stung his eyes, balls of spume skimmed across his path. Pym ignored them. Reaching the porch of a house marked "No Vacancies" he pressed the bell and waited, first for the outside light to go on, then for the chains to be unfastened from inside . . .

"Why Mr. Canterbury, it's you," an old lady's voice objected sharply as the door opened behind him. "You bad man. You caught the night sleeper again, I can tell. Why ever didn't you telephone?"

Le Carré, master of the spy novel, creates a mysterious place where a mysterious man acts in a mysterious manner. Notice all the clues that tell you he is leading a double, perhaps a triple life. Read it and you will find out.

....

ALICE WALKER

A writer delights in the glorious diversity of literature. What a change of pace from Le Carré to Alice Walker and the incredible beginning of *The Color Purple*, (Harcourt Brace, 1992), which takes the reader inside the life—and head—of a fourteen-year-old African American living in the rural South shortly after the turn of the century.

Dear God,

I am fourteen years old. I have always been a good girl. Maybe you can give me a sign letting me know what is happening to me.

Last spring after little Lucious come I heard them fussing. He was pulling on her arm. She say It too soon, Fonso, I ain't well. Finally he leave her alone. A week go by, he pulling on her arm again. She say Naw, I ain't Donna. Can't you see I'm already half dead, an all of these chilren.

She went to visit her sister doctor over Macon. Left me to see after the others. He never had a kine word to say to me. Just say You gonna do what your mummy wouldn't. First he put his thing up gainst my hip and sort of wiggle it around. Then he grab hold my titties. Then he push his thing inside my pussy. When that hurt, I cry. He start to choke me, saying You better shut up and git used to it.

But I don't never git used to it. And now I feels sick every time I be the one to cook. My mama she fuss at me an look at me. She happy, cause he good to her now. But too sick to last long.

ALICE MUNRO

If I had to choose the best short-story writer today—a choice I would hate to make—I would pick Alice Munro, a Canadian short-story writer who creates worlds and characters in those worlds that are entire. They are not cardboard flat, but multidimensional people you know and care about. Recently I discovered her first short story and was astonished to see that her talents were all there in "A Basket of Strawberries." Note the power and authority; note how well you know these people and their marriage in a few lines; note the sense of narrative, how the writer has drawn you into the story. Why is she at the window? What does she see? What is wrong? What's going to happen next?

> *Mr. Torrance had not slept well. The night had been unusually warm for June, and quite still, without the faintest wind. In his light sleep he had had an uneasy sensation of not being able to breathe as deeply as he should, and the darkness above his closed eyelids had seemed to have a reddish tinge, to be aglow with heat, impatience, and anguish of weariness. His wife was fretful, too; he was aware, all night long, of her great soft, heaving movements and the mumbling, childish noises she made in her sleep. He lay beside her, quite still and motionless, and at dawn there was an ache and heaviness in all his bones; he felt as if he were made of rusty and ill-fitted lengths of iron pipe. He opened his eyes—he would not try to sleep anymore. His wife was standing at the window. She was in her nightgown, with a mauve silk wrapper tied loosely at her soft bulging waist, and her gray dark-streaked hair loose down her back.*

BARRY LOPEZ

I am attracted to the Arctic for some reason so deep I cannot name it, and my favorite book on the subject is *Arctic Dreams* (Bantam, 1987), written by one of America's best nature writers, no scratch that, one of our best writers, Barry Lopez. I had mentioned that description, in my opinion, can be high art and is the basic form of writing from which all other writing grows. I read and reread his descriptions to go to the Arctic, to be inspired and instructed as a writer.

> *Like other landscapes that initially appear barren, Arctic tundra can open suddenly, like the corolla of a flower, when any intimacy with it is sought. One begins to notice spots of brilliant red, orange, and green, for example, among the monotonic browns of a tundra tussock. A wolf spider lunges at a glistening beetle. A shred of muskox wool lies inert in the lavender blooms of a saxifrage. . . .*
>
> *The wealth of biological detail on the tundra dispels any feeling that the land is empty; and its likeness to a stage suggests impending events. On a summer walk, the wind-washed air proves deathlessly clear. Time and again you come upon the isolated and succinct evidence of life—animal tracks, the undigested remains of a ptarmigan*

in an owl's casting, a patch of barrenground willow nibbled nearly leafless by Arctic hares. You are afforded the companionship of birds which follow after you. (They know you are an animal; sooner or later you will turn up something to eat.) Sandpipers scatter before you, screaming tuituek, an Eskimo name for them. Coming awkwardly down a scree slope of frost-riven limestone you make a glass-tinkling clatter—and at a distance a tundra grizzly rises on its hind legs to study you: the dish-shaped paws of its front legs deathly still, the stance so human it is unnerving.

Lopez creates a poetry of specifics so that I see-feel-care about the Arctic. He gets out of the way and puts you on the tundra, seeing it with his authoritative eyes—pun very much intended.

BROCK DETHIER

The poet Brock Dethier also uses nature to move back and forth in time in a poem in which I find new things to enjoy each time I read it. If you are not familiar with poetry, do not be put off by the funny lines. Read it aloud in the following form, as prose, and then read it aloud with the line breaks, the basic unit of contemporary poetry, to see how those pauses and hesitations—beats—enrich the music and the meaning of the poem.

The View from Black Cap

The sun's setting over Cathedral and White Horse, over that new abomination of a hotel leching up on White Horse's neck, over the hardwood green of Moat's skirts, the blueberry bush bronze of Red Ridge's beckoning rocky shin where my parents saw their first pileated woodpecker. There's a road up Cathedral—paved even. We used to ski it. Once in Silvretta bindings and hiking boots I jump-turned it thirties style, thrilled by rhythm and control. Moat was a bear in Granny's day. They'd walk down the hill from the house, ford the Saco, trudge across the valley and hike up to the trailhead at Diana's Baths. That's why they loved Crawford Notch up there to the northwest. They could hop the up-train at the station a quarter-mile from the house, let the steam do the work, get off where they wanted as the train elbowed its way up the grade, climb Willey or Webster or Crawford, sun at the top, plunge sweaty faces into Saco at the bottom, flag down the train with someone's red petticoat. As beloved as it is, Crawford's shape confused us for half a century. From 302 in the Bartlett plains you see a mountain nose peeking above a ridge and Mother and her mother and maybe hers too always said, There's the friendly nose of Crawford, but from the Bear Notch Road vista you can see it's really Nancy, higher and across the Notch from Crawford. Every time I tell Mother that she says Really? in a disappointed voice. Just to the right of Nancy is Bemis where Mother and Granny got lost in the '50s trying to find the old fire tower. I suppose most of the rotting tinkertoys have disappeared but so many remains still stand—one on Carrigain, at the other end of that little range, others at Hale, just a few miles north, and Osceola, just to the south, one right over here on Kearsarge that may still function—at least I've seen people up there working on it. You can see that one from the house, or could before we let all those birches grow up. Last time we went up there, we got buzzed twice—once by a plane, once by a chopper—had to tiptoe around two attack dogs on the way down, eavesdropped three couples arguing about turning back. But from that tower when I was a kid at exactly one o'clock we would aim our tinny mirror towards a knoll in the valley, watch the reflected light sweep down the rock then out towards the house, delight in the answering dots of brightness, the sudden brief flashes from home.

The View from Black Cap

The sun's setting over Cathedral and White Horse,
over that new abomination of a hotel
leching up on White Horse's neck,
over the hardwood green of Moat's skirts,
the blueberry bush bronze of
Red Ridge's beckoning rocky shin
where my parents saw their first pileated woodpecker.

There's a road up Cathedral—
paved even. We used to ski it.
Once in Silvretta bindings and hiking boots
I jump-turned it
thirties style,
thrilled by rhythm and control.
Moat was a bear in Granny's day.
They'd walk down the hill from the house,
ford the Saco,
trudge across the valley
and hike up to the trailhead at Diana's Baths.

That's why they loved Crawford Notch
up there to the northwest.
They could hop the up-train at the station
a quarter-mile from the house,
let the steam do the work,
get off where they wanted
as the train elbowed its way up the grade,
climb Willey or Webster or Crawford,
sun at the top,
plunge sweaty faces into Saco at the bottom,
flag the train down with someone's red petticoat.

As beloved as it is,
Crawford's shape confused us
for half a century.
From 302 in the Bartlett plains
you see a mountain nose peeking above a ridge
and Mother and her mother and maybe hers too

always said, There's the friendly nose of Crawford,
but from the Bear Notch Road vista
you can see it's really Nancy,
higher and across the Notch from Crawford.
Every time I tell Mother that she says
Really? in a disappointed voice.

Just to the right of Nancy is Bemis
where Mother and Granny got lost in the '50s
trying to find the old fire tower.
I suppose most of the rotting tinkertoys have disappeared
but so many remains still stand—
one on Carrigain, at the other end of that little range,
others at Hale, just a few miles north,
and Osceola, just to the south,
one right over here on Kearsarge that may still function—
at least I've seen people up there working on it.

You can see that one from the house,
or could before we let all those birches grow up.
Last time we went up there,
we got buzzed twice—
once by a plane, once by a chopper—
had to tiptoe around two attack dogs on the way down,
eavesdropped three couples arguing about turning back.
But from that tower when I was a kid
at exactly one o'clock
we would aim our tinny mirror
towards a knoll in the valley,
watch the reflected light sweep down the rock
then out towards the house,
delight in the answering dots of brightness,
the sudden brief flashes from home.

It always surprises me how a writer who is deeply familiar with a world can recreate it with specific names so that we see it or transpose it to a place with which we are familiar. In reading and rereading this poem, I am impressed at how easily the poet takes us back and forth in time to his grandmother's day, perhaps before, and up to the present so that he—and the reader—see the area and its changes in his lifetime, in his mother's and his grandmother's, and, by implication, his son's and the time of his son's son.

There is something magical and terrifying about the end, when signals across time and space are no longer sent or received. Do I "understand" the poem? As a writer, I read without complete understanding, as I live without complete understanding. I understood the poem enough to enter and inhabit the world of the poet. It is writing that becomes part of my experience, because there is surprise each time I read it and the promise that no reading will eliminate all its mystery.

Read as writers do: to understand our craft, to improve your own craft, to be inspired, and, most of all, for delight. Celebrate what other writers do that is so difficult but reads so easily when the writers have packed up their tools, swept the workshop floor, and left us a final draft.

....

QUESTIONS ABOUT READING AS A WRITER

Do I have to like the kind of writing that turns you on?

Certainly not. Sometimes I don't like the writing that "turns me on," and I move on to other kinds of writing. The writing that I think is good keeps changing, and your idea of good writing will keep changing. We read to learn what we need to learn about life; we read to hear others confirm and articulate our thoughts and feelings; we read to escape, and depending what we are escaping our choice of reading changes; we read to see how other writers solve the problems we face at this stage of our writing development or on particular writing tasks. Those tasks and situations keep changing, and so what interests us in our reading changes. Follow your own needs.

I don't always see what you see in published writing. In fact, I never see it until after you point it out. But I do see things I do or should do in my writing. Do I have to see what you see?

No. You come to reading with your own autobiography. I read about only children in a different way than my daughters do, since I was an only child and they were not; I read crime stories in a different way than my neighbors, since I have been both a policeman and a police reporter. When I read as a writer, I usually read to see the writer's solutions to problems that face me at the moment: What would be the advantages of a long line in the poem I'm writing this week? How should I start my next novel? How can I write a column about a conflict when I think both sides are right—or wrong?

Don't you always read as a writer?

Not consciously. I read to see why the teachers in the next town have gone on strike, to become a female private detective in a Sue Grafton novel or a bird artist in 1911 Newfoundland in a novel by Howard Norman, to see why the Patriots won. I read for information, instruction, entertainment, but when I read a page that makes me think or feel or care or laugh or weep, I guess I go back and read, saying, "How did the writer do that?"

Doesn't that take the fun out of it?

No, it increases the fun. When I watch the replay of a great save by a hockey goalie, I enjoy it more because I played in the goal. That second look—or fourth or fifth—makes it better.

Where do you get that stuff to read? Do you have a reading list?

Not often. Occasionally, I'll write down a couple of titles people have mentioned, or after a TV interview with an author, a book review, or some library research, but mostly I follow my nose. I go in a bookstore almost every day and I discover books on the shelves there or in the library. When I was a freelance writer in New Jersey, I had cards from four libraries. When I read something by a writer that impresses me, I rush to find books by the same author and devour them.

If I read like you do in my English class, I'd get in trouble. Why don't my English teachers read this way?

Some do, but many don't because they are not writers. They read as readers. They are critics and scholars. They examine the trends in literature, evaluate the works and their authors, study literature in a context, for example, seeing it as an historical document, a social or political one. They study literature in an aesthetic setting or see a work in cultural, ethnic, or gender context. All these are important ways to look at reading and good ways to spend your life. Like most English teachers, I have taught literature as well as composition. But my strengths are in teaching students to write. I read as a maker. They teach how to read more effectively, and the purpose of this book is to teach how to write more effectively.

By the way, you can read without writing but you can't write without reading, word by word, line by line, as it appears on the page and is later revised and edited.

Who's your favorite author?

My father was in the fashion business, and we ate poorly or well according to what sold at Christmas or Easter. It was a silly game. Literature isn't a silly game. As a literature student, I spent a lot of time ranking poems, plays, short stories, essays, novels as works of art but I refuse to play that game any more. A piece of literature has value when it speaks to you of the human condition. By that measure, Lisa Miller is the greatest poet in the English language—for me, today, after I read an as-yet-unpublished poem of hers that moved my mind and my emotions. Who knows who will be my favorite writer when I pick up a book tonight.

I hear there are lists of books everyone should read. Should I get one and read through the list?

All the lists peddle a point of view. One is white Anglo Saxon male, another is white liberal female, another African American, or Asian or European or Third World or . . . Find your own literature, and when you are familiar with it, then read the literature of others.

`When do you get your reading done? I don't have whole days in which I do nothing but read.`

Neither do I. I always have a book with me, and I have trained myself to read in fragments of time. I read in the car waiting for my wife, in a hall waiting for a concert or lecture to begin, in bed, on the john, in front of the TV during commercials, in front of the TV during a game or a program, sitting on a rock wall, in the waiting room of a doctor or a car repair shop, on a bench at the mall, in the bath, on the plane, at the beach, in the mountains, in the city park, in a hotel room, when eating alone, on the porch, in my office.

`What should I do to start reading like a writer?`

Find a writer who is writing on the same subject as you are or in the same genre. Read to see how that person performed your task. Find writers who sound like you'd like to sound, who write what you'd like to write, and you'll discover you are reading as a writer.

ACTIVITIES FOR READING AS A WRITER

1. Have each member of your writing group choose a paragraph or two (no more than a page) that they like or strongly dislike from a magazine or a book. Have each person read their selection out loud, BUT with one condition: do not tell if you liked or disliked the writing. Each listener should write down in their daybooks or reading journals their first thoughts about the passages. What's the writer trying to say? Is it said clearly? What works? What needs work? How could it be focused differently? Could it be cut? Expanded? How could the voice be better tuned? After the reader listens to the group, then have the reader express his or her reasons for selecting the passage and give a response to the listeners' reactions.

2. Select a short piece (less than two pages) of a published work and read it aloud, making believe you are the author appearing at a reading in a bookstore or library. Tell the readers how you came to write the selection. What problems did you discover in writing it? How did you solve them? What other solutions did you consider? How would you write it differently today? Answer these and other questions about the selection as you believe the writer would answer.

3. Get an inside view of the making of a piece of writing. Read an interview with a writer in a publication such as the *Paris Review,* the *New York Times Review of Books,* the *Washington Post, Writer's Digest,* or *Writer;* listen to writer interviews on "The Today Show"; "Good Morning, America"; National Public Radio; or C-Span's Booknotes program; read writers'

interviews on the Internet at such sites as Amazon.com, AOL's Book Report, or the publishers' Web pages that talk about the making of a work; then read the work itself. You may also be able to find writers' autobiographies, published letters, or journal entries at the library. Write down in your daybook or reading journal what the writer said were problems in writing the piece. Then write down how the writer solved those specific problems. Imagine a conversation between an editor and the writer during the making of the work. Suggest alternative solutions to one chosen by the writer. Change an element in the work—make it science fiction instead of a mystery; make the hero a heroine or vice versa; increase the dialogue; make the voice your own.

4. Go to a bookstore and choose three to five books from the same genre—reportage, mystery, biography, science fiction, humor, computer manuals, outdoors, travel, drama, sports, science, business, literary fiction. Sit down in a comfortable chair, and compare the opening paragraphs of each book to those of the others. What were the different approaches used by the authors? How different were the voices between the authors? For whom were the authors writing? Are the audiences different? How can you tell? What techniques do the authors use to draw the reader in? Did they succeed? Write your answers in your daybook or reading journal.

5. Have each member of your writing group bring in an excerpt from a novel. The excerpt should be intriguing, or mysterious, or exciting. Ask each group member to read the passage out loud, then ask the others to write down what they think happened that led to that scene. Then have them write down what happened after that passage. Share your ideas with one another. Then have each member tell what really happened before and after the excerpt, and compare how close your guesses were to the real story.

6. Break into teams of two or three, and act out a scene from a favorite novel, then have the class/audience act as play director and suggest other ways the same scene might have been acted. Discuss the advantages and disadvantages of each approach.

7. Along with a writing partner, bring in a textbook selection that you don't understand. Read your partner's troublesome passage, then write down what you think it means. Discuss it with your partner, and see if your interpretations agree or disagree. Discuss why you think the passage does not work. Was the problem technical language used by the author? What style could the author have used to make the text more understandable? Does the author's voice make the passage difficult to understand? How could it be changed? Does the problem originate with the author's choice of an audience?

Interview professors in the textbook's field to find out what the author meant. What do the professors think of the textbook? How would they write the confusing passage?

If you still don't understand the passage, begin rewriting each paragraph until it makes sense. Change technical terms to more common terms. Break down complicated sentences into more understandable ones. Compare explanations of the same thing in three, four, or five textbooks. Which ones are most effective? Why? Least effective? Why? Imagine you are the textbook editor for the next edition, and write a memo that will help the author do a better job. Send it to the publisher.

8. Many writers write both newspaper or magazine articles and books. Ernest Hemingway's newspaper stories are published, as well as his short stories and novels. Anna Quindlan is another writer who writes both newspaper pieces and books. Find an article or essay written by a chosen author, and compare it to a book written by the same person. What are the most noticeable differences in the styles of the two pieces? What is similar? How are the voices different between the newspaper/magazine articles and the books? How does the length affect the sentence and paragraph structures? How does the voice change? What benefits has journalism experience given the book writer?

9. Select a passage of writing, and rewrite it. If the passage is in first person, rewrite it in third person. If the passage has dialogue, rewrite it with no dialogue. If there is no dialogue, rewrite it with dialogue. Change the point of view. Change the genre—make it a poem or a TV sit-com script or a speech, a romance novel or a history.

Speed up the passage. Slow it down. Develop it; make it fuller and more complete. Increase the tension between the characters or the forces in the passage. Add a new character. Change the focus, so the meaning is different. Vary the evidence or documentation, adding statistics or city authorities or scholarly references.

10. With a writing partner, take a long passage from a book, and imagine you are editors assigned to cut the piece in half. What words can you cut from the piece without changing its meaning? What sentences can you cut without changing its meaning? How might you reorder the piece to speed it up? Can you move in closer? Stand further back? Eliminate some documentation? What can be implied and not said? In cutting the piece, what have you discovered about the way the author put it together?

11. Pick a passage from a book that uses a lot of descriptive adjectives. Read the passage out loud to your writing group using all the adjectives, then read it out loud deleting all the adjectives. How is the meaning changed by deleting the adjectives? Have the group brainstorm some different

adjectives to use in the passage, and rewrite it. How does your version compare to the original? How does rewriting change the meaning? Try the same thing with adverbs. Cut the *ly* words; also, delete *would* and *that* and *ing* words to see what difference these changes make.

12. Many novels—such as *The Prince of Tides* by Pat Conroy, *The Joy Luck Club* by Amy Tan, *The Color Purple* by Alice Walker, and almost all the classics—have been made into movies. You can rent the videos or find the published versions of the movie scripts at the library or a bookstore. Individually or in teams, read and/or view both versions of a story, and compare them. How would you have made a different film? How did your reading of the book affect your reading of the script or vice versa? How would the movie change if it were to become an animated film, a musical, a play, a made-for-TV drama, a TV series?

In the case of such a movie as *The English Patient,* there are abundant interviews with the author of the book, the script writer, and the director; stories about the making of the book and the movie; reviews of both book and movie. Assign people to research some sources and report back on what they discovered and how it might affect their own writing. Compare the storytelling techniques used in each medium. Compare the way the book's author conveyed meaning with words in a particular scene and the way the movie makers portrayed the same scene. Which is more moving or funny?

13. *First Words: Earliest Writings from Favorite Contemporary Authors* (Edited by Paul Mandelbaum, Algonquin Books, 1993), is a wonderful collection of the earliest writings from many of today's popular writers: Amy Tan, Stephen King, John Updike, Pat Conroy. See if your local library carries this book, and compare these authors' early writings to their recent work. What are the most noticeable differences? If you were the writers' teachers or the editors of school literary magazines, would you have foreseen their future success as writers? Why? What qualities did they have as young writers? What did they have yet to learn? How have their styles changed? How have their voices changed? What do interviews with these authors reveal about what happened to them in school?

14. Use your reading journal or daybook to "converse" with an author you admire. Imagine how he or she might respond to your questions, and jot down the answers you think the writer would give. Then stage a mock interview with your writing partner. Play the role of the writer, and have the partner interview you. Answer your interviewer's questions from the perspective of the writer. Switch roles. Then play the role of editor, and imagine a helping conversation. Make believe you are going to write a

movie script, and ask the author for specific suggestions on scenes that must be included and why.

15. Preserve a special section in your daybook or reading journal for memorable, provocative, or disturbing passages from your readings. Share these with the class, and talk about why you selected them. Did they make you think? Have you had experiences that gave them special meaning? Did you find them beautiful, ugly, upsetting? What struck you as particularly significant about these passages?

16. I started recording quotations by writers on writing when I was in junior high school. A collection of those I have noted has been published in *Shoptalk* (Boynton/Cook/Heineman, 1990). There are many such books of quotations, often called *commonplace books*. Read some of them to discover what authors have said about the writing process, their problems and solutions. Start your own commonplace book with quotations on the parts of the writing craft that interest you or give you difficulty, and join the community of writers living and dead.

17. Choose a passage from a piece of autobiographical writing by a professional author, one that you think conveys a sense of his or her voice. Make copies and pass them around in a small group, omitting any information about the author or title of the piece; ask your group mates to do the same. Try to guess from the passages what the narrators are like. What kinds of voice do they have? How old do you think they are? Are they male or female? Write up a profile of each narrator in your daybook.

18. Retype a couple of pages from a published author's work. LISTEN to the rhythm of the sentences as you type them. Think of the words you are putting down and how the author chose them. Pay attention to punctuation and the stylistic choices the author has made. Then rewrite the passage. Change or add punctuation or leave it out; drop or add details, or go off on a tangent of your own. Move the middle paragraph to the beginning, or change the ending. Choose one scene or detail to write about extensively, and omit others. Note when and how the focus of the selection shifts as you fiddle with it. Take a piece of your own, and write as the published author might have written it.

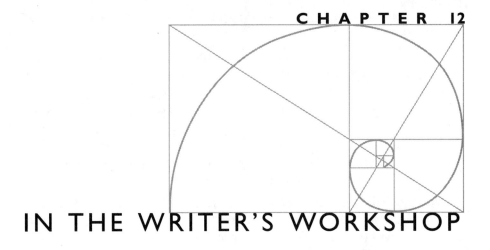

CHAPTER 12

IN THE WRITER'S WORKSHOP

Writing is not a mystical art; writing is a craft that can be understood, shared, learned. The best writers do have talent, but that talent is honed and developed. It is important for apprentice writers to join experienced writers at the workbench, to see how badly they write—good writing is the product of bad writing; the said that cannot yet be said—and how they find the good within the bad and develop it so that others can understand.

Fortunately there is a great deal of testimony by writers on how they write. The autobiographies and biographies of writers, their collected letters and published notebooks, their case histories and the reproductions of their manuscript pages, interviews with writers such as those published in the *Paris Review* and collected in the series *Writers at Work*—all of these sources document how writers work. You can also invite classmates to share their case histories, asking them to tell you how they have written pieces that you admire. Most of all, you should write your own case histories to discover what you have done when writing well, so that you can reinforce those habits and skills that work for you.

The case histories in this chapter reveal the narrative of writing samples, then the final drafts. You may want to skip ahead and read the final drafts, then go back to see how they were developed. Too few readers have had the opportunity to attend play or symphony rehearsals, watch artists or sculptors at work in their studios, and most of all—since writing is ordinarily a secret art—see writers alone with their pages. When Ernest Hemingway was asked where he worked, he reportedly said, "In my head." We can't open up the skulls of writers, but we can go into their workrooms and observe the process of "making" writing.

....

STUDENT CASE HISTORY: WRITING TO DESCRIBE—SARAH HANSEN

Sarah Hansen has written an excellent student case history that covers the entire writing process from finding a topic to completing a final draft. Her piece grew out of an assignment to write, with abundant detail, about a familiar place—her hometown.

· HOW I WROTE MY ESSAY ·
Sarah Hansen

This descriptive essay is the result of eight drafts, conferencing, workshopping, journal writing, thinking, and sharing. It was hard work—sometimes frustrating but mostly rewarding. I have learned to have confidence in my own writing. But I still have not tackled procrastination, and wonder if I ever will.

To come up with a topic, I brainstormed places and people that I would like to describe and that I know a lot about. I picked my hometown, Birch Grove, Illinois, because I have a lot to say about it, and at that point I was confused about my feelings for Birch Grove. My English teacher, Bruce Ballenger, says confusing topics are the best to write about because by writing about them a discovery might be made that will help to end the confusion.

Before I began a first draft, I brainstormed another list of Birch Grove people, places, and events. The list I made ended up in two piles: one bad and one good. This was something I hadn't expected.

I circled the most controversial and the weirdest things on the list. Directly after this, I began to free write about the circled things.

I thought about the paper for a few days then went to the computer to type what I had written during the free write. I added more stuff to it that had been in my head and took the first draft to my conference with Bruce. He liked it. But the point I was trying to make was not clear, because I didn't really know exactly what the point was. Ideas about a hometown are complex. This was the most difficult part of writing this essay: trying to find the point.

Also, my first draft had too much description. I had to find the places where the description didn't fit the purpose of the essay. I actually used scissors and tape on the first draft to cut out unnecessary description. The second draft had less description but was no closer to realizing a point than the first. I was frustrated.

Our writing class had group workshops where we shared our pieces with three or four other students. I read the Birch Grove paper to my workshop group, because I needed fresh perspectives. I also needed some positive reinforcement. All three students liked my paper—that made me feel more motivated to work on it. One woman in my workshop agreed with Bruce and me that the point of the essay needed to be clearer. The most valuable thing I learned from the workshop was that the topic of the essay wasn't clear until the middle. They suggested starting the essay with a paragraph or idea from the middle.

With this in mind, I changed the first paragraph and fiddled around with various parts of the essay. But I was still frustrated with the meaning. I knew that the essay was slowly progressing with each draft, but from drafts two to six, I made little progress finding exactly what it was I wanted to say without sounding boring, clichéd, or obvious. I started to share the essay with a lot of different people. Most close friends tend to like just about anything you do and aren't objective enough and don't give much criticism. Older English majors and my parents and their friends, people that read a good amount of writing, turned out to be the most helpful.

With each successive draft, the second to the sixth, my English teacher and I became more and more discouraged. I couldn't reach exactly what it was about Birch Grove I wanted to say. Did I want to say how I felt; did I want to say something to the people of Birch Grove; did I want to make a point about all hometowns; did I want to make a statement about the world by talking about one hometown? My biggest mistake was not writing in my journal enough. I procrastinated writing about my feelings for Birch Grove, because it was too frustrating.

Around draft four or five, I couldn't look at the paper with objectivity anymore. I was too close to my subject and practically had the words memorized, as did my English teacher. Finally, after draft five, Bruce gave the draft back to me with questions written all over it about what it was I was trying to say. In my journal I wrote answers to his questions. It was this way, by talking to myself in my journal, and by answering questions, that I nearly found what I wanted to say.

I wrote that the good in Birch Grove I had realized by going away far outweighed the bad. The energy of the good things is what makes Birch Grove all right. When people realize this, then Birch Grove will be safe. We decided that this would be the final draft. I thought I was done.

But when my father read the essay out loud that night, I realized what I had wanted to come across did not. In the sixth draft it seemed I had forgotten the racism and the close-mindedness. I intended just the opposite. I wanted to say that I have realized the good in Birch Grove, but that the bad needs to be changed.

The biggest problem I had writing this essay was attempting to find exactly what the meaning was. I also needed to spend more time talking to myself about the essay in my journal. In hand with this, I needed to spend more time writing than thinking about the essay. A good idea can sometimes surprise me as I write, but that rarely happens when I think about my writing without a pen in my hand.

I learned to share my work with as many people as I could who were willing to take the time to read it and give their responses. It is motivating to hear fresh and new ideas. The conferences helped in that Bruce and I would talk about what it was I was trying to say. The discussions helped each draft to come closer and closer. It was also good to hear someone give positive comments about my writing.

Writing a descriptive essay can help with any other kind of writing. Description is about saying things so that other people can see, feel, hear, and smell what you have. These things are revealed through specific details. It is exactly the same concrete writing that is needed to critique a novel or write a term paper.

Sarah's daybook started out with the following entry:

I have to write a paper for a book—a descriptive essay—to be published. I have no idea what to write about—just knowing it's for a book makes me nervous. I've even been avoiding thinking about it. Dad—Heather—East H—commune—expectations—grandma—Birch Grove—Berry Farm—trip to France—second semester at UNH.

She starts out with a writer's apprehension and makes a list of possible topics. She did put a mark like a rising sun after "Birch Grove," and then she wrote a draft that plunged into the subject: "The round and friendly minister of the Methodist Church of Birch Grove, Illinois, was found in Sanderson's three-story department store stealing a large pair of light brown corduroys."

In her daybook Sarah wrote:

I showed my first draft of the essay for the book today. Bruce liked it. I was so relieved. He's really helped me to be more confident about my writing. We decided that the point of the paper wasn't too clear. He said that I need to "peel the onion." In class we talked about how the layers of the onion are like layers of ideas and points to an essay or a piece of writing. The deeper into the onion layers you get, the closer you are to your main point. I know a few things that I am pointing out but I don't know exactly how to say them. I think my main point is about how Birch Grove was all bad to me at first, and then, as I went to UNH, I realized the better things about it. But the better things don't excuse the bad things. I'm still confused about it. I don't think this paper is very interesting. I don't think it will keep the reader's interest. We also talked about how there are too many descriptions.

I find this sort of writing to myself important. It helps to put into words what you got from a conference and to identify your feelings about the text and about the process of writing.

The next page in Sarah's daybook showed a typical jumble of doodling and writing. She listed potential specifics as a form of recovering memories and discovering what she may write.

Later she wrote in her daybook:

I've decided to show my paper on Birch Grove to my workshop group. I don't know where to go with it. I have been thinking a lot about the focus of this paper and it's getting me nowhere. Hopefully, they'll have some insight to it that will get me motivated for revising this paper. I spend too much time just thinking—I should be writing in this journal more but don't have discipline—I procrastinate too much.

• • •

My workshop group really liked my paper. Lin said it reminded her of her hometown which is cool cause that's sort of a point I'm trying to make—every hometown for every person is both good and bad—end up blaming hometown for everything—have bitterness towards it. A love-hate thing. I don't know that's quite what I want to say though—seems cliché. Brian and _____ both thought that the beginning isn't clear—maybe begin with paragraph that starts, "I moved to Birch Grove, where life offers more, when I was four. . . ." They said as it stands now it's a little unclear what I'm talking about. So I'll try to rework that into the beginning and Brian thought that my point was perfectly said—that I shouldn't add more but said I should make my point clearer. I agree more with _____ cause at this point I don't even know what my main point is. I asked them if they thought it was boring and if it caught and kept their attention. They said it was interesting and kept their attention well so that made me feel better. Asked if there was too much description and they said no.

In all her daybook entries Sarah reveals the way a writer's mind—and emotions—work. I certainly feel the same way about my drafts as Sarah does about hers. To learn to write effectively you need to be open and realize your feelings and how to deal with them. Later in her daybook Sarah writes:

I'm annoyed with my paper about Birch Grove. I'm sick of it. I'm too close to it and can't see it correctly any more. It seems so trite and boring and cliché. Bruce seems to not like it much either. That's really discouraging. I don't know what exactly I want my point to be that's creative and fresh.

These excerpts from her account reveal the writer at work, what goes on backstage that is essential to the creation of an effective piece of writing. Space limitations here preclude reproducing her drafts, sometimes marked up with her comments, other times with the comments of her readers, but they document the evolution of her essay. In the third draft, for example, Sarah begins, "When I was four, my mother, my dog, and I moved to Birch Grove, Illinois. I've spent all my time there minus the summers which I've spent with my father. Passing the town border a cheap billboard reads: 'Life offers more in Birch Grove.'"

By the fifth draft her lead reads, "Passing over the town border into Birch Grove, Illinois, a billboard, paint peeling off, reads: 'Life offers more in Birch Grove.' When I was four years old my mother, my dog, and I moved to this Midwestern town. As I grew up, I'd pass the fading billboard ~~faded as was along with~~ and my tolerance for BIRCH GROVE~~, my bitterness and anger seen in a grimace as I thought, 'Life offers less in Birch grave.'~~ faded along with it." By the eighth draft the lead was as it appears below. Writers have to learn by writing and by considering what they have written and how it can be improved.

Here is Sarah's final draft as it was turned in:

· SIMPLE BIRCH GROVE ·
Sarah Hansen

Passing over the town border into Birch Grove, Illinois, a billboard, paint peeling off, reads: "Life Offers More In Birch Grove." When I was four years old my mother, my dad, and I moved to this Midwestern town. As I grew up, I'd pass the fading billboard, and my tolerance for Birch Grove faded along with it.

The owner of Sanderson's three-story department store found the round and friendly minister, Donald Morison, of the Methodist Church of Sycamore stealing a pair of brown corduroys. Most of the bank presidents and company founders and Mercedes Benz owners of Birch Grove belonged to the Methodist Church on the corner of Third and Main. They put up a big fuss about having a kleptomaniac as a minister. There was great pressure on Don to leave. These influential people weren't seen at Sunday services anymore to listen to Don with his brown, shining eyes give the sermon. Only a few members forgave Don, told him so, and asked him to stay. One Sunday, a woman slowly stood up and told the churchgoers that the Bible says to forgive, and that we should forgive Don, and help him out, because his problem is a disease, just as alcoholism is a disease. Don left the Methodist Church two long months after the incident, and the members are now content to sit in the pews and sing out of the worn, red, cloth-covered hymnals.

Miss Gooch, the assistant counselor at Birch Grove High School, wears her thin, gray-brown hair in a tight curl perm. I was the student council president my senior year, and we were discussing some upcoming activities. Miss Gooch liked to gossip; she asked me how my friend Peggy was doing. Peggy has fair, freckled skin and blond, curled hair—like most other girls at Birch Grove High School. Her boyfriend is thin and has beautiful, chocolate brown skin. What Miss Gooch meant was, "How is she dealing with having a black boyfriend?" Miss Gooch said, "I am not prejudiced, but I don't think the races should intermingle . . . and I hate Mexicans." Sixteen black students and forty Mexican students attend Birch Grove High School, where Miss Gooch is the counselor and student council advisor.

At age eleven, my sister Traci walked to the Save And Shop, three blocks down Walnut Street from our house, to buy groceries. As she crossed the supermarket parking lot, a little girl, not over seven years old, was left alone in a beat-up station wagon. The girl rolled down the front seat window. "Nigger," she said to Traci, my adopted sister, now one of the sixteen black students at the high school. Traci is startled as she looks in the mirror to see her own black face. Her eyes are so accustomed to whiteness.

Sam Ritchel was salutatorian of my class. Now, when I come home for Christmas or Easter vacation, I see Sam wandering around Birch Grove, or staring off in a booth in the Coffee Shop. He's taken too much acid, refuses to get a job, dropped out of the University of Wisconsin, shaves his eyebrows, wears black lipstick, black eyeliner, and black clothing. He listens to Jim Morrison on his tape recorder, and says nothing but "black, melancholy, darkness, despair . . ." In the Weston Elementary School, Sam's nickname was Happy.

I hated everything about Birch Grove. I hated its conservatism, its hypocrisy, its ignorance, its racism, its close-mindedness, and its ugliness. I hated what it did to bright, open-minded people who could not escape. In Birch Grove, I could only think about itchy, depressing, angering things. Times when snotty Claire Saunders knocked over my newly painted three-speed bike in the fifth grade, when the whole of Birch Grove watched *Top Gun* perpetually for weeks after it came out on video, when high school students egged our house five times in two months because my stepfather is the assistant principal of the high school—a fair, kind man who must punish students for skipping a study hall, for smoking in the music wing.

But since I've been at college, far away from my hometown, I can remember eating macaroni and cheese on Kiersten's sunny, white porch with her mother and mine, enjoying the lunch hour before returning back to the third grade. I can remember the annual January snow sculpture competition in front of Prince's Restaurant across from Birch Grove Park. I remember my very first valentine in seventh grade from my very first boyfriend: shy, curly white-haired Jim Morse, a farm boy. The homemade card was caringly shaped and cut out of red, pink, and white construction paper. Two white rabbits kissed on the front; inside, pencil cursive writing read, "I'm glad that you're my valentine, Sarah."

I remember the annual Birch Grove Pumpkin Festival where all of Birch Grove competes in a pumpkin competition, decorating them as a scary monster with orange peels for hair and gourds for arms and legs or a pumpkinphone for goblins and ghosts to use. The Miller family won the grand prize one year and got to go on the Bozo Show. There was a pumpkin princess or prince award to the best essay in the junior high, and the grade-schooler with the best scary picture got to ride on the fire engine at the front of the Sunday Pumpkin Parade. I watched the parade from the Abbens' house on Somonauk Street with people from our church, eating warm carameled apples, and drinking hot apple cider sitting on fold-out chairs along the street. The huge oak, maple, and sycamore trees lining the street screamed autumn with their yellows, golds, reds, and oranges.

I remember Mrs. Munter, my junior and senior year English teacher, my most influential teacher, sneaking chocolate M&Ms out of the second drawer down. I remember her strong, clear, enunciated voice demanding and challenging us to accomplish more in her class than we ever had before.

I remember driving along the smooth and winding North River Road just after dusk on a hot summer day, windows rolled down and arms out waving, watching the thousands of tiny blinking lights of the fireflies just above the soybeans and wheat fields. Although I used to hate the flatness of the land, now as I return I appreciate the great big sky and lie in the middle of a cornfield with Steven and Pam, watching the silver-white shooting stars stream across the blue-black expanse.

I see Sean Allen in the store window of Ben Franklin, the five and dime, and wave back knowing he's still the same friendly, simple person he always was and will be. I know that every summer the woman with the wrinkled face will bring out her popcorn stand, and my mother and I'll buy sweet caramel-corn and eat the whole bag as we walk slowly home in the hot night air.

Mom says Birch Grove is a good place to bring up children. Maybe it is in some ways. Friendly Sean Allen, the sun on a white porch that makes the skin hum, and Mrs. Munter's deep, resounding voice are as pure and warm as the wealthy church-goers and close-minded Miss Gooch are tarnished and cold. But even as the sweet-smelling fields, the wide Midwest sky, the leaves of screaming colors that crackle under foot seek to balance this out, I know that Birch Grove still is no place to bring up my children.

....

PROFESSIONAL CASE HISTORY: WRITING TO ANALYZE—CHRISTOPHER SCANLAN

Christopher Scanlan is the writer I turn to first when I need help, diagnosis, encouragement, support, criticism, inspiration, comradeship.

He is a master writer of fiction and nonfiction who can write short and write long, write on hourly deadline and write over time. He can write on many subjects in many voices. He is—my greatest compliment—a pro.

He has been a staff member of the *Providence Journal,* the *St. Petersburg Times,* and Knight-Ridder Newspapers Washington Bureau. His stories, essays, and articles have appeared in *Redbook,* the *Washington Post Magazine,* the *Boston Globe Magazine,* and numerous other publications. He has won sixteen awards for writing, including a Robert F. Kennedy award for international journalism.

He is also a master teacher of writing. He is director of writing programs at The Poynter Institute for Media Studies in St. Petersburg, Florida, where he teaches professional writers to improve their writing. He also writes journalism texts for Harcourt Brace.

Now Chip Scanlan takes us into his workroom, showing just how he wrote a personal essay.

• HOW I WROTE MY ESSAY •
Christopher Scanlan

ORIGINS

"We've got the O. J. 911 tapes," the morning drive-time DJ promised. "Coming up. After these messages."

Like other commuters on this July morning, I was hooked. When the playback finally came over my car radio, I heard Nicole Brown Simpson's voice—fed-up, frightened, resigned—but that wasn't what brought tears to my eyes sitting at the downtown stop light. It was the voice in the background—the shouts of a man out of control, choking on contempt and rage, spewing abuse. I knew that sound.

I've heard it echoing off the walls in our house. I've felt the lump of remorse that screaming at the top of my lungs leaves in the back of my throat, the pit of my stomach. "I have to write about this," I thought.

After twenty years reporting for newspapers, big and small, I don't need both hands to count the times the first person singular appeared under my byline: a deadline account about a stint volunteering at a mental hospital during a state workers' strike; a recollection of a year in the Peace Corps; a Father's Day message to my unborn daughter; a travel piece about the search for a soldier's grave in Europe; a brief stint as a fill-in columnist. But in most of these I stayed back, little more than a personal pronoun. Like most journalists, I feared the word *I*.

I knew the rules, unwritten but oft-spoken, by cynical colleagues and fearsome editors:

"Reporters don't belong in their stories."

"Nobody cares about your personal opinions."

"If your life was really interesting, we'd be writing about you."

Writing about yourself is often difficult for reporters and editors whose work focuses on others. But writing about yourself, honestly, even painfully, can make you not only a better writer but a better person. The personal essay trains its sights on the writer's own life and the writer's emotional, psychological, and intellectual reactions to the most intimate experiences. As Phillip Lopate says in his introduction to his anthology *The Art of the Personal Essay* (Anchor Books Doubleday, 1994): "The personal essayist looks back at the choices that were made, the roads not taken, the limiting familial and historic circumstances, and what might be called the catastrophe of personality."

The DJ put on a song. The light changed. "But I don't want to write about it." I drove on.

THE PROCESS

The story began with handwritten notes in my journal and an assignment to myself. Don Murray, who has written hundreds of personal essays in his column for the *Boston Globe,* had come to Poynter in July 1994 to teach in a summer program for college graduates bent on a career in journalism. The assignment: to write a personal essay.

"Make a list of what you think about when you are not thinking," Murray advised. "What makes you mad? What makes you happy? What past events were turning points in your life that you'd like to understand?"

I had my subject. Or more accurately, it had me.

"The place you come from and how you remember it matters," says writer Robert Love Taylor. "It is your territory." Writing the personal essay requires you to seek out the territory that is your life and to explore it as deeply and honestly as possible. It means subjecting your own life to the same scrutiny that you train on your sources. It's here, at the beginning of the process, that I almost chickened out. My wife and I have three daughters, including a set of twins, who are always doing and saying cute things. I could write about being the father of twins, scattering my essay with funny anecdotes and the darndest things kids say.

I certainly wasn't going to write an essay that let anyone in on my dirty little secret, that I too often lost my temper with these three little girls. And then I remembered my reaction to O. J. Simpson's shouting on the 911 tapes, and I knew I couldn't keep my distance anymore. I began scribbling notes in my journal.

Temper, Temper

911 tape in car—tears at stop light. I have been there. My voice too.

Temper school

Male anger

Melvin Mencher, a professor at the Columbia University Graduate School of Journalism, had a simple cure for writer's block: "Whenever you are blocked," he said, "just stop and ask yourself, 'What am I trying to say?'"

The next day, I sat in front of a computer terminal with my students on all sides in a Poynter Institute computer lab, fingers frozen until I asked that question and the first tentative words began to appear on the screen.

I began, as usual, by babbling. Some call this *free writing*; putting words on the page without editing or even stopping to correct spelling or grammar. I prefer *Washington Post* feature writer Cynthia Gorney's description: "I start to babble, sometimes starting in the middle of the story and usually fairly quickly I see how it's going to start. It just starts shaping itself. I tell students, 'Don't think, write.'"

Don't think, I told myself. Write. Or rather, think but do it with your fingers. The idea is to race past the inner censor, the creature novelist Gail Godwin refers to as the "watcher at the gate." The next day, I put the notes aside and began typing. I began typing:

I do not want to write this.

I love my kids, but I have left my handprint, like a blush on the backs of their thighs.

I do not want to write this.

Like a child whistling by a cemetery, I typed as fast as I could, writing without thinking, trying to discover what I wanted to say by talking to myself on the page as honestly as I could. In thirty-seven minutes I wrote 960 words. And yes, I did count them. At this stage, that's the only way I can measure progress. First drafts are painful; I'm convinced every word is the wrong one. It's like the first time you ride a bike; there's a lot of wobbling, falling, scraping your knees. So I try to remember what Christine Martin, who directs the writing program at the University of West Virginia journalism school, tells writers: free writing is like turning on a faucet in an old house; you have to let it run a while to get the rust out.

The first draft was riddled with errors. Errors of fact. Errors of omission. I didn't let that stop me. When I wanted to include an entry from my journal, I simply wrote: "A sample entry: TK (for *to come*) and kept on typing. Spelling errors. Grammar. Syntax.

Any of the good newspaper copy editors I worked with would have been horrified. I didn't let that bother me. Like Frank O'Connor, the Irish short story writer, any garbage will do. "Get black on white," Guy de Maupassant, the French short story writer, counseled. "Get anything down," the legendary editor Maxwell Perkins told one of his authors (they included Hemingway and Fitzgerald), "then we can work on it."

I printed out the draft and read it over. The computer and word processing software, which allow constant revisions without having to make an entire new draft, has made me less of a "copy editor's nightmare," the way an early job evaluation described me. Even so, I like to make a hard copy after my first writing session. Changing the writing surface to paper makes it easier to spot mistakes and to read the piece the way it will be read. On the screen everything looks perfect, even mistakes, and it's important for me to know that it's not, so I can make it better.

I try to read the first draft as a reader but inevitably my hand begins to itch for a pen. I started marking up the page. One line read ". . . fed up with the thousands frustrations that stud the ordinary workday."

I crossed out "fed up with" and replaced it with "choking on." One less word. More important, a vivid image that suggested the inner rage work produced in me. Not surprisingly, much of my thinking was disjointed. I drew arrows connecting paragraphs and made notes to "move up" paragraphs. I could have started with an outline but I prefer to discover what I'm trying to say first and then see how I can rearrange things.

The real key to writing success is learning how to read your manuscript with a discriminating eye—and ear. You have to discover what you want to say by writing it and then be willing to jettison it all when it doesn't work. So I reread what I wrote. I read it aloud to my wife. I choked back my usual disgust at my first draft. I rewrote. I jettisoned entire pages. I worked over paragraphs until just one phrase remained. I made my endings my beginnings. I added new material. I gave them to readers I trusted—my wife, Don Murray, Tom French at the *St. Petersburg Times,* and my colleagues at the Poynter Institute. I listened to their reactions and cut and added and re-ordered and wrote again.

It was beginning to look like a story, but I knew it still wasn't there. It was time to risk ridicule, to confront the possibility that I had failed.

I submitted the essay to the *New York Times* "over the transom," as they say. They turned it down. Then I contacted *Newsday.* They liked the piece but asked for a few changes. The refrain "I don't want to write this" helped me get the first draft done, but it didn't work for the editor. She also wanted the piece to be more topical, more newsy. I rewrote the lead using material from the O. J. Simpson case and added a description of St. Petersburg in summer. The story appeared in *Newsday,* but I wasn't finished with the subject.

GETTING NAKED

"If you can't tell an honest story about yourself, you're a long way from telling an honest story about someone else," Walt Harrington, staff writer for the *Washington Post Magazine,* says in *The Complete Book of Feature Writing,* edited by Leonard Witt (Writer's Digest Books, 1991). All writers have a territory, a landscape of experience and emotional history unique to them. Like any land-scape, there are safe havens and dangerous places. I could easily write a light-hearted piece about being the father of three girls. But the topic that needed exploring was my darker side: my temper with my kids.

"You can't write a personal column without going to some very deep place inside yourself, even if it's only for four hours," says essayist Jennifer Allen in *Speaking of Journalism,* edited by William Zinsser (Harper Collins, 1994). "It's almost like psychotherapy, except you're doing it on your own. You have to pull something out of yourself and give away some important part of yourself. . . . It's a gift you have to give to the reader, even if it's the most light-hearted piece in the world."

After the essay appeared in *Newsday,* I got a call from Evelynne Kramer, the editor of the *Boston Globe Magazine,* who invited me to submit an essay. When I mentioned the *Newsday* piece she expressed an interest—not about the Simpson case connection which wasn't timeless enough for a magazine's longer lead time—but on male anger. She'd like to see something on that.

Back to the computer, where I found myself writing about a starkly etched memory:

> It's late at night, and I'm screaming at my kids again. Yelling at the top of my lungs at three little girls, lying still and terrified in their beds. Like a referee in a lop-sided boxing match, my wife is trying to pull me away, but I am in the grip of a fury I am unwilling to relinquish. "And if you don't get to sleep right now," I shout, "there are going to be consequences you're not going to like."

In this version, I also used passages from a journal I'd been keeping about my temper. In the *Newsday* version, I had mentioned my father, who had died when I was a boy, his drinking and his own angry outbursts. But most of the focus in this draft was on my children and me.

I can look at my favorite stories and tell exactly where and how an editor improved it. In this case, Evelynne Kramer of the *Boston Globe Magazine* liked my initial submission but added, "It doesn't seem resolved in a literary way." (There aren't many newspaper editors who talk this way.) My father played a role that she felt I only hinted at.

For me, that meant trying to recreate an unforgettable moment that oc-curred nearly forty years ago and which I became convinced held answers to my own battles with anger.

I am no more than nine, and I am standing just outside our family kitchen. My father has come home drunk again. He is in his mid-forties, (about the age I am today). By now, he has had three strokes, land mines in his brain that he seems to shrug off, like his hangovers, but which in a year will kill him. He has lost his job selling paper products, which he detested, and has had no luck finding another. He and my mother begin arguing in the kitchen. Somehow he has gotten hold of her rosary beads. I hear his anger, her protests, and then, suddenly, they are struggling over the black necklace. (Has he found her at the kitchen table, praying for him? I can imagine his rage. "If your God is so good, why are the sheriffs coming to the door about the bills I can't pay? Why am I broke? Why can't I find a job? Why am I so sick? Why, dammit? Why?") Out of control now, he tears the rosary apart. I can still hear the beads dancing like marbles on the linoleum.

Evelynne's questions led me to confront why I was so mad at him. Writing about my temper led me to an unexpected insight—and a new peace—about my relationship with my father, who died when I was a boy. Whatever psychic wounds my father's death caused when I was ten seem to have frozen over my recollection of him. I have few conscious memories; those I have are starkly etched scenes of drunkenness, grief, and rage that left me with a reservoir of unresolved anger. This limitless supply feeds the frustrations of my own life, as do my templates of parental behavior that I, the loyal son, can reenact with my own children. For many years, I thought that I hated the dimly remembered stranger who was my father. I believed that I hated him for dying before I could learn who he was, for scaring me when he was drunk, but now I realize I hate him only because he left me before I could say "I love you."

Evelynne is one of those rare editors who doesn't feel she has to take over the writing, but instead leaves that responsibility with the writer. It's a lesson that Michael Crichton, the best-selling novelist, says he's learned about working with editors. "Ask for their reactions to what they find wrong, and not for their suggestions for how to fix it."

I owe the power of this piece to two people, Evelynne Kramer, who forced me to discover its true meaning, and my wife, Kathy Fair, who not only encouraged me to publish it, but insisted I do so.

FEEDBACK

Some of my friends cautioned me against publishing this piece; people might get the wrong idea about me. But writing the piece has helped me understand myself better and, more important, treat my family better. Judging from the letters and phone calls I've received from readers grateful to see a painful issue in their life aired publicly, it's helped others, too. Explore a dangerous region of your writer's territory by writing a piece nobody can write but you. By reporting on the central issues of the human condition—joy, loss, birth, anger, fear, death, hate, and love—you will give voice to the unspoken feelings and thoughts of your readers and draw each other into the human community.

JUDGMENT DAY

Writing about my temper with my kids was the easy part. Going public was the biggest risk. After it appeared, several letter writers to the *Boston Globe*

Magazine denounced me. "I am outraged that the *Globe Magazine* devoted space to a domestic-violence apologist," wrote one. "Temper tantrums are excusable for two-year-olds, not for grown men," another agreed.

Be ready to be judged, says my friend Mark Patinkin, a columnist for the *Providence Journal.* "When you use the letter *I,* for every supportive letter you get from someone who related to your one-year-old having a scene at a restaurant, you'll get another from a reader tired of hearing about your kid."

Their criticism was softened by other letters from parents who said they recognized their own family struggles with temper in my story. One mother from Maine planned to share the piece with her siblings "so they can tackle the trait sooner and hopefully more effectively." Another woman said she wished her father were still alive so he could read it.

Stylistically, recreating my parents' argument over her rosary beads and my father's anguished questions seems a bit risky. I make it clear it's a product of memory and imagination, though, and several people tell me they find it the most affecting part of the piece.

I have gotten more reaction—letters to the editor, phone calls, personal comments—from personal essays than from any single story in my entire career.

TIP SHEET

A personal essay is an attempt to understand. You don't have to find the answer. Like any quest, the experience of writing and rewriting will change you, whether or not you find the grail.

What do you need to understand?

About yourself?

About life?

What are you most afraid to write?

What is the story that nobody else can write but you?

This is the first and most important step. And if it's not close to the bone, keep looking. It's the willingness to explore something that is very personal and even painful that will serve you and the reader. I think it's best to write about something you feel deeply about but which you don't yet fully understand. Write what you don't know or know you don't know but which you need to know. The stuff of everyday life, meticulously observed and described, is what sets the personal essay apart. At Poynter, seminar participants have written haunting, wrenching, funny, and inspiring essays about a thirty-year-old prom dress, the minefield of personal relationships, a friend's suicide, the pain of racism, the trials of living with a pack rat, their children, their marriages, their parents' lives and deaths. "There are common human experiences, and journalists strike a chord when they write about them," says Ruth Hanley, an assistant city editor for the *Dispatch* in Columbus, Ohio.

I have written essays about my pathetic boyhood athletic career and how it made me a nonsports watcher ("Stupor Bowl" in the *Boston Globe Magazine*) and how my wife and I ask the parents of our children's friends if they have guns in their homes ("It's 10 P.M. Do You Know Where Your Guns Are?" in the *Christian Science Monitor*), as well as the story about my temper which appeared in the Sunday magazines of the *Boston Globe*, the *Detroit Free Press* and the *Hartford Courant*.

At the *Boston Globe Magazine*, editor Evelynne Kramer, says she looks for writing "that plumbs a universal feeling that a reader can relate to on some level even though they might not have had that particular experience." Effective essays, she says, "explore universal themes although not necessarily experiences."

Recreate Pivotal Moments

Larry Bloom, editor of *Northeast*, the Sunday magazine of the *Hartford Courant* and author of *The Writer Within: How to Discover Your Own Ideas, Get Them on Paper, and Sell Them for Publication,* puts the form to a rigorous test. "You don't have a personal essay unless you have a religious experience," he says. "Then it's the task of the writer to re-create that moment."

Take Risks

The single most important lesson I learned in journalism school, from a taskmaster named Melvin Mencher, was a line he considered a throwaway: "Be counter-phobic." Do what you fear to do. In twenty-two years of reporting for a living, there were very few days I wasn't scared. Could I get the interview I needed? Could I write the story? Did I get it right? To succeed, counter-phobia was my only option. Imagine a tightrope, and every day walk across it. Who's the one person you're afraid to call? Where is the one place in town you've never been because you're afraid to go there? It may be a housing project, or it may be the top floor of the big bank. What's the riskiest way I can write this story? Ask yourself every day, "Have I taken a risk?"

Write

Writers write. It's that simple—and that hard. If you're not writing regularly (every day, three times a week, every Saturday, for just fifteen minutes before your day job), then you're not a writer. You're part of that vast universe of people who want to be writers, but don't want to do the work. (I'm talking to myself here, hoping I can start paying attention and stop procrastinating.)

Writers fail more than they succeed. Ask yourself, "How can I fail today?" Then give it your best shot. Get in the game. Submit your stories. Risk rejection or you'll never have a chance at success.

ROLE MODELS

My biggest struggle with writing is putting my butt in the chair. I keep reminding myself to swallow the bile that rises with the first draft and having faith that somewhere in a disorganized, unfocused, even sometimes deceptively coherent story there lurks the promise of a final draft. It's always easier to channel surf the TV or the World Wide Web.

I read for inspiration and motivation. Books, like this one, that introduce writers to the way professionals work are enormously helpful. *The Best American Essay* series and *The Art of the Personal Essay* are two ready sources of good writing and discussion of how the writing was made. Fortunately, personal essays are everywhere these days, in newspapers, magazines, and on the Internet. Start keeping your own collection of writing that makes you want to write. Every sentence you read is a writer's workshop. So is every sentence you write.

Go out and buy a blank notebook today and begin filling it with your ideas. Essays, like trees, begin with a single seed, nourished by time and effort.

We are deluged today by what novelist and short story writer A. Manette Ansay refers to as "public domain" images and language: clichés, commonplace descriptions, and derivative plots that blur any attempts at originality. Draw instead on your individual experiences by tapping the "private stock" of memory and feeling that is inside you. Search for the particulars, the telling details and observations that give resonance and meaning to your story and set it apart from all others, and the chances of producing a piece with universal appeal are strong.

We all have stories that only we can tell. Is there a message you think needs to be heard? A story in your "private stock" that needs tapping? One story that's telling you how it must be written? A dangerous territory worth exploring? An idea you've never lost faith in? Ask yourself, "What's the writing only I can do?" And then do it.

• LOVE AND ANGER •
Christopher Scanlan

It's late at night, and I'm screaming at my kids again. Yelling at the top of my lungs at three little girls, lying still and terrified in their beds. Like a referee in a lopsided boxing match, my wife is trying to pull me away, but I am in the grip of a fury I am unwilling to relinquish. "And if you don't get to sleep right now," I shout, "there are going to be consequences you're not going to like."

With that vague but ominous threat, I slam the door so hard that I hear plaster falling behind the walls, and I throw myself onto my own bed, out of breath, pulse jackhammering in my temples, throat bruised and burning, a tide of remorse and revulsion rising within. From the children's room, howls descend into sobs and then sniffling whimpers as my wife murmurs a lullaby of explanations. "Daddy loves you very much," I hear Kathy tell them, a bedtime story in which I appear as a monster whose true, kinder side is obscured by fatigue and worry. "He's just tired, and he wants you to go to sleep. No, you're right, he shouldn't lose his temper, but sometimes parents get upset and they do things they shouldn't."

All my life I have struggled with anger, and its manifestations in fits of temper.

In college, I once punched a kitchen cabinet in anger, and, while I no longer recall what I was so frustrated about, I have never forgotten how, for months afterward, I couldn't shake hands without wincing. But it was only after I became a parent—we have a seven-year-old and five-year-old fraternal twins— that my rages grew worse and more frequent.

I have never hit my wife, but I have punched walls during arguments with her.

I love my kids, but I have left my handprint, a faint blush, on the backs of their thighs when I've spanked them. I have seen them recoil from me in terror.

At the office, I'm friendly, easy-going, generally considered a nice guy. It's only at home that I display this vein-popping, larynx-scraping rage. It's not just that I never show this secret, ugly side of my personality to others; I don't even seem to feel it in any other spheres of my life. Why must loved ones bear the brunt of anger?

It's 6:15 A.M. Two of the kids are slurping their way with a solemn determination through their Ripple Crisps and Cheerios. The laggard remains in bed, curled under her comforter, thumb planted firmly in her mouth.

"I'm counting to three," I call up from the landing. Silence.

"One."

The whiny protest is muffled, by the blanket and the finger. "Don't count!"

"You're going to miss the bus. You can't be late. Two."

Nothing.

"If I get to three, no 'Scooby Doo' tonight." Denying them this inane cartoon, their latest favorite, has proven a potent threat, and from the howl it sparks, I know I have hit a nerve. She doesn't move. Inside my head, some unseen force is unleashed, and my anger spews forth, like a race car's fiery exhaust. "That's it," I roar, my anger all out of proportion to the offense. "THREE-EEEE."

With that, the recalcitrant child is howling, and her twin joins in, while the eldest begins berating me. The peaceful breakfast is now a war zone.

I didn't want to believe anything was wrong. I shrugged off my wife's complaints that I had become the out-of-control parent her father had been. "I don't want my kids to have a father they're afraid of," she said after one of my outbursts.

"Wait a minute," I countered. "The kids know I love them." Didn't I always apologize after my anger had spent itself? Wasn't I unstinting with hugs and kisses?

"Maybe you should talk to somebody about it," she said, but I rebuffed that gentle hint. Everybody loses his temper sometimes. People get angry. Kids can drive you crazy. It's not as if I beat my wife or kids.

Kathy began clipping the occasional newspaper article about anger and pinning it to the refrigerator door. Eventually, she told me flat-out that she wouldn't tolerate any more verbal abuse. Her ultimatum, along with a particularly awful late-night screaming assault on the kids that left me ashamed, and, most of all, afraid, finally broke through the wall of denial. I did what I always do when I'm trying to get hold of something elusive: I wrote about it. Two years ago, I sat down in front of my computer and began what became a series of meditations. I called it my Temper Log.

I didn't write in it every day or every week, not even every month. But a pattern emerged from the sporadic entries. I was then working as a newspaper reporter in Washington, D.C. I constantly felt under the gun of deadlines at work, worries about supporting a family of five on a single paycheck, and the incessant demands of the children. I seemed to lose it most often early in the morning, in the rush to get sleepy children to school, or at the end of a long day and a deadening ride home on the Metro. I was usually tired, hungry, overwhelmed by the frustrations that studded my workday, beset by the responsibilities of a family. Half of me wanted to be Super Dad; the other half wanted to be left alone. And for the first time, I had someone I could yell at without immediate consequences—someone who wouldn't fire me, or hang up and give the story I was after to a competitor, someone who loved me so much that they took this crap that they shouldn't have to take.

FROM THE TEMPER LOG:

"Tuesday night, shortly before midnight. The last two days, I have lost my temper with the children as I got ready for work and tried to get them up. Today I got so furious with Michaela when she wouldn't put on her OshKosh jumper, I picked her up and dropped her on the bed against the bunched-up comforter. This is how 'normal' people wind up on the child-abuse hot line, accused of mistreating their children. I am sick at heart for acting this way. I love my children so much, and I don't want them to remember bad things about me, the way I remember Daddy breaking the rosary that night in the kitchen."

I am no more than nine, and I am standing just outside our family kitchen. My father has come home drunk again. He is in his mid-fortys (about the age I am today). By now, he has had three strokes, landmines in his brain that he seems to shrug off, like his hangovers, but which in a year will kill him. He has lost his job selling paper products, which he detested, and has had no luck finding another. He and my mother begin arguing in the kitchen. Somehow he has gotten hold of her rosary beads. I hear his anger, her protests, and then, suddenly, they are struggling over the black necklace. (Has he found her at the kitchen table, praying for him? I can imagine his rage. "If your God is so good, why are the sheriffs coming to the door about the bills I can't pay? Why am I broke? Why can't I find a job? Why am I so sick? Why, dammit? Why?") Out of control now, he tears the rosary apart. I can still hear the beads dancing like marbles on the linoleum.

I don't want to make this another one of those "It's all my parents' fault" stories, the convenient apologia of the Adult Child of an Alcoholic. Like me, my father was the product—and the victim—of his own upbringing: the only child born to a mother who had numerous miscarriages before him and a second-generation Irish-American father who squandered several fortunes and ended up alone with his memories in a furnished room at the YMCA.

While my own memories of my father are fragmentary, my mother's stories describe a vibrant, winning man, rich with an aura of promise that became deadened by alcohol and the burden of supporting a large family on a salesman's uncertain salary. No wonder he was angry.

Whatever psychic wounds my father's death caused when I was ten seem to have frozen over my recollection of him. I have few conscious memories; those I have are starkly etched scenes of drunkenness, grief, and rage that left me with a reservoir of unresolved anger. This limitless supply feeds the frustrations of my own life, as do my templates of parental behavior that I, the loyal son, can reenact with my own children. For many years, I thought that I hated the dimly remembered stranger who was my father. I believed that I hated him for dying before I could learn who he was, for scaring me when he was drunk, but now I realize I hate him only because he left me before I could say "I love you."

FROM THE TEMPER LOG:

"I told Caitlin that I am trying to control my temper because I don't want to frighten her and Lianna and Michaela. Last night, she angered me because she didn't want to go to bed, but I tried to put myself in her shoes and realized she was worried because Mommy wasn't home yet. So I lay down with her until she fell asleep.

"It's a balancing act, I see now, between my needs and theirs. Sometimes mine will have to take precedence. And sometimes, like last night when Caitlin just wasn't ready to sleep because she was afraid, I have to let the anger go and focus on what they need."

They read like confessions, these recitations of my outbursts, and the act of setting them down, however painful, has helped me. I've also gotten better, with my wife's help, at recognizing the flashpoints; like an early warning system, she can detect the first signs of a blow-up—the edge in my voice, my impatience with the bedtime-delaying antics of the children—and steer me clear.

I've finally begun to take her advice to just walk away, shut the door, go for a walk, without feeling guilty. Unlike, or perhaps because of, my father, I rarely drink. I talk about my temper with the kids. They know Daddy has a problem and he's working on it. I'd like to be able to say that I never lose my temper anymore, but I can't. Kids are constantly testing you, and often, I know now, they can inspire deserved anger.

The night my father broke my mother's rosary, my younger brother and I lay crying in our beds. The door opened, and light spilled in. In the placid cruelty of what passes for reason in a drunk's mind, he told us, "Don't worry, boys, your mother and I are getting a divorce," which, of course, sent our wails even higher. There have been moments when I have remembered that scene, and the memory has checked me from saying something equally terrible to my own children huddled in their beds.

Even then, I knew that he was terrified of something, and now I see that my worst anger seems to come when I am most deeply afraid—about work, about money, about whether I will amount to anything or if I will die as he did, bitter and unfulfilled. I don't want my children to remember me the way I remember my father, as this looming, frightened man.

"At every corner," the poet Robert Lowell wrote, "I meet my father, my age, still alive." The other morning, the barber who cuts my hair stood behind me with an oval mirror to show off his handiwork. I found myself looking at the same bald spot on the back of my head that I used to stare at from the back seat of our family Ford, when my father was at the wheel. There are mornings when I wake up afraid and wonder: How many mornings was he afraid? How many nights was he squeezed to the breaking point?

I meet my father now in the dark of my children's bedroom, hearing in my shouts the echoes of his rage, the legacy of anger passed from father to son. As our children have grown from cribs to their own beds, I have begun to hear myself in their outbursts: temper tantrums from the oldest, impulsive slaps from the youngest. Rivers of rage run from one generation to another, and it may be impossible to staunch the flow. But I have to keep trying. One breakfast, one bedtime, one day at a time.

....

STUDENT CASE HISTORY: WRITING TO PERSUADE—EMMA TOBIN

• HOW I WROTE MY ESSAY •
Emma Tobin

It all started with a letter. Donald Murray wrote to me one day, asking if I'd be interested in writing a piece for the new edition of his book, *Write to Learn*. Thrilled by this proposal, I immediately responded with an enthusiastic "yes." Don asked me to come up with a list of topics and a somewhat sketchy outline for each. Really having no idea what I wanted to write about, this proved to be harder than it at first sounded.

It took a while, but I did get a list. The topics included: comparing gay and lesbian rights to other minority groups' rights, animal rights, how contemporary music affects teens, rock musicals, and age discrimination on the Internet.

A few days later I got an "OK'' from Don to go ahead on any of these topics, but he was leaning toward the one on age discrimination on-line—mostly because all the communication we had done was on the computer. I considered this. I had written a more developed paragraph outlining what I would write about on this particular topic, and I felt I would be able to continue writing about it. So I did just that; I had my topic.

I'm an Internet user from pretty far back. I use it for research, communication with friends, and, yes, I do go into chat rooms more than I probably should. But it's from being in these chat rooms that I've noticed the incredible amount of discrimination that goes on. There is almost always someone who is hating someone else about something. It can be anywhere from one fourteen-year-old who is trashing another for being a skateboarder or an entire chat room ganging up on one individual for being a different race. But whatever it is, it's almost always there, in one form or another.

I had lots to say the first time I sat down at the computer to begin writing my paper . . . maybe a little too much. After about a half-hour of furiously pounding away at the keyboard, I finally stopped, looked back, and realized I had three pages filled with jumbled opinions, terrible spelling, some random punctuation, and not a single paragraph. This, I realized, was definitely NOT my essay.

I made several more lame attempts at starting a draft on this topic, until I sat back, realized this wasn't working, and took a new approach. I probably wouldn't have come to this conclusion so quickly if it weren't for Don, actually. After e-mailing him all of my first attempts, he told me that, while I did have good ideas, they were totally disorganized and not very well focused. Organization has never been a strong point for me, but I was determined to improve.

Don's advice to organize my thinking got me sitting down in front of the screen the next day with a plan just to write a good, solid lead. And that's what I did. I wrote a clearly focused, organized lead, went back, edited it, spell-checked it, and saved it. "There," I thought. "There's the first part of my essay I will actually be able to use."

My paper progressed. I kept writing. I discussed every aspect of age discrimination I could think of. Problem was, I couldn't really think of a whole lot. Where it had seemed that I had a lot of ideas on the topic in my original outline and in my first writing attempts, when I actually decided to get organized, there didn't seem a whole lot to say. I only got about three pages. Dead end. From that point on, I could not think of one, single thing to add, and the only thing I could think to blame was my topic. It was time, I realized, for sane reconsideration.

It was then, in my first exasperated stage, that I came to an on-line article about the law that the government had passed but that had been blocked by the courts in 1996. The law would have made it impossible for teens under eighteen to access a lot of information on the Internet. This, quite honestly, outraged me. I consider myself an adult, and the fact that the government was going to keep one from ANYTHING online had me furious. (But also a little thankful because I then had more to add to my piece.)

The first draft was the most difficult. After discussing the law the government was working to pass, I ran out of ideas again and rambled my way through another couple of pages. But there were definite sections that were usable, definite paragraphs, sentences, words even that I liked. So even before I sent the first draft off to Don, I began making changes. I was so embarrassed in fact by my first full-length attempt that I decided to wait until I had a second draft complete to send along with the first, including a note that I knew the first one was not exactly up to par.

But even in the second draft, it again seemed that organization was the key problem. Nothing was in any kind of order that made sense. That's when I decided to come up with a detailed outline that I could follow for the whole essay. I already had the sections written, even if they were a little sketchy. But before I could work on improving them, I needed them to be in place.

Basically, my outline divided my paper into three sections, the first being "What are parents, teachers, and politicians doing to limit teenage [Internet] access?" The second was "Why they shouldn't limit teenage access, and what's wrong with the way some adults view teen Internet use." That was the section that needed the most revision. When I start going off about something I feel strongly about, there's really not much stopping me. I'll ramble for pages before I realize I'm doing it.

The third section was "What I'm proposing." It took me a while to get this one done. To be honest, I didn't know what I was proposing. I wasn't sure what I thought should happen in the end. I guess maybe if I were more sure from the beginning, the piece would have been easier to write.

The main thing I learned about while I was writing this essay was the importance of revision. I certainly did enough of it anyway. Something that I wrote that sounded good one day would sound awful to me the next. An opinion that I had at one point would seem outrageous to me later. I not only had to revise to make the writing better; I had to revise to make my actual opinions different. I kept changing my mind so often on so many issues that it really became difficult to revise my piece.

One thing I changed my opinion on fairly drastically was the issue of pornography on-line. I kept shying away from the topic to begin with. I didn't want to discuss it in a way that made me sound inhuman, just reciting facts and figures, but I also didn't want to get into too many details and make it too explicit. Finding a place in the middle was kind of difficult.

When I started writing this paper, I was sure it was hard to get pornography on-line if you were a teenager, though I really hadn't tried to find out. But when I actually began letting other people (besides Don) read my work, they would read that section, look at me critically, and say "Is that true? Isn't it easy to find pornography on-line?" I would tell them it was in fact true, hoping and hoping that I was right. One day I made the decision to find out for sure.

This is what I discovered: If you want pornography on-line, you can get it regardless of your age. That's when I had to almost totally rewrite that section of any paper. My position changed from "It's difficult to get porn," to "Most teenagers don't really spend their time doing that kind of thing on-line anyway." In general, this is true, but I feel I would have made a stronger point if pornography really WAS difficult to come by . . . which it's not.

The pornography issue definitely tested my revising skills. I was stretched to make a good point, where maybe there was not such a good point to make (or at least not a point in my favor).

It was around this time that I met with Don. Before now, we hadn't conferred in person, only on-line and on the phone. By then, he had read my first and second drafts, and he came to the conference prepared with a list of changes to be made. But, his were very open-ended suggestions. Nothing was "And this part should be more like this . . ." It was more like him telling me how to look for what didn't work, instead of showing me what he thought didn't work. It turned out that, in Don's opinion, my lead didn't work. It had con-sisted of a sort of sketchy picture of what a typical day for me on-line looks like. "This piece is about safety is-sues on-line," he said to me. "There has to be some element of danger. Some feeling that something COULD happen." It turned out that he was absolutely right. Conveniently, my second paragraph worked very well as a lead, with a few changes. So in the end, it turned out that the first thing I wrote that I thought could be used really couldn't be used at all.

After working through and reworking an entire essay more times than I can count, I came up with my "third draft" which was really more like my tenth. If I had printed it out and sent my piece to Don every time I made drastic changes, he would have gotten far too many drafts in the end. I was sure that this was it; I had finally produced an essay worth reading.

HOW I HELPED EMMA TOBIN WRITE *HER* ESSAY—
DON MURRAY

I invited Emma Tobin to write a freshman English paper for me for entirely self-ish reasons. I wanted to work directly with a student assigned to write a college freshman paper. I never expressed any doubts that she would do a good job, because I did not feel any. I found that most students see themselves—and their potential—reflected in the teacher's eyes. Confidence on the part of the teacher and writer is as important as confidence in the writer. Another word for this is *faith*. I had faith that Emma Tobin would produce a good paper.

Teachers who hold opposite views think that such confidence—the student is capable of good work until proven guilty of poor work—pampers the student, that the method is touchy feely. I disagree. My confidence that Emma would produce a publishable paper put extraordinary pressure on her.

I had two principal approaches I would apply that appear contradictory. First, I would give Emma a lot of room to teach herself. I wanted her to find her own subject so that she would be motivated to pursue it. I also wanted her to write *without* instruction so that I would not waste time teaching her what she already knew. I would, however, reinforce her natural writing abilities so that she would know she possessed those skills. Then I wanted to give her a chance to learn to write on her own, knowing that what she taught herself would be truly learned and would remain with her all her life.

I would be available to nudge, encourage, direct, support, rescue, stimulate during her own learning if necessary. When she produced a draft, I would respond with a candid, professional response that would encourage her to solve the problems I spotted in her own way.

She first showed me a long list of topics. Her first one seemed the most likely. It was better thought through, a significant topic that would interest readers of my textbook and could be completed in a few weeks. I nudged her toward this topic, revealing my interest in it, but emphasizing she had to make her own choice; she was the one who had to live with the topic.

Here is her proposal:

• AGE DISCRIMINATION ON THE INTERNET •

From my experience, the average person in a chat room is a teenager or young adult. Many of us spend more time on-line than adults, and understand how it works better than they do. But still, we are considered "the lower level being" on-line. For example, we are thought to be less intelligent, unimportant, even silly or annoying. Some adults even go so far as to imply or suggest that we "leave the area."

It's a type of discrimination that is not considered "bad" or "unkind" because the ageist person uses the excuse "I was young once too." By saying this, it means they believe that they have the right to dislike us, because they were in our place once. Ageism shows through in everyday life, but much more strongly on the Internet. I believe I could produce a good paper defending teens on-line, but taking the adults point of view, and trying to understand it.

Hands off criticism can be frustrating for most students. They are used to being told exactly what to do, but instruction external to the piece often doesn't work. Each writing situation has its own context. The writing has its own focus, the point of view of the writer, its own meaning, and a specific form and order that carries that meaning to the intended audience. The writer doesn't just apply rules; the writer thinks, defining the subject and its writing and solving problems that vary with the writer, the writing task, and the writer's experience with the task. My job was to create an environment that gave Emma the confidence to discover and solve her own problems, certain I would be on hand if she needed me. We all know the basic model for teaching and editing: When a baby starts to walk, we hold out our hands close enough to help, far enough to encourage—and we laugh when the baby falls, cheer when it doesn't, and keep increasing the distance. I gave Emma room, hid my impatience, and waited while she wrote several drafts before she gave me one.

Now I had to give her a professional response. I read the draft quickly and phoned her that it was good but needed work and we made a date to get together. Then I read the draft carefully, doing some line-by-line editing on page two. I did not want to "correct" the entire piece because I would make it mine, and it was her subject and her language. I wanted to show her what I would do but make it clear she had to find her own way to solve the problems I saw in the piece.

Here is her draft:

· TALKING TO STRANGERS OR AT-RISK ON-LINE? TEENS IN CYBERSPACE ·

It's been a long day, and I drop into the chair in front of the screen with relief. Point-and-clicking my way through folders and files, I find what I am looking for right where I know that it would be. After following seven "quick and easy" steps, I hear the familiar voice.

"Welcome. You have mail!" No surprise. Clicking into the mail center, I open my personal America On-line "mail box" to reveal the list of letters that await me . . . all twenty-four of them. No joke. Scanning the list, I figure out that only about ten of them are real or of any importance to me, and the rest are junk mail: "Make a million dollars in six months!" "Lose ten pounds a week!" I quickly delete them.

After responding to letters from friends I've met off- and on-line, I head my way into "Instant Novelist" to get some feedback on my latest short story. I have four responses; three please me, one doesn't. After a moment of consideration, I decide to tell "Mr. Critical" just what I think of his latest story. I quickly type up my thoughts and post them for him to find later. I've had enough of this for one day, and almost without even looking at the screen, I have myself into a chat room—"Lobby 216"—within seconds. I settle back to chat.

And so goes another average day on AOL.

• HOW ADULTS PERCEIVE AND RESPOND TO TEENAGE INTERNET USE •

A newspaper article headline jumps out at me from the page. "Girl Kidnapped from Home by Internet 'Romeo.'" Immediately dropping the comic I was just starting, I turn my attention to the story. . . . Same old stuff. Thirteen-year-old girl leaves her home willingly with a strange man she met on-line. Girl is underage, becomes sexually active, police get notified by parents, strange Internet guy gets found, girl returns home, admits she made a stupid choice. Story ends with parents saying the problem is solved because their daughter "No longer has Internet access."

This type of story convinces many non-Internet using adults that the Internet is not safe for their kids. Right there is a huge reason why parents don't want their kids hanging out unsupervised on-line. They believe that they are going to get molested or sexually harassed by some screwed up forty-year-old guy lurking on the Net. And if they have no other way of knowing what the Internet is like, then they will become certain that it is a dangerous or risky place for their children to be.

Now I mark up this page.

Pornograph~~y. The word certainly catches your attention, doesn't it? It's also a word~~ comes up ~~fairly~~ often in discussion of teens and the Net. Even

I cut here to show Emma how to get out of the way of the text. She was running around, waving her arms, calling attention to herself, getting between the reader and the text. I find that I only have to do this a few times for the writer to understand.

adults who don't worry that teens will encounter sexual predators on-line worry that they will be exposed to inappropriate and disturbing images and information.

I wrote in the margin: "Good direct sentence." It is important to point out what works as well as what doesn't yet work.

Finally, there are some adults who think of the Internet as a big computer or video game which teens waste their time and energy on.

I wrote: "Good but that's another point" followed by some words I can't translate. My bad handwriting was an asset; my students had to figure out what I meant. They had to think.

So what actions are these adults taking to limit teenage access to the net?

In the margin I wrote, "Let's discuss rhetorical sentences." Inexperienced writers try to make a connection with the reader in this way but it doesn't work. The questioner knows the answer. It is insulting. Questioner doesn't listen to answer. Nurse: "We want to take our shot don't we."

Many kids and teens whose families own computers are not ~~even~~ allowed to use chat rooms or the World Wide Web when there are no parents home. Some parents ~~even~~ insist ~~that~~ they sit by the computer and supervise their kids.

I cut some unnecessary words and suggested she start a new paragraph below.

The other place where a large population of teens can use the Internet is at school. ~~Many schools across the country have net access so students can use it for research on the Web and for communication with other classrooms in other schools. Of course, teens could get themselves into the same kind of situation just as easily at school as they could at home. This being what teachers~~ I INSERTED "Because of cyberfear ~~students have~~ many schools limit~~ed~~ access, ~~and many schools~~ block all chat room use completely, and strictly ~~limit~~ control [?] Web use.

Here I wrote: "Let's talk about transitions—not needed if information is in the right place."

~~These are some of the reasons that parents and teachers don't want kids on the Internet, but it goes to an even higher level than that I~~ In 1996 the state of Pennsylvania passed a law, the Communications Decency Act, that would make it illegal for any one under eighteen to obtain or access anything on-line that is considered offensive.

I wrote: "Develop. Clarify."

That obviously includes sexual images and sexual text. Fortunately for teens across America, the law was challenged,

"What was challenged?"

argued before the Supreme Court in the spring of 1997, and eventually overturned. But this does not mean that the

government is through. The law was not adopted because the
court thought that it was too vague. ~~It is safe to assume
that I~~ In the near future, HOWEVER, a more specific law ~~will~~
MAY be proposed and passed in other states.
~~The point is that~~ Adults are making decisions to limit Internet access to teens . . .

*I did not mark up any more pages, but I did give her the following written
response, telling her these were just suggestions:*

Response to Emma Tobin's Draft August 21, 1997

As I said in the e-mail last night I am glad you are doing this. We have something
to work on. I am going to give this a professional, line-by-line reading, and I will
be specific about what I think needs to be done. I think it is important for me to
be directive at this time. But I want you to have room to disagree, to solve the
problems in your own way. I want to be clear so you will understand my concerns
but I do not want to be dictatorial.

As I used to tell my students, this kind of careful response is a compliment.
Most drafts, my own included, do not deserve this attention.

I will have marked the draft in spots to show how I might do it. Do it your
own way.

1. Title. You're getting there, but I think it will be helpful if you sharpen the title
with some tension or at least an implied conflict.

> Why Parents Should Fear Cyberspace
>
> Why Should Mom and Dad NOT Fear Cyberspace?
>
> Should Mom and Dad Fear Cyberspace?
>
> Should Cyberspace Be Off Limits for Teens?
>
> Is ~~Parents'~~ Mom and Dad's Cyberfear Justified?
>
> Is Cyberfear Justified?
>
> Are Teenagers at Risk in Cyberspace?

Play with some more as a focusing device, trying to get to the central issue in
as few words as possible. This is too important to be taken seriously: Play.

2. Lead. The lead is well-written but it would not compel me to read on. Nothing happens. If that's your message, the reader has to go on with the fear that
something may happen. The first paragraphs may be scaffolding, what you
needed to write to get to the lead, and it may be a scene you can use later to allay
fears about cyberspace.

Your lead may be in paragraph beginning "A newspaper ~~article~~ headline
jumps ~~out at me~~ off the page: "Girl Kidnapped . . . ""

3. Orwell's Pane of Glass. Get out of the way of the information. This is hardest to learn, but you are right on the verge of learning it. Let the information speak. George Orwell said, "Good writing is like a window pane." You should see the subject, not the author.

I'll point out what I mean on page two. Good writers always do what you do, writing about what you are going to say. You'll learn just to say it.

You have to write with authority, in specific terms with specific evidence.

4. Answer the Reader's Questions. Anticipate the questions the reader will ask and answer them when they ask them.

5. Line-by-Line Editing. When your draft is finished—you have your topic, a sequence or order that carries the reader from point-to-point, and you have provided evidence for each point—then you should read line-by-line:

Are my nouns specific?

Are my verbs active?

Are my sentences, sentences—usually subject–verb–object?

Is each word the right word?

Is everything clear to an uninformed, intelligent reader?

Is my voice clear and tuned to support what I am saying the way a movie score supports the action?

Have I emphasized what is important, usually placing the most important information at the end or the beginning of the paragraph or section?

Do I move fast enough to keep the reader reading, slow enough to allow the reader to absorb what I have said.

Have I given the reader enough or too much information?

Do I only break tradition when it's necessary for clarity or emphasis?

Also, I gave Emma the Will Strunk and George Orwell quotations cited on page 233 and page 232.

Here is her final article:

· WHY TEENS SHOULD BE ALLOWED IN CYBERSPACE ·
Emma Tobin

A newspaper article headline jumps off the page. "Girl Kidnapped from Home by Internet 'Romeo.'" Immediately dropping the comic I was just starting, I turn my attention to the story. . . . Same old stuff. Thirteen-year-old girl leaves her home willingly with a strange man she met on-line. Girl is underage, becomes sexually active, police get notified by parents, strange Internet guy gets found, girl returns home, admits she made a stupid choice. Story ends with parents saying the problem is solved because their daughter "No longer has Internet access."

This type of story convinces many non-Internet-using adults that the Internet is not safe for their kids. They are convinced that their children are going to get molested or sexually harassed by some screwed up forty-year-old-guy lurking on the Net. And if they have no other way of knowing what the Internet is like, then they will become certain that it is a dangerous or risky place for their children to be.

Of course, there are other reasons why parents might limit their teenagers' access to the Internet. Some think of computers the way they think of video games or television—as a giant waste of time and energy. But for the majority of parents, it is pornography that dominates their thinking about teenagers and the Internet. Even adults who don't worry that teens will encounter sexual predators online worry that they will be exposed to inappropriate and disturbing images and information. For this reason, many kids and teens whose families own computers are not allowed to use chat rooms or the World Wide Web when there are no parents home. Other parents insist they sit by the computer and supervise their kids.

Teens have even less on-line freedom at school. Many classrooms and libraries across the country have Net access so students can use it for research and for communication with other classrooms in other schools. But teachers and librarians worry that teens could get themselves into the same kind of situation just as easily at school as they could at home. Because of cyberfear, many schools limit access, block all chat room use completely, and strictly control Web use.

Many politicians have the same idea: In 1996 the United States Congress almost unanimously passed and President Clinton signed the Communications Decency Act, a law that, among other things, criminalizes "the use of any 'interactive computer service to 'see' or 'display in a manner available' to a person under eighteen any communication that 'depicts or describes, in terms patently offensive as measured by contemporary community standards, sexual or excretory activities or organs" ("Complaint," 2). Fortunately, for teens across America, the law was challenged, argued before the Supreme Court in the spring of 1997, and eventually overturned. But this does not mean that the government is through. The law was not adopted because the court thought that it was too vague and that limited adults' freedom of speech. In the near future, however, more specific laws limiting teenage access to information on the Internet may be proposed and passed.

Adults are making decisions to limit Internet access to teens partially out of a misunderstanding of what the Internet has to offer and partially out of an overreaction to sensational stories they've read or heard. Most of these adults just don't have a realistic idea about how most teens spend their time on-line and about what are the relative dangers of an on-line life.

Let's start with the risk of sexual molestation and kidnapping. Even if we admit that there is some risk of meeting a dangerous sexual predator on-line, is this danger greater than the one teens face every day in "real life"? This same parent who won't let a child go into a chat room may let a son or daughter walk to the convenience store two blocks away, where their child may not just talk to a child molester through a screen, but actually encounter one. When looking at the things that can happen to kids and teens on the Internet, some adults seem to forget that these same— or much worse—things can happen off the Internet just as easily. There are dangerous people in the world; there are people on the Internet. Therefore, you are going to end up with some dangerous people on the Internet. It is fine for parents to take that into account, but they need to understand that most Internet interactions are positive and completely safe.

Of course, that's not the impression you get from reading newspapers or magazines. For example, a 1997 *People* magazine story described case after case of teenagers who left their homes to meet up with on-line correspondents. If you read the piece carefully, you see that a majority of the stories were about teens who met up with other teens who turned out to be perfectly safe and friendly. Of course, there were also some stories of teens who met up with middle-aged sexual predators, but in those cases, is the Internet to blame? It's really just juveniles making unwise, uninformed decisions. When a person goes somewhere on their own will, it does not mean that they were kidnapped. Teenagers can make a bad decision to leave home with someone they meet in person just as easily as with someone they meet on-line. Something is definitely wrong in these cases, but the Internet is not the source of the problem. Teenagers who have a desire to run away with someone they have never met must already have a pretty good motive for wanting to leave home.

Adults who want to limit teen use of the Net because of the easy access to pornography also have several misleading beliefs—that pornography is forced on children, that teenagers spend all of their time surfing erotic Web sites, and that older teens would be as traumatized by sexual material as young children are. There is no denying that pornography is available on the Net. There are hundreds or even thousands of Web sites featuring explicit photographs, videos, and stories

ranging from soft-core erotica to hard-core child pornography. And even though a teenager has to go through an "age
check" and waiver statements to enter most of these Web sites,
pornography is pretty easy to get your hands on, if one
chooses to do so. But "chooses" is the key word there. When
one does end up with sexual content, it is almost always de-
liberate. You could erase every letter or ad that porn sites
send out, you could simply not reply to any on-line users who
are looking for someone who wants to "trade pics" (send and
receive pornographic pictures), and you could leave any chat
area where the topic is sex. If you did not go out of your way
to get pornography, you probably never would.

But pornography is not the reason most teenagers go on-
line most of the time. While some teens spend some of their
on-line time looking at porn, the average seventeen-year-old
doesn't come from school, sit at their computer, and start
searching for pornographic pictures. Some adults seem to believe that since there is access to pornography on-line that
every teenage person in the entire world is going to do all
they can to get to it and is going to end up using the computer for nothing else.

But let's assume that some teenagers are spending most of
their on-line time viewing pornography. We could still ask
what harm is taking place? Is there any evidence that proves
that teenagers are hurt by talking about sex with other
teenagers in chat rooms or by looking at pictures of naked
people on Web sites? Many teens are actually having sex
themselves. One would think that if a person could actually
have sex, then they could write or read about it. Same thing
with pictures. If a teenager has seen (or done) off the Net
all the things they see on it, then the Internet is not the
problem.

The law that Congress tried to pass in 1996 would keep a
person under eighteen from getting their hands on anything
even vaguely related to sex. If an eighteen-year-old person
can vote, serve in the armed forces, and drive, then certainly a seventeen-year-old can surf the Net. In fact, many
seventeen-year-olds are sexually active, some are married,
most have jobs, and some are freshmen in college. If our
culture gives teens the freedom and responsibility to do
adult things, then it's ridiculous to deny them full access
to everything on the Internet.

If the Communications Decency Act had been adopted, then
it could have been illegal for some teenager to get information on AIDS and HIV, because it is sexual material. It
could have been illegal for a homosexual teenager to get any
information that they may not feel comfortable asking someone for in person. It could have been illegal for a pregnant
teen to get information about pregnancy or abortion. Teens

suddenly would have been cut off from a whole world of valuable information.

Let's imagine there is a fifteen-year-old girl named Ann who has just had her first sexual experience. And let's say that she soon begins to worry that she may be pregnant or may have picked up a sexually transmitted disease. Let's assume that she doesn't want to talk to either of her parents about it or anyone at all, for that matter. The thought of going to a doctor or to Planned Parenthood has her terrified, so she looks into the only anonymous source she knows: the Internet.

If the 1996 law had not been overturned, Ann would find once she was on-line that she might not be able to get access to any information on STDs or pregnancy or AIDS. There would be barriers to "protect" her from this information. While adults may think that they are helping Ann by denying her this information on-line, I do not think they understand how wrong they are. Of course, this is exactly the kind of argument that the plaintiffs in the Supreme Court case made to overturn the law. Groups including Planned Parenthood, the Queer Resource Directory, ACLU, and American Library Association all argued that teens have a need for as well as a constitutional right to this information.

The other problem with adults' perceptions of the Internet is that they not only point out everything that's wrong and exaggerate those points, they also seem to ignore all of the good things that the Internet has to offer teenagers. For example, you never see a story written up on the thirteen-year-old girl who puts out a newsletter every month on animal rights. Or an article on how two fourteen-year-old kids meet twice a week to discuss poetry. And you'll never see anything on the sixteen-year-old boy who has started his own successful graphic design business on the Net. You only see the stories of destruction the Internet has caused.

And what about that side of teenage Internet use that no one could have a problem with: the academic side. It's eleven o'clock at night. You have a paper due the next morning. Frantic for information on the Spanish Armada, you turn to the Internet. There in front of you is an encyclopedia article, plus many other write-ups. You take the notes and produce a good paper without setting foot inside a library. Now, of course, I am not saying this is the best way to get a paper written. One should look in many places and sources of information for a well-rounded piece. But it is a life-saving way to get something done when you have no time. And even when you do have the time, the Internet is an excellent source. They will have information on all the aspects of what you're looking for. What could be better?

Some adults believe that there is no educational side to chat rooms such as those found on America On-line. Totally wrong. Just to get the basics out of the way first, there is really no better way to learn typing than being in an interactive conversation where you have to respond quickly, or your chatting partner will quickly be bored with you. One learns how to argue maturely and effectively and how to relate to people through the written word. Then we come to chat rooms that are especially designed for learning, such as AOL's "Thinkers," a room for pondering life, or really—whatever else is on your mind. Next are chat rooms where you are able to work one-on-one with a teacher on the subject you need help with. Many times I have tackled complicated math work I never thought I could do using someone I found on the Internet as my tutor. The flow of information coming from the Internet is endless. There are so many sides to it, so many possibilities.

For someone like me who has a great interest in writing, the Net has been incredibly enriching. For instance, through AOL's "Instant Novelist" site, I have had a chance to be part of a writing community. You can respond to anything you read, both positively and negatively. When you post a story of your own, it is read by hundreds of little editors across the country, all there to help you improve your work. Many participants develop e-mail relationships with fellow on-line writers. I, personally, do not see one thing that could be considered dangerous about this and most other Internet sites. What I do see are a million ways to learn, to find useful information, and to connect to other people.

When ten-year-old children wind up with pornography in their grasp, we have a problem. But when seventeen-year-old young adults are not allowed access to information that they may need for their education and even health, then we have another problem. Many schools, government agencies, and computer companies are all working now to develop guidelines and new technology to keep kids away from dangerous material on the Internet without limiting adults' freedom to information. Parents can buy "smut-blocker" software, like "Cyper Patrol" or "Net Nanny," which restricts and records a child's use of the Internet. And libraries can now buy Web software and search engines that keep children "from turning up unwanted risqué sites while looking for information on that report on The Chile Pepper through History" (Powers, 2).

But as *Boston Globe* columnist Ellen Goodman has said, the key is to "protect children, without shackling adults." And, in this area, teens ought to be treated as adults. Parents, teachers, and politicians have a good motive: protecting young people from the dangers of the Internet. But they need to step back and distinguish between children and teens. Again, if a seventeen-year-old can work, drive, and attend college (not to mention, have sex and even have children), how can you keep full access to the Internet off that list?

• WORKS CITED •

Electronic Privacy Information Center, "Complaint," U.S. District Court, Eastern District of Pennsylvania, Civ. No. 96-963, http://www.epic.org./free_speech, p. 2.

Goodman, Ellen. "'The Boston Solution' to Pornography on the Internet," *Boston Globe,* July 24, 1997.

Powers, Kate. "DO YOU Know Where Your Children Are Surfing," *Parent Soup: Family and the Intent,* http://www.parentsoup.com.

Rogers, Patock. "Snared By the Net," *People* 48, No. 6, August 11, 1997: 48-53.

....

STUDENT CASE HISTORY: WRITING TO INFORM—TINA WINSLOW

The research paper is the fundamental building block of academic discourse—and it is the composition assignment most dreaded by the students who have to write research papers and the instructors who have to read them. Most research papers are dull, because the students have not yet done research on a topic important to them and the form becomes more important than the message.

Yet students need experience in gathering information, building the information into a significant meaning, and presenting it so that the reader not only understands the message but has access to the sources of information the writer used.

Tina Winslow demonstrates that a student can prove a knowledge of academic research conventions while writing a lively, interesting report that places scholarly material in a human context.

Her assignment was to "Inform readers by completing a five- to ten-page [1,500–2,500 word] research report that will demonstrate your ability to use scholarly techniques to investigate a topic and reveal its significance to them."

She was told to keep a journal that would reveal her writing problems and how she solved them. The student was given time to find a territory, then a topic, sharpening her research question in consultation with the instructor and classmates, then to write several drafts. She was to have at least a dozen sources with footnotes and a bibliography that follows Modern Language Association guidelines. Tina was also referred to the "Tips on Writing to Inform" (pp. 251–252).

The case history shows how she moved from the vague and general to the specific, finding a way to combine several aspects of her topic so that the final article had a clear, documented focus. She moved toward this clarity of vision while achieving an increasing grace. Her work is a demonstration of good thinking as well as good writing, as all effective prose should be.

In her journal she first brainstormed (pp. 20–23) on animal rights looking for a focus line (pp. 95–100) that contained enough tension to spark a research report:

- Animal rights—where is the line?
- Who decides whose rights get to be violated—the chemical industry at odds with the natural order or is it the natural order?
- Would people buy the products if they saw the process it goes through?
- Do animals have rights—historical/religious implications—meat industry—health implications
- Pumping poultry, beef with hormones
- Is the meat industry lying about the health requirements and how far down the line does it go?
- Feel passionately about not eating meat without bias, why?
- No meat has helped achieve my goals to trim down—why? What does meat do psychologically or physiologically that slims people?
- Moods are evened out—hormones in meat?
- No guilt with eating healthy, cheaper
- In small way have stopped poor treatment of animals
- Read a book that describes the process
- People live too much of their life with spurts of unrealistic violence or softened reality
- Would you enjoy chicken if you watched the man rip his feet off because the nails had grown around the bars of the cage back into his feet?

This is an excellent way to begin. Tina doesn't worry about the writing, she is scouting the territory to find a way into her subject, and the journal entries show her ranging across the whole area, looking for the most important material—the material she needs to explore and that her reader needs to know. Her final topic is deeply hidden in her list, and the approach that makes her final paper distinctive does not appear. But this step was essential to her thinking process.

Now let us listen in as she continues talking to herself in her journal. Remember that the direction in which she thinks she is headed is not the direction in which she will go. Elizabeth Bowen said: "The writer . . . sees what he did not expect to see. . . . Inattentive learner in the schoolroom of life, he keeps some faculty free to hear and wonder. His is the roving eye. By that roving eye is his subject found. The glance, at first only vaguely caught, goes on to concentrate, deepen; becomes the vision." In Tina's journal, we catch a rare but important glimpse of the writer in the act of thought, catching her unexpected vision.

• JOURNAL •

When I think about animal rights many issues shoot through my head. My two kitties waiting on my bed, waking up with a lazy stare that pretty much lays out the law—"You have the right to scratch my ears and why you are at it the bowl in the other room is a bit empty." Those are their rights but they are lucky cause I'm a sucker for a good mew and milk breath. Society's definition of animal rights extends more into our comfort zone as human beings. Not only my comfort zone about what I will use on my body but what goes into my body and the realities that went into mundane things I take for granted. My true experience in this issue began when my roommates a year or so ago were very much into the movement of animal rights. They were adamant about how cruel vivisection was and that it should cease immediately for all products. While I struggle as a compassionate human who has done volunteer work with animals to comprehend the exact reality of vivisection, which in essence needs a proper definition this issue becomes one of limits. Flipping in the handy Miriam-Webster the definition alone of vivisection bothers me inside—"the cutting of or operation on a living animal usually for physiological or pathological investigation" or worse, definition two, "animal experimentation especially if considered to cause distress to the subject." Who gave us the power to take that animal's life? Or worse keeping it alive to test it's reactions. I understand the theory that it's an us or them kind of world but in reality where people are just vain creatures how much does it matter if the deodorant and the makeup don't look just right or don't exist especially when everyone will not be wearing it. It's just a layer of protection anyway.

> *Tina's final paper will not focus on animal rights, but she needs to start here to find her ultimate focus. Her journal reveals the writer talking to herself, and what some people might describe as bad or sloppy writing is good writing here, appropriate to the task. It is courageous of Tina to allow us to see a good writer doing the rough, pre-draft writing that is essential but not usually revealed to a reader.*
>
> *Let's listen further to Tina talking to herself. She is at once the appropriately floundering writer allowing her evolving text to carry her toward meaning and the draftsperson standing back and watching herself working. This split vision—being in the writing act and observing and standing back watching herself in the act—is essential for good writing.*

The paper I want to write needs a focus line. Something that creates a tension. I think if you take the normal person who wasn't attacked by vicious dogs as a child and who was socialized with animals normally and show them the process from start to finish they will understand the brutality of the process. To take something living and breathing and warp it for our needs doesn't seem right. Do the end results, a juicy piece of chicken or tube of lipstick, really make the process OK? In a world filled with lawsuits on product liability, companies are scrambling to find proof that this product when accidently swallowed, poked in an eye or applied incorrectly won't adversely affect humans. If there is so much concern with humans why aren't humans used to test these results and why is there such a lack of concern with humans when their food is concerned. If they don't want to harm people why would they pump pesticides onto the eventual food of cows and poultry, pump hormones into animals for better growth, keep them in deplorable conditions and then wonder why Americans are getting fatter, madder and sicker. It all comes back to a basic respect for other things.

This paper will be about the realities involved in everyday products that involve animals. It could go two ways right now. With vivisection you have the brutality of pictures and there is a plenty of tension about it with animal righters and research industry. When I visited a pharmaceutical company my friend worked in she told me not to even joke about freeing the animals. They had them locked up in a special room you had to have four keys to get into. When I asked her why she didn't mind testing on them she was like well they throw poop on me and are mean but ultimately her argument was humans first, everything else "bah." She didn't realize that if someone put me in a cage and shot me full of drugs I would have a very similar reaction. Mean as spit and proud of it. The other direction of the paper could be on when we eat, what is the process of the food. The chickens and cows we eat aren't exactly running around the yard, they are chemicals through and through from the minute they are born.

Focus lines—potential:

Chemical food—what are we eating? Whose rights are they anyway

Food industry—provider or killer?

In consultation with her classmates and a conference with her instructor, Tina came to realize she didn't really have anything new to say about animal rights but that she had strong feelings about her new decision to be a vegetarian, a decision that was tested on a cruise with her parents and confirmed two weeks later when her mother—a life-long meat eater—suffered a heart attack. Tina felt uncomfortable about using her personal feelings and her personal experience in a research paper but was encouraged to try to find a way to combine objective research information with personal experience.

Writing is often like a tunnel that is wide at the beginning but narrows as you follow it. Here you will see Tina as the tunnel narrows and she finds her focus and begins to work within it.

OK, focus line:

Solidifying Vegetarianism—the hard way. Or why I am still a Vegetarian today. Or Taming the Taco Urges.

But really the focus although it doesn't sound focused is that the after shocks of my Mom's heart attack solidified never eating meat again for me. I guess I need to trim it into a more readable state but basically this issue to me is like a spark to gasoline. For the record, when I shared this topic with my parents they were not exactly thrilled. To defend my mother, who really wants to know that an incident in her life scared everyone down to their belief foundations. To defend my father, well he just likes to argue. Basically, he wants to vent that you can't be a vegetarian for purely health reasons because he believes that you can be unhealthy, heartwise, and eat no meat. For instance, chicken and turkey and low fat/cholesterol meats can be eaten and still be healthy or did you hear the one about the vegetarian who died of a heart attack. He maintains you are a vegetarian for ethical—not health reasons. My point for my focus is that although I was a brand new vegetarian before the heart attack (Wait till I tell you the taunts that a week cruise with my family brought me a week and a half before my mother's run in with her arteries), the material I read after the scare solidified that I will never again put meat in my mouth. I guess the ethical part is there as back up but after what I learned I see meat and the industry as killers and beyond that totally unnecessary.

(Title)
- Momma, Me and Meat
- Scaring the Meat out of Me
- Meat Stinks
- A Tube in the Nose Is Meat out of Me
- Vegetarians Unite
- You Don't Get a Chest Pain Eating Broccoli (Unless You Swallow a Stalk)
- Reeducation of My Mouth and My Mom
- Liar, Liar Heart on Fire
- If It Had a Mother I Won't Eat It—Mom
- Moo Cow and Then Shoo
- You Don't Have to Beat Me with a Carrot to Make Me Give Up Meat
- Thicken Your Clogged Arteries with Lies

(Lead)
Understand what will stop me from ever putting meat in my
mouth again, was my mother in an ICU bed after her heart attack.

. . .

Well that's part of it. But after reading up on heart attacks and what they are about, I realized she didn't have to
be in that bed and that keeps me focused in my non-meat eating habits.

. . .

(Lead—2)
Nothing made being a vegetarian easier than realizing that
my mother having a heart attack didn't have to be a reality.

(Trail)
• mother has heart attack

• already a vegetarian but very new

• in learning more about heart attacks read book after book
  which detailed what meat is and what it isn't both from
  heart aspect as well as healthy living aspect

• realization it's a lie—meat industry

• based on what it does to your body, what is in it and the
  benefits of other types of protein—meat stinks

• I realize this isn't an ethical attack on meat eater's way
  of life but I personally feel betrayed

(End)
You don't have to not eat meat to be heart healthy but
after realizing what goes into the process and how close you
are to being a vegetarian why would you eat meat.

(Possible first paragraph)
Through the mist that are tears unshed, I look wildeyed at
my mother in an ICU bed with slightly green, thick tubes in
her nose. ICU has no room for deep personal talks with the
doors flung wide open and everyone's heartbeeps beating loud
enough for the staff behind the desks to hear. Her nails are
purple as well as her lips. She looks an off color like someone walked in and sucked the oxygen out of her skin. Pale and
tired, with wide brown eyes, she pleads with me not to be
scared—its just a minor life threatening procedure.

**Good writing is promiscuous; writers do not write one draft but many. We
do not have the space to show each of Tina's drafts, but we can listen to
her journal as she reacts to completing her first draft.**

OK, the first rough draft is out. It's weak in some areas ad-
mittedly but I feel better having the thoughts in a rough

diving board for better work. I just hate, hate, hate showing other people work that I don't consider finished. The
hardest part for me in this critique sessions is admitting
that I have to write just like everyone in stages and that
the first things out of my typewriter/computer look just
like everyone else's. I guess I want to be brilliant and perfect on the first shot. "BULLS EYE! the crowd roared as they
tossed the first draft writer roses." But alas, I need more
work on the quotations and the integration of paraphrases
not to mention documentation style at this early stage is a
enough to make MLA come out and personally tweak me on the
nose. But at least I have exorcised the demons onto paper at
this point all while on Tylenol for sinus and cold.

Better flow and tighter in beginning paragraphs, Smoother
flow in Paragraph 2. More quotes, direct in Paragraph 3, check
for logic flow LOGIC FLOW in paragraph 4 with more sources,
more sources and another quote or two. Summary needs more bite.

So . . . round two is done but I have to cut cut cut.

· · ·

I guess I am going to have to cut the chemicals paragraph
but I do this under duress.

> *It was not cut. She found a way to keep it in the piece by making it support
> her focus on why vegetarianism is important to health. Later, in her jour-
> nal, Tina debates a cut her peer readers suggested. Ultimately the decision
> has to be the writer's but she expresses the insecure response to a critical
> suggestion that is natural in a writer.*

I like that paragraph, I feel it has merit and geez, it
grosses me out and I wrote the thing. I was hoping to get my
punch in quick and well I guess as a being with somewhat rational thought I realize it doesn't fit in with the mom-had-
a-heart-attack motif. I really like the mixture of personal
vignettes mixed in with writing of a more research nature. I
find it really interesting the process this had been. I
started out with animal rights and have it nuzzled, pushed
and CUT It down to just vegetarianism.

For next draft:

- Finish getting the references pinned down to MLA style
- Re-arrange the chemical paragraph out of the paper and work
  out the flow
- Go through with a fine tooth grammar comb and get all of it
  laying down without obvious cowlicks (pun intended)

> *A complete case history would reproduce draft after draft, and space pro-
> hibits reprinting each one of them. Also, it would probably be boring to all
> but the most interested students. The important element in the process is*

the astonishment expressed by the writer in her journal at what she has written, discovering that writing is not recording previous thoughts but thinking by writing. Her understanding of the subject changes as she captures and clarifies meaning through language. This is the most important lesson of her writing course.

Man, oh, man. Whew! Done, finis, end of papyrus! OK, so I feel guilty at being relieved that I'm done with the paper. It is not what I would have conceived at the beginning but it wound it's way down the paper trail to completedom. I wanted a paper that bit and nickered at lies and then spit it out in a huge cavalcade of burning all consuming truth. What I got was a paper that resembled "What I Did over the Summer" tone with a vegetarian twist.

Now, now, I can hear that voice now. (How come this voice always resembles my mother's voice?) "If you aren't happy with the paper then change it." The truth is I will never be happy with the paper. I can put it in my treasure box and dig it up 10 years from now and say (in my knowing and critical tone, of course) "This seems so pedantic and stiff," "What was I trying to say here?"

Why did I pick that word or phrase?" Hopefully, buried in that chest is also my good critic who reads it and nods her head and whispers, "Because that's where you were. The paper is done I can look at it and see the legitimate course it took. I started off worried by what I would write, how to say it perfectly, WHERE AM I GOING TO FIND THE TIME and now I can look at it and realize I created something.

Each of Tina's drafts clarified what she had to say and allowed her to say it in with increasing liveliness and fluency. At first, she wrote each paragraph separately, moving the information to a position that answered the reader's questions. Then she had to consider the pace and proportion: How much of her mother? How much research information? Throughout the process she had to listen to her peer readers and her instructor but make her own way.

Compare the drafts of the lead in her journal with the final, disciplined example of good writing. She had to go from the bland statement of her first effort ("Understand what will stop me from ever putting meat in my mouth again, was my mother in an ICE bed after her heart attack.") to purple prose ("Through the mist that are tears unshed, I look wild eyed at my mother in an ICU bed with slightly green, thick tubes in her nose.") to the fine, professional beginning that moves the reader ("I look at my mother in the Cardiac Care Unit bed with pale green, plastic tubes in her nose.")

In her first draft, Tina moved from her mother to this paragraph:

Defining what a heart attack is, how it occurs and how to prevent it/ takes research It's not as cut and dry as eating to much fatty fried stuff, arteries clogging and then the next moment you are grabbing your arm and clutching your chest calling for an ambulance as you go down. In essence, it is an artery clogging that causes heart attacks but as more and more research is done, it's about a whole lifestyle. Several papers can be written on the technical medical reasons behind a heart attack, why meat is morally wrong, what is wrong with the meat industry but the focus for this paper is on why eating meat and dairy products is unhealthy for the body. Every fork of meat and dairy product have harmful chemicals present, a meat and dairyless diet automatically trims weight off people and a vegetarian diet makes having a heart attack hard to do. Accordingly the premise that being a vegetarians while only one aspect of the whole heart attack chain reaction and still a controversial one, is one worth merit and consideration.

As Tina said in her journal, she is embarrassed at readers seeing her early drafts, but it is important for students who imagine that others write well the first time to observe how real writing emerges, draft after draft, until the final draft has this excellent paragraph:

The first step is to look at meat and dairy products for what they really are. Meat and dairy are primarily vehicles for fat and cholesterol. Most of the established health organizations, as well as the Surgeon General, recommend reducing the fat in your diet to 30 percent (Robbins, *May All* 89). Studies indicate that this number should be even lower to prevent cancer, strokes, diabetes, hypertension and heart disease risks, and to eliminate or drastically reduce cholesterol (Robbins, *May All* 89). But Dr. T. Colin Campbell, director of one of the most comprehensive and informative diet and health studies ever undertaken (Chen et al.) and on the committee that set the 30 percent guideline, states it would have been impractical to recommend less than 30 percent, as most people would have to drop the animal foods from their diet and go vegetarian (Robbins, *May All* 90).

Every piece of information, whether it comes from personal experience or library research, moves the meaning of the paper forward. The result is a moving, significant, well-documented research paper that both pleases and educates the reader. Here is her final draft:

• TAKE A BITE OF LIFE •
Tina Winslow

I look at my mother in the Cardiac Care Unit bed with pale green, plastic tubes in her nose. CCU has no room for personal whisperings with the doors flung wide and everyone's heartbeeps beating loud enough for the staff behind the desk to hear. Her nails are purple as well as her lips. She looks an off color as if someone sucked the oxygen out of her skin. Pale and tired, with wide brown eyes, she pleads with me not to be scared: it's just a minor lifethreatening illness.

The initial prognosis was a minor heart attack, which calmed everyone until the tests revealed three of her arteries were more than 65 percent blocked. This new prognosis, terrible and threatening, was the one thing that would force change into my Mom's life so dramatically and so thoroughly. Having married a Nebraska "meat and potatoes man" her response from the beginning was not one of compromise but rather pouty resistance to a new way of life forced upon her.

Even with a monitor recording her heartbeat she was upset by the chicken and pasta they gave her for lunch.

"It is so bland."

"Mom, you're in a hospital."

"But you think they could put some cheese on this stuff."

"Mom, you just had a heart attack."

I had just become a vegetarian shortly before my mother's heart attack and I discovered through the research I did—both before becoming a vegetarian and after my mother's heart attack—that a diet with no meat and dairy products automatically trims weight and reduces the chances of a heart attack. I also learned that a vegetarian diet prevents the harmful ingestion of chemicals that are present in meat and dairy products and provides a good defense against disease. With benefits like these, being a vegetarian seems the only logical choice for a healthy life.

The first step is to look at meat and dairy products for what they really are. Meat and dairy are primarily vehicles for fat and cholesterol. Most of the established health organizations, as well as the Surgeon General, recommend reducing the fat in your diet to 30 percent (Robbins, *May All* 89). Studies indicate that this number should be even lower to prevent cancer, strokes, diabetes, hypertension and heart disease risks, and to eliminate or drastically reduce cholesterol (Robbins, *May All* 89). But Dr. T. Colin Campbell, director of one of the most comprehensive and informative diet and health studies ever undertaken (Chen et al.) and on the committee that set the 30 percent guideline, states it would have been impractical to recommend less than 30 percent, as most people would have to drop the animal foods from their diet and go vegetarian (Robbins, *May All* 90).

Even chicken, the most common alternative consumers choose when trying to cut fat from their diet, derives 35 percent of its calories from fat and that's without the skin (*PETA Guide* 1). Beef, on the high end of the scale, has about 22 grams of saturated fat in an average 8-oz. serving (*PETA Guide Compassionate Living* 17). And as Dean Ornish points out in his book *Reversing Heart Disease,* "eating fat makes you fat" (255).

Why does eating vegetarian naturally cut weight and reduce the chances of a heart attack? According to Martin and Tenenbaum, authors of *Diet against Disease,* most of the fat we eat is in the form of meat and dairy products, so reducing our fat consumption in these areas will reduce the total fat and saturated fat in our diets (16). Conversely, vegetarian foods are primarily complex carbohydrates and are hard for your body to convert into fat (Ornish 257), so the less cholesterol you eat, the lower your risk of developing coronary heart disease (Ornish 263). As advised by the Physicians Committee for Responsible Medicine, a diet without meat and dairy products makes low cholesterol easy "since cholesterol is found only in animal products such as meat, dairy and eggs" (2). Your body also makes all the cholesterol it needs naturally so "it's the excessive amounts of cholesterol and saturated fat in the diet that lead to coronary heart disease" (Ornish 263).

Two months after becoming a vegetarian and two weeks before my mother's heart attack, my entire family went on a cruise. I guess on a cruise, where every meal is supposed to be about reckless abandon without regard to waist size, waste or what you're eating, a vegetarian feeling uneasy isn't going to be the most popular topic.

"What do you mean the French onion soup made you sick?"

"Mom, once you don't eat meat, your body gets used to not having it and I didn't think about French onion soup being made with beef broth."

"There is no way broth can make you sick."

My mom, looking concerned but unbelieving, eyed me suspiciously and tried to make light of it.

"Look, honey, I just ate a whole side of cow, tail and all and I'm fine. How can a soup broth made of beef make you sick?"

The vegetarian target on my forehead grew as my mother's tone drew my entire family's attention at the dinner table. That week spent with my family trapped on board a floating buffet table, just two weeks before my mother had a heart attack, was a study of open hostility at the mention of not eating meat or cheese. My mother—at the head of that committee—was unbelieving that meat could be so harmful. "My quirky daughter, what's next?" seemed to be the question asked without realizing she was less than fourteen days away from a full-blown heart attack—not realizing that it was also the same thing making us both sick.

But it is not just the fat and cholesterol we need to be aware of in meat and dairy products: "Most of us, with images in our minds of the cows of yesteryear, could hardly believe the extent to which the meat industry today relies on chemicals, hormones, antibiotics and a plethora of other drugs" (Robbins, *Diet New America* 109). The image of a cow chewing on grass in a field is an image of the past as is the pecking and scratching chicken of the barnyard, and the loving mother cow letting the farmer squeeze milk into the pail. They are all misconceptions of what meat and dairy consumers are actually internalizing each time they consume these products. Today's cows used for meat are fed a diet with the strict purpose of fattening them up the cheapest way possible (Robbins, *Diet New America* 110). "It is impossible to raise animals in intensive confinement without continual reliance on antibiotics, sulfa drugs and other substances" (*Fund Facts* 2).

Chickens are also fed a diet of chemicals to produce more fat and thus more profit. With "over 90% of today's chickens" fed arsenic compounds (Mason and Singer 56—58) and virtually every chicken raised in the United States being fed a diet of antibiotics, it is hard to believe chicken is being sold as a health food (Robbins, *Diet New America* 65). Furthermore, "up to 90% of federally inspected poultry is infected with salmonella bacteria" (*PETA Guide* 1). Chicken is not health food as presented to Americans everyday.

The ad campaign "Milk: It Does A Body Good" is also a lie. With the introduction of the Bovine Growth Hormone (rBGH), milk, cheese, butter, ice cream, yogurt and infant formula are now being contaminated without the U.S. Food and Drug Administration testing the long-term health effects on consumers (*Vegetarian Voice* 12). Furthermore, the FDA admits that "use of rBGH in cows may lead to increased amounts of pus and bacteria in milk" and that "powerful antibiotics and other drugs used to fight increased disease in rBGH-injected cows may lead to greater antibiotic and chemical contamination of milk and dangerous resistance to antibiotics in the human population" (*Vegetarian Voice* 12). And because these drugs present in these forms of meat and dairy products "form toxic residues in animal tissue, they pose a harm to human consumers" (*Fund Facts* 2). In other words, what they eat, you eat.

After her heart attack, I tried to help my mother understand the vegetarian lifestyle—which means no meat and dairy products of any kind.

"Tina, you can pick the chicken out."

"WHAT!? Mom, it's tortilla soup with shredded chicken not to mention it's in a chicken broth."

"Well it's got lots of vegetables in it. Maybe you can pick those out."

"It's OK, Mom, I'll just make a cucumber sandwich and be fine."

"But I did put in extra veggies for you."

"And for you, too, Mom, you get the benefits, too."

Since the heart attack she has resigned herself to retiring the *Cooking Beef: A Recipe a Day* cookbook and has even had lessons in low-fat cooking, but it hasn't occurred to her that as she moves away from fat and cholesterol she is also moving into vegetarianism. We are making progress, though. After realizing that fat and cholesterol make eating meat and dairy so bad for us, she also understands what makes them a double jeopardy for everyone.

Meat and dairy products add chemicals, saturated fat, and cholesterol to a diet. So what will vegetarian foods add to a diet? Beyond reducing fat and cholesterol as previously discussed, a diet without meat or dairy products will reduce cancer risks, reduce protein levels, and add fiber. A vegetarian diet higher in fiber than meat-based diets "helps to dilute, bind, inactivate, and remove many of the carcinogens and toxic substances found in our food supply" (McDougall 120). Due to these properties and other considerations involving fiber "a diet high in fiber helps prevent colon cancer as well as cancers of other parts of the body" (McDougall 120). "An additional benefit of a [vegetarian diet] is that it contains generous amounts of substances with 'anticancer' properties" (McDougall 128). Some of these include Vitamin A, Vitamin C, Vitamin E, and minerals. Thus a vegetarian diet, "complemented with vegetables and fruits, provides a multitude of overlapping mechanisms for preventing cancer and keeping us healthy" (McDougall 130).

According to Martin and Tenenbaum, "there is no known nutritional need for the amount of protein we eat" (27). Americans typically eat roughly twice the amount of protein as the Recommended Dietary Allowance sets for healthy people (Martin and Tenenbaum 27) and much of this protein comes in the form of meat and dairy products. Too much protein lowers the body's ability to naturally absorb calcium and "as surprising as it sounds, one major culprit in osteoporosis may be protein" (Barnard 19). Furthermore, high protein "intakes have been found to contribute to progressive kidney damage" (Barnard 24). Through eating more whole grains, fruits, and vegetables, which naturally reduces saturated fat—and maintains the same level of protein intake—an alteration in the ratio of animal to vegetable protein inevitably will occur" (Martin and Tenenbaum 26). The shift allows more reasonable protein intake without the fat.

I couldn't believe it. My mother was defending my beliefs to my aunts. It was a humorous and satisfying scene.

"Tell them, Tina, what is that Bovine Hormone thing you were telling me about. GROSS, pus in my milk."

"Well, the milk farmers put . . ."

"And what about McDonald's cows eating the rain forests" she interrupted.

"See to support the cows used in . . ."

"And the chicken, Tina, tell them about cholesterol in chicken. The whole industry of meat has hoodwinked us all. It's all a mass market sell."

I know she hasn't eliminated meat entirely but I have watched her over the past four months gently guide herself and our family from taco salad, hamburgers, and sausage to red beans and rice, lentil soup, and other vegetarian meals as she discovers the hidden benefits of vegetarianism on her own.

The choice of a vegetarian lifestyle with all the perceived sanctimonious philosophy can be traced back to the simple fact that eating meat and dairy products is bad for you. A constant reminder to me is remembering someone I love with a monitor on her heart now sitting across from me laughing as she puts another bite of life into her mouth.

• WORKS CITED •

"Altered Bovine Hormone Makes Milk, Dairy Products Even Riskier." *Vegetarian Voice* 20.3 (1994): 12.

Barnard, Neil, M.D. *Food for Life: How the New Four Food Groups Can Save Your Life.* New York: Crown, 1993.

Chen, J., et al. *Diet, Lifestyle, and Mortality in China: A Study of the Characteristics of 65 Countries.* New York: Oxford UP, Cornell UP, and the China People's Medical, 1990.

Fund for Animals, *The Fund Facts: Animal Agriculture Fact Sheet* #2. Houston: Fund for Animals, 1992.

Martin, Alice A., and Frances Tenenbaum. *Diet against Disease.* Boston: Houghton Mifflin, 1980.

Mason, J., and P. Singer. *Animal Factories.* New York: Crown, 1980.

McDougall, John, M.D., and Mary McDougall. *The McDougall Plan.* Piscataway: New Century, 1983.

Ornish, Dean, Dr. *Dr. Dean Ornish's Program for Reversing Heart Disease.* New York: Ballantine, 1990.

PETA Guide to Animals and the Meat Industry, The. Washington, D.C.: PETA, 1993.

PETA Guide to Compassionate Living, The. Washington, D.C.: PETA, 1993.

Robbins, John. *Diet for a New America.* Walpole: Stillpoint, 1987.

Robbins, John. *May All Be Fed: Diet for a New World.* New York: Avon, 1992.

....

QUESTIONS ON WRITING A CASE HISTORY

Will writing a case history really help me with the kind of writing I will do in other classes than my writing class?

Writing case histories means reflecting, analyzing, and interpreting. Since writing is learning and thinking, a case history is a microcosm of the educational process itself. It replicates everything you do in school: taking subjects apart, examining their components, holding them up to the light, exploring them, and then putting them back together and viewing them from an enlightened perspective. You follow this process in almost any class—whether it be math, science, English, history, or economics.

But won't picking apart my writing ruin my spontaneity? If I analyze my writing too much, I'm afraid I'll start to sound boring and stilted.

Athletes play hard, putting body, soul, *and* mind into their work. Writing a case history is like being an athlete who reviews videotapes of a game in order to improve his or her performance. Fast forwarding, rewinding, or pausing at crucial points in the tape, the athlete analyzes key parts of the game and reflects on what he or she sees, taking stock of what went right of wrong in a game, what worked and what didn't. This kind of analysis does not ruin the athlete's ability to enjoy him or herself on the field; it allows the athlete to act spontaneously while engaging the mind.

When you write a case history you are like the informed athlete. The more you analyze and reflect on the process of writing a piece, the more informed about your own skills you will be as you approach writing tasks of different kinds. You will know what you do best and what you need to work on. You will know what methods work with one type of writing and not with another. This knowledge will make you a more confident writer, one who can adapt skills to almost any assignment. The more confidence you gain, the more spontaneous and creative you will be.

How can I write a case history if I haven't kept track of the way I wrote the piece?

Often we tell or write stories about ourselves or others from memory. In fact, writing itself is a way of reclaiming memory and bringing it into the present. While your case history may not be "scientifically" accurate if based solely on memory, it will still allow you to reflect, to think back on how you write and what you have learned.

I can remember some details, but memory alone won't help me write a complete history.

That may be true. As you sit down to write your case history, you will probably find that you have much more to go on than memory alone. If you have followed this text and completed some of the activities in previous chapters, you will
have a variety of sources to interpret and analyze. You may also have kept a daybook or journal, or your writing partner may have kept notes on stories and essays
you have written. If you have worked extensively with a partner or writing group,
you might want to interview them to get *their* perspectives on your writing process
and the pieces you have written throughout the semester. Look also at any comments your teacher has written on your papers. If you have had conferences with
your teacher, you might want to think back on those conversations, as well.

CASE HISTORY ACTIVITIES

1. Reflect in your daybook about writing a particular piece. Don't go back
   yet to your notes or conversations with your writing partners. Instead,
   write from your "gut." What were your strongest feelings about the
   piece? What did you love about it, hate about it? What in it pleased you
   or frustrated you? Where did you get stuck and how did you move on?
   How did you feel as you started the piece? Continued it? Finished it?
   How do you feel about the piece in retrospect?

2. Research your own case history as a writer of a particular piece. Consult
   your daybook and go back to comments your classmates or teacher
   wrote on earlier drafts. Interview your writing partner, your groupmates,
   your dorm neighbors, friends, or parents—anyone and everyone to
   whom you talked about your piece. Ask them what they remember
   about your writing process and what you told them about your topic.
   Review the activities that you completed in this text that may have
   helped you as you wrote your piece. Sort through outlines, maps, brainstorming lists, and freewrites as ways of tracing your writing process.

3. Write a collaborative case history with your writing partner. Trace how
   you helped each other as you wrote, what kind of feedback you got, and
   how sharing your writing influenced your final draft. Interview one another and share notes from your daybooks, drafts, outlines, and free
   writes. Vow to be as honest as possible with each other about what worked
   and what didn't.

4. Compile a booklet of case histories with your writing group. Have each
   member write a history about an essay he or she composed in a particular genre—a reflective essay, a persuasive essay, a research essay, and so
   on. Don't let any two members select the same genre. When the case
   histories are finished, exchange them within the group, read them as

editors, and prepare them for "publication." Make sure to include final drafts of each member's genre essay with his or her case history.

5. Select one of the case histories in this chapter—Sarah Hansen's, Chip Scanlan's, Emma Tobin's, or Tina Winslow's—and make an outline of the steps each writer took while reflecting on his or her writing experience. Jot down the questions each writer asked while compiling his or her history. Use this outline and these questions as starting points for your own case history. Add your own steps and questions as you proceed.

6. Look back through this text at the steps you followed in writing a particular piece, and organize your case history around them. You may, for instance, want to begin with brainstorming as your first point, and then move on to focusing, exploring, planning, and so on. As you address each point, go back through your notes and drafts to find the information that best reflects how you approached each step. Organize this information under the appropriate headings.

7. Visit a writer's bulletin board on the Internet, and trace one writer's journey through a single essay or story. Read all of the writer's posts, and keep a list of the writer's main concerns and how she or he resolved particular problems. Think of the writing process and outlined in this text, and ask yourself how each concern relates to a particular step in that writer's process. Then use this list to begin compiling your own case history.

8. Write a case history of one particular step in your writing process (brainstorming, focusing, planning, drafting, revising, etc.). Choose a step that you always have difficulty with, no matter what you write. Using your notes and conversations with classmates, reflect on the ways you approached this step, the obstacles it presented, and how you negotiated those obstacles. Interview classmates about their own experiences with this step and then reflect on what you have learned about it.

9. Compare and contrast the first draft of a paper you wrote with a final draft. Make a copy of your first draft on your computer or word processor and triple space between lines. In the margins and spaces, note where you made significant changes to the draft as you revised it. Retrace the steps you took to get from the first to last draft. How and why did you make the changes you did? What effect did those changes have on the final draft? What did you learn about your writing process while revising the original draft?

10. Find an interview with a writer in the *Paris Review* or the series *Writers at Work*. Write a case study about that writer, focusing on the writer's particular composing process and how he or she goes about revising. Then compare that process with your own.

11. Write a case history of an editorialist or columnist for a local or school newspaper. Ask if you can sit in on meetings in which editorials or columns are discussed. Then interview the writer several times over a period of weeks and at every stage of writing. Ask the writer to save drafts and proofread copies of his or her work. Interview the writer's coworkers—other writers, editors, support staff, and so on—about the writer's process and what they know about how the writer works.

12. Use the headings of your original outline to build a case history. Under each heading retrace your steps in writing the paper, and review how you adhered to or digressed from your outline. Explain why. Did feedback from your writing partner or group influence your decisions? How many revisions did you do before you made the changes? At what point in the outline did you become stuck? Where did you find it easy to move forward? Think of your outline as a series of stepping stones to your final draft; explain how you used, or skipped these stones or moved them around as you wrote.

13. Draw lines down the centers of two sheets of paper in your daybook. At the top of the first sheet write, "Things that Worked." On the left-hand side of this sheet, list the parts of your essay that you had fun writing or that you found easy to compose. On the right-hand side, reflect on how and why you went about composing these sections. At the top of the second sheet, write, "Things I Found Difficult." On the left-hand side of the page, list all the parts of your essay that seemed hard to write or that frustrated you. On the right-hand side, reflect on the reasons for your difficulties and how and when you overcame them. Use these observations as the basis for your case history.

14. Write a case history of writing projects by your roommates or friends. Ask to see drafts of essays they have written for their classes. Interview them about the steps they took in writing their essays. Observe them in action and ask them to reflect—either by talking or on paper—about their writing processes. Have them tell you what they liked or disliked about writing their essays, what worked and didn't work, and why.

15. Choose someone you know who absolutely hates to write, and study his or her process of composing a single essay for a class. Ask the writer to describe the difficulties he or she has with writing. What obstacles did the writer encounter? Did he or she overcome them? If so, how? If not, why? Using the writer's drafts and interviews, compose a case history.

16. Choose someone who is in love with writing, and repeat Activity 15. Then write a case history comparing the avid writer with the frustrated

writer. See if you can pinpoint specific features of both writers' processes that made writing particular pieces good or bad experiences for them.

17. Write a case history of a laboratory problem you have solved in a science class. Trace your steps in the procedure, and recall how you thought the problem through, where you got stuck, and how you finally resolved it. Adapt the same procedure to a successful essay you have written, tracing your journey from draft to draft. Then write a few paragraphs examining the similarities and differences in the two case histories.

18. Choose several observations from the writers whose case histories are included in this chapter that sum up aspects of your own writing. Use them to make an outline for your own case history, and make sure to bring in examples and details from your writing.

19. Ask your partner to write a case history of you as a writer. When he or she finishes it, alter the case history as needed so that it more closely reflects how you think of yourself as a writer. Select one essay or story you have written to use as the central piece in this case history.

20. Go back to the activities you have completed for each chapter in this text, and use them as the basis for your case history.

AFTERWORD

....

THE JOY OF A CRAFT THAT
CAN NEVER BE LEARNED

You have explored a craft that can never be learned. Be grateful—writing will bring you a lifetime of discovery and surprise. I have been writing for more than fifty years, but each morning at my writing desk, I am again seventeen. I face the page with just enough fear to make it exciting and little enough expectation to allow me to write what I do not expect.

Writing has allowed my voice to be heard. I have been able to participate in our society, arguing for new ways to teach writing, arguing against old ways of resolving differences and against war, speaking out on the satisfactions and concerns of my generation. At my writing desk, I have been able to discover and explore the mysteries of life and survive the tragedies that enter each life—hurt and loss, sickness and death. I have been able to complain and to celebrate, mourn and laugh, imagine and learn. Writing has also brought me the gift of concentration as I become lost in my craft, searching for the right word, creating the phrase that gives off sparks of meaning, constructing sentences that flow and paragraphs that satisfy, tuning the music of my voice to my evolving meaning.

Readers have told me that I have articulated their feelings and their thoughts allowing them to feel like participating members of the human community.

Writing began as play and it remains play. I hope you will be as fortunate and find a lifetime of play, fooling around with language, and finding yourself surprised by a meaning that clarifies your life.

INDEX